MARSHALLING OF SECURITIES

MARSHALLING OF SECURITIES

EQUITY AND THE PRIORITY-RANKING OF SECURED DEBT

PAUL A. U. ALI

CLARENDON PRESS · OXFORD

OXFORD

UNIVERSITY PRESS

Great Clarendon Street, Oxford OX2 6DP

Oxford University Press is a department of the University of Oxford
It furthers the University's objective of excellence in research, scholarship,
and education by publishing worldwide in

Oxford New York

Athens Auckland Bangkok Bogotá Buenos Aires Calcutta
Cape Town Chennai Dar es Salaam Delhi Florence Hong Kong Istanbul
Karachi Kuala Lumpur Madrid Melbourne Mexico City Mumbai
Nairobi Paris São Paulo Singapore Taipei Tokyo Toronto Warsaw

with associated companies in Berlin Ibadan

Oxford is a registered trade mark of Oxford University Press
in the UK and in certain other countries

Published in the United States
by Oxford University Press Inc., New York

British Library Cataloguing in Publication Data

Data available

Library of Congress Cataloging in Publication Data

Data available

ISBN 0–19–826865–3

1 3 5 7 9 10 8 6 4 2

Typeset by Hope Services (Abingdon) Ltd.
Printed in Great Britain
on acid-free paper by
Biddles Ltd., Guildford and King's Lynn

PREFACE

This book is a recension of the thesis, for which I received the degree of Doctor of Juridical Studies from the University of Sydney in 1996. I have endeavoured to state the law from the sources available to me in October 1998.

I was particularly fortunate to have Ms Dimity Kingsford Smith of the University of Sydney as my supervisor. This book is in no small measure due to her generosity with her time throughout the course of my degree and her incisive observations on the various drafts of my thesis. I would also like to express my gratitude to my examiners, the Solicitor-General for England and Wales, Professor Ross Cranston QC MP (in his then position as Cassel Professor of Commercial Law at the London School of Economics) and Ms Barbara McDonald of the University of Sydney, whose comments on my thesis encouraged me to take the first, tentative steps towards publication.

Thanks are also due to Professor Barry Rider, Director of the Institute of Advanced Legal Studies, London who kindly permitted me to make use of the Institute's research facilities during August 1998. I am, in addition, deeply grateful to Mr Philip Clark, Managing Partner of Minter Ellison, Sydney and my erstwhile supervising partner, Justice Robert Austin of the Supreme Court of New South Wales (Equity Division) for their support of this book. It has also been a pleasure to work with Mr Christopher Rycroft, Commissioning Editor, Law, Mr Nigel Sleight, Assistant Editor, Law, and the staff at Oxford University Press.

Finally, I should like to thank Mr Thomas Moloney and Ms Virginia Wise, Mr Martin Gold, Dr Roger Magnusson, Mr Thomas Russell, and Dr Geofrey Stapledon for their assistance during the writing of this book.

Paul A. U. Ali

Sydney
February, 1999

CONTENTS

Table of Cases   xi
Table of Legislation   xxix

PART I. INTRODUCTION

1. Introduction

A. What is Marshalling of Securities?   3
B. Organisation of this Text   7

PART II. GENERAL PRINCIPLES – HISTORY AND OPERATION OF MARSHALLING OF SECURITIES

2. The History of the Equitable Doctrine of Marshalling of Securities   11

A. Origins of Marshalling of Securities   12
B. Establishment of the General Principles of Marshalling of Securities   17
C. Affirmation of the General Principles of Marshalling of Securities   32
D. Recent Developments in Marshalling of Securities   36

3. How Does Marshalling Work?

A. Two Competing Theories about Marshalling of Securities   39
B. Coercion Theory of Marshalling of Securities   40
C. Post-Realisation Theory of Marshalling of Securities   46
D. Purported Revival of the Coercion Theory   51

vii

PART III. GENERAL PRINCIPLES – JURIDICAL
NATURE OF MARSHALLING OF SECURITIES

4. **Marshalling of Securities and the Law of Subrogation**

A. Introduction 59
B. Marshalling of Securities as a Redistributive Remedy 60
C. Marshalling of Securities as a Subrogation Remedy 63
D. A Comparison of Marshalling of Securities and the Established
Categories of Subrogation 65
E. Marshalling of Securities, Subrogation and the Law of
Restitution 69

5. **Marshalling of Securities and Other Equitable Doctrines and
Remedies** 78

A. Marshalling of Securities and Consolidation of Mortgages 79
B. Marshalling of Securities and Contribution 89
C. Marshalling of Securities and Specific Performance 97

6. **The Rationale for Marshalling of Securities**

A. Introduction 101
B. Natural Justice Basis of Marshalling of Securities 102
C. Marshalling of Securities and Theories of Security 104
D. Functional and Private Property-Based Theories of Security 107
E. Monitoring and Informational Theories of Security 110
F. Marshalling of Securities and the Conventional Theory of
Security 114

PART IV. PRE-REQUISITES OF MARSHALLING
OF SECURITIES

7. **Marshalling of Securities and the Common Debtor Rule**

A. Introduction 121
B. Requirement of a Common Debtor 124
C. Status of Assets subject to Senior and Junior Securities 128
D. Requirement of Equal Rights of Recourse to Assets Subject to
Senior Security 129

8. **Exceptions to the Common Debtor Rule**

A. Introduction 133
B. Surety Exception to the Common Debtor Rule 134

C. Questioning the Efficacy of the Surety Exception 142
D. Piercing the Corporate Veil and Marshalling of Securities 147

9. **Marshalling of Securities and the Requirement of Proprietary Securities**

A. Introduction 154
B. Proprietary and Non-Proprietary Securities 155
C. *Webb v Smith* and the Requirement of Proprietary Securities 160
D. Extension of Marshalling to Non-Security Rights 163
E. Marshalling of Securities and Quasi-Securities 166

PART V. LIMITATIONS ON MARSHALLING OF SECURITIES

10. **Marshalling of Securities and the Rights of Unsecured Creditors**

A. Introduction 171
B. Extension of Marshalling Rights to Unsecured Creditors 172
C. Unsecured Creditors and Extinguishment of Marshalling Rights 176

11. **Marshalling of Securities and Third Parties**

A. Introduction 179
B. Marshalling in the Presence of Third Party Rights 181
C. Third Party Security Holders and Marshalling by Apportionment 185
D. Third Party Transferees or Disponees and Exclusion of Marshalling Rights 193

12. **Covenants Against Marshalling and Other Contractual Constraints**

A. Introduction 201
B. Covenants Against Marshalling 202
C. Priority Arrangements between a Senior Creditor and Third Parties 204
D. Purchase Money Security Arrangements between a Debtor and Third Parties 205

Bibliography 208
Index 223

TABLE OF CASES

AUSTRALIA

Alliance Acceptance Company Limited v Graham (1974) 10 SASR 220 ....3.16

Austin v Royal (unrep 14 May 1998, Sup Ct of NSW) 4.14, 4.34, 4.35, 11.13

Australia and New Zealand Banking Group Limited v Bangadilly Pastoral
    Company Pty Limited (1978) 139 CLR 195 ....3.12

Australia and New Zealand Banking Group Limited v Bendigo Building Society
    (unrep 5 Oct 1992, Sup Ct of Vic)..2.53, 7.05

Australia and New Zealand Banking Group Limited v Carnegie (unrep 16 June
    1987, Sup Ct of Vic) 9.14

Aylwin, Re [1938] VLR 105..2.52, 2.57

Balkin v Peck (unrep 24 July 1998, C of A (NSW)) 4.35, 4.53

Bank of New South Wales v City Mutual Life Assurance Society Limited [1969]
    VR 556...4.14

Barns v Queensland National Bank Limited (1906) 3 CLR 942 ....3.12

Browne v Cranfield (1925) 25 SR (NSW) 443 ....5.08

Challenge Bank Limited v Mailman (unrep 14 May 1993, C of A (NSW))............4.14

Chase Corporation (Australia) Pty Limited v North Sydney Brick and Tile
    Company Limited (1994) 12 ACLC 997 ....2.52, 2.54, 3.08, 3.20, 3.23,
                3.26, 3.31, 5.36, 5.49, 6.02, 11.13, 11.20, 11.28, 11.56

Citicorp (Australia) Limited v McLoughney (1984) 35 SASR 375 ....3.13

Commonwealth Trading Bank v Colonial Mutual Life Assurance Society
    Limited (1970) 26 FLR 338 ....2.52, 2.54, 2.57, 2.58, 3.02, 3.08, 3.23,
          3.31, 4.14, 7.04, 8.40, 9.24, 11.03, 11.08, 11.13, 11.20, 11.25, 11.28

Composite Buyers v State Bank of New South Wales (1990) 3 ACSR 196...........12.17

Corozo Pty Ltd v Total Australia Ltd [1987] 2 Qd R 11 ....5.04

Crothers, In re [1930] VLR 49...2.53, 10.01, 11.01, 11.20

D J Fowler (Australia) Limited v Bank of New South Wales [1982] 2 NSWLR
    879...2.29

DM & BP Wiskich Pty Ltd v Saadi (unrep 16 Feb 1996, Sup Ct of NSW) ...2.53, 10.01

Deta Nominees Pty Limited v Discount Plastic Products Pty Limited [1979]
    VR 167..2.52, 3.26, 3.31, 5.54

English Scottish and Australian Bank Limited v Phillips (1937) 57 CLR 302.........5.08

Expo International Pty Ltd v Chant [1979] 2 NSWLR 820 ....3.13

Finance & Investments Pty Limited v Van Kempen (1986) 6 NSWLR 305 .... 5.45
Finance Corporation of Australia Limited v Bentley (1991)
    5 BPR 97412 .... 1.04, 2.53, 3.26, 5.44, 5.45, 7.05, 8.26, 8.27
Forsyth v Blundell (1973) 129 CLR 477 .... 3.10

Gattuso v Geelong Building Society [1989] ATR 69,281 .... 3.12
Greig v Watson (1881) 7 VLR (E) 79 .... 5.08

Henry Roach (Petroleum) Pty Limited v Credit House (Vic) Pty Limited [1976]
    VR 309 .... 3.10
Holland, Re (1928) 28 SR (NSW) 369 .... 2.53, 7.05, 7.25, 7.27

Latec Investments Ltd v Hotel Terrigal Pty Ltd (1965) 113 CLR 265 .... 3.12

McColl's Wholesale Pty Ltd v State Bank of NSW [1984] 3 NSWLR 365 .... 6.02
McKean v Maloney [1988] 1 Qd R 628 .... 3.12
Miles v Official Receiver (1963) 109 CLR 501 .... 2.53, 7.05, 7.25, 7.27
Mir Bros Projects Pty Limited v Lyons [1977] 2 NSWLR 192 ... 2.52, 2.54, 3.20, 3.26,
                                                                                       3.31, 11.18, 11.28
Mir Bros Projects Pty Limited v Lyons [1978] 2 NSWLR 505 .... 2.52, 2.54, 3.26,
                                                                                       3.31, 11.28

O'Day v Commercial Bank of Australia Limited (1933) 50 CLR 200 .... 9.14
O'Leary, Re (1985) 61 ALR 674 .... 2.52, 2.53, 3.31, 7.05
Oamington Pty Limited v Commissioner of Land Tax (unrep 24 Nov 1997,
    Sup Ct of NSW) 2.52, 3.26, 3.31, 7.04
Official Trustee in Bankruptcy v Citibank Savings Limited (1995) 38 NSWLR
    116 .... 5.33

Patrick Stevedores No 2 Pty Limited v MV Skulptor Konenkov (1996) 136 ALR
    211 .... 2.52, 3.20, 3.26, 3.31, 9.15
Pendlebury v CML Assurance Society Limited (1912) 13 CLR 676 .... 3.12
Porter v Associated Securities Limited (1976) 1 BPR 97027 .... 11.49
Pullen v Abalcheck Pty Limited (1990) 20 NSWLR 732 .... 9.38

Ramsay v Lowther (1912) 16 CLR 1 .... 5.39

Sarge Pty Limited v Cazihaven Homes Pty Limited (1994) 34 NSWLR 658 .... 1.04,
    1.05, 2.53, 3.08, 4.14, 5.27, 5.48, 5.55, 6.02, 7.05, 8.07, 8.13, 8.26, 8.27, 8.40, 11.13
Selvas Pty Limited, Re (1989) 52 SASR 449 .... 9.14
Sherwin v McWilliams (1921) 17 Tas LR 16 .... 5.32

Underwood, In the Will of (1889) 10 LR (NSW) Eq 227 .... 5.04

W, In re (1901) 11 QLJ 108 .... 2.53, 7.05

Wertheim, In re [1934] VLR 321 ....2.53, 7.05
Westpac Banking Corporation v Daydream Island Pty Limited [1985] 2 Qd R
   330 ....5.53, 7.04
White v Colonial Bank of Australasia (1871) 2 VR 96..2.13
White v London Chartered Bank of Australia (1877) 3 VLR 33 ....2.13, 2.46, 11.27, 11.28
Wood, Re [1949] St R Qd 17 ....10.01

CANADA

Adams v Keers (1919) 51 DLR 514..2.54, 11.28
Allison, Re (1998) 38 OR (3d) 337 ....2.52, 2.53, 3.26, 7.05, 8.14

Bank of British Columbia v Tamavi Holdings Limited (1978) 29 CBR (NS)
   111 ....2.53, 7.05, 8.14
Bank of Nova Scotia v Adriatic Development Limited [1985]
   2 WWR 627 ....2.53, 10.01
Bank of Nova Scotia v Bartrop [1983] 4 WWR 91..5.10
Bread Man Inc., Re (1979) 89 DLR (3d) 599 ....2.53, 9.25, 10.01, 10.02, 11.03
Brown v Canadian Imperial Bank of Commerce (1985)
   50 OR (2d) 420..2.53, 7.05, 8.14

Canada v French (unrep 15 Jan 1985, Ont HCJ) 2.53, 7.05
Canadian Trustco Mortgage Company v Wenngatz Construction & Holdings
   Limited (1986) 1 BCLR (2d) 302 ....2.52, 2.53, 3.26, 7.05, 7.24
Clark v Bogart (1880) 27 Gr 450 ....2.50, 11.56
Credit Foncier Franco-Canadien v Walker [1938] OWN 339...............................5.10

Dominion Lumber v Gelfand (1916) 34 WLR 624.......................................2.53, 7.05

Ernst Brothers Company v Canadian Permanent Mortgage Corporation (1920)
   47 OLR 362; (1920) 57 DLR 500 (on appeal) 2.52, 2.53, 2.54, 3.26, 7.04,
                                    7.05, 8.11, 8.12, 8.19, 11.55

Farm Credit Corporation v McLane (1983) 30 Sask R 320 ....2.53, 7.05, 7.24, 10.09
Farm Credit Corporation v Nelson (1993) 102 DLR (4th) 743 ....2.52, 3.26
Fiatallis North America Inc v Pigott Construction Limited (1992) 3 PPSAC
   (2d) 30 ....2.52, 2.53, 3.26, 7.05, 8.11
First Investors Corporation Limited v Veeradon Developments Limited (1988) 47
   DLR (4th) 446 ....2.52, 3.26
Fraser v Nagle (1888) 16 OR 241 ....2.50, 11.56

G Ruso Construction Limited v Laviola (1976) 27 Chitty's LJ 136 ......2.53, 7.05, 8.14
Goodman v Keel (1923) 4 DLR 468 ....5.32
Goodman v Parkhurst [1980] 6 WWR 601...............................2.52, 3.26, 5.10
Granville Savings & Mortgage Corporation v Bob B Company Holdings Limited
   (1996) 24 BCLR (3d) 348...2.53, 7.05, 11.01

Hamilton, Re (1895) 10 Man R 573..2.13, 2.32, 5.10, 7.05
Hongkong Bank of Canada v Shrimp Projectors Inc [1993] 3 WWR 484..............3.26

Invesco Holdings Limited v Kendall [1979] 4 WWR 571 ....2.53, 7.05

Johal v Sahota (1986) 2 BCLR (2d) 218..2.54, 11.55
Jones v Beck (1871) 18 Gr 671 ....2.13, 2.50, 11.56

Lake Apartments Limited v Bootwala (1973) 37 DLR (3d) 523 ....3.10

Maritime Warehousing & Dock Company v Nicholson (1884) 24 NBR 170........5.10
Montmor Investments Limited v Montreal Trust Company (1984) 53 BCLR
    275...2.53, 7.05, 7.24, 8.50, 10.09
Montreal Trust Company v Montreal Trust Company of Canada (1988) 24
    BCLR (2d) 238 ....2.53, 7.05
Montreal Trust Company v Newberry Energy Limited (1983) 147 DLR (3d)
    189...5.10

National Bank of Canada v Makin Metals Limited [1993] 3 WWR 318;
    (1994) 116 Sask R 236 (on appeal)..2.53, 9.25
Nova Scotia Savings & Loan Company v O'Hara (1979)
    7 RPR 281 ....2.52, 2.53, 3.26, 10.01

Ontario Inc v Allison (1995) CBR (3d) 144......................................2.53, 7.05, 10.01

Pierce v Canavan (1882) 7 OAR 187 ....2.50, 11.56
Project Research Group Limited v Acumen Investments Limited (1986) 43 RPR
    50..5.10

Quay v Sculthorpe (1869) 16 Gr 449..2.35, 8.14

Renwick v Berryman (1886) 3 Man R 387..2.50, 11.56
Richmond Savings Credit Union v Zilbershats (1997)
    35 BCLR (3d) 136 ....2.53, 2.54, 3.35, 5.10, 7.05, 11.05, 11.20, 11.28
Royal Bank of Canada v Izen [1921] 2 WWR 929 ....2.53, 7.05
Royal Trust Company v H A Roberts Group Limited [1995]
    4 WWR 305..2.52, 3.26, 9.25
Roynat Limited v Denis (1982) 139 DLR (3d) 265......................................9.14
Rutherford v Rutherford (1896) 17 PR 228 ....2.13, 2.26

Seel Investments Limited v Greater Canadian Securities Corporation Limited
    (1967) 65 DLR (2d) 45....................................2.52, 2.54, 3.26, 11.28
Silverthorn v Glazebrook (1899) 30 OR 408...5.03
Slayter v Johnson (1864) 5 NSR 502...5.10
Steacy, Re (1917) 39 OLR 548 ....2.53, 7.05

Steinbach Credit Union Limited v Manitoba Agricultural Credit Corporation
(1991) 72 Man R (2d) 161...2.53, 3.26, 9.25

Toronto-Dominion Bank v Whitaker (unrep 4 July 1986, Alta QB) 2.53, 7.05, 7.24

Victor Investment Corporation v Fidelity Trust Company (1973) 41 DLR (3d)
65..2.54, 11.03, 11.28
Victoria & Grey Trust Company v Brewer (1971) 14 DLR (3d) 28 ....2.54, 11.28

Westcoast Savings Credit Union v P E DeVito & Associates Limited (unrep 24
Feb 1986, BCSC)..2.53, 7.05
Williamson v Loonstra (1973) 34 DLR (3d) 275 ....2.52, 2.53, 3.26, 10.01, 10.02

Yorkshire Trust Company v Armwest Development Limited [1986]
1 WWR 478..2.52, 3.26

ENGLAND and WALES

Abbey National Building Society v Cann [1991] AC 56..12.16
Adams v Cape Industries plc [1990] 2 WLR 657 ....8.53, 8.55
AIB Finance Limited v Debtors [1997] 4 All ER 677; [1998] 2 All ER 929
(on appeal) 3.12, 3.13, 3.15, 3.17
Airedale Co-operative Worsted Manufacturing Society Limited, Re [1933]
Ch 639 ....4.29
'Albazero', The [1977] AC 774 ....8.53
Aldrich v Cooper (1803) 8 Ves Jun 382 ....2.05, 2.21, 2.22, 2.58, 3.20,
3.26, 5.32, 8.31, 11.07, 11.08
Aldridge v Forbes (1839) 9 LJ Ch 37..............................2.50, 2.56, 5.55, 11.27, 11.51
Aldworth v Robinson (1840) 2 Beav 287...5.04
Allen v De Lisle (1857) 5 WR 158 ....12.05
Alston, *Ex parte* (1868) 4 Ch App 168..............2.26, 2.40, 2.42, 3.26, 7.02, 8.01, 8.31,
9.15, 10.02, 11.02
American Surety Company of New York v Wrightson (1910) 103 LT 663 ....5.32
Andrew v City Permanent Benefit Building Society (1881)
44 LT 641 ....5.04, 5.19
Anonymous (1557) Cary 1 ....5.43
Anonymous (1679) 2 Ch Cas 5 ....2.02
Anstey v Newman (1870) 39 LJ Ch 769..............2.30, 2.50, 5.55, 10.01, 11.43, 11.51
'Arab', The (1859) 5 Jur (NS) 417 ....2.23, 2.40, 7.03
Arcedeckne, Re (1883) 24 Ch D 709 ....5.31, 5.32
Arcedeckne v Howard, Lord (1875) 45 LJ Ch 622 ....5.31
Attorney-General v Tyndall (1764) Amb 614.......................................2.04, 2.05, 2.21

Bacon v Vesey (1677–1678) 79 Selden Society 660..5.03
Baglioni v Cavalli (1900) 83 LT 500 ....2.54, 11.20, 11.25
Baldwin v Belcher (1842) 3 Dr & War 173..............................2.42, 7.02, 10.02, 11.02

Bank of Credit and Commerce International SA (No 8), Re [1998]
1 BCLC 68....................................2.57, 2.60, 2.61, 3.02, 3.32, 3.33, 3.35, 3.38, 9.29
Bank of Tokyo v Karoon [1986] 3 All ER 468 ....8.53
Bannatyne v MacIver [1906] 1 KB 103 ....4.31
Banner v Berridge (1881) 18 Ch D 254 ....5.45
Banque Financière de la Cité v Parc (Battersea) Limited [1998]
1 All ER 737...3.08, 4.03, 4.34, 4.35, 9.32
Barclays Bank plc v O'Brien [1993] 4 All ER 417 ....4.27
Barker v Gray (1875) 1 Ch D 491..5.19
Barnes v Racster (1842) 1 Y & C Ch Cas 401 ....2.26, 2.42, 2.46, 3.26, 5.48, 7.10,
9.28, 10.02, 11.18, 11.20
Baroness Wenlock v River Dee Company (1887) 19 QB D 155 ....4.29, 4.30
Bartholomew v May (1737) 1 Atk 487 ....5.42
Beevor v Luck (1867) LR 4 Eq 537 ....5.21
Belton v Bass Ratcliffe & Gretton Limited [1922] 2 Ch 449 ....3.10
Berridge v Berridge (1890) 44 Ch D 168 ....5.32
Best, In re [1924] 1 Ch 42...2.54, 5.31, 5.34, 11.43, 11.52
Bilbie v Lumley (1802) 2 East 469 ....2.29
Binns v Nichols (1866) LR 2 Eq 256...2.26, 3.26
Bishop v Bonham [1988] 1 WLR 742...3.12
Blaauwpot v Da Costa (1758) 1 Edn 130 ....2.29
Blackburn Benefit Building Society v Cunliffe, Brooks & Company (1882) 22
Ch D 61 ....4.29, 4.30
Blackett v Bates (1865) LR 1 Ch 117 ....5.51
Bligh v Darnley, Earl of (1731) 2 P Wms 619 ....2.05
Boazman v Johnston (1830) 3 Sim 377 ....5.55
Boscawen v Bajwa [1996] 1 WLR 328 ....4.34
Bovey v Skipwith (1671) 1 Ch Cas 201 ....2.02, 5.21, 11.20
Bowker v Bull (1850) 1 Sim (NS) 29..5.04, 8.32
Bradford v Foley (1791) 3 Bro C C 351n..2.05
Brandon v Brandon (1859) 28 LJ Ch 147 ....12.05
Brecon Corporation v Seymour (1859) 26 Beav 548 ....5.04
Breeds, Re (1841) 2 Mont D & De G 328..5.04
Broadbent v Barlow (1861) 3 De G F & J 570.............................2.40, 8.01, 9.15
Brown v Cork [1985] BCLC 363 ....4.14, 5.32, 5.44, 5.46
Bugden v Bignold (1843) 2 Y & C Ch Cas 377 ....2.46, 5.48, 11.18, 11.20
Bullock v Knight (1682) 2 Ch Cas 117 ....2.02
Burge, Woodall & Company, Re [1912] 1 KB 393........2.54, 8.01, 9.15, 11.43, 11.52
Burgh v Francis (1673) Rep temp Finch 29..2.02, 10.01
Bute, Marquis of v Cunynghame (1826) 2 Russ 275 ....5.32
Butlers Wharf Limited, Re [1995] 2 BCLC 43..................5.32, 5.47, 8.10, 8.30, 8.32

Cargo ex Galam (1863) Br & Lush 167..9.15
Carter, *Ex parte* (1773) Amb 733 ....5.17
Carter v Barnadiston (1718) 1 P Wms 506...2.05, 5.36, 5.55

Castle Phillips Finance Limited v Piddington (unrep 7 Dec 1994, C of A).............4.27
Chappell v Rees (1839) 9 LJ Ch 37 ....2.49, 5.36, 11.43
Charge Card Services Limited, Re [1986] 3 WLR 697 ....9.29
Chatterton v Maclean [1951] 1 All ER 761 ....5.32
Chesworth v Hunt (1880) 5 CPD 266......................................5.03, 6.02
China & South Sea Bank Limited v Tan [1990] 1 AC 536 ....3.10, 3.12, 3.15
'Chioggia', The [1898] P 1 ....2.26, 2.32, 2.40, 3.26, 7.02, 8.41, 11.07, 11.08
Clifton v Burt (1720) 1 P Wms 678...2.05
Cohen, Re [1960] Ch 179...2.52, 3.26
Collins v Prosser (1823) 1 B & C 682 ....5.29, 5.32
Commercial Union Assurance Company Limited v Hayden [1977] QB 804 ....5.32
Company, Re A (1985) 1 BCC 99, 421 ....8.53
Conley, Re [1938] 2 All ER 127..7.19
Cook's Mortgage, Re [1896] 1 Ch 923...........................2.50, 5.36, 11.52
Coope v Twynam (1823) Turn & R 426 ....5.31
Cope v Cope (circa 1710) 2 Salk 449 ....5.43
Cork and Youghal Railway, Re (1869) LR 4 Ch App 748 ....4.29
Cracknall v Janson (1879) 11 Ch D 1 ....2.46, 5.03, 5.04, 5.17, 11.20
Craythorne v Swinburne (1807) 14 Ves Jun 160 ....2.29, 5.29, 5.31
Crickmore v Freeston (1870) 40 LJ Ch 137 ....5.03
Crisp, *Ex parte* (1744) 1 Atk 133..2.29
Cuckmere Brick Company Limited v Mutual Finance Limited [1971]
    Ch 949 ....3.10, 3.12, 3.13, 3.15
Culpepper v Aston (1682) 2 Ch Cas 115.....................................2.02
Cummins v Fletcher (1880) 14 Ch D 699.........................5.03, 5.04, 5.21

Dallas v Walls (1873) 29 LT 599 ....5.32
Darby's Estate, In re [1907] 2 Ch 465....................2.54, 5.33, 11.43, 11.52
Davidson v Case (1820) 2 Brod & B 379 ....2.29
Davies v Humphreys (1840) 6 M & W 153 ....5.29, 5.32
Davis v Gardiner (1723) 2 P Wms 187 ....5.43
Debtor, In re A [1976] 1 WLR 952..5.33, 8.31
Denton's Estate, Re [1904] 2 Ch 178....................5.31, 5.32, 5.39
Dering v Winchelsea, Earl of (1787) 1 Cox Eq Cas 318 ....2.29, 5.29, 5.31, 5.43
Dixon v Steel [1901] 2 Ch 602...8.40
Dolphin v Aylward (1870) LR 4 E & I 486.....2.26, 2.32, 2.42, 2.50, 3.26, 5.55, 7.02,
                                            10.02, 11.07, 11.08, 11.43, 11.51
Donald v Suckling (1866) LR 1 QB 585 ....9.09
Drew v Lockett (1863) 32 Beav 499..8.31
Duncan Fox & Company v North and South Wales Bank (1880) 6 App Cas 1 .....5.29
Dunlop, Re (1882) 21 Ch D 583 ....5.32

'Edward Oliver', The (1867) LR 1 A & E 379 ....2.32, 2.40, 7.02
Ellesmere Brewery Company v Cooper [1896] 1 QB 75.................5.29, 5.32
Ellis v Emmanuel (1876) 1 Ex D 157..5.32

Ennis, Re [1893] 3 Ch 238 ....5.31
'Eugenie', The (1873) LR 4 A & E 123..2.40
Evans v Bremridge (1855) 2 K & J 174...5.32

Faircharm Investments Limited v Citibank International plc (unrep 6 Feb 1998,
   CA) 3.08
Farebrother v Wodehouse (1856) 26 LJ Ch 81...5.03, 8.32
Farrar v Farrars Limited (1888) 40 Ch D 395 ....3.10, 3.14
Farrington v Forrestor [1893] 2 Ch 461 ....5.55
Fernandes, Re (1844) 6 H & N 717..12.05
FG (Films) Limited, Re [1953] 1 WLR 483 ....8.53
Finch v Shaw (1854) 19 Beav 500 ....5.36, 11.52
Finch v Winchelsea (1718) 1 P Wms 399n 2.05, 2.30, 10.01
Firestone Tyre and Rubber Company Limited v Lewellin [1957] 1 WLR 464 ....8.53
Fleetwood v Charnock (1629) Nelson 10 ....5.43
Flint v Howard [1893] 2 Ch 54 ....2.23, 2.42, 2.46, 7.02, 10.02, 11.02,
                                                11.03, 11.20, 11.25
Ford v Tynte (1872) 41 LJ Ch 758 ....2.46, 5.26, 11.20
Forrester v Leigh, Lord (1753) Amb 171 ....2.05
Foster v Cook (1791) 3 Bro C C 347 ....2.05
Freemoult v Dedire (1718) 1 P Wms 429 ....2.05
Fry, Re [1912] 2 Ch 86..2.53, 9.25

Galton v Hancock (1743) 2 Atk 428 ....2.05, 5.34, 5.55
Gee v Liddell [1913] 2 Ch 62...5.33
Gee v Smart (1857) 8 El & Bl 313 ....5.33
Gibbs v Ougier (1806) 12 Ves 413..7.04
Gibson v Seagrim (1855) 20 Beav 614 ....2.21, 2.42, 2.46, 2.59, 10.02, 11.20
Gifford, *Ex parte* (1802) 6 Ves 805...5.29
Godin v London Assurance Company (1758) 1 Burr 489 ....5.43
Goodwin v Gray (1874) 22 WR 312...5.32
Goss v Withers (1758) 2 Burr 683..2.29
Gray v Stone & Funnell (1893) 69 LT 282 ....2.30, 2.42, 10.02
Greerside v Benson (1745) 3 Atk 248..2.29
Gregg v Arrott (Chitty, Index to All the Reported Cases Decided in the Several
   Courts of Equity and Bankruptcy in England and Ireland, 4048–4049)....2.26, 3.26
Gregson, Re (1887) 36 Ch D 223 ....5.04
Griffith v Pound (1890) 40 Ch D 553 ....5.03, 5.04
Gwynne v Edwards (1825) 2 Russ 289n...........................2.26, 2.50, 3.26, 7.08, 11.52

Hall v Hall [1911] 1 Ch 487 ....5.33
Hamilton v Mendes (1761) 2 Burr 1198..2.29
Hamilton v Royse (1804) 2 Sch & Lef 315 ....2.30, 2.42, 10.02
Hamly v Fisher (1757) 1 Dick 104..2.05
Hanby v Fisher (1757) 2 Coll 512..:...2.05

Hanby v Roberts (1751) Amb 127 ....2.05
Harbert's Case (1584) 3 Co Rep 11b...1.05, 5.43
Harris v Lee (1718) 1 P Wms 482...2.29
Harris v Tubb (1889) 42 Ch D 79...5.17
Harris Calculating Machine Company, Re [1914] 1 Ch 920.........................4.30, 4.31
Harter v Colman (1882) 19 Ch D 630.......................................5.17, 5.19, 5.20, 5.21
Hartley v O'Flaherty (1813–1830) Beat 61 ....2.49, 11.43
Hay v Carter [1935] Ch 397 ....5.29
Haynes v Forshaw (1853) 11 Hare 93 ....2.42, 10.02, 11.01, 11.52
Herle v Harrison (1674–1675) 73 Selden Society 138...5.43
Heyman v Dubois (1871) LR 13 Eq 158....................7.02, 8.27, 8.31, 8.39, 8.45
Higgins v Frankis (1848) 15 LJ Ch 329..5.04
Hitchman v Stewart (1855) 3 Drewery 271...5.32
Hoare v Contencin (1779) 1 Bro C C 27 ....2.05
Hodgson v Hodgson (1837) 2 Keen 704 ....5.32
Hole v Harrison (1673) 1 Ch Ca 246..5.43
Holmes v Williamson (1817) 6 M & S 158..5.29
Hotchkin, *Ex parte* (1875) LR 20 Eq 746...5.21
Hughes v Britannia Permanent Benefit Building Society [1906]
   2 Ch 607 ....5.04, 5.16, 5.19
Hughes v Williams (1852) 3 Mac & G 683...........2.50, 5.36, 5.55, 7.02, 11.43, 11.51
Huntington v Huntington (1702) 2 Bro Parl Cas 1...5.43
Hyde v Hyde (1708) 3 Ch Rep 155 ....2.05

International Life Assurance Society, Re (1876) 2 Ch D 476.........................2.32, 7.02
Irvin v Ironmonger (1831) 2 R & M 531...5.36

Jarrett v Barclays Bank Limited [1947] Ch 187 ....3.16
Jennings v Jordan (1881) 6 App Cas 698................................5.04, 5.19, 5.20, 5.21
Johnson v Child (1844) 4 Hare 87 ....5.32
Jones, In re [1893] 2 Ch 461 ....2.50, 5.36, 11.52
Jones v Griffith (1845) 2 Coll 207..5.04
Jones v Lipman [1962] 1 WLR 832...8.53
Jones v Smith (1794) 2 Ves Jun 372...5.03, 5.04, 5.17

Kearsley v Cole (1846) 16 M & W 153...5.32
Kemp v Falk (1882) 52 LJ Ch 167 ....8.31
Kendall, *Ex parte* (1811) 17 Ves 514 ....2.21, 2.32, 2.33, 2.35, 2.36, 7.02, 8.07,
                                  8.08, 8.23, 8.44, 11.01
Kendall v Hamilton (1879) 4 App Cas 504 ....2.32, 7.02
Kennedy v De Trafford [1896] 1 Ch 762...3.10
Kensington, Lord v Bouverie (1854) 19 Beav 39 ....5.04
King v Jones (1814) 5 Taunt 518...5.55
Kirkham v Smith (1749) 1 Ves Sen 258 ....5.34
Kirkham v Smith (1749) Amb 518...2.05
Kulen Kemp v Vigne (1786) 1 TR 304 ....2.29

'La Constancia', The (1845) 2 Wm Rob 403..2.40
Lanoy v Athol, Duke & Duchess of (1742) 2 Atk 444.......2.04, 2.05, 2.06, 2.21, 2.22,
                                             2.58, 7.02, 10.02, 11.02
Lawrance v Galsworthy (1857) 3 Jur (NS) 1049....................2.23, 3.08, 3.26, 7.04
Lawson v Wright (1786) 1 Cox 275 ....5.43
Leonino v Leonino (1879) 10 Ch D 460...5.32
Lipscomb v Lipscomb (1868) LR 7 Eq 501 ....5.32, 11.27
Liverpool Marine Credit Company v Wilson (1872) 7 Ch App 507............2.46, 11.20
Lloyd v Cox (1676–1677) 79 Selden Society 531 ....5.03
Lloyd v Johnes (1804) 9 Ves 37..5.33
Loder's Trusts, In re (1886) 56 LJ Ch 230 ....2.21
Lomas v Wright (1833) 2 My & K 769 ....5.55, 10.01
London Assurance Company v Sainsbury (1783) 3 Dougl 245................................2.29
Loosemore, Re (1843) 3 Mont D & De G 464 ....5.04
Lowe v Dixon (1885) 16 QB D 455..5.32
Lutkin v Leigh (1734) Cases T Talbot 53...2.05

McHugh v Union Bank of Canada [1913] AC 299.......................................3.12, 3.15
Mackreth v Walmesley (1884) 51 LT 19..5.31
Mainwaring, In re [1937] Ch 96 ....2.54, 5.32, 5.34, 8.20, 11.43
Mallott v Wilson [1903] 2 Ch 494..2.54, 5.55, 11.43, 11.52
Manks v Whiteley [1911] 2 Ch 448 ....2.52, 3.19, 3.26
Marcon v Bloxam (1856) 11 Exch 586...5.04
Margrave v Le Hooke (1690) 2 Vern 207...5.03, 5.04
Marsh v Lee (1670) 2 Ventris 337 ....5.03
'Mary Ann', The (1845) 9 Jur 94 ....2.32, 2.40, 7.02
Mason v Bogg (1827) 2 My & Cr 443 ....2.26, 2.32, 3.26, 7.02
Mason v Sainsbury (1783) 3 Dougl 61 ....2.29
Masters v Masters (1717) 1 P Wms 421 ....2.05
Merchandise Transport Limited v British Transport Commission [1962] 2 QB
    173...8.53
Middleton v Middleton (1852) 15 Beav 450 ....5.32
Midland Banking Company v Chambers (1869) 4 Ch App 398...........................12.05
Milles v Fletcher (1779) 1 Dougl 231..2.29
Mills v Eden (1725) 10 Mod 487 ....2.05
Minter v Carr [1894] 3 Ch 498...5.19, 5.20, 5.21
Morgan v Seymour (1637/1638) 1 Chan Rep 120 ....2.29, 5.43
Mower's Trusts, Re (1869) LR 8 Eq 110......................................2.46, 11.20, 11.27
Moxon v The Berkeley Mutual Benefit Building Society (1890)
    59 LJ Ch 524 ....2.26, 2.46, 3.26, 9.21, 11.01, 11.02, 11.03, 11.20, 11.23
Multinational Gas & Petroleum Company v Multinational Gas & Petroleum
    Services Limited [1983] 3 WLR 492 ....8.55
Mutual Life Assurance Society v Langley (1886) 32 Ch D 460.............5.12, 5.17, 5.19

National Permanent Benefit Building Society, Re (1869) LR 5 Ch App 309 ....4.29

National Provincial Bank v Brackenbury (1906) 22 TLR 797 ....5.32
Neave v Alderton (1695) 1 Eq Ca Ab 144 ....2.02
Neve v Pennell (1863) 2 H & M 170 ....5.04
Newby v Reed (1763) 1 W Bl 416 ....5.43
Newton v Chorlton (1853) 10 Hare 646 ....8.31
Noyes v Pollock (1886) 32 Ch D 466 ....2.26, 3.26

Offley v Johnson (1584) 2 Leon 166 ....5.43
Oneal v Mead (1720) 1 P Wms 694 ....5.43

Paget v Paget (1898) 1 Ch 470 ....5.33
Paley v Field (1806) 12 Ves 435 ....3.04
Palk v Mortgage Services Funding plc [1993] Ch 330 ....3.12, 3.15
Palmer v Barclays Bank Limited (1971) 23 P & CR 30 ....3.10
Parker Tweedale v Dunbar Bank plc [1991] Ch 12 ....3.13, 3.15
Parsons & Cole v Briddock (1708) 2 Vern 608 ....2.29
Pearce v Loman (1796) 3 Ves 135 ....2.05
Pearl v Deacon (1857) 24 Beav 186..5.32
Peirs v Peirs (1750) 1 Ves Sen 521...5.43
Pelly v Wathen (1849) 3 Hare 351 ....5.03
Pendlebury v Walker (1841) 4 Y & C Ex 424 ....5.29, 5.31, 5.32
Peter v Rich (1629/1630) 1 Chan Rep 34 ....5.43
Peters v Erving (1789) 3 Bro C C 55...2.05
Pittortou, Re [1985] 1 WLR 58 ....5.33
Pledge v White [1896] AC 187 ....5.04, 5.20, 5.21
Pocock v Lee (1707) 2 Vern 604 ....5.43
Polly Peck International plc, Re [1996] BCC 486 ....8.53, 8.55
Pooley's Trustee v Whetham (1886) 33 Ch D 111 ....3.10
Pope v Onslow (1692) 2 Vern 286...5.17
Porey v Marsh (1690) 2 Vern 182 ....2.02
Povye's Case (1680) 2 Free 51 ....2.02
Praed v Gardiner (1788) 2 Cox Eq Cas 86 ....3.28, 5.03, 8.31
Pringle v Hartley (1744) 3 Atk 195 ....2.29
'Priscilla', The (1859) Lush 1..2.32, 2.40, 7.02
Professional Life Assurance Company, Re (1867) LR 3 Eq 668......................2.32, 7.02
Prowse v Abingdon (1736) 1 Atk 482...2.05

R v Doughty (1702) Wight 3 ....2.29
Raggett, Re (1880) 16 Ch D 117 ....5.03, 5.04
Rancliffe, Lord v Parkyns, Lady (1818) 6 Dow 149...2.21
Randal v Cockran (1748) 1 Ves Sen 98 ....2.29
Reliance Permanent Building Society v Harwood-Stamper [1944] Ch 362 ....3.10
Repington, Re [1904] 1 Ch 811 ....5.33, 5.34, 5.55
Riley v Hall (1898) 79 LT 244 ....5.04
Robinson v Tonge (1739) 1 P Wms 679n 2.05

Rochefort, De v Dawes (1871) LR 12 Eq 540 ....11.27
Rogers v Mackenzie (1799) 4 Ves Jun 752 ....2.29
Rooke v Kensington, Lord (1856) 21 Beav 470 ....2.50, 11.51
Rumbold v Rumbold (1796) 3 Ves Jun 65 ....5.34

Sagitory v Hyde (1687) 1 Vern 455...2.02
Salmon, Re [1903] 1 KB 149 ....5.04, 5.17
Salting, *Ex parte* (1883) 25 Ch D 148 ....8.26, 8.27, 8.31
Scott v Scott (1760) Amb 383 ....2.05
Scott's Estate, Re (1863) 14 L Ch R 63 ....2.26, 3.26
Selby v Pomfret (1861) 7 Jur (NS) 835 ....5.03, 5.04, 5.17, 5.20, 5.21
Shalcross v Dixon (1838) 7 LJ (NS) 180 ....2.46, 11.20, 11.25
Sharp v Rickards [1909] 1 Ch 109 ....5.04
Smit Tak International Zeesleepin Bergingsbedrijf BV v Selco Salvage Limited
    [1988] 2 Ll Rep 398...........................2.57, 2.59, 2.61, 2.62, 3.02, 3.32, 3.33, 3.34,
        3.35, 3.38, 9.01, 9.21, 9.26, 9.27, 9.28, 9.29, 9.30, 9.31, 9.32, 9.33, 9.34, 9.36
Smith v Wood [1929] 1 Ch 14...5.32, 5.46
Snowdon, *Ex parte* (1881) 17 Ch D 44 ....5.29
Softley, Re (1875) LR 20 Eq 746 ....5.04
South v Bloxam (1865) 2 H & M 457 ....3.08, 8.27, 8.40
Southard & Company Limited, Re [1979] 1 WLR 1198 ....8.55
Spalding v Rudding (1846) 15 LJ Ch 374..8.31
Spalding v Thompson (1858) 26 Beav 637..5.03
Sproule v Prior (1826) 8 Sim 189..2.40, 9.15
Standard Chartered Bank Limited v Walker [1982] 3 All ER 938 ....3.16
State Fire Insurance Company, Re The (1863) 32 LJ Ch 300 ....2.32, 7.02
Steel v Dixon (1881) 17 Ch D 825 ....5.31, 5.32
Stephenson, Re (1866) 3 De G M & G 969.....................2.40, 10.02, 11.49, 11.55
Stirling v Burdett [1911] 2 Ch 418 ....5.29
Stirling v Forrester (1821) 3 Bli 575...2.29, 5.29
Stringer v Harper (1858) 26 Beav 33...5.32
Stronge v Hawkes (1859) 4 De G & J 632..5.36, 11.26
Swain v Wall (1641) 1 Rep Ch 149...5.31, 5.43

Tassell v Smith (1858) 2 De G & J 713 ....5.03, 5.04
Thorneycroft v Crockett (1848) 2 HLC 239 ....5.04
Thorpe v Jackson (1837) 2 Y & C Ex 553...2.32, 7.02
Tidd v Lister (1853) 3 De G M & G 857...2.21, 7.02
Tipping v Tipping (1721) 1 P Wms 729...2.05
Titley v Davies (1743) 2 Y & C Ch Cas 399 ....2.07, 2.08, 2.09, 5.12
Tombs v Roch (1846) 2 Coll 490..5.28, 5.39
Townley, Re [1922] 1 Ch 154..2.53, 7.02
Trestrail v Mason (1878) 7 Ch D 665 ....5.32
'Trident', The (1839) 1 Wm Rob 29..2.40
Trimmer v Bayne (1803) 9 Ves 209 ....2.21, 2.40, 9.15

Tristram, Re (1825) 1 Deac 288..2.42, 10.02, 11.02

Trumper v Trumper (1872) LR 14 Eq 295 ....2.46, 11.20

Tse Kwong Lam v Wong Chit Sen [1983] 1 WLR 1349................................3.12, 3.15

Turner, *Ex parte* (1796) 3 Ves 243 ....3.04, 5.43

Turner v Davies (1796) 2 Esp 478..5.43

Tweedale v Tweedale (1857) 23 Beav 341 ....5.03, 5.04, 5.20, 5.21

Vint v Padget (1858) 2 De G & J 611.............................5.04, 5.20, 5.21

Walhampton Estate, Re (1884) 26 Ch D 391 ....2.50, 11.51

Wallis v Woodyear (1855) 2 Jur (NS) 179 ....2.25, 2.32, 3.19, 3.26, 7.02

Ward v National Bank of New Zealand (1883) 8 App Cas 755 ....5.29, 5.32

Waring v Ward (1802) 7 Ves 332 ....5.33, 5.34

Warner v Jacob (1882) 20 Ch D 220 ....3.10

Watts v Symes (1851) 1 De G M & G 240 ....5.03, 5.04, 5.17

Webb v Hewitt (1857) 3 K & J 438...5.32

Webb v Smith (1885) 30 Ch D 192.......1.10, 2.23, 2.30, 2.32, 2.39, 2.40, 2.62, 3.26,
                            7.02, 7.03, 7.25, 7.26, 7.32, 9.01, 9.02, 9.03, 9.04, 9.05,
                            9.12, 9.15, 9.16, 9.17, 9.18, 9.19, 9.20, 9.21, 9.22, 9.23,
                                     9.24, 9.26, 9.27, 9.34, 11.07, 11.08, 11.25

Webster v Alsop (1791) 3 Bro C C 352n..2.05

Wellesley v Mornington, Lord (1869) 17 WR 355.......................2.46, 11.20

Westzinthus, In re (1833) 5 B & Ad 817..8.31

White v Hillacre (1839) 3 Y & C Ex 597 ....5.04, 5.20

Willie v Lugg (1761) 2 Eden 78 ....5.17

Wilson v Mitchell [1939] 2 KB 869 ....5.29

Wisden v Wisden (1854) 2 Sm & G 396 ....5.31

Wolmershausen, Re (1890) 62 LT 541...5.32

Wolverhampton and Walsall Railway Company v London and NW Railway
    Company (1873) LR 16 Eq 433...5.51

Wood v West (1895) 40 Sol Jo 114...............................2.46, 11.20

Wrexham Mold and Connah's Quay Railway Company, Re [1899]
    1 Ch 440 ....4.29, 4.30, 4.31

Wright v Morley (1805) 11 Ves Jun 12........................2.29, 8.31

Wright v Nutt (1791) 3 Bro C C 326 ....2.05

Wright v Simpson (1802) 6 Ves 714 ....2.26, 3.26

Yonge v Reynell (1852) 9 Hare 809..5.32

IRELAND

Archer's Estate, In re [1914] 1 IR 285 ....2.54, 11.25, 11.28

Averall v Wade (1835) L & G temp Sugd 252.................2.13, 2.21, 2.30, 2.49, 5.36,
                                            10.01, 11.08, 11.25, 11.55

Buckley v Buckley (1887) 19 LR Ir 544.......................................2.40, 9.15

Chute's Estate, In re [1914] 1 IR 180...5.36, 5.49

Fox, Re (1856) 5 Ir Ch R 541 ....3.26

Hales v Cox (1863) 32 Beav 118 ....2.42, 2.50, 5.55, 10.02, 11.43, 11.55, 11.56
Hollinshead v Devane (1914) 49 ILT 87..2.54, 11.55

Ker v Ker (1869) 4 IR Eq 15 ....1.05, 2.49, 5.34, 5.36, 5.49, 11.55

Lawder's Estate, Re (1861) 11 Ir Ch R 346 ....2.21, 2.46, 3.26, 11.28
Lombard & Ulster Banking Limited v Murray & Murray
   [1987] ILRM 522...2.53, 7.05
Lynch's Estate, Re (1867) 1 Ir R Eq 396 ....2.42, 10.02
Lysaght's Estate, In re [1903] 1 IR 235...........................2.54, 5.49, 5.55, 11.55, 11.56

McCarthy v M'Cartie (No 2) [1904] 1 IR 100........................2.54, 5.36, 11.55, 11.56

Ocean Accident & Guarantee Corporation Limited and Hewitt v Collum [1913]
   1 IR 337...2.54, 5.36, 11.55

Roche's Estate, Re (1890) 25 LR Ir 284 ....2.46, 5.36, 11.28
Roddy's Estate, Re (1861) 11 Ir Ch R 369 ....2.46, 5.36, 11.28
Rorke's Estate, In re (1865) 15 Ir Ch R 316..2.50, 11.56

Scott's Estate, In re (1862) 14 Ir Ch R 63 ....2.42, 10.02
Smyth v Toms [1918] 1 IR 338..2.54, 11.25, 11.28

Tighe v Dolphin [1906] 1 IR 305 ....5.36, 11.26

NEW ZEALAND

Australian Guarantee Corporation (NZ) Limited v Nicholson (1995) 7 NZCLC
   260, 932...12.17

Bisset v ANZ Bank Limited [1961] NZLR 687....................................2.52, 3.23, 3.26
Brigham v Chambers (1880) OB & F 66 ....2.13, 2.26, 3.26

Clark v National Mutual Life Association of Australia Limited [1966] NZLR
   196..3.16
Clark v UDC Finance [1985] 2 NZLR 636 ....3.12

Manawatu Transport Limited, Re (1984) 2 NZCLC 99,084 .....2.52, 2.55, 3.26, 7.05,
                                            8.02, 8.11, 8.36, 8.42, 8.44, 8.46, 8.63

National Bank of New Zealand Limited v Caldesia Promotions Limited and
   Jenkins Roberts & Associates Limited [1996] 3 NZLR 467....2.52, 2.54, 3.26, 4.14,
                                                       5.44, 5.48, 11.28

National Bank of New Zealand Limited v Chapman [1975] 1 NZLR 480.............9.14

New Zealand Loan & Mercantile Agency Company Limited v Loach (1912)
   31 NZLR 292 ....2.55, 3.08, 8.02, 8.26, 8.27, 8.36, 8.37, 8.38,
                              8.39, 8.40, 8.41, 8.42, 8.44, 8.45, 8.46, 8.47, 8.63

Olivier v Colonial Bank (1887) 5 NZLR 239......................................2.13, 2.46, 11.28

Stephenson, Re (1911) 30 NZLR 145..5.55, 11.55

Taylor, Re [1934] NZLR 117 ....7.05

Tremain, Re [1934] NZLR 369 ....2.52, 3.26, 10.01, 11.01

Watkins, Re [1938] NZLR 847...2.53, 10.01

Wilkin v Deans (1886) 6 NZLR 425...5.09

UNITED STATES OF AMERICA

AEI Corporation, In re 11 BR 97 (1981).............................8.52, 8.64, 10.05

American National Insurance Company v Vine-Wood Realty Company 199 A 2d
   449 (1964) 3.35

Anderson v Engwall 149 NW 611 (1914) 10.12

Ayres v Husted 15 Conn 504 (1843)...8.17

Beacon Distributors, Inc., In re 441 F 2d 547 (1971)......................................2.02, 2.13

Borges, In re 184 BR 874 (1995)...10.07

Careful Laundry, Inc., In re 104 A 2d 813 (1954)...................................10.04

Carter v Tanners' Leather Company 81 NE 902 (1907)...8.17

Center Wholesale, Inc., In re 759 F 2d 1440 (1985) 10.11, 10.13, 10.16

Chase Manhattan Bank v Gems-by-Gordon Inc 649 F 2d 710 (1981) 9.38

Cheesebrough v Millard (1815) 1 Johns Chan 408..11.13

Childers, In re 44 BR 23 (1984)..8.62

Coast Bank v Minderhout 392 P 2d 265 (1964) 9.38

Computer Room, Inc., In re 24 BR 732 (1982) 8.52, 8.55, 8.64, 10.04

Dealer Support Services International, Inc., In re 73 BR 763 (1987).............8.52, 8.64

Dig It, Inc., In re 129 BR 65 (1991) 10.07

DuPage Lumber & Home Improvement Center Company, Inc v Georgia-Pacific
   Corporation 34 BR 737 (1983) 8.52, 8.62, 8.64

'Edith', The 94 US 518 (1876)...10.04

El Paso Truck Center, Inc., In re 129 BR 109 (1991) 10.07

Enloe v Franklin Bank & Trust Company 445 NE 2d 1005 (1983)......................8.62

Equitable Savings & Loan Association v 20th Avenue Corporation 235 NYS 2d
   394 (1962) 11.29

Equitable Trust Company v Imbesi 412 A 2d 96 (1980) 9.38

Farmers & Merchants Bank v Gibson 7 BR 437 (1980) 8.49, 8.52, 8.55, 8.64
First National Bank of Boston v Proctor 40 F 2d 841 (1930) 10.04

Gibson Group, Inc., In re 151 BR 133 (1993) 10.04
Greenwich Trust Company v Tyson 27 A 2d 166 (1942)......................................10.04

Hale, In re 141 BR 225 (1992)..10.04
Hall v Hyer 37 SE 594 (1900)..8.62
Harvest Milling Company, In re 221 F Supp 836 (1963)..8.52
House v Thompson 3 Head 512 (1859) 8.17

Ingersoll v Somers Land Company 89 A 288 (1913) 10.12, 11.29

Jack Green's Fashions for Men – Big & Tall, Inc., In re 507 F 2d 130
    (1979) 8.52, 8.64, 10.05, 10.06, 10.07, 10.08
James Stewart & Company v National Shawmut Bank of Boston 196 NE 169
    (1935) 10.12
Jenkins v Smith 48 NYS 126 (1897) 8.62
Johnson v Lentini 169 A 2d 208 (1961) 10.04

Langdel v Moore 168 NE 57 (1929) 10.12
Lewis v United States 92 US 618 (1875) 10.04
Liberty Outdoors, Inc., In re 204 BR 746 (1997)..10.05
Ludwig Honold Manufacturing, In re 33 BR 724 (1983)............................8.62, 10.05

McElwaney, In re 40 BR 66 (1984)..10.04, 10.07
Maimone, In re 41 BR 974 (1984)...8.62
Mason v Hull 45 NE 632 (1896) 8.62, 8.63
Merrill v National Bank 173 US 131 (1899) 10.04
Mesa Intercontinental, Inc., In re 79 BR 669 (1987)...10.04
Meyer v United States 375 US 233 (1963) 2.13, 8.49, 8.62, 10.14, 11.29
Multiple Services Industries, In re 18 BR 635 (1982) 8.52, 8.55, 8.64

Neff v Miller 8 Pa (Barr) 347 (1848) 8.17
Newsom v McLendon 6 Ga 392 (1849) 8.17

Plad, Inc., In re 24 BR 676 (1982) 8.52, 8.64

Rich Supply House, Inc., In re 43 BR 68 (1984).......................................8.52, 8.65

Sanborn, McDuffee Company v Keefe 187 A 97 (1936) 10.12, 11.29
Savings & Loan Corporation v Bear 154 SE 587 (1930) 8.17
Schraff v Meyer 35 SW 858 (1896)..10.04
Shedoudy v Beverly Surgical Supply Company 161 Cal Rptr 164 (1980).............10.05
Spectra Prism Industries, Inc., In re 28 BR 397 (1983) 10.11, 10.13, 10.14, 10.15

Speer v Home Bank 206 SW 405 (1918) 8.62
Stickel v Atwood 56 A 687 (1903)..10.04
Swift & Company v Kortrecht 112 F 709 (1902)...................................8.62

Tahoe National Bank v Phillips 480 P 2d 320 (1971) 9.38
Tampa Chain Company, Inc., In re 53 BR 772 (1985)...............8.52, 8.55, 8.56, 8.65

Union Bank v Laird 15 US 390 (1817) 10.04
United Medical Research, Inc., In re 12 BR 941 (1981).......................8.52, 8.55, 8.65

Vermont Toy Works, Inc., In re 82 BR 258 (1987) 8.52, 8.65

Weaver v TriCity Credit Bureau 557 P 2d 1072 (1976)..........................9.38
Weiss, In re 34 BR 346 (1983)...8.62
Wenatchee Production Credit Association v Pacific Fruit & Produce Company 92
    P 2d 883 (1939) 10.04
West Coast Optical Instruments, Inc., In re 177 BR 720 (1992)....10.11, 10.13, 10.16
Wilson Dairy Company, In re 30 BR 67 (1983)....................................8.62

TABLE OF LEGISLATION

AUSTRALIA

New South Wales

Conveyancing Act 1919
  s 97 ....5.07
Law Reform (Miscellaneous Provisions) Act 1965
  s 3..2.29

Queensland

Property Law Act 1974-1985
  s 98..5.07

Victoria

Property Law Act 1958
  s 93 ....5.07
Supreme Court Act 1986
  s 52 ....2.29

Western Australia

Property Law Act 1969-1979
  s 66 ....5.07

CANADA

British Columbia

Property Law Act, RSBC 1996
  s 31 ....5.10

Ontario

Land Titles Act, RSO 1990
  s 97 ....5.10
Mercantile Law Amendment Act, RSO 1980
  s 2 ....2.29
Registry Act, RSO 1990
  s 72 ....5.10

Saskatchewan

Queen's Bench Act, RSS 1978
s 44 ....5.10

IRELAND

Conveyancing Act 1881
  s 17(1) 5.06

NEW ZEALAND

Judicature Act 1908
  s 85 ....2.29
Property Law Act 1952
  s 85 ....5.09

UNITED KINGDOM

Companies Act 1985
  s 24 ....8.53
  s 227 ....8.53
  Pt XII 1.02
    Ch 1 ....3.36
Companies Act 1989
  Pt IV 3.36
Conveyancing Act 1881
  s 17 ....5.05
Income and Corporation Taxes Act 1988 ....8.53
Insolvency Act 1986
  s 214(7) 8.53
  Pt VI 1.02, 8.53
  Pt IX
    Ch V 1.02, 8.53
Law of Property Act 1925
  s 93 ....5.05, 5.06
Mercantile Law Amendment Act 1856
  s 5 ....2.29

UNITED STATES OF AMERICA

Bankruptcy Reform Act 1978
  s 544(a)(1) 10.07, 10.09, 10.14

PART I

INTRODUCTION

1

INTRODUCTION

What is Marshalling of Securities?	**1.01**	The inverse order rule	1.05
The singular nature of marshalling of securities	1.02	**Organisation of this Text**	**1.07**
The treatment of marshalling of securities	1.03	Other jurisdictions	1.12
Confusion about marshalling of securities	1.04	Terminology	1.13

A. What is Marshalling of Securities?

1.01 The equitable doctrine of marshalling of securities is the label given to the process by which equity intervenes to protect the secured status or priority-ranking of a creditor holding *mesne* or junior-ranking security following the enforcement of a prior-ranking security.

The doctrine typically applies where one creditor (the 'senior creditor') holds first-ranking security over two or more assets of a debtor as security for the repayment of a common debt, and another creditor (the 'junior creditor') holds a second-ranking security over one of those assets. Should the senior creditor recoup its secured debt by enforcing its security against that asset, which is also subject to the junior creditor's security, the doctrine of marshalling will permit the junior creditor to 'marshall' the senior creditor's security. By this is meant that the junior creditor will, *via* the intervention of equity, be placed in the position of the senior creditor, as against those other assets of the debtor which are subject to only the senior creditor's security, to the extent of any deficiency in the junior creditor's security.[1]

Thus, by allowing the junior creditor to effectively exchange its own eroded security for the intact security of the senior creditor, the doctrine acts to preserve the junior creditor's priority-ranking *qua* the debtor. Equity, in this manner, ensures that a paramount-ranking creditor does not, in the course of recovering its secured debt, prejudice the ability of *puisne* secured creditors to recover their debts and,

---

[1] See, for example, the description of marshalling of securities in W F Beddoes, *A Concise Treatise on the Law of Mortgages* (2nd ed 1908 Stevens & Sons), 105: 'a second mortgagee gets the benefit of a fund not included in his security as compensation for the loss of his own security'.

consequently that, as far as possible, the assets of a common debtor are made available to satisfy the claims of its secured creditors.[2]

The singular nature of marshalling of securities

1.02 The law of securities is, to a large degree, concerned with the problem of priorities. This requires an examination of the relative merits of competing claims against a common debtor and a determination of the order in which the debtor's assets should be applied in satisfying those claims.

The doctrine of marshalling is, however, of an entirely different character from the rules that typically regulate the order in which the claims of competing creditors are to be met.[3] Marshalling is not determinative of whether or not the claim of one creditor deserves precedence over that of another,[4] but merely accepts the priorities generated by those rules. Nor does marshalling affect the quantum of assets available for distribution.[5] Marshalling acts instead to preserve the existing priority-ranking of *puisne* secured creditors, by conferring upon such creditors the benefit of a security held by a prior-ranking creditor.

The treatment of marshalling of securities

1.03 The doctrine of marshalling of securities boasts a recorded history of at least some three hundred years and has, moreover, since the mid-nineteenth century, been the subject of comment in the leading English texts on equity and securities.[6] However, for the most part, these cases and texts have been content merely to describe the operation of the doctrine, without attempting to resolve the conflicting lines of authority as to the pre-requisites[7] and ambit[8] of marshalling.[9] Nor to date has any substantive inquiry been undertaken into marshalling's relationship with the equitable doctrine of subrogation[10] or the veracity of those disparate

---

[2] Marshalling does not sacrifice full payment of the senior creditor's debt to ensure recovery of the junior creditor's debt; if the asset subject to the junior creditor's security is insufficient to meet the senior creditor's debt, the senior creditor will be entitled to look to the other assets encompassed by its security, free of any marshalling claim: e g J J Shalhoub, *Marshaling: Equitable Rights of Holders of Junior Interests* (1986) 38 Rutgers L Rev 287, 289n18.

[3] e g Shalhoub, *Marshaling: Equitable Rights of Holders of Junior Interests*, 287–288; B MacDougall, *Marshalling and the Personal Property Security Acts: Doing Unto Others . . .* (1994) 28 UBCLR 91, 91–92.

[4] e g the priority provisions of Part XII of the *Companies Act 1985*.

[5] e g the voidable transactions provisions of Part VI, and Chapter V of Part IX, of the *Insolvency Act 1986*.

[6] See further Chapter 2.

[7] e g the apparent requirement that the securities held by senior and junior creditors must be proprietary in nature: see further Chapter 9.

[8] e g the issue of the persistence of marshalling in the face of competing third party rights: see further Chapters 10 and 11.

[9] c f R P Meagher, W M C Gummow & J R F Lehane, *Equity Doctrines and Remedies* (3rd ed 1992 Butterworths), Chapter 11.

[10] See further Chapter 4.

claims which see marshalling as derivative of consolidation, contribution or specific performance.[11]

The following comments are demonstrative of this treatment of marshalling: '[there is] no reason to look for a deeper principle than that equity will not allow a first incumbrancer . . . to satisfy or disappoint a second at his election'.[12] The absence of a coherent explanation of the doctrine of marshalling of securities is, however, inexplicable in the face of marshalling's ability to intervene in the affairs of a debtor for the benefit of *puisne* secured creditors and the predilection of borrowers to raise funds by granting multiple securities to different financiers. The characterisation of marshalling in this text as an equitable doctrine, which protects the priority-ranking of *puisne* secured creditors by effecting a redistribution of a debtor's assets for their benefit, thus represents a radical departure from existing treatments of marshalling.[13]

Confusion about marshalling of securities

The label 'marshalling of securities', in a manner inconsistent with the right of a **1.04** *puisne* secured creditor to obtain access to a prior-ranking security, has been used to describe the following disparate rights:[14]

    (1) A surety's right, upon the discharge of the guaranteed debt, to be subrogated to the securities held by a creditor for that debt.[15]

    (2) A surety's apparent rights in respect of a security held by a creditor, for a debt other than the guaranteed debt, in circumstances where that security can be consolidated with the security held by the creditor for the guaranteed debt.[16]

    (3) The rights of co-sureties to share, as between themselves, the securities held by a creditor for the guaranteed debt.[17]

    (4) The right of a voluntary disponee of an asset to throw liability for a secured debt onto the transferor of the asset.[18]

    (5) The 'inverse order rule'.[19]

---

[11] See further Chapter 5.

[12] H G Hanbury & C H M Waldock, *The Law of Mortgages* (1938 Stevens & Sons), 182.

[13] See further Chapter 3.

[14] There is support in Australia for a further instance of 'marshalling', that encompasses 'cases which are not within the doctrine of marshalling, but [which] can be decided on the same general principles of equity from which the principles of marshalling have been derived' (*Sarge Pty Ltd v Cazihaven Homes Pty Ltd* (1994) 34 NSWLR 658, 663; q v *Finance Corp of Australia Ltd v Bentley* (1991) 5 BPR 97412, 11,834 and 11,841). It is not, however, clear whether this *dictum* relates to those situations in which equitable doctrines similar to marshalling, such as contribution, apply (see further Chapter 5) or supports the view that, in certain circumstances, the doctrine of marshalling of securities should be applied other than *strictu sensu*.

[15] See further paragraph 8.27.

[16] See further paragraphs 8.29–8.32.

[17] See further paragraphs 5.46 and 5.47.

[18] See further paragraph 5.55.

[19] *Sarge Pty Ltd v Cazihaven Homes Pty Ltd* (1994) 34 NSWLR 658, 662.

These ostensible instances of marshalling of securities are, with the exception of (5), considered in Chapters 5 and 8.

The inverse order rule

1.05   The inverse order rule,[20] in contrast to the other instances of 'marshalling' identified above, is an almost exclusively American doctrine,[21] although its origins may be traced back to English law.[22]

The inverse order rule encompasses situations where a debtor has granted a security over two or more of its assets to a creditor and has subsequently transferred some or all of those assets to third parties without having obtained a release of the security. A third party transferee may apply this rule to require the creditor to satisfy its secured debt out of the assets retained by the debtor in priority to the transferred assets.[23] Only if the assets retained by the debtor are insufficient to discharge the secured debt may the creditor resort to the transferred assets, and then only in the inverse order of their transfer, *viz.* the asset transferred last must be first exhausted before the creditor may resort to the asset that was the subject of the penultimate transfer, and so on.[24]

1.06   The United States courts have taken the view that the inverse order rule, although related to marshalling, is not an instance of marshalling.[25] There is one fundamental, irreconcilable difference between the doctrine of marshalling of securities

---

[20]   This rule is usually described as the 'inverse order of alienation doctrine' or 'doctrine of sale in the inverse order of alienation': *American Jurisprudence* (1996 Lawyers Co-operative Publishing), para 53:8. See also L A Jones, *A Treatise on the Law of Mortgages of Real Property* (1878 Houghton, Osgood & Co), paras 1630–1631 and C F Beach Jr., *Commentaries on Modern Equity Jurisprudence* (1892 Baker, Voorhis & Co), para 795.

[21]   The inverse order rule is not recognised by English law. Nonetheless, the equitable doctrine of exoneration, under English law, does permit a prior transferee, in a limited range of circumstances, to be exonerated from liability for a secured debt at the expense of a subsequent transferee. In contrast to the inverse order rule, the prior transferee cannot interfere with the enforcement by the creditor of its security and, moreover, the prior transferee must have contracted to take its asset free of the creditor's security (see further paragraph 5.36).

[22]   *Am Jur*, para 53:8. *Harbert's Case* (1584) 3 Co Rep 11b is cited in connection with the inverse order rule by *Sarge Pty Ltd v Cazihaven Homes Pty Ltd* (1994) 34 NSWLR 658, 662 (whilst the rule may have been derived from that case, the case itself is only authority for the principle that the transferees of assets subject to a common security are rateably liable for the secured debt: see *Ker v Ker* (1869) 4 Ir Eq 15, 24–29).

[23]   *Am Jur*, paras 53:33 and 53:37.

[24]   *Am Jur*, paras 53:33 and 53:38. See also Shalhoub, *Marshaling: Equitable Rights of Holders of Junior Interests*, 288n13. A subsequent transferee against whom the rule is sought to be enforced by a prior transferee must have had actual or constructive notice of the prior transfer: *Am Jur*, para 53:40. The United States courts are divided as to whether the transferee seeking to apply the rule must have expressly contracted to take its asset free of the creditor's security: *Am Jur*, para 53:39.

[25]   See, in particular, the cases cited at *Am Jur*, para 53:8n61. The two doctrines are considered analogous under United States law as they both act to compel a secured creditor to realise the assets subject to its security in a particular order: *Am Jur*, para 53:8. The version of marshalling, generally accepted by English law, does not act in that manner: see further Chapter 3.

and the inverse order rule. The right of a transferee to apply the inverse order rule, by requiring the creditor to enforce its security against an asset owned by the debtor or another transferee, is dependent upon the time at which that transferee acquired its asset *qua* the other transferees.[26] Further, that right, once it arises, is indefeasible.[27] In contrast, a junior creditor's right to marshall the senior security is dependent upon the circumstances prevailing at the time that right is sought to be enforced, and may be qualified or displaced by the conduct of the debtor subsequent to the grant of the security to the junior creditor.[28]

B. Organisation of this Text

Part II considers the history, and operation, of the doctrine of marshalling of securities. The development of marshalling of securities under English law and the general principles that govern its application are described in Chapter 2. This chapter provides the historical context for the later discussion in this text of the nature and incidents of marshalling. **1.07**

There are two distinct theories as to how the doctrine of marshalling should act to protect the priority-ranking of *puisne* secured creditors. Should the doctrine compel the prior-ranking creditor to realise the assets subject to its security in a particular order? Or should the doctrine only intervene if the secured status of a *puisne* secured creditor has deteriorated as a result of the prior-ranking creditor's recovery of its debt? Chapter 3 discusses the two theories and the competing lines of authority in support of each theory. **1.08**

Following the consideration of this key issue, Part III examines the juridical nature of marshalling of securities. Chapter 4 discusses whether marshalling of securities should be regarded as a sub-set of the equitable doctrine of subrogation rather than a distinct doctrine, on the basis that subrogation acts by substituting one party to the rights of another. Chapter 5 inquires into the relationship between marshalling of securities, on the one hand, and consolidation, contribution and specific performance, on the other, all of which have been claimed as precursors of marshalling. Chapter 6 considers the underlying rationale for marshalling of securities. **1.09**

Part IV examines the requirements that a *puisne* secured creditor must satisfy before equity will permit it to marshall the security held by a prior-ranking **1.10**

---

[26] *Am Jur*, paras 53:8, 53:33, 53:36 and 53:38. Simultaneous transferees of different assets cannot invoke the inverse order rule as against one another, but are instead liable rateably for the secured debt (should the assets retained by the debtor prove insufficient): *Am Jur*, paras 53:8, 53:36 and 53:38.

[27] *Am Jur*, paras 53:8 and 53:36.

[28] See further Chapter 11.

creditor. Chapter 7 discusses the requirements prescribed by the 'common debtor rule' and Chapter 8 discusses the exceptions to that rule. Chapter 9 considers the requirement, said to be established by *Webb v Smith*,[29] that marshalling of securities will only be available where the securities held by the prior-ranking and *puisne* creditors are proprietary securities.

1.11 Finally, Part V examines the limits of marshalling of securities. Chapter 10 discusses the position of unsecured creditors and, in particular, their ability to curtail a *puisne* secured creditor's marshalling rights. Chapter 11 considers the persistence of marshalling in the face of competing third party rights and the circumstances in which the right to marshall security will be qualified or abrogated by such rights. Chapter 12 examines the efficacy of contractual constraints, such as covenants against marshalling, upon marshalling of securities.

Other jurisdictions

1.12 The principal focus of this text is the law of England and Wales. In addition, this text considers the doctrine of marshalling of securities as it is applied under the laws of Australia, Canada, Ireland and New Zealand. The laws of the United States and Scotland are also considered, to the extent that they illuminate the application of marshalling of securities under English law.

Terminology

1.13 As regards the terminology used in this text, the term 'senior creditor' describes the creditor who holds prior-ranking security over two or more assets of the debtor, while the term 'junior creditor' describes the creditor who is seeking to marshall the senior creditor's security. The terms 'senior debt' and 'senior security' refer to the debt owed by the debtor to the senior creditor and the security held by the senior creditor for that debt respectively. The terms 'junior debt' and 'junior security' refer to the debt owed by the debtor (or, as in Chapter 8, a third party) to the junior creditor and the security held by the junior creditor for that debt respectively.

---

[29] (1885) 30 Ch D 192.

PART II

GENERAL PRINCIPLES – HISTORY AND OPERATION OF MARSHALLING OF SECURITIES

2

THE HISTORY OF THE EQUITABLE DOCTRINE OF MARSHALLING OF SECURITIES

Origins of Marshalling of Securities

Seventeenth-century cases   2.02
Eighteenth-century cases   2.05
Consolidation as the basis for marshalling:
   introduction   2.07
   Ashburner's argument   2.08
Alleged Roman law origins   2.10

Establishment of the General Principles of Marshalling

Nineteenth-century cases   2.14
Marshalling as a post-realisation remedy:
   introduction   2.19
   dominance of coercion theory   2.21
   reaction   2.23
priority-preservation without coercion of
   senior creditor   2.24
   developments in subrogation   2.28
Conditions on the availability of marshalling:
   introduction   2.30
   common debtor rule   2.32
   requirements (1) and (2) of common
     debtor rule   2.33

surety exception   2.35
requirement (3) of common debtor rule   2.37
requirement (4) of common debtor rule   2.38
proprietary securities   2.39
Undermining or excluding right to marshall:
   introduction   2.41
   transfers or dispositions by way of
     security   2.44
   absolute transfers or dispositions   2.48

Affirmation of General Principles of Marshalling   **2.51**

Acceptance of post-realisation theory   2.52
Common debtor rule   2.53
Marshalling and third parties   2.54

Recent Developments in Marshalling

Recent developments:
   competing rights of surety   2.55
   revival of coercion theory   2.57
   extension to non-security interests   2.62

2.01   The purpose of this chapter is to provide the foundations for the discussion, later in this text, of the competing juridical views as to how marshalling should preserve the priority-ranking of junior creditors, and the conditions and limitations which presently govern the application of marshalling.

A. Origins of Marshalling of Securities

Early cases on marshalling of securities—seventeenth-century cases

2.02 The equitable doctrine of marshalling of securities is first encountered in English law, in two decisions of the Court of Chancery in the late seventeenth century:[1] *Bovey v Skipwith*[2] and *Povye's Case.*[3] In both cases, the courts considered that the doctrine of marshalling of securities was a broad remedy generally available at equity to protect the second-ranking security held by a junior creditor.

A senior creditor, who held first-ranking security over two or more assets belonging to the same debtor would thus be prevented, by the intervention of marshalling, from undermining the ability of the junior creditor to recover from one of those assets the debt due to it.

2.03 The doctrine of marshalling depicted in the very first reported cases on marshalling is a remedy which impinges upon the right of the senior creditor to enforce its securities. Although the courts, in the above two cases, were clearly cognisant of the role performed by marshalling as a priority-preservation device, there is nothing in their decisions to suggest that they were advocating a remedy which operated – as does the modern version of marshalling – by redistributing the assets of a debtor.

2.04 Marshalling, as it first appears in English law, ensures that a junior creditor's secured claim against a debtor is protected by denying the senior creditor the discretion to realise the assets subject to its security in the order it sees fit. The emphasis is thus on preventing the senior creditor from adversely affecting the junior creditor, rather than on redressing the impact of a prejudicial enforcement by the senior creditor, by restoring the junior creditor to its original position once the debt owed to the senior creditor has been satisfied.[4]

---

[1] It is also in this period that the related doctrine of marshalling of beneficiaries and legatees first makes its appearance in English law: *Burgh v Francis* (1673) Rep temp Finch 29; *Anonymous* (1679) 2 Ch Cas 5; *Culpepper v Aston* (1682) 2 Ch Cas 115; *Bullock v Knight* (1682) 2 Ch Cas 117; *Sagitory v Hyde* (1687) 1 Vern 455; *Porey v Marsh* (1690) 2 Vern 182; *Neave v Alderton* (1695) 1 Eq Ca Ab 144. See A L Goodhart & H G Hanbury (eds), *Holdsworth's History of English Law* (7th ed Methuen & Co), Vol VI, 656–657. It should be noted that in the United States case, *In re Beacon Distributors, Inc* 441 F 2d 547 (1971), the origins of marshalling of securities were erroneously traced back to *Culpepper v Aston* (1682) 2 Ch Cas 115, a case which dealt with marshalling of legatees not marshalling of securities.

[2] (1671) 1 Ch Cas 201.

[3] (1680) 2 Free 51.

[4] This interpretation is supported by the fact that these two cases were followed by *Lanoy v Duke & Duchess of Athol* (1742) 2 Atk 444 and *A-G v Tyndall* (1764) Amb 614, in which the coercive nature of marshalling was made explicit.

Early cases on marshalling of securities—eighteenth-century cases

This characterisation of the doctrine of marshalling, as a device which is coercive **2.05** of the senior creditor, is far more explicit in the two major eighteenth-century English cases on marshalling of securities.[5] In *Lanoy v Duke & Duchess of Athol*,[6] marshalling was described by Lord Hardwicke as follows:[7]

> Is it not then the constant equity of this court that if a creditor has two funds he shall take his satisfaction out of that fund upon which another creditor has no lien . . . Suppose a person, who has two real estates, mortgages both to one person, and afterwards only one estate to a second mortgagee, who had no notice of the first; the court, in order to relieve the second mortgage, *have directed the first to take his satisfaction out of that estate only which is not in mortgage to the second mortgagee*, if that is sufficient to satisfy the first mortgagee, in order to make room for the second mortgagee (emphasis added).

The same view was also expressed by Lord Henley in *A-G v Tyndall*:[8]

> [W]here a person had a double fund to resort to, and another person had a demand upon one of those funds, *the Court has turned the person having the double security upon that fund, which was not liable to the other person's demand,* in order to leave the fund open which was (emphasis added).

The doctrine of marshalling, as it was applied in the eighteenth century, protects **2.06** the security held by the junior creditor by restricting the senior creditor's freedom of action, rather than by substituting the junior creditor to the security of the senior creditor (and, in so doing, effecting a redistribution of the debtor's

---

[5] The following eighteenth-century cases are also relevant to marshalling: (i) *Carter v Barnadiston* (1718) 1 P Wms 506 and *Galton v Hancock* (1743) 2 Atk 428 are concerned with the apparent right of a volunteer to marshall (see further paragraph 5.55); (ii) *Finch v Winchelsea* (1718) 1 P Wms 399n, appears in the notes to Volume 24 of the English Reports (24 ER 277) as one of a number of authorities for the proposition that unsecured creditors have no standing to marshall the security of a senior creditor. This case has not, however, been otherwise reported. The particular issue raised in that case is considered in Chapter 10. A fourth case from this period, *Robinson v Tonge* (1739) 1 P Wms 679n, is not considered in this text as it was overruled by *Aldrich v Cooper* (1803) 8 Ves Jun 382.

[6] (1742) 2 Atk 444. There are also a large number of cases from the eighteenth century, which deal with the marshalling of beneficiaries and legatees: *Hyde v Hyde* (1708) 3 Ch Rep 155; *Masters v Masters* (1717) 1 P Wms 421; *Freemoult v Dedire* (1718) 1 P Wms 429; *Clifton v Burt* (1720) 1 P Wms 678; *Tipping v Tipping* (1721) 1 P Wms 729; *Mills v Eden* (1725) 10 Mod 487; *Bligh v Earl of Darnley* (1731) 2 P Wms 619; *Lutkin v Leigh* (1734) Cases T Talbot 53; *Prowse v Abingdon* (1736) 1 Atk 482; *Kirkham v Smith* (1749) Amb 518; *Hanby v Roberts* (1751) Amb 127; *Forrester v Lord Leigh* (1753) Amb 171; *Hamly v Fisher* (1757) 1 Dick 104; *Hanby v Fisher* (1757) 2 Coll 512; *Scott v Scott* (1760) Amb 383; *Hoare v Contencin* (1779) 1 Bro C C 27; *Peters v Erving* (1789) 3 Bro C C 55; *Wright v Nutt* (1791) 3 Bro C C 326; *Foster v Cook* (1791) 3 Bro C C 347; *Bradford v Foley* (1791) 3 Bro C C 351n; *Webster v Alsop* (1791) 3 Bro C C 352n; *Pearce v Loman* (1796) 3 Ves 135. See also J Fonblanque, *A Treatise of Equity* (1820 J & W T Clarke), 286–301 for an early discussion of marshalling of beneficiaries and legatees.

[7] *Lanoy v Duke & Duchess of Athol* (1742) 2 Atk 444, 446.

[8] (1764) Amb 614, 615–616.

assets) once the senior debt has been recouped. The risk of loss to the junior creditor is dealt with by compelling the senior creditor to look first to those assets, over which only it holds security, for the satisfaction of its debt.[9]

Consolidation as the basis for marshalling—introduction

2.07 Perhaps the most significant development in the eighteenth century may be attributed to *Titley v Davies*.[10] In Chapter 1, it was noted that there were a number of claims that had been made concerning the origins of marshalling. The most significant of these relates to the categorisation of marshalling as a form of, or derivative from, the equitable doctrine of consolidation of mortgages.

In contrast to the other cases discussed in the body of this chapter, *Titley v Davies*[11] was not concerned with the marshalling rights of a junior creditor. It was, instead, concerned with the ability of a junior creditor, having taken an assignment of the senior security, to 'consolidate' the senior and junior securities.[12] On the debtor tendering payment of the senior debt, the doctrine of consolidation permitted the junior creditor to refuse to release the asset that was encumbered by only the senior security; instead the junior creditor was entitled to decline redemption of the senior security until the debts secured by both the senior and junior securities had been discharged.

Consolidation as the basis for marshalling—Ashburner's argument

2.08 What renders *Titley v Davies*[13] of significance is that Ashburner, in his *Principles of Equity*,[14] claims to see common ground between the doctrine of consolidation, as applied in that case, and the doctrine of marshalling.[15]

Ashburner argues that the right of a junior creditor to marshall senior security is merely a special case of its broader right, as the ultimate beneficiary of the junior and senior securities, to consolidate all its securities. The junior creditor, by marshalling the senior security, is in fact ensuring that both the senior and junior securities are given effect to and, consequently, that the debts secured by those securities are repaid. This, according to Ashburner, is no different from the

---

[9] In *Lanoy v Duke & Duchess of Athol* (1742) 2 Atk 444 marshalling was effected *via* a direction from the court compelling the senior creditor to enforce its security against the asset over which only it held security. This direction is essentially a form of mandatory injunction: q v n55.

[10] (1743) 2 Y & C Ch Cas 399 (this case is sometimes cited as *Titley v Jenyns* (1743) 2 Y & C Ch Cas 399).

[11] Ibid.

[12] See further Chapter 5.

[13] (1743) 2 Y & C Ch Cas 399.

[14] D Browne, *Ashburner's Principles of Equity* (2nd ed 1933 Butterworths).

[15] Ibid, 212–214.

doctrine of consolidation which allows a secured creditor to insist upon the redemption of all securities held by it.[16]

This categorisation of marshalling would be of little import were it not for the fact **2.09** that consolidation has been substantially curtailed by statute in England and abolished in other common law jurisdictions (such as Australia and New Zealand). If Ashburner's interpretation of *Titley v Davies*[17] is correct, it is likely that the marshalling rights of junior creditors are, in England, subject to the same statutory curtailment as consolidation (or have, as in the case of Australia and New Zealand, been abrogated by statute). Ashburner's argument is considered in detail in Chapter 5.

Alleged Roman law origins of marshalling

That the doctrine of marshalling of securities is indigenous to English law is not, **2.10** however, a proposition that is universally accepted. Story, in his *Commentaries on Equity Jurisprudence*, asserts that the origins of the doctrine are to be found not in English equity cases from the seventeenth and eighteenth centuries but in Roman law.[18] He considers that there is evidence in the *Digest* of Justinian of a remedy equivalent to the equitable doctrine of marshalling of securities:[19]

> It is not improbable that this doctrine of marshalling securities or funds, which under another form had its existence in the Roman law, and was therein called subrogation or substitution, was derived into the jurisprudence of equity from that source, as it might well be, since it is a doctrine belonging to an age of enlightened policy, and refined although natural justice.

Story bases his claims upon the following passage from a text by the Roman jurist **2.11** Paulus,[20] fragments of which have been preserved in the *Digest*:[21]

---

[16] It makes no difference to Ashburner's argument whether the coercion theory or the post-realisation theory is accepted as the correct version of marshalling. In both instances, the doctrine of marshalling is seeking to preserve the priority-ranking of the junior creditor; the two theories are only in disagreement as to the means that should be employed to accomplish that objective.

[17] (1743) 2 Y & C Ch Cas 399.

[18] M M Bigelow, *Story's Commentaries on Equity Jurisprudence* (13th ed 1886 Little, Brown & Co), paras 635–636. Beyond the evidence proffered by Story, the only support for Story's claims may be found in three articles (in which Story's comments are merely reproduced or referred to): (i) M W Mosman, *The Proper Application of Marshaling on Behalf of Unsecured Creditors* [1983] Brigham Young ULR 639, 639; (ii) M Lachman, *Marshaling Assets in Bankruptcy: Recent Innovations in the Doctrine* (1985) 6 Cadozo L Rev 671, 671n1; and (iii) B MacDougall, *Marshalling and the Personal Property Security Acts: Doing Unto Others . . .* (1994) 28 UBCLR 91, 91n1 where it is stated: 'There is no way of knowing exactly what the origin of marshalling is. According to one author, the doctrine of marshalling was derived from Roman and civil law and found its way into English law in the mid-seventeenth century'.

[19] Bigelow, *Story's Commentaries on Equity Jurisprudence*, para 635.

[20] *Quaestiones*. Story also relies, albeit to a far lesser degree, upon a second text by Marcianus (*Ad Formulam Hypothecariam*): Bigelow, *Story's Commentaries on Equity Jurisprudence*, para 635n2. For a history of Roman jurisprudence and, in particular, an analysis of those works of the Roman jurists which have survived into the present time see F Schulz, *History of Roman Legal Science* (1946 Oxford). Schulz deals with these two texts at 202, and 238 and 325 respectively.

[21] D.20.4.16. The relevant passage from Marcianus may be found at D.20.4.12.

*Plane, cum tertius creditor primum de sua pecunia dimisit, in locum ejus substituitur in ea quantitate quam superiori exsolvit.*²²

2.12 This excerpt, however, fails to corroborate the Roman law antecedents of the doctrine of marshalling. An examination of it reveals that Paulus is concerned with the situation where two creditors hold securities over the same asset and the creditor holding lower-ranking security has discharged the debt owed to the other creditor. In those circumstances, Paulus argues, the lower-ranking creditor should be entitled to substitute the higher-ranking security for its own security. Although Paulus' statement is demonstrative of the right, under Roman law, of one secured creditor to be substituted or subrogated to the security held by another, it is not evidence of the recognition, by Roman law, of a principle equivalent to the doctrine of marshalling of securities.²³ The doctrine of marshalling, as it is presently applied by the courts, effects the substitution of the junior creditor to the rights of the senior creditor in respect of an asset, over which only the latter holds security.²⁴ In contrast, the principle enunciated by Paulus allows the junior creditor to exchange its security over an asset for the security held by the senior creditor over the same asset.²⁵

2.13 There is, moreover, in the earliest English cases on marshalling no indication that marshalling is something other than a creation of English law. In addition, it is English law, not Roman law, to which responsibility for the doctrine of marshalling is accorded in both subsequent English cases²⁶ and the cases in which

---

²² This has been translated by T Mommsen, P Krüger & A Watson, *The Digest of Justinian* (1985 Penn), Volume II, 594 as '[o]f course, when the third pays the first, he takes the place of the first as regards the amount paid'.

²³ In contrast, it is generally accepted that the equitable doctrine of subrogation, itself, is derived from the Roman law concept of substitution. See W W Buckland, *Equity in Roman Law* (1911 Cambridge), 47–55; S R Derham, *Subrogation in Insurance Law* (1985 Law Book Company), 4; R P Meagher, W M C Gummow & J R F Lehane, *Equity Doctrines and Remedies* (3rd ed 1992 Butterworths), para 901; Lord Goff of Chieveley & G Jones, *The Law of Restitution* (4th ed 1993 Sweet & Maxwell), 589–591, 589n5 and 602n5; J O'Donovan & J C Phillips, *The Modern Contract of Guarantee* (3rd ed 1996 Law Book Company), 653. C f Note, *Subrogation – An Equitable Device for Achieving Preferences and Priorities* (1933) 31 Mich L Rev 826 where the French, as opposed to Roman, origins of this doctrine are argued for. For a list of the early English subrogation cases, see n56. It is also of interest that the surety's access to the creditor's securities was effected under Roman law by the legal fiction of a sale of the securities between the creditor and the surety: Bigelow, *Story's Commentaries on Equity Jurisprudence*, paras 494, 500, 501 and 635; C Mitchell, *The Law of Subrogation* (1994 Oxford), 57n30; R Zimmerman, *The Law of Obligations: Roman Foundations of the Civilian Tradition* (1996 Oxford), 134–136; P K Jones Jr, *Roman Law Bases of Suretyship in Some Modern Civil Codes* (1977) 52 Tulane L Rev 129, 134–135. For a recent discussion of the borrowing of civil law principles by the common law, see D J Seipp, *The Reception of Canon Law and Civil Law in the Common Law Courts before 1600* (1993) 13 OJLS 388.

²⁴ Moreover, the principle propounded by Paulus is obviously different from the coercion theory of marshalling, which is the earliest form of marshalling known to English law.

²⁵ For an overview of the Roman law of securities, see e g R J Goebel, *Reconstructing the Roman Law of Real Security* (1961–62) 36 Tulane L Rev 29; D E Phillipson, *Development of the Roman Law of Debt Security* (1968) 20 Stan L Rev 1230.

²⁶ These cases are considered in the following sections of this chapter.

marshalling first makes its appearance in the major common law jurisdictions outside England,[27] *viz.* Australia,[28] Canada,[29] Ireland,[30] New Zealand[31] and the United States of America.[32] This is similarly the case with those texts on the marshalling of securities that date from the formative years of the doctrine.[33] It may, on the basis of these authorities, be safely accepted that marshalling is peculiar to the common law and is not a legal transplant from Roman law.

B. Establishment of the General Principles of Marshalling of Securities

Major developments in marshalling—nineteenth-century cases

The nineteenth century, in stark contrast to the two preceding centuries of **2.14** English law, is a watershed in the evolution of the doctrine of marshalling of securities. The meagre number of cases on marshalling which emerged from the seventeenth and eighteenth centuries are uniformly of the view that marshalling

---

[27] The mere fact that the doctrine of marshalling is recognised by Scots law does not undermine this claim. While Scots law retains many features of Roman law it has also been heavily influenced by the common law. There is nothing in the leading Scottish texts, on equity and securities, to suggest that marshalling is the creation of Roman law as opposed to the common law: e g Lord Kames, *Principles of Equity* (3rd ed 1825 Edinburgh), 79–80; T B Smith, *A Short Commentary on the Law of Scotland* (1962 W Green & Sons), 470; A M Johnston & J A D Hope (eds), *Gloag & Henderson's Introduction to the Law of Scotland* (7th ed 1969 W Green & Sons), 218–219; D M Walker, *Principles of Scottish Private Law* (4th ed 1989 Oxford), Volume III, 190–191. See generally W M Gordon, *Roman Influence on Scots Law of Real Property* in R Evans-Jones (ed), *The Civil Law Tradition in Scotland* (1995 Edinburgh). Scots law, however, gives effect to marshalling *via* assignment: see further paragraphs 3.28 and 3.29.
[28] *White v Colonial Bank of Australasia* (1871) 2 VR 96; *White v London Chartered Bank of Australia* (1877) 3 VLR 33.
[29] *Jones v Beck* (1871) 18 Gr 671; *Re Hamilton* (1895) 10 Man R 573; *Rutherford v Rutherford* (1896) 17 PR 228.
[30] *Averall v Wade* (1835) L & G temp Sugd 252.
[31] *Brigham v Chambers* (1880) OB & F 66; *Olivier v Colonial Bank* (1887) 5 NZLR 239.
[32] The copious United States authorities may be found in *American Digest* (1658–1896), 354–390. The view that the doctrine of marshalling is of English origin may be found in two more recent United States cases: *Meyer v United States* 375 US 233 (1963); *In re Beacon Distributors, Inc* 441 F 2d 547 (1971) (c f n1). See also H Karasik & R Kolodney, *The Doctrine of Marshaling Under the Bankruptcy Code* [1984] Com LJ 102, 102.
[33] e g G Spence, *The Equitable Jurisdiction of the Court of Chancery* (1849 Stevens & Norton), 833–837; T A Roberts, *Principles of Equity* (1852 Butterworths), 176–177; W W Watson, *A Practical Compendium of Equity* (1873 H Sweet), 36–38; C Cavanagh, *The Law of Money Securities* (2nd ed 1885 W Clowes & Sons), 550–552; E Chitty, *Index to All the Reported Cases Decided in the Several Courts of Equity and Bankruptcy in England and Ireland* (1886 Stevens & Sons), 4048–4052; T Brett, *Leading Cases in Modern Equity* (1887 W Clowes & Son), 222–223; D M Kerly, *An Historical Sketch of the Equitable Jurisdiction of the Court of Chancery* (1890 Cambridge), 215–217; L G G Robbins, *A Treatise on the Law of Mortgages, Pledges and Hypothecations* (1897 Stevens & Sons, Sweet & Maxwell), 777–789; A Thomson, *A Compendium of Modern Equity* (1899 W Clowes & Sons), 420.

functions as a coercive remedy, *viz.* it insulates the holders of *mesne* security from the consequences of the conduct of the holders of paramount-ranking security by compelling the latter to enforce their security in a particular manner. Furthermore, the bald statements of principle in those earlier cases are sufficiently wide to permit any creditor who holds security over an asset of the debtor to marshall the security held by a prior-ranking creditor over that and other assets of the debtor.

2.15 Neither of these propositions is left unchallenged in the nineteenth century. Although the characterisation of marshalling as a coercive remedy continues to receive favourable comment during the course of the nineteenth century, the majority of the cases evince an alternative view of the manner in which the doctrine of marshalling operates. These cases propose a concept of marshalling that leaves the senior creditor free to recover the secured debt owed to it as it sees fit and which intervenes only after the senior debt has been discharged, and then only if the junior creditor's priority-ranking has been adversely affected by the senior creditor's conduct.

In those circumstances, the doctrine of marshalling will attempt to make good the loss suffered by the junior creditor by granting the junior creditor access to the senior creditor's security with the aim of restoring the junior creditor to the position it enjoyed before the enforcement of the senior security. This substitution effects a redistribution of the assets of the debtor amongst the junior creditor and the debtor's other remaining creditors.

2.16 In addition, the class of creditors considered eligible to invoke the doctrine of marshalling is sharply reduced during the course of the nineteenth century from all creditors who hold *mesne* security to a select group of such creditors whose security is of a specific type. A junior creditor can no longer avail itself of the doctrine of marshalling solely by reason of the fact that it held *mesne* security.

2.17 The attention of the courts was not, however, confined to rewriting the earlier cases on marshalling. The courts also explored the limits of marshalling, such as whether or not marshalling rights could be eroded by the subsequent introduction of third parties by the debtor. Moreover, it was not only the courts that were concerned with the nature and limits of marshalling; for the first time the doctrine of marshalling was subjected to analysis in the leading texts on equity and securities.[34]

---

[34] See n33 for a list of the nineteenth century texts on equity and securities law. There is no mention of marshalling (either in its own right or as an alleged instance of subrogation) in the major eighteenth century works on equity: R Francis, *Maxims of Equity* (4th ed 1746 Sweet & Maxwell); H Ballow, *A Treatise of Equity* (1793–1794 Strahan & Woodfall).

There are three major themes which emerge from the nineteenth-century cases on marshalling of securities: **2.18**

- The acceptance of marshalling as a 'post-realisation' remedy.
- The imposition of conditions on the availability of marshalling.
- The ability of the debtor to undermine or exclude marshalling rights.

Marshalling as a post-realisation remedy—introduction

The doctrine of marshalling, in its original form, was coercive in nature. The cases   **2.19**
on marshalling from the seventeenth and eighteenth centuries all espoused the notion that the priority-position of the junior creditor was capable of being protected by dictating the manner in which the senior creditor could realise the assets subject to its security. It was recognised that a senior creditor, whose security extended to two or more assets of the debtor, possessed the power to jeopardise the repayment of a debt owed to a junior creditor, who was secured over only one of those assets. The courts chose to protect the junior creditor by forestalling any risk of damage being inflicted upon it by the senior creditor's conduct, rather than attempting to rectify any such damage.

Accordingly, where a junior creditor found itself in a situation where its secu-   **2.20**
rity was both lower in priority and narrower in scope than that of a senior creditor, it could protect its security by invoking the doctrine of marshalling. The intervention of the doctrine of marshalling meant that the senior creditor would be required to recoup the debt owed to it out of those assets over which only it held security. By doing so, the senior creditor would leave undiminished the asset that was encumbered by both the senior and junior securities. The law thus insulated the security held by the junior creditor from any action which the senior creditor might take to recover the senior debt, by depriving the latter of the right to freely elect between the various assets subject to its security.[35]

Marshalling as a post-realisation remedy—the dominance of the coercion theory of marshalling

This 'coercion theory' of marshalling, as expressed in *Lanoy v Duke & Duchess of Athol*[36] and *A-G v Tyndall*,[37] struck a responsive chord with the courts in several of   **2.21**

---

[35] A major flaw with the coercion theory of marshalling was that it assumed that a junior creditor would have advance warning of the senior creditor's intention to enforce the senior security.
[36] (1742) 2 Atk 444.
[37] (1764) Amb 614.

the nineteenth-century cases on marshalling.[38] In *Aldrich v Cooper*[39], Lord Eldon described marshalling in the following terms:[40]

> . . . if a party has two funds . . . a person having an interest in one only *has a right in equity to compel* the former to resort to the other; if that is necessary for the satisfaction of both (emphasis added);

and further:[41]

> . . . it is the ordinary case to say a person having two funds shall not by his election disappoint the party having only one fund; and equity, to satisfy both, will throw him, who has two funds on that, which can be affected by him only; to the intent that the only fund, to which the other has access, may remain clear to him.

Similar sentiments were expressed in *Trimmer v Bayne*,[42] and by Lord Eldon in *Ex parte Kendall*:[43]

> If A has a right to go upon two funds, and B upon one, having both the same debtor, A shall take payment from that fund to which he can resort exclusively.

and:[44]

> The equity is clear upon the authorities, that, if two funds of the debtor are liable to one creditor, and only one fund to another, the former shall be thrown upon that fund, to which the other cannot resort; in order that he may avail himself of his only security: where that can be done without injustice to the debtor or the creditor.

2.22 This conceptualisation of marshalling as a pre-emptive or coercive remedy enjoyed virtually unanimous support until the mid-nineteenth century. In all this time, however, the courts in articulating the coercion theory of marshalling did not – save for two exceptions – explicitly refer to the fact that they were compelling the senior creditor to act in a manner that was perhaps contrary to its wishes. That marshalling operated in such a manner was made obvious only in *Lanoy v Duke & Duchess of Athol*[45] (where Lord Hardwicke held that he would direct the senior creditor to recover its debt from the asset over which only it held

---

[38] In addition to the cases cited in paragraph 2.21, see *Lord Rancliffe v Lady Parkyns* (1818) 6 Dow 149; *Tidd v Lister* (1853) 3 De G M & G 857; *Gibson v Seagrim* (1855) 20 Beav 614; *In re Loder's Trusts* (1886) 56 LJ Ch 230. See also Spence, *The Equitable Jurisdiction of the Court of Chancery*, 833–834; Roberts, *Principles of Equity*, 176–177; Watson, *A Practical Compendium of Equity*, 36–37; Thomson, *A Compendium of Modern Equity*, 420. Support for the coercion theory of marshalling can also be found in Ireland; in *Averall v Wade* (1835) L & G temp Sugd 252, 253, Sugden L.C. stated: 'The general doctrine is this. Where one creditor has a demand against two estates, and another a demand against one only, the latter is entitled to throw the former on the fund that is not common to them both'; and in *Re Lawder's Estate* (1861) 11 Ir Ch R 346.

[39] (1803) 8 Ves Jun 382.

[40] Ibid, 388.

[41] Ibid, 395.

[42] (1803) 9 Ves 209.

[43] (1811) 17 Ves 514, 520.

[44] Ibid, 527.

[45] (1742) 2 Atk 444.

security) and in *Aldrich v Cooper*[46] (where Lord Eldon adopted the formulation of marshalling set out in *Lanoy v Duke & Duchess of Athol*[47]).

The courts, in those other cases, spoke instead of the ability of the junior creditor to 'throw' the senior creditor upon the asset that was encumbered by only the senior security. These cases nonetheless provide support for the coercion theory of marshalling as in each case *Lanoy v Duke & Duchess of Athol*[48] was considered and followed.

Marshalling as a post-realisation remedy—the reaction to the post-realisation theory of marshalling

It was not until the emergence in the mid-nineteenth century of a theory of mar- **2.23** shalling that was antagonistic to the coercion theory (*viz.* the notion of marshalling as a post-realisation remedy) that the judicial proponents of the coercion theory progressed to more strident language. In those cases, the courts castigated the rival post-realisation theory and made explicit their support for the view that the marshalling conferred on the junior creditor the 'right to compel' the senior creditor to resort to payment out of that asset in respect of which only the senior creditor held security. Examples of this new language may be found in the judgment of Stuart V.C. in *Lawrance v Galsworthy*:[49]

> [I]t was a well-established doctrine of this Court that the second mortgagee of property which was held by the first mortgagee under his security, along with other property to which the second mortgagee was not entitled, had a right to *compel the first mortgagee to resort to payment out of that fund to which the second mortgage did not extend* (emphasis added);

in that of Dr Lushington in *The 'Arab'*:[50]

> It is undoubtedly true, that if one party has the security of several funds, and another but of one, the Court will compel the former to elect that security which will permit of the latter being paid;

in Cotton L.J.'s judgment in *Webb v Smith*:[51]

> [I]f A has a charge upon Whiteacre and Blackacre, and if B also has a charge upon Blackacre only, A must take payment of his charge out of Whiteacre, and must leave

---

[46] (1803) 8 Ves Jun 382.

[47] (1742) 2 Atk 444.

[48] Ibid.

[49] (1857) 3 Jur (NS) 1049, 1050. See also Chitty, *Index to All the Reported Cases Decided in the Several Courts of Equity and Bankruptcy in England and Ireland*, 4050.

[50] (1859) 5 Jur (NS) 417, 417.

[51] (1885) 30 Ch D 192, 200. Counsel in this case argued that marshalling operated by way of substitution ((1885) 30 Ch D 192, 198): 'the creditor with one fund shall not be prejudiced by the choice of the creditor with two funds to take payment out of the doubly charged fund, and that if the creditor with the two funds, does so elect, as he may do, the other creditor shall *stand in his shoes* against the debtors' (emphasis added). This argument was rejected by the Court of Appeal.

Blackacre, so that B, the other creditor, may follow it and obtain payment of his debt out of it: in other words, if two estates, Whiteacre and Blackacre, are mortgaged to one person, and subsequently one of them, Blackacre, is mortgaged to another person, unless Blackacre is sufficient to pay both charges, *the first mortgagee will be compelled to take satisfaction out of Whiteacre*, in order to leave to the second mortgagee Blackacre, upon which alone he can go (emphasis added);

and that of Kay L.J. in *Flint v Howard*:[52]

[I]f a person having two estates mortgaged both to A and then one only to B, who had no notice of A's mortgage, B might, as against the mortgagor, *compel the payment of the first mortgage out of the estate on which he had no charge*, according to the ordinary doctrine of marshalling (emphasis added).

Marshalling as a post-realisation remedy—priority-preservation without coercion of the senior creditor

2.24 Despite the weight of precedent arrayed on the side of the coercion theory, the English courts in the mid-nineteenth century began to develop a theory of marshalling that did not interfere with the manner in which a senior creditor sought to recover the debt due to it. This theory may be described as the 'post-realisation' theory of marshalling. As will be seen from the next section of this chapter, the post-realisation theory of marshalling is now accepted in preference to the coercion theory in England, Australia, Canada and New Zealand. The coercion and post-realisation theories of marshalling are considered in detail in Chapter 3.

2.25 Although the post-realisation theory of marshalling does not affect the right of senior creditors to enforce their securities as they see fit, it, in common with the coercion theory, has as its objective the preservation of the priority-ranking of junior creditors. The post-realisation theory of marshalling argues that this can be accomplished by redressing any damage which a junior creditor might suffer as a consequence of the order in which a senior creditor has chosen to realise the assets subject to its security. The concept of marshalling developed in those cases accepts as axiomatic the proposition that the senior creditor, as paramount-ranking creditor, is not to be hindered by the holders of *mesne* security in the recovery of its debt.[53]

2.26 It is only where the recovery of the senior debt causes loss to the junior creditor (by the recoupment of the senior debt out of that asset which is subject to the junior creditor's security) that the doctrine of marshalling will be available to the junior creditor. The doctrine of marshalling, according to the post-realisation theory, will seek to rectify the junior creditor's loss by substituting the junior creditor to

---

[52] [1893] 2 Ch 54, 72.
[53] *Wallis v Woodyear* (1855) 2 Jur (NS) 179.

the security held by the senior creditor *vis-à-vis* those assets, which are encumbered by only the senior security.[54]

Although the ultimate objective of the post-realisation theory is no different from that of the coercion theory – both seek to preserve the priority-position of junior creditors – the two theories achieve that common objective in radically different ways. The post-realisation theory thus advances a concept of marshalling, which is reactive in nature rather than pre-emptive or pro-active, as is the case with the coercion theory.   **2.27**

The post-realisation theory leaves untouched the senior creditor's freedom of action whereas that freedom is substantially curtailed by the coercion theory. Under the post-realisation theory, equity will only intervene if the junior creditor suffers loss as the result of the senior creditor's conduct; the particular order in which the senior creditor *has elected* to realise the assets subject to its security is prevented from prejudicing the junior creditor's ability to recover its debt. The coercion theory, in contrast, does not attempt to prevent the consequences of such an election from disappointing the junior creditor's expectation that its debt will be repaid. Instead, the coercion theory prevents the senior creditor *from making that election.*[55]

Marshalling as a post-realisation theory—developments in subrogation

The post-realisation theory of marshalling makes use of subrogation to grant the junior creditor access to the senior security. Subrogation, too, is a 'post-realisation'   **2.28**

---

[54] *Wright v Simpson* (1802) 6 Ves 714; *Gwynne v Edwards* (1825) 2 Russ 289n; *Mason v Bogg* (1827) 2 My & Cr 443; *Barnes v Racster* (1842) 1 Y & C Ch Cas 401; *Re Scott's Estate* (1863) 14 L Ch R 63; *Binns v Nichols* (1866) LR 2 Eq 256; *Ex parte Alston* (1868) 4 Ch App 168; *Dolphin v Aylward* (1870) LR 4 E & I 486; *Noyes v Pollock* (1886) 32 Ch D 466; *Gregg v Arrott* (noted in Chitty, *Index to All the Reported Cases Decided in the Several Courts of Equity and Bankruptcy in England and Ireland*, 4048–4049); *Moxon v The Berkeley Mutual Benefit Building Society* (1890) 59 LJ Ch 524; *The 'Chioggia'* [1898] P 1. This is also the position in New Zealand: *Brigham v Chambers* (1880) OB & F 66; and Canada: *Rutherford v Rutherford* (1896) 17 PR 228. Moreover, in common with those cases in which the coercion theory was first developed, none of the nineteenth-century cases that support the post-realisation theory of marshalling attribute non-English origins to that view of marshalling.

[55] The doctrine of marshalling, in terms of the coercion theory, is given effect to by way of mandatory injunction. The jurisdiction of the court to issue a mandatory injunction in favour of a junior creditor arises from the court's inherent equitable jurisdiction which permits the issuance of an injunction in the enforcement of any equitable right: I C F Spry, *The Principles of Equitable Remedies* (5th ed 1997 Law Book Company), 323–335. Although both the mandatory injunction and specific performance have the effect of requiring the party, the subject of the order, to act in the manner directed by the court, the two remedies are very different. Specific performance is concerned with the enforcement of contractual obligations and requires a pre-existing contractual relationship. A mandatory injunction does not require such a relationship. See generally Browne, *Ashburner's Principles of Equity*, 336–338; Spry, *The Principles of Equitable Remedies*, 534–539; Meagher, Gummow & Lehane, *Equity Doctrines and Remedies*, paras 2191–2197. This is particularly relevant to the discussion of the nature of marshalling in Chapter 5: the coercion theory of marshalling does not support the view that marshalling is a form of specific performance.

style remedy in the sense that it does not pre-empt conduct but, instead, adjusts the rights of the affected parties once that conduct has occurred.

2.29 However, there is no evidence[56] to suggest that the sudden transformation of marshalling from a coercive remedy into a post-realisation remedy in the 1850s had anything to do with parallel developments in the law relating to subrogation.[57] The relationship between marshalling and subrogation is examined in Chapter 4.

Conditions on the availability of marshalling—introduction

2.30 The second major development of the nineteenth-century English courts was the rejection of an absolute entitlement to marshall on the part of the class of holders of *mesne* security.

While the earliest cases[58] on marshalling took it as a matter of course that the doctrine they were applying was available only to junior creditors, there was an implicit understanding that all such creditors – provided their security encompassed only one of the assets over which the senior creditor held security – could avail themselves of the doctrine of marshalling. Not only did the nineteenth

---

[56] The doctrine of subrogation, in contrast to marshalling, has always operated by substituting one party to the rights of another: *Morgan v Seymour* (1637/1638) 1 Chan Rep 120; *R v Doughty* (1702) Wight 3; *Parsons & Cole v Briddock* (1708) 2 Vern 608; *Harris v Lee* (1718) 1 P Wms 482; *Ex parte Crisp* (1744) 1 Atk 133; *Pringle v Hartley* (1744) 3 Atk 195; *Greerside v Benson* (1745) 3 Atk 248; *Randal v Cockran* (1748) 1 Ves Sen 98; *Blaauwpot v Da Costa* (1758) 1 Edn 130; *Goss v Withers* (1758) 2 Burr 683; *Hamilton v Mendes* (1761) 2 Burr 1198; *Milles v Fletcher* (1779) 1 Dougl 231; *Mason v Sainsbury* (1783) 3 Dougl 61; *London Assurance Co v Sainsbury* (1783) 3 Dougl 245; *Kulen Kemp v Vigne* (1786) 1 TR 304; *Dering v Earl of Winchelsea* (1787) 1 Cox Eq Cas 318; *Rogers v Mackenzie* (1799) 4 Ves Jun 752; *Bilbie v Lumley* (1802) 2 East 469; *Wright v Morley* (1805) 11 Ves Jun 12; *Craythorne v Swinburne* (1807) 14 Ves 160; *Davidson v Case* (1820) 2 Brod & B 379; *Stirling v Forrester* (1821) 3 Bli 575. See also Browne, *Ashburner's Principles of Equity*, 243–245; Baker & Langan, *Snell's Equity*, 421; M L Marasinghe, *An Historical Introduction to the Doctrine of Subrogation: the Early History of the Doctrine* (1975) 10 Val UL Rev 45 and 275; C Mitchell, *The Law of Subrogation* [1992] LMCLQ 483, 483–493.

[57] O'Donovan & Phillips, *The Modern Contract of Guarantee*, 653–654 and 666–668 states that it was not until the enactment of section 5 of the *Mercantile Law Amendment Act 1856* (UK) that a surety, in England, was entitled to be subrogated, upon the payment of the principal debt, to the securities held by the creditor over the property of the debtor (section 5 has been adopted by all Australian jurisdictions (e g section 3 of the *Law Reform (Miscellaneous Provisions) Act 1965* (NSW) and section 52 of the *Supreme Court Act 1986* (Vic)), New Zealand (section 85 of the *Judicature Act 1908* (NZ)) and Canada (e.g section 2 of the *Mercantile Law Amendment Act, RSO 1980* (Ontario)). Although the enactment of the *Mercantile Law Amendment Act* coincided with the advent of the post-realisation theory, it is difficult to see, in section 5, the impetus for the evolution of that theory. Section 5 did not create a new right of subrogation to a creditor's securities (see the cases cited in n56); its impact was largely procedural. It removed the technical bar at equity which prevented a surety from being subrogated to a security that had been discharged by the surety's payment of the principal debt. It thus 'artificially keeps alive, if necessary, the security and lets the person who has paid the debt in effect get his hands on it' (*D J Fowler (Australia) Limited v Bank of New South Wales* [1982] 2 NSWLR 879, 885). It also removed the need for concurrent actions at law and equity by resolving the discrepancy between law and equity; before section 5, a surety was not entitled, at law, to the securities that a creditor might possess against a debtor.

[58] See *Finch v Winchelsea* (1718) 1 P Wms 399n (discussed at n5).

century witness explicit statements to the effect that only junior creditors, and not unsecured creditors,[59] had standing to marshall, it also saw the imposition on those junior creditors of two strict conditions which had to be satisfied before they would be granted the right to marshall the security held by the senior creditor following the enforcement of the senior security:[60]

- the 'common debtor' rule;
- the securities held by both the senior and junior creditors must be 'proprietary securities'.

Thus, during the course of the nineteenth century, the English courts trans-   **2.31**
formed the doctrine of marshalling from an amorphous remedy, seemingly available to all holders of *mesne* security, that dictated the order of realisation of the paramount-ranking security, into a narrower remedy that only some secured creditors were eligible to summon in aid.

Conditions on the availability of marshalling—the common debtor rule

The common debtor rule stipulates that: **2.32**

(1) the debts, whose repayment is secured by the securities held by the senior and junior creditors, must be owed to both creditors by the same or 'common' debtor;[61]
(2) the assets, over which both the senior and junior creditors hold security, must be owned by the common debtor;[62]
(3) the assets in (2) must be in existence at the time the junior creditor asserts its right to marshall the senior security;[63] and
(4) the senior creditor must have equal rights of recourse against each of the assets in (2).[64]

The requirements of the common debtor rule are discussed in Chapter 7.

---

[59] *Anstey v Newman* (1870) 39 LJ Ch 769. This is also the position in Ireland: *Averall v Wade* (1835) L & G temp Sugd 252.

[60] *Hamilton v Royse* (1804) 2 Sch & Lef 315; *Webb v Smith* (1885) 30 Ch D 192; *Gray v Stone & Funnell* (1893) 69 LT 282. This is also the position in Ireland: *Averall v Wade* (1835) L & G temp Sugd 252.

[61] *Ex parte Kendall* (1811) 17 Ves 514; *Mason v Bogg* (1827) 2 My & Cr 443; *Thorpe v Jackson* (1837) 2 Y & C Ex 553; *Wallis v Woodyear* (1855) 2 Jur (NS) 179; *Dolphin v Aylward* (1870) LR 4 E & I 486; *Kendall v Hamilton* (1879) 4 App Cas 504. This is also the position in Canada: *Re Hamilton* (1895) 10 Man R 573.

[62] *Ex parte Kendall* (1811) 17 Ves 514; *Thorpe v Jackson* (1837) 2 Y & C Ex 553; *Dolphin v Aylward* (1870) LR 4 E & I 486; *Kendall v Hamilton* (1879) 4 App Cas 504; *The 'Chioggia'* [1898] P 1; c f *The 'Edward Oliver'* (1867) LR 1 A & E 379.

[63] *Re The State Fire Insurance Company* (1863) 32 LJ Ch 300; *Re Professional Life Assurance Co* (1867) LR 3 Eq 668; *Re International Life Assurance Society* (1876) 2 Ch D 476.

[64] *The 'Priscilla'* (1859) Lush 1; *Dolphin v Aylward* (1870) LR 4 E & I 486; *Webb v Smith* (1885) 30 Ch D 192; c f *The 'Mary Ann'* (1845) 9 Jur 94; *The 'Edward Oliver'* (1867) LR 1 A & E 379.

Conditions on the availability of marshalling—requirements (1) and (2) of the common debtor rule

2.33 Requirements (1) and (2) are derived from *Ex parte Kendall*,[65] in which Lord Eldon stated:[66]

> ... if A has a right to go upon two funds, and B upon one, having both the same debtor, A shall take payment from that fund, to which he can resort exclusively; that by those means of distribution both may be paid. That course takes place, where both are creditors of the same person, and have demands against funds, the property of the same person ...;

and:[67]

> ... much less have persons, who are not common creditors of the same debtor, a right to compel the creditors of both funds to resort to the other: in order to leave a larger dividend for those, who can claim only against the other.

Thus marshalling will only be available where both the senior and junior creditors are 'creditors of the same person, and have demands against funds, the property of the same person'.[68]

2.34 These two requirements have been justified on the basis of preventing a junior creditor from marshalling the senior security to the prejudice of 'strangers'.[69] To permit the junior creditor to marshall the senior security over an asset owned by a party other than the debtor would, *prima facie*, be manifestly unfair to that party. If marshalling were permitted, the junior creditor would be able to impose the burden of the junior debt on a party who is a *stranger* to the debtor-creditor relationship between the debtor and the junior creditor.

Conditions on the availability of marshalling—the 'surety exception'

2.35 The nineteenth-century cases on marshalling, however, recognised one exception to requirements (1) and (2). A junior creditor would be permitted to marshall the senior security where the party over whose asset the junior creditor held security was a *surety* of the senior debt.[70] This exception is discussed in detail in Chapter 8.

2.36 The surety exception is derived from the following statement of Lord Eldon in *Ex parte Kendall*:[71]

---

[65] (1811) 17 Ves 514. See also Roberts, *Principles of Equity*, 177.

[66] (1811) 17 Ves 514, 520.

[67] Ibid, 527.

[68] Ibid.

[69] See Cavanagh, *The Law of Money Securities*, 550–551.

[70] *Ex parte Kendall* (1811) 17 Ves 514. See also the Canadian case of *Quay v Sculthorpe* (1869) 16 Gr 449. See further Roberts, *Principles of Equity*, 177; Chitty, *Index to All the Reported Cases Decided in the Several Courts of Equity and Bankruptcy in England and Ireland*, 4048 and 4051.

[71] (1811) 17 Ves 514, 520.

... but it was never said, that, if I have a demand against A and B, a creditor of [B (sic)] shall compel me to go against A; without more; as, if B himself could insist, that A ought to pay in the first instance; as in the ordinary case of drawer and acceptor, or principal and surety; to the intent, that all the obligations, arising out of these complicated relations, may be satisfied: but, if I have a demand against both, the creditors of B have no right to compel me to seek payment from A; if not founded upon some equity, giving B the right for his own sake to compel me to seek payment from A.

Conditions on the availability of marshalling—requirement (3) of the common debtor rule

Requirement (3) is self-explanatory. The right to marshall the senior security will **2.37** avail the junior creditor nothing unless there is an asset in existence to which the junior creditor can obtain access *via* the senior security.

Conditions on the availability of marshalling—requirement (4) of the common debtor rule

The last requirement of the common debtor rule developed in the nineteenth cen- **2.38** tury requires the senior creditor to have equal rights of recourse against both the asset over which the junior creditor also holds security and the asset over which the security the junior creditor is seeking to marshall is held.

If, for example, the senior creditor is secured over the latter of the above two assets only to the extent that the former asset is inadequate security for the senior debt, the junior creditor (as the holder of a lower-ranking security over the former asset) will be unable to marshall the senior security.

Conditions on the availability of marshalling—proprietary securities

The second of the conditions on the availability of marshalling is derived from **2.39** *Webb v Smith*.[72] The following statement of Cotton L.J. has been taken to pre-scribe the rule that the doctrine of marshalling requires the securities held by both the junior and senior creditors to confer upon their holders proprietary interests in the assets which are encumbered by those securities:[73]

> [T]here were two funds: but the [junior creditors] had no claim against or lien over the fund . . . they could only have a set-off as to it, and the doctrine of marshalling applies only where there are claims or charges upon both funds.

Prior to *Webb v Smith*,[74] it was considered that the nature of the securities held by **2.40** the senior and junior creditors made no difference to the junior creditor's ability

---

[72] (1885) 30 Ch D 192.
[73] Ibid, 200.
[74] (1885) 30 Ch D 192.

to invoke the doctrine of marshalling (provided, of course, that the requirements of the common debtor rule had been complied with).[75] *Webb v Smith*,[76] however, confines the doctrine of marshalling to proprietary securities. The effect of this is that some junior creditors will be able to marshall the senior security whilst others will not solely on the basis that the latter hold non-proprietary securities,[77] such as pledges or possessory liens.[78]

This apparent requirement of proprietary securities is examined in Chapter 9.

Undermining or excluding the right to marshall—introduction

2.41   The third major contribution of the nineteenth century to the jurisprudence of marshalling is the recognition that a debtor could, by its subsequent conduct, undermine or exclude a junior creditor's right to marshall.

Consistent with the imposition of conditions on the right to marshall, the nineteenth-century courts took the view that marshalling rights were not inviolate. A junior creditor, who satisfied the common debtor rule and the apparent requirement of proprietary securities, might nonetheless find that its marshalling rights had been undermined or excluded by competing third party claims—introduced subsequently by the debtor—to the asset subject to the security sought to be marshalled.

2.42   Not all third parties were, however, capable of defeating the marshalling rights of a junior creditor. The nineteenth-century courts were emphatic that the right to marshall was to be considered sacrosanct as against all third parties whose interests in the asset (over which the security sought to be marshalled was held) were not derived by way of security or absolute transfer. Receivers, liquidators, trustees in bankruptcy, personal representatives and unsecured creditors of the debtor were

---

[75]   Prior to the nineteenth century, the cases on marshalling were concerned only with mortgages over land. In the nineteenth century the doctrine of marshalling was extended to (i) bottomry bonds: *The 'Trident'* (1839) 1 Wm Rob 29; *The 'La Constancia'* (1845) 2 Wm Rob 403; *The 'Mary Ann'* (1845) 9 Jur 94; *The 'Priscilla'* (1859) Lush 1; *The 'Arab'* (1859) 5 Jur (NS) 417; *The 'Edward Oliver'* (1867) LR 1 A & E 379; *The 'Eugenie'* (1873) LR 4 A & E 123; *The 'Chioggia'* [1898] P 1. See further Robbins, *A Treatise on the Law of Mortgages, Pledges and Hypothecations*, 789. For a general discussion of bottomry (and the related respondentia), see M Davies & A Dickey, *Shipping Law* (2nd ed 1995 Law Book Company), 132–135; (ii) possessory liens: *Trimmer v Bayne* (1803) 9 Ves 209; *Sproule v Prior* (1826) 8 Sim 189; *Buckley v Buckley* (1887) 19 LR Ir 544; and (iii) non-possessory liens: *Broadbent v Barlow* (1861) 3 De G F & J 570; *Ex parte Alston* (1868) 4 Ch App 168.
[76]   (1885) 30 Ch D 192.
[77]   The distinction between proprietary and non-proprietary securities is elaborated upon in Chapter 9.
[78]   The requirement of proprietary securities is entirely at odds with those cases in which the doctrine of marshalling has been applied to possessory liens (q v n75). The position of the non-possessory lien is ambiguous and is considered in more detail in Chapter 9.

therefore impotent to resist the claims of a junior creditor to marshall the security of a senior creditor.[79]

There were two categories of third party rights that the nineteenth-century courts **2.43** recognised as effective to modify or defeat a junior creditor's marshalling rights. These were third parties whose rights arose pursuant to:

    (a) a transfer or disposition by way of security; or

    (b) an absolute transfer or disposition,

of the debtor's interest in one or more of the assets subject to the senior security. The impact of third party rights upon a junior creditor's marshalling rights is considered in detail in Chapter 11.

Undermining or excluding the right to marshall—transfers or dispositions by way of security

The mere presence of a third party security holder will not, however, completely **2.44** abrogate the junior creditor's ability to marshall the senior security. All it does is prevent the junior creditor from using the doctrine of marshalling to impose the entire burden of the senior debt upon the asset over which the third party holds security.

If the doctrine of marshalling were to apply in a completely unmodified form the junior creditor would be able to effectively destroy the third party's security; the junior creditor would thus be accomplishing the very thing that is the subject of its complaint against the manner of the senior creditor's recovery of the senior debt.[80]

Moreover, in terms of the post-realisation theory, the application of the doctrine **2.45** of marshalling would result in the substitution of the junior creditor to the security—and priority position—held by the senior creditor over the asset, which is subject to the third party's security. The substitution of the junior creditor to the senior creditor's security would confer upon it priority, in respect of an asset over which it does not hold security, over a third party who does.

---

[79] *Hamilton v Royse* (1804) 2 Sch & Lef 315; *Re Tristram* (1825) 1 Dec 288; *Barnes v Racster* (1842) 1 Y & C Ch Cas 401; *Baldwin v Belcher* (1842) 3 Dr & War 173; *Haynes v Forshaw* (1853) 11 Hare 93; *Gibson v Seagrim* (1855) 20 Beav 614; *Re Stephenson* (1866) 3 De G M & G 969; *Ex parte Alston* (1868) 4 Ch App 168; *Dolphin v Aylward* (1870) LR 4 E & I 486; *Flint v Howard* [1893] 2 Ch 54; *Gray v Stone & Funnell* (1893) 69 LT 282. This is also the position in Ireland: *In re Scott's Estate* (1862) 14 Ir Ch R 63; *Hales v Cox* (1863) 32 Beav 118; *Re Lynch's Estate* (1867) 1 Ir R Eq 396.

[80] If the senior creditor had enforced its security against the asset subject to the third party's security, the junior creditor would be in the same position *qua* the third party as the third party is now *qua* the junior creditor.

2.46 To prevent such a result, the nineteenth-century courts developed a modified form of marshalling, sometimes referred to as 'marshalling by apportionment'.[81] A leading example is *Gibson v Seagrim*,[82] where Romilly M.R. held:[83]

> I agree with what was decided by the Vice-Chancellor Knight Bruce in *Barnes v Racster* . . . that if two estates are mortgaged to A, and one is afterwards mortgaged to B, and the remaining estate is afterwards mortgaged to C, B has no equity to throw the whole of A's mortgage on C's estate, and so destroy C's security. As between B and C, A is bound to satisfy himself the principal, interest and costs due to him out of the two estates *rateably, according to the respective values of such two estates*, and thus to leave the surplus proceeds of each estate to be applied in payment of the incumbrances thereon (emphasis added).

Further examples of this approach may also be found in the judgments of Kay J. (as he then was) in *Moxon v The Berkeley Mutual Benefit Building Society*:[84]

> If a person mortgages estates X and Y to A, and then mortgages or assigns estate X to B, and Y to C, the rights between B and C are to compel the payment of the first debt out of the two estates *rateably, and throw it on them rateably*, so that there shall be left of those estates, the proper proportion for each of the separate assigns (emphasis added);

and, as a Lord Justice of Appeal, in *Flint v Howard*:[85]

> But if there was a second mortgage of one estate to B, and also subsequently a second mortgage of the other estate to C, the matter is more complicated. C, although he had no notice of the prior mortgage on both properties to A, would not then be able to throw it on the property mortgaged to B, *but the equity between B and C would be to apportion the first mortgage between the two properties according to their respective values* (emphasis added).

2.47 Rather than conferring the entire benefit of the senior security on the junior creditor, the benefit of the senior security is apportioned rateably amongst the junior creditor and the third party security holder. Each creditor therefore receives a share of the senior security in proportion to the value of the asset over which it holds security. Thus the rights of the junior creditor and the third party are

---

[81] In addition to the cases cited in this paragraph, see: *Shalcross v Dixon* (1838) 7 LJ (NS) 180; *Barnes v Racster* (1842) 1 Y & C Ch Cas 401; *Bugden v Bignold* (1843) 2 Y & C Ch Cas 377; *Wellesley v Lord Mornington* (1869) 17 WR 355; *Re Mower's Trusts* (1869) LR 8 Eq 110; *Ford v Tynte* (1872) 41 LJ Ch 758; *Liverpool Marine Credit Co v Wilson* (1872) 7 Ch App 507; *Trumper v Trumper* (1872) LR 14 Eq 295; *Cracknall v Janson* (1879) 11 Ch D 1; *Wood v West* (1895) 40 Sol Jo 114. This is also the position in Ireland: *Re Lawder's Estate* (1861) 11 Ir Ch R 346; *Re Roddy's Estate* (1861) 11 Ir Ch R 369; *Re Roche's Estate* (1890) 25 LR Ir 284; Australia: *White v London Chartered Bank of Australia* (1877) 3 VLR 33; and New Zealand: *Olivier v Colonial Bank* (1887) 5 NZLR 239. See generally Spence, *The Equitable Jurisdiction of the Court of Chancery*, 834–836; Thomson, *A Compendium of Modern Equity*, 420.

[82] (1855) 20 Beav 614. See Chitty, *Index to All the Reported Cases Decided in the Several Courts of Equity and Bankruptcy in England and Ireland*, 4050.

[83] (1855) 20 Beav 614, 619.

[84] (1890) 59 LJ Ch 524, 526.

[85] [1893] 2 Ch 54, 72.

adjusted *vis-à-vis* one another, as opposed to permitting one of them to abrogate the security held by the other.

Undermining or excluding the right to marshall—absolute transfers or dispositions

The exclusion of marshalling rights by way of absolute transfer or disposition **2.48** to a third party constitutes the most complex of the changes wrought by the nineteenth-century courts to the doctrine of marshalling.[86] The courts were concerned with the persistence of marshalling rights where a debtor, having already granted security over two assets to a senior creditor and security over one of those assets to a junior creditor, disposes of the other asset to a third party: could the junior creditor marshall the senior security, despite the fact that the security sought to be marshalled encumbered an asset now owned by a third party?

The nineteenth-century courts agreed that the debtor could, by the subsequent **2.49** transfer or disposition of the asset that was subject to only the senior security, exclude the junior creditor's right to marshall *provided* that the transfer or disposition was on terms which contained a 'covenant against encumbrances' (i.e. the third party had agreed to take the asset free from the senior security).[87] This was on the basis that the transferee or disponee had bargained for, and obtained, clear title.

Thus once the transfer or disposition was perfected there was no longer a security subsisting over the transferred asset, to which the junior creditor could be substituted. The doctrine of marshalling does *not* create security where no security previously existed; all it does is permit a junior creditor, whose priority-ranking has been eroded, to take up another creditor's security.

It was in circumstances where a covenant against encumbrances was absent from **2.50** the terms of the transfer or disposition that the position as regards the persistence of marshalling rights was less clear.

There was support for the proposition that, in the absence of a covenant against encumbrances, the persistence of marshalling rights was dependent upon whether or not the third party had notice of the junior security at the time of the transfer or disposition.[88] Only if the third party had notice, would the junior creditor be able to marshall the senior security.

---

[86] See Cavanagh, *The Law of Money Securities*, 551–552.

[87] *Hartley v O'Flaherty* (1813–1830) Beat 61; *Chappell v Rees* (1839) 9 LJ Ch 37. This is also the position in Ireland: *Averall v Wade* (1835) L & G temp Sugd 252; *Ker v Ker* (1869) 4 IR Eq 15.

[88] *Aldridge v Forbes* (1839) 9 LJ Ch 37; *Hughes v Williams* (1852) 3 Mac & G 683; *Rooke v Lord Kensington* (1856) 21 Beav 470; *Anstey v Newman* (1870) 39 LJ Ch 769; *Dolphin v Aylward* (1870) LR 4 E & I 486; *Re Walhampton Estate* (1884) 26 Ch D 391. This is also the position in Canada: *Jones v Beck* (1871) 18 Gr 671; *Clark v Bogart* (1880) 27 Gr 450; *Pierce v Canavan* (1882) 7 OAR 187; *Renwick v Berryman* (1886) 3 Man R 387; *Fraser v Nagle* (1888) 16 OR 241.

The opposing position was that notice was irrelevant and all that mattered were the terms of the transfer or disposition. If the third party took the asset subject to the senior security it would have to bear the risk that a junior creditor might subsequently be entitled to marshall that security. [89]

C. Affirmation of the General Principles of Marshalling of Securities

2.51 The history of marshalling of securities in the twentieth century is characterised by a mood of consolidation or affirmation, rather than one of innovation. Apart from three notable exceptions (which will be described in the next section) and developments in the law of marshalling in the United States, the cases that have emerged during this century from the major common law jurisdictions have been content to confirm the developments of the English courts of the previous century. Accordingly, the law governing the doctrine of marshalling of securities in England, Australia, Canada, Ireland and New Zealand is essentially that which was applied in England in the latter half of the nineteenth century. [90]

---

[89] *Gwynne v Edwards* (1825) 2 Russ 289n; *In re Jones* [1893] 2 Ch 461; *Re Cook's Mortgage* [1896] 1 Ch 923. This is also the position in Ireland: *Hales v Cox* (1863) 32 Beav 118; *In re Rorke's Estate* (1865) 15 Ir Ch R 316.

[90] Due to the static nature of the doctrine, the contemporary English texts on equity (H A Smith, *A Practical Exposition of the Principles of Equity* (5th ed 1914 Stevens & Sons), 613–614; E P Hewitt, *White & Tudor's Leading Cases in Equity* (9th ed 1928 Sweet & Maxwell), 40–59; Browne, *Ashburner's Principles of Equity*, 212–214; G W Keaton & L A Sheridan, *Equity* (2nd ed 1976 Professional Books), 303–307; P V Baker & P St J Langan, *Snell's Equity* (29th ed 1990 Sweet & Maxwell), 421–422; Lord Hailsham of St Marylebone (ed), *Halsbury's Laws of England*, Vol 16 ('*Equity*') (4th ed reissue 1992 Butterworths), paras 876–878) and securities (Beddoes, *A Concise Treatise on the Law of Mortgages*, 102–106; W F Webster, *Ashburner's Concise Treatise on Mortgages, Pledges and Liens* (2nd ed 1911 Butterworths), 465–467; Hanbury & Waldock, *The Law of Mortgages*, 176–182; R L Ramsbotham, *Coote's Treatise on the Law of Mortgages* (9th ed 1927 Stevens & Sons, Sweet & Maxwell), 803–813; G G G Robb, *Nokes' Outline of the Law of Mortgages and Receiverships* (1951 Estates Gazette), 84–85; *Halsbury's*, Vol 32 ('*Mortgage*') (4th ed 1980 Butterworths), paras 915–918; D G M Marks & G S Moss, *Rowlatt on the Law of Principal and Surety* (4th ed 1982 Sweet & Maxwell), 149–150; E L G Tyler, *Fisher & Lightwood's Law of Mortgage* (10th ed 1988 Butterworths), 530–533; E F Cousins, *The Law of Mortgages* (1989 Sweet & Maxwell), 434–438) which consider marshalling of securities are content to merely describe its requirements and operation. This is similarly the case in Ireland (J C W Wylie, *Irish Land Law* (1975 Professional Books), paras 13.075-[13].080 (sic)), in Australian equity (J Leslie, *Leslie's Equity and Commercial Practice* (1998 Prospect), para M24:10; M Evans, *Outline of Equity and Trusts* (3rd ed 1996 Butterworths), para 11–1; G E Dal Pont & D R C Chalmers, *Equity and Trusts in Australia and New Zealand* (1996 Law Book Company), 263–267; B McDonald, *Marshalling* in P Parkinson (ed), *The Principles of Equity* (1996 Law Book Company); B McDonald, *Marshalling* in J A Riordan (ed), *The Laws of Australia* (1997 Release Law Book Company), Vol 15:3, paras 23–33; J D Heydon & P L Loughlan, *Cases and Materials on Equity and Trusts* (5th ed 1997 Butterworths), Chapter 16) and securities texts (E A Francis & K J Thomas, *Mortgages and Securities* (3rd ed 1986 Butterworths), 369–371; W D Duncan & L Willmott, *Mortgages Law in Australia* (1996 Federation Press), 154–155; E I Sykes & S Walker, *The Law of Securities* (5th ed 1993 Law

Acceptance of the post-realisation theory of marshalling

The version of marshalling that is applied in those jurisdictions (with the excep- **2.52**
tion of Ireland where the issue remains unsettled[91]), does not interfere with the
senior creditor's rights to enforce its security as it sees fit. The junior creditor is
thus only entitled to marshall the senior security where the conduct of the senior
creditor has prejudiced the junior creditor's priority-ranking.[92]

The post-realisation theory, which was advanced in the mid-nineteenth century
as an alternative to the then dominant coercion theory of marshalling, has now
largely been accepted as the preferred version of the doctrine of marshalling of
securities.[93] The courts have therefore rejected the notion that marshalling protects *mesne* security by regulating the conduct of the senior creditor. They have,
instead, adopted a version of marshalling which protects *mesne* security, by redistributing the residue of the debtor's assets that remains after the senior debt has
been discharged.

Book Company), 182–185; E L G Tyler, P W Young & C E Croft, *Fisher & Lightwood's Law of
Mortgage* (Aust ed 1995 Butterworths), paras 30.8–30.14). The Australian equity text, Meagher,
Gummow & Lehane, *Equity Doctrines and Remedies*, Chapter 11, is a notable exception.

[91] See further paragraph 3.26.

[92] *Manks v Whiteley* [1911] 2 Ch 448; *Re Cohen* [1960] Ch 179. This is also the position in
Australia: *Mir Bros Projects Pty Ltd v Lyons* [1977] 2 NSWLR 192; *Mir Bros Projects Pty Ltd v Lyons*
[1978] 2 NSWLR 505; *Deta Nominees Pty Ltd v Discount Plastic Products Pty Ltd* [1979] VR 167;
Re O'Leary (1985) 61 ALR 674; *Chase Corp (Australia) Pty Ltd v North Sydney Brick and Tile Co Ltd*
(1994) 12 ACLC 997; *Patrick Stevedores No 2 Pty Ltd v MV Skulptor Konenkov* (1996) 136 ALR
211; *Oamington Pty Ltd v Commissioner of Land Tax* (unrep 24 Nov 1997, Sup Ct of NSW). C f *Re
Aylwin* [1938] VLR 105 and especially *Commonwealth Trading Bank v Colonial Mutual Life
Assurance Society Ltd* (1970) 26 FLR 338; New Zealand: *Re Tremain* [1934] NZLR 369; *Bissett v
ANZ* [1961] NZLR 687; *Re Manawatu Transport Ltd* (1984) 2 NZCLC 99,084; *National Bank of
NZ Ltd v Caldesia Promotions Ltd and Jenkins Roberts & Associates Ltd* [1996] 3 NZLR 467; and
Canada: *Ernst Bros Co v Canadian Permanent Mortgage Corp* (1920) 57 DLR 500; *Seel Investments
Ltd v Greater Canadian Securities Corp Ltd* (1967) 65 DLR (2d) 45; *Williamson v Loonstra* (1973)
34 DLR (3d) 275; *Nova Scotia Savings & Loan Co v O'Hara* (1979) 7 RPR 281; *Goodman v
Parkhurst* [1980] 6 WWR 601; *Canadian Trustco Mortgage Co v Wenngatz Construction & Holdings
Ltd* (1986) 1 BCLR (2d) 302; *Yorkshire Trust Co v Armwest Development Ltd* [1986] 1 WWR 478;
First Investors Corporation Ltd v Veeradon Developments Ltd (1988) 47 DLR (4th) 446; *Fiatallis
North America Inc v Pigott Construction Ltd* (1992) 3 PPSAC (2d) 30; *Farm Credit Corporation v
Nelson* (1993) 102 DLR (4th) 743; *Royal Trust Company v H A Roberts Group Limited* [1995] 4
WWR 305; *Re Allison* (1998) 38 OR (3d) 337.

[93] Beddoes, *A Concise Treatise on the Law of Mortgages*, 105; Hewitt, *White & Tudor's Leading
Cases in Equity*, 40 and 52–53; Hanbury & Waldock, *The Law of Mortgages*, 178; Ramsbotham,
Coote's Treatise on the Law of Mortgages, 802–803 and 804; *Halsbury's*, Vol 16 ('*Equity*'), para 876n1
and Vol 32 ('*Mortgage*'), para 915; Keaton & Sheridan, *Equity*, 304; Baker & Langan, *Snell's Equity*,
421–422; Tyler, *Fisher & Lightwood's Law of Mortgage*, 530–531; Cousins, *The Law of Mortgages*,
436; W Strahan, *The Marshalling of Mortgages* (1906) 22 LQR 307, 307. C f Smith, *A Practical
Exposition of the Principles of Equity*, 613; Robb, *Nokes' Outline of the Law of Mortgages and
Receiverships*, 84–85. This is also the case in Australia: Francis & Thomas, *Mortgages and Securities*,
369–370; Meagher, Gummow & Lehane, *Equity Doctrines and Remedies*, paras 1102–1106;
McDonald, *Marshalling* (1996), para 1604; McDonald (1997), *Marshalling*, paras 23 and 27; and
Canada: Rayner & McLaren, *Falconbridge on Mortgages*, 314.

The common debtor rule

2.53 The requirements of the common debtor rule and the inability of unsecured creditors to marshall the senior security have met with even less discussion. [94] The
courts in England and the other major common law jurisdictions have simply
assumed that a junior creditor who wishes to marshall the security of a senior creditor must satisfy the several components of the common debtor rule (or avail itself
of the surety exception),[95] and that unsecured creditors lack standing to invoke the
doctrine of marshalling.[96]

---

[94] Hewitt, *White & Tudor's Leading Cases in Equity*, 41; Hanbury & Waldock, *The Law of
Mortgages*, 177–178; *Halsbury's*, Vol 16 ('*Equity*'), para 877; Keaton & Sheridan, *Equity*, 304–305;
Cousins, *The Law of Mortgages*, 436; This is also the position in Australia: Francis & Thomas,
Mortgages and Securities, 370; Meagher, Gummow & Lehane, *Equity Doctrines and Remedies*, paras
1108–1109 and 1111–1113; Sykes & Walker, *The Law of Securities*, 183; McDonald, *Marshalling*
(1996), paras 1605–1607; McDonald, *Marshalling* (1997), paras 26, 28 and 29. Moreover, in this
period, the doctrine of marshalling is extended to equitable charges for the first time: *Re Fry* [1912]
2 Ch 86.

[95] *Re Townley* [1922] 1 Ch 154. This is also the position in Ireland: *Lombard & Ulster Banking
Limited v Murray & Murray* [1987] ILRM 522; Australia: *In re W* (1901) 11 QLJ 108; *Re Holland*
(1928) 28 SR (NSW) 369; *In re Wertheim* [1934] VLR 321; *Miles v Official Receiver* (1963) 109
CLR 501; *Re O'Leary* (1985) 61 ALR 674; *Finance Corporation of Australia Ltd v Bentley* (1991) 5
BPR 97412; *Australia and New Zealand Banking Group Ltd v Bendigo Building Society* (unrep 5 Oct
1992, Sup Ct of Vic); *Sarge Pty Ltd v Cazihaven Homes Pty Ltd* (1994) 34 NSWLR 658; and
Canada: *Dominion Lumber v Gelfand* (1916) 34 WLR 624; *Re Steacy* (1917) 39 OLR 548; *Ernst
Brothers Co v Canadian Permanent Mortgage Corp* (1920) 57 DLR 500; *Royal Bank of Canada v Izen*
[1921] 2 WWR 929; *G Ruso Construction Ltd v Laviola* (1976) 27 Chitty's LJ 136; *Bank of British
Columbia v Tamavi Holdings Ltd* (1978) 29 CBR (NS) 111; *Invesco Holdings Ltd v Kendall* [1979]
4 WWR 571; *Farm Credit Corp v McLane* (1983) 30 Sask R 320; *Montmor Investments Ltd v
Montreal Trust Co* (1984) 53 BCLR 275; *Canada v French* (unrep 15 Jan 1985, Ont HCJ); *Brown
v Canadian Imperial Bank of Commerce* (1985) 50 OR (2d) 420; *Westcoast Savings Credit Union v P
E DeVito & Associates Ltd* (unrep 24 Feb 1986, BCSC); *Toronto-Dominion Bank v Whitaker* (unrep
4 July 1986, Alta QB); *Canadian Trustco Mortgage Co v Wenngatz Construction & Holdings Ltd*
(1986) 1 BCLR (2d) 302; *Montreal Trust Co v Montreal Trust Co of Canada* (1988) 24 BCLR (2d)
238; *Fiatallis North America Inc v Pigott Construction Ltd* (1992) 3 PPSAC (2d) 30; *Ontario Inc v
Allison* (1995) CBR (3d) 144; *Granville Savings & Mortgage Corp v Bob B Co Holdings Ltd* (1996)
24 BCLR (3d) 348; *Richmond Savings Credit Union v Zilbershats* (1997) 35 BCLR (3d) 136; *Re
Allison* (1998) 38 OR (3d) 337.

[96] See the Australian case: *DM & BP Wiskich Pty Ltd v Saadi* (unrep 16 Feb 1996, Sup Ct of
NSW); the New Zealand case: *Re Watkins* [1938] NZLR 847; and the Canadian cases: *Williamson
v Loonstra* (1973) 34 DLR (3d) 275; *Nova Scotia Savings & Loan Co v O'Hara* (1979) 7 RPR 281;
Re Bread Man Inc (1979) 89 DLR (3d) 599; *Bank of Nova Scotia v Adriatic Development Ltd* [1985]
2 WWR 627; *Ontario Inc v Allison* (1995) CBR (3d) 144. Cf there is a line of Canadian authority
which purportedly limits the application of marshalling to real property securities: *Steinbach Credit
Union Ltd v Manitoba Agricultural Credit Corp* (1991) 72 Man R (2d) 161; *National Bank of
Canada v Makin Metals Ltd* [1993] 3 WWR 318 (doubted on appeal in *National Bank of Canada v
Makin Metals Ltd* (1994) 116 Sask R 236) (see further paragraph 9.25). Cf the Australian case of *In
re Crothers* [1930] VLR 49, in which marshalling by apportionment was applied in favour of unsecured creditors.

Marshalling of securities and third parties

In similar fashion, the limitations that were imposed on the scope of marshalling **2.54** by the nineteenth-century courts have been acceded to without demurrer. It is considered beyond doubt that a junior creditor's right to marshall is capable of being undermined or excluded by the subsequent introduction of third party rights by the debtor.[97]

A junior creditor will therefore enjoy only a modified right to marshall where the asset, to which the junior creditor is attempting to gain access *via* the doctrine of marshalling, is subject to a security in favour of a third party.[98] Alternatively, should that asset be the subject of an absolute transfer or disposition to a third party, on terms which contain a covenant against encumbrances, the junior creditor will be prevented from marshalling the senior security.[99]

---

[97] Hewitt, *White & Tudor's Leading Cases in Equity*, 47–49 and 53–54; Browne, *Ashburner's Principles of Equity*, 214; Hanbury & Waldock, *The Law of Mortgages*, 179–181; Ramsbotham, *Coote's Treatise on the Law of Mortgages*, 803–804, 806 and 811–813; Robb, *Nokes' Outline of the Law of Mortgages and Receiverships*, 85; *Halsbury's*, Vol 32 ('*Mortgage*'), paras 916 and 918; Keaton & Sheridan, *Equity*, 305–306; Baker & Langan, *Snell's Equity*, 422; Tyler, *Fisher & Lightwood's Law of Mortgage*, 531–532; Cousins, *The Law of Mortgages*, 436–438; Strahan, *The Marshalling of Mortgages*, 308–310. This is also the position in Ireland: Wylie, *Irish Land Law* at paras 13.079 and [13].080 (sic); and Australia: Meagher, Gummow & Lehane, *Equity Doctrines and Remedies*, paras 1122–1130; Sykes & Walker, *The Law of Securities*, 183–185; McDonald, *Marshalling* (1996), para 1611; McDonald, *Marshalling* (1997), para 33.

[98] *Baglioni v Cavalli* (1900) 83 LT 500. This is also the position in Australia: *Commonwealth Trading Bank v Colonial Mutual Life Assurance Society Ltd* (1970) 26 FLR 338; *Mir Bros Projects Pty Ltd v Lyons* [1977] 2 NSWLR 192; *Mir Bros Projects Pty Ltd v Lyons* [1978] 2 NSWLR 505; *Chase Corp (Australia) Pty Ltd v North Sydney Brick and Tile Co Ltd* (1994) 12 ACLC 997; New Zealand: *National Bank of NZ Ltd v Caldesia Promotions Ltd and Jenkins Roberts & Associates Ltd* [1996] 3 NZLR 467; and Canada: *Adams v Keers* (1919) 51 DLR 514; *Seel Investments Ltd v Greater Canadian Securities Corp Ltd* (1967) 65 DLR (2d) 45; *Victoria & Grey Trust Co v Brewer* (1971) 14 DLR (3d) 28; *Victor Investment Corporation v Fidelity Trust Company* (1973) 41 DLR (3d) 65; *Richmond Savings Credit Union v Zilbershats* (1997) 35 BCLR (3d) 136. In Ireland, see *Smyth v Toms* [1918] 1 IR 338; c f *In re Archer's Estate* [1914] 1 IR 285 – this case is doubtful authority for the proposition that a junior creditor's marshalling rights may be exercised to their fullest extent in the presence of a third party security holder. This case was found to be inconsistent with the English precedents in *Smyth v Toms* [1918] 1 IR 338 a case which, as Ross J. noted (at 345 and 346), was indistinguishable from *In re Archer's Estate* [1914] 1 IR 285. See further Tyler, *Fisher & Lightwood's Law of Mortgage*, 532n(x).

[99] *Mallott v Wilson* [1903] 2 Ch 494; *In re Darby's Estate* [1907] 2 Ch 465; *Re Burge, Woodall & Co* [1912] 1 KB 313; *In re Best* [1924] 1 Ch 42; *In re Mainwaring* [1937] Ch 96. This is also the position in Ireland: *In re Lysaght's Estate* [1903] 1 IR 235; *McCarthy v M'Cartie (No 2)* [1904] 1 IR 100; *Ocean Accident & Guarantee Corp Ltd and Hewett v Collum* [1913] 1 IR 337; *Hollinshead v Devane* (1914) 49 ILT 87; and Canada: *Ernst Brothers Co v Canadian Permanent Mortgage Corp* (1920) 57 DLR 500; *Johal v Sahota* (1986) 2 BCLR (2d) 218.

D. Recent Developments in Marshalling of Securities

Recent developments—marshalling and the competing rights of the surety

2.55 The first major divergence from the strictures imposed on the doctrine of mar-shalling by the nineteenth-century English courts comes in two New Zealand cases, *New Zealand Loan & Mercantile Agency Co Ltd v Loach*[100] and *Re Manawatu Transport Ltd.*[101] These two cases are reviewed in Chapter 8.

Both these cases have called the efficacy of the 'surety exception' into question. As noted above, the surety exception constitutes the sole occasion on which English courts will permit a junior creditor to marshall the senior security even though the requirements of the common debtor rule have not been met.

2.56 The two New Zealand cases do not deny that a junior creditor, who holds security over the asset of a surety of the senior debt, may marshall the security held by the senior creditor over the asset of the debtor. They, instead, question whether the surety exception is as effective as the nineteenth-century cases have made it out to be.[102] The surety exception, it is pointed out, is premised on the proposition that the right of a junior creditor to marshall the senior security is superior to any rights that the surety might possess, and that this proposition rarely reflects reality. The significance of this view is immediately obvious: if the two cases have been cor-rectly decided, the surety's competing subrogation rights will generally preclude the junior creditor from marshalling the senior security over the surety's asset.

Recent developments—the revival of the coercion theory

2.57 A second challenge to the body of nineteenth-century case law (and, in particular, the case law from the latter half of that century) is to be found in two recent English cases, *Smit Tak International Zeesleepin Bergingsbedrijf BV v Selco Salvage Ltd*[103] and *Re Bank of Credit and Commerce International SA (No 8)*,[104] and an Australian case, *Commonwealth Trading Bank v Colonial Mutual Life Assurance Society Ltd.*[105]

2.58 In the earliest of the three cases, *Commonwealth Trading Bank v Colonial Mutual Life Assurance Society Ltd*,[106] the Supreme Court of Tasmania cited with approval the chief authorities supporting the view of marshalling as a coercive remedy (such

---

[100] (1912) 31 NZLR 292.
[101] (1984) 2 NZCLC 99,084.
[102] q v n70.
[103] [1988] 2 Ll Rep 398. See further Meagher, Gummow & Lehane, *Equity Doctrines and Remedies*, paras 1114–1119.
[104] [1998] 1 BCLC 68.
[105] (1970) 26 FLR 338; q v *Re Aylwin* [1938] VLR 105.
[106] (1970) 26 FLR 338, 343–344.

as *Lanoy v Duke & Duchess of Athol*[107] and *Aldrich v Cooper*[108]), in seeming igno-rance of the more recent authorities in favour of the post-realisation theory of marshalling.

Similarly, the following statement of Warner J. in the *Smit Tak* case[109] is inconsis- **2.59**
tent with the prevalent view of marshalling as a post-realisation remedy:[110]

> [T]he court will give effect to the doctrine of marshalling in a way that will *bind the first claimant* . . . where the first claimant has satisfied himself *before* proceedings are brought, the court will confine itself to *giving effect to the equities as between the subsequent claimants* (emphasis added).

Further life has been breathed into the coercion theory by the recent *BCCI* case.[111] **2.60**
Although Lord Hoffmann decided that marshalling had no application in the case, the following comments lend support to the view of marshalling as a coercive remedy:[112]

> This is a principle for doing equity between two or more creditors, each of whom are owed debts by the same debtor, but one of whom can enforce his claim against more than one security or fund and the other can resort to only one. *It gives the latter an equity to require that the first creditor satisfy himself (or be treated as having satisfied himself) so far as possible out of the security or fund to which the latter has no claim.* I am at a loss to understand how this principle can have any application in the present case. There is only one debt and that is owed to BCCI by the principal borrower. . . . There is no basis upon which the depositors can assert an equity to require BCCI to proceed against their deposits before claiming against the principal debtors (emphasis added).

This purported revival of the coercion theory of marshalling is considered in Chapter 3.

However, it is important to note that the coercion theory, as articulated in the **2.61**
Smit Tak[113] and *BCCI*[114] cases, differs significantly from the coercion theory that held sway in the first half of the nineteenth century. While, in both instances, the courts accepted that a junior creditor's marshalling rights might be given effect to *via* the coercion of the senior creditor, it is explicit in the former case and implicit in the latter that time is of the essence. If the senior creditor enforces its security before the junior creditor asserts its right to marshal the senior security, the court will utilise the post-realisation version of marshalling. Accordingly, the junior

---

[107] (1742) 2 Atk 444.
[108] (1803) 8 Ves Jun 382.
[109] [1988] 2 Ll Rep 398.
[110] Ibid, 407. Note that *Gibson v Seagrim* (1855) 20 Beav 614 is incorrectly cited as *Gibson v Marshall*.
[111] [1998] 1 BCLC 68.
[112] Ibid, 81.
[113] [1988] 2 Ll Rep 398.
[114] [1998] 1 BCLC 68.

creditor's ability to require the senior creditor to enforce its security in a particular manner is vulnerable to dilatoriness or a want of vigilance on the part of the junior creditor.

Recent developments—the extension of marshalling to non-security interests

2.62 The *Smit Tak* case[115] is also responsible for undermining the requirement, apparently established in *Webb v Smith*,[116] that the senior and junior securities must confer upon their holders proprietary interests in the assets of the debtor.

Warner J. in *Smit Tak*[117] was of the opinion that *Webb v Smith*[118] was only authority for a much narrower proposition, *viz.* the doctrine of marshalling does not apply where the senior creditor possesses unequal or different rights of recourse to the assets subject to the senior security. On this basis, a junior creditor would be able to assert the right to marshall where the senior creditor holds *equal non-security* rights (such as rights of set-off) in respect of two or more assets of the debtor.[119]

The requirement of proprietary securities and the purported extension of marshalling to non-security interests are considered in detail in Chapter 9.

---

[115] [1988] 2 Ll Rep 398.
[116] (1885) 30 Ch D 192.
[117] [1988] 2 Ll Rep 398.
[118] (1885) 30 Ch D 192.
[119] [1988] 2 Ll Rep 398, 406.

3

HOW DOES MARSHALLING WORK?

Two Competing Theories about Marshalling	3.01	Post-Realisation Theory of Marshalling	
		Introduction	3.18
Coercion Theory of Marshalling		Nature of marshalling as a post-realisation remedy	3.21
Introduction	3.03	Acceptance of post-realisation theory in England and other jurisdictions	3.26
Encroachment on senior creditor's freedom of action	3.05	Alternative means of giving effect to post-realisation theory	3.28
Enforcement of securities by secured creditors	3.07	**Purported Revival of Coercion Theory**	
Secured creditor's duty:			
to act in good faith	3.10	Introduction	3.30
to obtain a fair price	3.12	A hybrid model of marshalling	3.35

A. Two Competing Theories about Marshalling of Securities

The historical account of marshalling of securities in the preceding chapter reveals **3.01** two conflicting views as to how marshalling should protect the priority-ranking of the holders of *mesne* security. The first (and older) of these views—labelled the 'coercion theory of marshalling'—holds that marshalling preserves priority-ranking by dictating the order of realisation of the assets subject to the senior security. In contrast, the second view—labelled the 'post-realisation theory of marshalling'—contends that priority-ranking is preserved by granting the junior creditor access to the senior security following the recoupment of the senior debt.

However, as is clear from Chapter 2, the antagonism between the coercion and **3.02** post-realisation theories of marshalling was essentially a nineteenth-century affair. By the end of that century, the coercion theory was, for all practical purposes, merely an historical curiosity. This is evidenced by the fact that, since the turn of the century, virtually every reported case on marshalling of securities in England and Australia, Canada and New Zealand has adopted the view of marshalling embodied in the post-realisation theory.[1]

---

[1] q v the cases cited in n32 and nn34–36.

Nonetheless, it has now become necessary to consider the merits of the coercion theory *qua* the post-realisation theory as a result of the statements in favour of that theory, by the Supreme Court of Tasmania in *Commonwealth Trading Bank v Colonial Mutual Life Assurance Society Ltd*,[2] the High Court in *Smit Tak International Zeesleepin Bergingsbedrijf BV v Selco Salvage Ltd*,[3] and, most recently, the House of Lords in *Re Bank of Credit and Commerce International SA (No 8)*.[4]

B. Coercion Theory of Marshalling of Securities

Introduction

3.03   The coercion theory of marshalling declares that marshalling's objective of priority-preservation is achieved by the pre-emption of the conduct of the senior creditor. Marshalling permits the junior creditor to require the senior creditor to enforce the senior security in a manner which leaves the junior security intact i e by compelling the senior creditor to recoup its debt out of the asset, to which only the senior security extends, rather than that asset which is subject to securities in favour of both the senior and junior creditors. The senior creditor is thus required to leave the asset, over which the junior creditor holds security, intact for the benefit of the junior creditor.

3.04   Marshalling effectively circumscribes the senior creditor's freedom to enforce the senior security as it sees fit. This constraint, in contrast to the typical legal impediments to the exercise by a secured creditor of the remedies available to it under its security, is not to be found in the debtor-creditor relationship. Nor is it a right capable of being asserted by the debtor.[5] The beneficiary of the protection afforded by marshalling is, instead, a lower-ranking secured[6] creditor of the debtor. Further, marshalling does not require a pre-existing contractual relationship between the junior and senior creditors,[7] nor does it require the privity of contract between the creditors.

Encroachment on the senior creditor's freedom of action

3.05   The version of marshalling supported by the coercion theory substantially detracts from the position of the senior creditor, as the paramount-ranking creditor of the debtor. The senior creditor, by virtue of its priority position, enjoys the right to have the debt owed to it satisfied out of the assets of the debtor over which

---

[2]   (1970) 26 FLR 338.
[3]   [1988] 2 Ll Rep 398.
[4]   [1998] 1 BCLC 68.
[5]   *Ex parte Turner* (1796) 3 Ves 243; *Paley v Field* (1806) 12 Ves 435.
[6]   Only secured creditors have standing to marshall the senior security: see further Chapter 10.
[7]   c f the equitable remedy of specific performance: see further Chapter 5.

it holds security, before those assets may be applied to meet the claims of any other creditor of the debtor (with the exception of creditors preferred by statute). The coercion theory, however, subjects the enforcement of that right to the interests of lower-ranking secured creditors.

Any one of those secured creditors, should it hold security that is narrower in scope than the senior creditor's security, would be entitled to dictate to the senior creditor the order in which the latter may resort to the various assets encompassed by the senior security. The issue arises as to whether this encroachment on the senior creditor's freedom of action is consistent with the general principles of English law that regulate the enforcement of securities by secured creditors. **3.06**

Enforcement of securities by secured creditors

The coercion theory of marshalling prevents a senior creditor from insisting upon its strict legal rights against a debtor. However, such a broad right, on the part of one secured creditor, to interfere with the legitimate exercise by a higher-ranking secured creditor of its security rights, is inconsistent with those principles of English law governing the enforcement of securities. **3.07**

The English law of securities recognises only a limited range of circumstances in which it will permit a secured creditor to be impeded by another creditor in recouping the secured debt, in the absence of a pre-existing contractual relationship. As regards this relationship, the junior creditor will invariably be a stranger to the grant of security in favour of the senior creditor (and the underlying creditor-debtor relationship). Nor, as noted above, will the junior creditor usually be in a contractual relationship,[8] or enjoy privity of contract, with the senior creditor.[9]

Those cases supporting the coercion theory aside, the law evinces considerable reluctance as regards intervention in the process of enforcement where the junior creditor is a stranger *qua* the senior creditor. In the absence of a contractual or other relationship between the junior creditor and the senior creditor, the law will generally not consider the senior creditor obligated to the junior creditor in respect of the enforcement by the senior creditor of the rights conferred upon it by the senior security. In *Commonwealth Trading Bank v Colonial Mutual Life Assurance Society Ltd*,[10] Neasey J. rejected any notion that the doctrine of marshalling constituted the senior creditor a trustee for the junior creditor of the **3.08**

---

[8] The impact on the right to marshall of covenants against marshalling and priority/subordination arrangements is considered in Chapter 12.

[9] There is no indication in any of the cases on marshalling of securities that a junior creditor's right to marshall is predicated on a contractual nexus between the junior and senior creditors: q.v. the discussion of marshalling and specific performance in Chapter 5.

[10] (1970) 26 FLR 338. See further Meagher, Gummow & Lehane, *Equity Doctrines and Remedies*, paras 1104–1106 and 1130.

senior secured asset subject to the junior security.[11] Nor, Neasey J. held, was the senior creditor a trustee for the junior creditor of any balance of proceeds of realisation of the senior security following repayment of the senior debt.[12]

3.09   The senior creditor will, as a general rule, be entitled to look after its own interests in the recovery of the senior debt, irrespective of the junior creditor's interest in the matter.[13] There are only two instances in which the law of securities will, in the

----

[11] (1970) 26 FLR 338, 339–342 and 349–350. Neasey J. noted that both Ramsbotham, *Coote's Treatise on the Law of Mortgages*, 803 and Hanbury & Waldock, *The Law of Mortgages*, 178 had cited *South v Bloxam* (1865) 2 H & M 457 as establishing the principle that a senior creditor held such balance on trust for the junior creditor (this is also the case with Robbins, *A Treatise on the Law of Mortgages, Pledges and Hypothecations*, 779). Neasey J. considered (349) that *South v Bloxam* concerned the rights of a surety of the mortgagor as against a subsequent mortgagee and, as the first mortgagee was not involved, could not see how any principle affecting first mortgagees could be derived from that case. A similar view regarding Coote's interpretation of *South v Bloxam* can be found in the New Zealand case of *New Zealand Loan & Mercantile Agency Co Ltd v Loach* (1912) 31 NZLR 292, 298–302. See also Meagher, Gummow & Lehane, *Equity Doctrines and Remedies*, para 1104; O'Donovan & Phillips, *The Modern Contract of Guarantee*, 682.

[12] (1970) 26 FLR 338, 349–350. The views of Neasey J. in *Commonwealth Trading Bank v Colonial Mutual Life Assurance Society Ltd* have since been adopted, subject to one qualification, in Australia in *Sarge Pty Ltd v Cazihaven Homes Pty Ltd* (1994) 34 NSWLR 658 and *Chase Corp (Australia) Pty Ltd v North Sydney Brick and Tile Co Ltd* (1994) 12 ACLC 997. The Supreme Court of New South Wales in those two cases accepted that marshalling conferred no equitable or other proprietary right on the junior creditor (q v n31), but noted that, on the basis of *Lawrance v Galsworthy* (1857) 3 Jur (NS) 1049, the senior creditor would be liable, as a fiduciary, to compensate the junior creditor for any loss occasioned to the junior creditor by the senior creditor's release of the assets subject to the senior security following repayment of the senior debt ((1994) 34 NSWLR 658, 664–665; and (1994) 12 ACLC 997, 1,010–1,011). Cohen J. in *Chase Corp (Australia) Pty Ltd v North Sydney Brick and Tile Co Ltd* (1994) 12 ACLC 997 considered (1,011) that this duty arose in circumstances analogous to 'a creditor releasing a security given by a debtor after payment of the debt by the surety, and before any claim of subrogation in respect of that security has been made by the surety' but noted (1,011) that liability would be limited to 'circumstances where it would be regarded as inequitable or unconscionable to release the security, that is with full knowledge of the right being asserted by the other mortgagee [the junior creditor]'. Accordingly, the obligation of the senior creditor to release to the debtor assets no longer encumbered by the senior security would be circumscribed by this duty if the senior creditor had knowledge that another creditor was claiming one of those assets by way of marshalling; q v *Faircharm Investments Ltd v Citibank International plc* (unrep 6 Feb 1998, CA). However, this is unlikely to be a significant issue following the House of Lords' decision in *Banque Financière de la Cité v Parc (Battersea) Ltd* [1998] 1 All ER 737, 749 which has resolved doubts about the efficacy of subrogation to discharged securities: see further Chapter 4. C f Webster, *Ashburner's Concise Treatise on Mortgages, Pledges and Liens*, 465, which suggests that where a senior creditor has notice of the junior security, it may be under a duty to resort to the asset encumbered by only the senior security. Similarly, Bigelow, *Story's Commentaries on Equity Jurisprudence*, para 633n(b) indicates that marshalling is predicated upon the fact that the senior creditor had notice of the junior security.

[13] A Berg, *Duties of a Mortgagee and a Receiver* [1993] JBL 213; A Clarke, *Mortgagee's Powers of Sale: Contract or Statute* [1997] LMCLQ 329. For the position in Ireland, see: P Devonshire, *The Mortgagee's Power of Sale: A Case for the Equitable Standard of Good Faith* (1995) 46 NILQ 182; in Australia, see: J Bryson, *Restraining Sales by Mortgagees and a Curial Myth* (1993) 11 ABR 1; P Butt, *Is a Mortgagee Free to Choose how it will Apply the Sale Proceeds* (1994) 68 ALJ 814; S Rodrick, *The Response of Torrens Mortgagors to Improper Mortgagee Sales* (1996) 22 Mon L R 289; in New Zealand, see: P Devonshire, *The Mortgagee's Power of Sale: New Perspectives on an Old Theme* (1995) 16 NZULR 251.

absence of a contractual or other relationship between the relevant parties, regard the secured creditor as owing a duty to the debtor (and other parties with interests in the assets subject to the creditor's security, such as lower-ranking creditors) in respect of the realisation of the secured assets.

Secured creditor's duty to act in good faith

The first such instance is where the secured creditor has not acted in good faith in enforcing its security:[14] **3.10**

> [the power of sale] is a power given to him for his own benefit, to enable him the better to realise his debt. If he exercises it *bona fide* for that purpose, without corruption or collusion with the purchaser, the Court will not interfere, even though the sale be very disadvantageous, unless, indeed the price is so low as in itself to be evidence of fraud.

The fact that a senior creditor has elected to recoup the senior debt out of assets, which are subject to a security in favour of a junior creditor, is not, of itself, evidence of *male fides* on the part of the senior creditor. It is therefore difficult to see how the right to compel the senior creditor to act in a particular manner is coeval with this duty to act in good faith. **3.11**

Secured creditor's duty to obtain a fair price

The second of the two instances in which the law will consider a secured creditor as owing a duty to the debtor (and lower-ranking creditors) arises in relation to the price obtained by the secured creditor upon the realisation of the assets subject to its security. As noted above, a secured creditor does not, even when acting in good faith, enjoy an unfettered discretion in recovering the secured debt.[15] The secured creditor is required to take reasonable care to obtain a fair price for the assets against which it is enforcing its security.[16] **3.12**

---

[14] Kay J. (as he then was) in *Warner v Jacob* (1882) 20 Ch D 220, 224. See also *Pooley's Trustee v Whetham* (1886) 33 Ch D 111; *Farrar v Farrars Ltd* (1888) 40 Ch D 395; *Kennedy v De Trafford* [1896] 1 Ch 762; *Belton v Bass Ratcliffe & Gretton Ltd* [1922] 2 Ch 449; *Reliance Permanent Building Society v Harwood-Stamper* [1944] Ch 362; *Cuckmere Brick Co Ltd v Mutual Finance Ltd* [1971] Ch 949; *Palmer v Barclays Bank Ltd* (1971) 23 P & CR 30; *China and South Sea Bank Ltd v Tan* [1990] 1 AC 536. This is also the position in Australia: *Forsyth v Blundell* (1973) 129 CLR 477; *Henry Roach (Petroleum) Pty Ltd v Credit House (Vic) Pty Ltd* [1976] VR 309; and Canada: *Lake Apartments Ltd v Bootwala* (1973) 37 DLR (3d) 523.

[15] See Francis & Thomas, *Mortgages and Securities*, 119–121.

[16] *McHugh v Union Bank of Canada* [1913] AC 299; *Cuckmere Brick Co Ltd v Mutual Finance Ltd* [1971] Ch 949; *Tse Kwong Lam v Wong Chit Sen* [1983] 1 WLR 1349; *Bishop v Bonham* [1988] 1 WLR 742; *China and South Sea Bank Ltd v Tan* [1990] 1 AC 536; *Palk v Mortgagee Services Funding plc* [1993] Ch 330; *AIB Finance Ltd v Debtors* [1998] 2 All ER 929. This is also the position in Australia: *Barns v Queensland National Bank Ltd* (1906) 3 CLR 942; *Pendlebury v CML Assurance Society Ltd* (1912) 13 CLR 676; *Latec Investments Ltd v Hotel Terrigal Pty Ltd* (1965) 113 CLR 265; *ANZ Banking Group Ltd v Bangadilly Pastoral Co Pty Ltd* (1978) 139 CLR 195; *McKean v Maloney* [1988] 1 Qd R 628; *Gattuso v Geelong Building Society* [1989] ATR 69,281; and New Zealand: *Clark v UDC Finance* [1985] 2 NZLR 636. See further Sykes & Walker, *The Law of Securities*, 118 and 275–277.

3.13 The law in this regard is taken as having been authoritatively articulated by Salmon L.J. in *Cuckmere Brick Co Ltd v Mutual Finance Ltd* in the following terms:[17]

> Given that the power of sale is for the benefit of the mortgagee and that he is entitled to choose the moment to sell which suits him, it would be strange indeed if he were under no legal obligation to obtain what I call the true market value at the date of the sale;

and:[18]

> . . . a mortgagee in exercising his power of sale does owe a duty to take reasonable precautions to obtain the true market value of the mortgaged property at the date on which he decides to sell it.

3.14 However, it is recognised that the secured creditor's duty to obtain a fair price is itself subject to an important qualification, *viz.* that once the secured creditor becomes entitled to enforce its security, the timing of the enforcement is a matter for the secured creditor:[19]

> Once the power has accrued the mortgagee is entitled to exercise it for his own purposes whenever he chooses to do so. It matters not that the moment may be unpropitious and that by waiting a higher price could be obtained. He has the right to realise his security by turning it into money when he likes.

3.15 That these principles are well settled is evidenced by their affirmation by the Court of Appeal in *Palk v Mortgage Services Funding plc*,[20] *Parker Tweedale v Dunbar Bank plc*[21] and, most recently, *AIB Finance Ltd v Debtors*,[22] and the Privy Council in *China and South Sea Bank Ltd v Tan*.[23] The following statement of

---

[17] [1971] Ch 949, 966. Doubts have, however, been raised in Australia as to the correctness of this decision in terms of damages being the appropriate remedy for a breach by the mortgagee of its duty to obtain a proper price: see, in particular, *Expo International Pty Ltd v Chant* [1979] 2 NSWLR 820; *Citicorp (Australia) Ltd v McLoughney* (1984) 35 SASR 375. See further Meagher, Gummow & Lehane, *Equity Doctrines and Remedies*, para 230. It is now clear in England that this duty is an equitable duty rather than a tortious duty: *Parker Tweedale v Dunbar Bank plc* [1991] Ch 12; *AIB Finance Ltd v Debtors* [1998] 2 All ER 929.

[18] [1971] Ch 949, 968–969.

[19] Ibid, 965. Support for this may also be found in *Farrar v Farrars Ltd* (1888) 40 Ch D 395 where Lindley L.J. stated (411): 'every mortgage confers upon the mortgagee the right to realize his security and to find a purchaser if he can, and if in exercise of his power he acts *bona fide* and takes reasonable precautions to obtain a proper price, the mortgagor has no redress, even although more might have been obtained for the property if the sale had been postponed'.

[20] [1993] Ch 330.

[21] Nourse L.J. in *Parker Tweedale v Dunbar Bank plc* [1991] Ch 12, 18–19.

[22] Nourse L.J. in *AIB Finance Ltd v Debtors* [1998] 2 All ER 929, 937. Carnwath J., whose decision was affirmed in part by the Court of Appeal, expressly cited the passage in paragraph 3.15 with approval: [1997] 4 All E R 677, 685–686.

[23] Lord Templeman in *China and South Sea Bank Ltd v Tan* [1990] 1 AC 536, 545. Similarly, express support for the duty outlined in *Cuckmere Brick Co Ltd v Mutual Finance Ltd* [1971] Ch 949 may be found in the decision of the Privy Council in *Tse Kwong Lam v Wong Chit Sen* [1983] 1 WLR 1349.

Nicholls V.C. in the *Palk* case well illustrates the duties owed by a secured creditor:[24]

> ... a mortgagee does owe some duties to a mortgagor. As Lord Templeman noted in *China and South Sea Bank* case, at p545, a mortgagee can sit back and do nothing. He is not obliged to take steps to realise his security. But if he does take steps to exercise his rights over his security, common law and equity alike have set bounds to the extent to which he can look after himself and ignore the mortgagor's interests. In the exercise of his rights over his security the mortgagee must act fairly towards the mortgagor. His interest in the property has priority over the interest of the mortgagor, and he is entitled to proceed on that footing. He can protect his own interest, but he is not entitled to conduct himself in a way which unfairly prejudices the mortgagor ... if he sells the property: he cannot sell hastily at a knock-down price sufficient to pay off his debt ... He must exercise reasonable care to sell only at the proper market value. As Lord Moulton said in *McHugh v Union Bank of Canada* [1913] AC 299, 311: 'It is well settled law that it is a duty of a mortgagee when realising the mortgaged property by sale to behave in conducting such realisation as a reasonable man would behave in the realisation of his own property, so that the mortgagor may receive credit for the fair value of the property sold.'

3.16 This duty to obtain a fair price is owed to all parties who are interested in the proceeds of realisation of the assets[25] i e the debtor as well as lower-ranking creditors (such as the junior creditor). Nonetheless, it is difficult to see how the duty imposed on a secured creditor to obtain a fair price for the assets subject to its security translates into a right that permits a junior creditor to dictate which of those assets should be realised first. The senior creditor is legally entitled to recover the senior debt out of any of the assets which are encumbered by the senior security, including any asset subject also to the junior security. Should the senior creditor elect to do so, it does not necessarily follow that it has been derelict in its duty, to the junior creditor, to take reasonable care to obtain a fair price for the assets being realised.

3.17 Furthermore, this duty—even more so than the duty to act in good faith—is directed at circumstances diametrically opposed to those with which the coercion theory is concerned. The 'duty to obtain a fair price' envisages the situation where the senior creditor has enforced its security against an asset that is also subject to the junior security, and a party such as the junior creditor is unhappy with the quantum of the proceeds of realisation. While the 'duty to act in good faith' is superimposed upon the entire period from crystallisation of the right to enforce to enforcement, the 'duty to obtain a fair price' is relevant only at the time of enforcement. The senior creditor is under no duty to preserve the value of the

---

[24] [1993] Ch 330, 337–338.

[25] *Jarrett v Barclays Bank Ltd* [1947] Ch 187; *Standard Chartered Bank Ltd v Walker* [1982] 3 All ER 938. This is also the position in Australia: *Alliance Acceptance Co Ltd v Graham* (1974) 10 SASR 220; and New Zealand: *Clark v National Mutual Life Assoc of Australia Ltd* [1966] NZLR 196. See further L Hogg, *No Duty to Enforce Securities* (1990) 1 JBFLP 150, 150–152.

secured property ahead of the enforcement of its security.[26] That is definitely not the case with the coercion theory; the coercion theory permits the junior creditor to dictate the conduct of the senior creditor *before* the process of enforcement has even commenced.

C. Post-Realisation Theory of Marshalling of Securities

Introduction

3.18 The version of marshalling advocated by the post-realisation theory, in contrast to that advanced by the coercion theory, does not interfere with the freedom of the senior creditor to realise the assets subject to its security in whichever manner it deems fit. The doctrine of marshalling cannot therefore be employed by the junior creditor to enjoin a senior creditor from recovering the senior debt out of an asset of the debtor that is subject to the junior security.

While the doctrine of marshalling will not interfere with the measures undertaken by the senior creditor to recover its debt, it will not permit that creditor to deprive the junior creditor of the benefit of the junior security. Should the senior creditor satisfy the senior debt out of that asset which is subject to the junior security, marshalling will redress the loss sustained by the junior creditor by granting the junior creditor access to the senior creditor's security.

3.19 The preference for the post-realisation theory has been expressed by English courts in the following terms; by Wood V.C. in *Wallis v Woodyear*:[27]

> [The senior creditor] has a right to take the first money that is realised by any of his securities which first comes to hand;

and by Parker J. in *Manks v Whiteley*:[28]

> The equitable right of marshalling has never been held to prevent a prior mortgagee from realising his securities in such manner and order as he thinks fit.

3.20 Similar preference for the post-realisation theory of marshalling has been expressed by the Australian courts; by Waddell J. of the Supreme Court of New South Wales, in *Mir Bros Projects Pty Ltd v Lyons*:[29]

> The simplest example of the application of this . . . doctrine is where X has a charge over two funds, and Y a subsequent charge over only one of them. If X satisfies his charge out of the fund which is subject to Y's charge and the result is to deprive Y of the whole or the part of the benefit of his security, he is, in effect, subrogated to X's

---

[26] Mummery L.J. in *AIB Finance Ltd v Debtors* [1998] 2 All ER 929, 936.
[27] (1855) 2 Jur (NS) 179, 180.
[28] [1911] 2 Ch 448, 466.
[29] [1977] 2 NSWLR 192, 196.

rights against the other fund and has recourse to the other to the extent necessary to satisfy his charge;

and more recently by Cohen J. of the Supreme Court of New South Wales, in *Chase Corporation (Australia) Pty Ltd v North Sydney Brick and Tile Company Ltd:*[30]

> Although reference was there made [in *Aldrich v Cooper*] to compelling the person having the two funds to resort to the one which the other party cannot resort to, it is clear from the authorities that the double mortgagee can satisfy his claim against either of the funds or securities available to it. It is not bound to seek to have its debt paid only from the fund in which the other mortgagee has no interest. What follows however is that the single claimant is entitled to recover from the single fund if the double fund has been exhausted by the double claimant exercising its rights.

The nature of marshalling of securities as a post-realisation remedy

Should the senior creditor, of its own volition, choose to satisfy the debt owed to **3.21** it out of the asset, which is subject to only the senior security, the junior creditor's marshalling rights will remain dormant; the junior creditor will have effectively been accorded the status of paramount-ranking creditor, *vis-à-vis* the asset which is subject to the junior security, by this course of action. It is only in the event that the senior creditor recovers its debt out of the asset, over which both the senior and junior creditors hold security, that the junior creditor will be prejudiced and that the doctrine of marshalling will apply.

In such circumstances, the junior creditor may find itself in a position no different from that of the debtor's unsecured creditors (to the extent that there is a short-fall as a result of the asset, subject to the junior security, having been appropriated to the repayment of the senior debt). It is in this situation, according to the post-realisation theory, that the doctrine of marshalling will intervene for the purpose of preserving the priority-ranking of the junior creditor. The post-realisation theory states that marshalling achieves this objective by permitting the junior creditor to resort to the security rights of the senior creditor in respect of that asset of the debtor, over which only the senior creditor holds security.

Marshalling thus allows the junior creditor to exchange its security for the security **3.22** held by the senior creditor. This has the effect of preserving the status of the junior creditor's claim against the assets of the debtor.

---

[30] (1994) 12 ACLC 997, 1,008–1,009. Significantly, Cohen J. read down the language of compulsion in *Aldrich v Cooper* (1803) 8 Ves Jun 382 (see further paragraph 2.21). Support in Australia for the post-realisation characterisation of marshalling may also be found in the *obiter* comments of the Federal Court of Australia in *Patrick Stevedores No 2 Pty Ltd v MV Skulptor Konenkov* (1996) 136 ALR 211, 225–226 where Snell's description of marshalling (as a post-realisation remedy) was adopted.

3.23 The senior creditor has, by the recoupment of its debt out of the asset over which the junior creditor holds security, eroded the junior security. Although the actual claim of the junior creditor against the debtor has been left intact, the conduct of the senior creditor has undermined the preferential status of that claim *vis-à-vis* the other creditors of the debtor. The doctrine of marshalling redresses this by allowing the junior creditor to replace its diminished secured claim against an asset with the intact secured claim of the senior creditor against another asset. Thus, in effect, the doctrine of marshalling has conferred upon the junior creditor a security over an asset against which it did not originally enjoy a secured claim:[31]

> Marshalling is a doctrine which enables a person who has no security in law or equity against [an] asset . . . to become subrogated to such a claim, if the creditor entitled to resort to this and other assets by his election deprives him of security. It is of the very essence of the doctrine that the creditor invoking it has otherwise no claim upon the fund freed by the actual course of realisation.

3.24 The junior creditor is by the process of marshalling able to regain its priority-ranking *vis-à-vis* the other creditors of the debtor. The doctrine of marshalling effectively places the junior creditor in the position it would have been in had the senior creditor elected to enforce its security against the asset of the debtor that was subject only to the senior security.

3.25 The result attained by the post-realisation theory is therefore no different from that which would have been obtained by the adoption of the coercion theory: both theories are concerned with the preservation of the priority-ranking of the junior creditor. They do, however, achieve that objective in radically different ways. The post-realisation theory leaves the senior creditor's freedom of action uninhibited. It does not impinge upon the status of the senior creditor as the paramount-ranking creditor of the debtor. Instead, it attempts to reverse the consequences of the senior creditor's actions in so far as the enforcement of the senior

---

[31] *Bisset v ANZ Bank Ltd* [1961] NZLR 687, 693–694 (Turner J. of the High Court). The security in question is that of the senior creditor. Marshalling does not confer on the junior creditor a new security or other proprietary interest: *Commonwealth Trading Bank v Colonial Mutual Life Assurance Society Ltd* (1970) 26 FLR 338, 341–342, 343 and 346. This is made explicit by Neasey J. (341–342): '. . . the argument is in effect that the right in equity to marshall confers an equitable right of property in the alternative fund of the debtor over which the plaintiff had, before the right to marshall arose, no security. I have already observed that this proposition is apparently bare of authority to support it, but in my opinion a number of considerations make it plain that it is not sustainable' and later (346): 'the doctrine depends not upon the creation of any equitable right of property in the fund over which the claimant otherwise has no security, but upon the grant by the court of an equitable remedy in certain circumstances'. Cohen J. in *Chase Corp (Australia) Pty Ltd v North Sydney Brick and Tile Co Ltd* (1994) 12 ACLC 997, 1,010–1,011 concluded, applying this case, that marshalling did not give the junior creditor a proprietary right in the asset subject only to the senior security. See also Tyler, *Fisher & Lightwood's Law of Mortgage*, 531; Meagher, Gummow & Lehane, *Equity Doctrines and Remedies*, paras 1105, 1122, 1123, 1129 and 1130. This does not necessarily exclude the possibility of an inchoate equitable interest: see further paragraphs 11.12 to 11.14.

security has adversely impacted upon the junior security. The doctrine of marshalling comes into force 'post-realisation' of the senior security in order to prevent the election by the senior creditor, of a particular sequence of recourse to the assets subject to its security, from eroding the security held by the junior creditor. The coercion theory, on the other hand, prevents such an election from ever being made; the senior creditor, at the junior creditor's behest, is directed to look first to those assets, whose only encumbrance is the senior security.

Acceptance of the post-realisation theory in England and other jurisdictions

The post-realisation theory has been accepted by the majority of the English cases[32] and virtually all the major English texts[33] concerned with marshalling of securities. This is similarly the case in Australia,[34] Canada[35] and New Zealand.[36] In Ireland, the position remains unsettled.[37]   **3.26**

---

[32] *Wright v Simpson* (1802) 6 Ves 714; *Gwynne v Edwards* (1825) 2 Russ 289n; *Mason v Bogg* (1827) 2 My & Cr 443; *Barnes v Racster* (1842) 1 Y & C Ch Cas 401; *Wallis v Woodyear* (1855) 2 Jur (NS) 179; *Re Scott's Estate* (1863) 14 L Ch R 63; *Binns v Nichols* (1866) LR 2 Eq 256; *Ex parte Alston* (1868) 4 Ch App 168; *Dolphin v Aylward* (1870) LR 4 E & I 486; *Noyes v Pollock* (1886) 32 Ch D 466; *Gregg v Arrott* (noted in Chitty, *Index to All the Reported Cases Decided in the Several Courts of Equity and Bankruptcy in England and Ireland*, 4048–4049); *Moxon v The Berkeley Mutual Benefit Building Society* (1890) 59 LJ Ch 524; *The 'Chioggia'* [1898] P 1; *Manks v Whiteley* [1911] 2 Ch 448; *Re Cohen* [1960] Ch 179.

[33] Robbins, *A Treatise on the Law of Mortgages, Pledges and Hypothecations*, 778 (c f Robbins, 783 where the description of marshalling in *Flint v Howard* [1893] 2 Ch 54 as a coercive remedy is quoted with approval); Beddoes, *A Concise Treatise on the Law of Mortgages*, 105 (c f Beddoes, 102, 103 and 106 where the coercive view of marshalling is stated); Hewitt, *White & Tudor's Leading Cases in Equity*, 40 and 52–53; Ramsbotham, *Coote's Treatise on the Law of Mortgages*, 802–803 and 804 (c f Ramsbotham, 807 where the coercive view of marshalling is stated); Browne, *Ashburner's Principles of Equity*, 214; Hanbury & Waldock, *The Law of Mortgages*, 178; *Halsbury's*, Vol 16 (*'Equity'*), para 876n1 and Vol 32 (*'Mortgage'*), para 915 (*Aldrich v Cooper* (1803) 8 Ves Jun 382 is incorrectly cited at para 915n10 in support); Keaton & Sheridan, *Equity*, 304 (again, *Lawrance v Galsworthy* (1857) 3 Jur (NS) 1049 is incorrectly cited at 304n3 in support); *Halsbury's*, Vol 32 (*'Mortgage'*), para 915n9; Baker & Langan, *Snell's Equity*, 421–422; Tyler, *Fisher & Lightwood's Law of Mortgage*, 530–531; Cousins, *The Law of Mortgages*, 436–437; P R Wood, *Comparative Law of Security and Guarantees*, para 10–17; Strahan, *The Marshalling of Mortgages*, 308 (*Webb v Smith* (1885) 30 Ch D 192 is incorrectly cited at 308n2 in support of the post-realisation version of marshalling); S R Derham, *Set-Off Against an Assignee: the Relevance of Marshalling, Contribution and Subrogation* (1991) 107 LQR 126, 129–130. C f (i) Smith, *A Practical Exposition of the Principles of Equity*, 613 and Robb, *Nokes' Outline of the Law of Mortgages and Receiverships*, 84–85 which support the coercion theory of marshalling; and (ii) Cavanagh, *The Law of Money Securities*, 550 and Webster, *Ashburner's Concise Treatise on Mortgages, Pledges and Liens*, 465–466 where a hybrid model incorporating the coercion and post-realisation theories is advanced; this is considered in more detail in paragraphs 3.35–3.39.

[34] *Mir Bros Projects Pty Ltd v Lyons* [1977] 2 NSWLR 192; *Mir Bros Projects Pty Ltd v Lyons* [1978] 2 NSWLR 508; *Deta Nominees Pty Ltd v Discount Plastic Products Pty Ltd* [1979] VR 167; *Re O'Leary* (1985) 61 ALR 674; *Chase Corp (Australia) Pty Ltd v North Sydney Brick and Tile Co Ltd* (1994) 12 ACLC 997; *Patrick Stevedores No 2 Pty Ltd v MV Skulptor Konenkov* (1996) 136 ALR 211; *Oamington Pty Ltd v Commissioner of Land Tax* (unrep 24 Nov 1997, Sup Ct of NSW). See Francis & Thomas, *Mortgages and Securities*, 369–370; Meagher, Gummow & Lehane, *Equity Doctrines and Remedies*, paras 1102–1106; Sykes & Walker, *The Law of Securities*, 182 (this text is ambiguous with respect to this issue); McDonald, *Marshalling* (1996), para 1604; McDonald,

3.27   The major reason for the preference of the post-realisation theory is that, unlike the coercion theory, it does not offend against the fundamental principle of securities law: once a security becomes enforceable, the secured creditor is entitled to enforce it whenever, and realise the assets subject to it in whatever order, it pleases. Accordingly, it is difficult to see how an argument characterising marshalling as something other than a post-realisation remedy could be sustained before an English (or Australian, Canadian or New Zealand) court.

Alternative means of giving effect to the post-realisation theory

3.28   The mechanism of subrogation or substitution to the senior security is not, however, the sole means by which the post-realisation theory may be given effect.

Marshalling (1997), paras 23 and 27; W M C Gummow, *Marshalling and Protected Assets* (1965) 5 Syd LR 120, 122. c f O'Donovan & Phillips, *The Modern Contract of Guarantee*, 680 where the coercion theory is adopted. In *Finance Corp of Australia Ltd v Bentley* (1991) 5 BPR 97412, the Supreme Court of New South Wales expressly adopted the coercion theory of marshalling (at 11,840): 'The doctrine of marshalling expressly prohibits a mortgagee with two or more securities from taking his debt out of one of those securities if another creditor has a right, subject to the rights of the first creditor, as against that security only. The first creditor must satisfy his claim out of the property encumbered only by his interest'. However, the Supreme Court's decision was reversed on appeal. Although the NSW Court of Appeal did not consider this specific point, the result renders the comments of the lower court of little persuasive value. See further P Butt, *Is a Mortgagee Free to Choose how it will Apply the Sale Proceeds* (1994) 68 ALJ 814 for a discussion of this case.

[35]   *Ernst Bros Co v Canadian Permanent Mortgage Corporation* (1920) 57 DLR 500 (of the four judges of the Ontario Supreme Court, Appellate Division who decided this case, Riddell J. and Masten J. described marshalling as a post-realisation remedy (505 and 507) while Mulock C.J.Ex adopted the hybrid version of marshalling (503–504)); *Seel Investments Ltd v Greater Canadian Securities Corporation Ltd* (1967) 65 DLR (2d) 45; *Williamson v Loonstra* (1973) 34 DLR (3d) 275; *Nova Scotia Savings & Loan Co v O'Hara* (1979) 7 RPR 281; *Goodman v Parkhurst* [1980] 6 WWR 601; *Canadian Trustco Mortgage Co v Wenngatz Construction & Holdings Ltd* (1986) 1 BCLR (2d) 302; *Yorkshire Trust Co v Armwest Development Ltd* [1986] 1 WWR 478; *First Investors Corporation Ltd v Veeradon Developments Ltd* (1988) 47 DLR (4th) 446; *Fiatallis North America Inc v Pigott Construction Ltd* (1992) 3 PPSAC (2d) 30; *Farm Credit Corporation v Nelson* (1993) 102 DLR (4th) 743; *Royal Trust Company v H A Roberts Group Limited* [1995] 4 WWR 305; *Re Allison* (1998) 38 OR (3d) 337. See Rayner & McLaren, *Falconbridge on Mortgages*, 314; c f (i) *Steinbach Credit Union Ltd v Manitoba Agricultural Credit Corp* (1991) 72 Man R (2d) 161 in which the view of marshalling as a coercive remedy was expressed; and (ii) MacDougall, *Marshalling and the Personal Property Security Acts: Doing Unto Others . . .*, 120 and 120–122 where the adoption in Canada of the United States version of marshalling is argued for. Support for the hybrid model of marshalling may also be found in *Hongkong Bank of Canada v Shrimp Projectors Inc* [1993] 3 WWR 484.

[36]   *Brigham v Chambers* (1880) OB & F 66; *Re Tremain* [1934] NZLR 369; *Bisset v ANZ Bank Ltd* [1961] NZLR 687; *Re Manawatu Transport Ltd* (1984) 2 NZCLC 99,084; *National Bank of NZ Ltd v Caldesia Promotions Ltd and Jenkins Roberts & Associates Ltd* [1996] 3 NZLR 467. See G W Hinde, D W McMorland, N R Campbell & D P Grinlinton, *Butterworths Land Law in New Zealand* (1997 Butterworths), para 8.147; T Schumacher, *Marshalling* (1989) 5 BCB 89, 90; T Cleaver, *Marshalling* (1991) 21 VUWLR 275, 277–280.

[37]   There is support for both the coercion theory (*Re Lawder's Estate* (1861) 11 Ir Ch R 346) and the post-realisation theory (*Re Fox* (1856) 5 I Ch R 541) in Ireland, with no final decision having been reached in favour of one or the other. See also A Lyall, *Land Law in Ireland* (1994 Oak Tree Press), para 23.7.3.

Should the senior creditor elect to recover the senior debt out of the asset over which the junior creditor holds security, it has been contended that the junior creditor will be entitled to demand that the senior security be assigned to it.[38] Instead, therefore, of being placed in the position of the senior creditor *vis-à-vis* the assets, which are subject to only the senior security, the junior creditor will take an assignment of the senior security over those assets.

While an assignment of the senior security will confer upon the junior creditor **3.29** equivalent rights as being substituted to that security would, there is one crucial aspect in which assignment differs from the process of substitution envisaged by marshalling. An assignment is perfected by the voluntary act of the assignor[39] whereas the process of substitution envisaged by marshalling operates by law. Accordingly, an assignment is a far less efficacious means of acquiring the benefit of the senior security, as it depends upon the acquiescence of the senior creditor (who has little incentive to involve itself in the affairs of the debtor once the debt due to it has been discharged). The mechanism of assignment is thus unlikely to replace or even erode the substitution mechanism as the preferred means by which the post-realisation theory of marshalling grants the junior creditor access to the security of the senior creditor.

D. Purported Revival of the Coercion Theory

Introduction

As noted in Chapter 2 and in the first section of this chapter, the position of the **3.30** post-realisation theory as the preferred version of marshalling has been questioned in two English cases and one Australian case.

The Australian case, *Commonwealth Trading Bank v Colonial Mutual Life* **3.31** *Assurance Society Ltd*,[40] can be readily dismissed (to the extent that it deals with how marshalling operates). For one reason or another, Neasey J. saw fit to consider

---

[38] The sole support for this view is to be found in Scots law and in certain minority authorities in the United States (q v n54). See Lord Kames, *Principles of Equity*, 79–80; Bigelow, *Story's Commentaries on Equity Jurisprudence*, para 637; Smith, *A Short Commentary on the Law of Scotland*, 470; Johnston & Hope (eds), *Gloag & Henderson's Introduction to the Law of Scotland*, 218–219; Walker, *Principles of Scottish Private Law*, Vol III, 190–191. See also Mitchell, *The Law of Subrogation* (1994 Oxford), 57–58, where it is noted that, in the context of a surety's succession to the security rights of a creditor, the use by Scots law of assignment, as opposed to subrogation, is due to its Roman law antecedents. Also of relevance, is *Praed v Gardiner* (1788) 2 Cox Eq Cas 86 where a surety, upon discharging the liability of a debtor to a creditor, was entitled to stand in the place of the creditor as against the debtor and have the creditor's securities assigned to it.

[39] See Derham, *Subrogation in Insurance Law*, 23; Meagher, Gummow & Lehane, *Equity Doctrines and Remedies*, paras 602–603 and 609–611; K P McGuinness, *The Law of Guarantee* (2nd ed 1996 Carswell), para 7.12.

[40] (1970) 26 FLR 338.

only those authorities in favour of the coercion theory. In addition, since the decision in that case, the Australian courts have on several occasions opined in favour of the post-realisation theory.[41]

3.32 The statements in *Smit Tak International Zeesleepin Bergingsbedrijf BV v Selco Salvage Ltd*[42] and *Re Bank of Credit and Commerce International SA (No 8)*[43] are more difficult to reconcile with the line of English authorities in favour of the post-realisation theory.

3.33 Warner J. in the *Smit Tak* case[44], in his depiction of the doctrine of marshalling, reverted to the language of the coercion theory. He did not speak of redressing the loss sustained by the junior creditor but rather of preventing that loss eventuating by 'binding' the senior creditor. However, Warner J. went beyond the original formulation of the coercion theory; he glossed onto the coercion theory a refinement not evinced by any of the earlier English cases in which support for the coercion theory is to be found.[45]

Warner J. held that the manner in which the doctrine of marshalling operated depended upon the time at which the junior creditor invoked the doctrine. If, by the time the junior creditor sought to avail itself of the doctrine of marshalling, the senior creditor had already enforced its security and recouped its debt, the junior creditor would be too late to compel enforcement of that security against those assets which were encumbered by only the senior security. In such a situation, as pre-emption was no longer possible, the doctrine of marshalling would apply in accordance with the post-realisation theory. The junior creditor would therefore be placed in the position of the senior creditor *vis-à-vis* those assets. A similar approach to marshalling of securities is implicit in the *dicta* of Lord Hoffmann in the *BCCI* case.[46]

3.34 Nonetheless, the *Smit Tak* case[47] clearly prefers the coercion theory. Although Warner J. was not averse to employing the post-realisation theory, his preference was to preserve the priority-ranking of the junior security by binding or pre-

---

[41] *Mir Bros Projects Pty Ltd v Lyons* [1977] 2 NSWLR 192; *Mir Bros Projects Pty Ltd v Lyons* [1978] 2 NSWLR 508; *Deta Nominees Pty Ltd v Discount Plastic Products Pty Ltd* [1979] VR 167; *Re O'Leary* (1985) 61 ALR 674; *Chase Corp (Australia) Pty Ltd v North Sydney Brick and Tile Co Ltd* (1994) 12 ACLC 997; *Patrick Stevedores No 2 Pty Ltd v MV Skulptor Konenkov* (1996) 136 ALR 211; *Oamington Pty Ltd v Commissioner of Land Tax* (unrep 24 Nov 1997, Sup Ct of NSW).

[42] [1988] 2 Ll Rep 398. The relevant statement is quoted in paragraph 2.59.

[43] [1998] 1 BCLC 68. The relevant statement is quoted in paragraph 2.60.

[44] [1988] 2 Ll Rep 398.

[45] This version of marshalling was first argued for, in England, by Cavanagh, *The Law of Money Securities*, 550. By so doing, the *Smit Tak* case [1988] 2 Ll Rep 398 is attempting to rectify the shortcomings of the coercion theory: the coercion theory, in its original form, as a pre-emptive remedy, overlooked the situation where the senior security was enforced prior to the junior creditor's assertion of its marshalling rights.

[46] [1998] 1 BCLC 68.

[47] [1988] 2 Ll Rep 398.

empting the actions of the senior creditor. Accordingly, it is only where the senior creditor has, so to speak, stolen a march on the junior creditor that use will be made of the substitutive process of the post-realisation theory whereby the junior creditor will be permitted to exchange its security for the senior security.

A hybrid model of marshalling of securities

There is considerable support in the United States of America for the model of **3.35** marshalling envisaged by the *Smit Tak*[48] and *BCCI*[49] cases. The courts in the United States prefer, to the extent it is possible, to give effect to marshalling of securities *via* the coercion[50] of the senior creditor.[51] This preference is evident in the following statement of Story:[52]

> The general principle is, that if one party has a lien on, or interest in, two funds for a debt, and another party has a lien on, or interest in, only one of the funds for another debt; the latter has a right in equity to compel the former to resort to the other fund,

---

[48] Ibid.

[49] [1998] 1 BCLC 68. Support for the hybrid model of marshalling may also be found in Canada: *Richmond Savings Credit Union v Zilbershats* (1997) 35 BCLR (3d) 136; MacDougall, *Marshalling and the Personal Property Security Acts: Doing Unto Others . . .*, 117–116.

[50] There is one important qualification recognised in the United States to the ability of a junior creditor to dictate the order of realisation to the senior creditor: the risk of loss to the senior creditor will often prove a bar to the application of marshalling. A number of United States jurisdictions require the junior creditor to demonstrate that no such risk exists by establishing that the senior creditor has at its disposal another asset capable of providing for full repayment of the senior debt: the leading United States case on this point is *American National Insurance Co v Vine-Wood Realty Co* 199 A 2d 449 (1964). See further Jones, *A Treatise on the Law of Mortgages of Real Property*, para 1628; *Am Jur*, paras 53:14 and 53:30; Shalhoub, *Marshaling: Equitable Rights of Holders of Junior Interests*, 294–295.

[51] J Ram, *Law of Assets, Debts and Incumbrances* (2nd ed 1837 Baker Voorhis & Co), Chapter 28; Jones, *A Treatise on the Law of Mortgages of Real Property*, para 1628; Beach Jr., *Commentaries on Modern Equity Jurisprudence*, paras 781 and 789; *Am Jur*, paras 53:1, 53:29 and 53:32; *Corpus Juris Secundum* (1948 American Book Co), para 55:1; *Corpus Juris Secundum* (1990 American Book Co), para 21:110; D R Cowans, *Cowans Bankruptcy Law and Practice* (6th ed 1994 West Publishing), Vol 3, 152–155.

[52] Bigelow, *Story's Commentaries on Equity Jurisprudence*, para 633; see also para 499. C f (i) Pomeroy Jr., *Equity Jurisprudence*, para 1414, which expressly adopts the post-realisation theory and the English authorities supporting it (Pomeroy Jr., para 1414n6 states further that the coercion of the senior creditor is unwarranted; this is, however, inconsistent with other statements by Pomeroy where the coercion theory is adopted: Pomeroy Jr., *Equity Jurisprudence*, para 396; Pomeroy Jr., *A Treatise on Equitable Remedies*, paras 865–866); and (ii) J D McCoy, *Bispham's Principles of Equity* (11th ed 1931 Baker, Voorhis & Co), para 316 where a much narrower role for the coercive theory in the hybrid model is proposed, *viz.* that marshalling should only operate by way of coercion where the secured assets are in court or under the immediate control of the court: '. . . it would appear to be unjust that a creditor who had taken pains to obtain ample security should be limited in his rights of enforcement, and exposed to delay . . . A paramount encumbrancer ought to be allowed to choose the method of collecting his debt, and all that a junior creditor can fairly ask is that he shall have liberty to resort to another source of payment in place of one of which he has been deprived. Of course, where both funds are in court, or under its immediate control, the case is different. The rights of every one can be protected, and there is no harm in throwing the paramount creditor at once on the singly-charged fund'.

in the first instance for satisfaction, if that course is necessary for the satisfaction of the claims of both parties.

Similarly, the *Restatement of the Law of Security* provides:[53]

> Where a debt is secured by chattels which can be conveniently sold in parcels and as to some of the chattels a third person has a junior security interest, the pledgee can be compelled by a court of equity to sell first the chattels in which he has the exclusive security interest . . .

3.36   It is only where a junior creditor invokes the doctrine of marshalling, subsequent to the senior creditor having enforced its security against the asset over which the junior creditor also holds security, that American law will resort to a mechanism equivalent to that depicted by the post-realisation theory.[54] Again, this is because in that situation it is obviously impossible to pre-empt the order of realisation of the assets subject to the senior security. Accordingly, equity, to preserve the priority-ranking of the junior security, will, instead, place the junior creditor in the position of the senior creditor *vis-à-vis* that asset, in respect of which the senior creditor alone holds security.

3.37   This hybrid model of marshalling is not, however, a viable alternative to the post-realisation theory of marshalling under English (or Australian, Canadian or New Zealand) law.

3.38   It is, in essence, no different from the original coercion theory of marshalling; although the version of marshalling contemplated by the *Smit Tak*[55] and *BCCI*[56] cases does not reject the post-realisation theory, it only has recourse to that theory in circumstances where the use of the coercion theory is no longer feasible. The hybrid model is thus not a compromise between what are, in any event, two mutually exclusive concepts of marshalling: the coercion theory depicts marshalling as essentially a pre-emptive doctrine while the post-realisation theory portrays it as a reactive doctrine. It is, rather, nothing but a recapitulation of the

---

[53]   (1941 American Law Institute), para 53C.

[54]   See *Am Jur*, paras 53:29 and 53:32; *CJS*, paras 21:120b and 55:21; B Schwartz, *Marshaling Assets for Benefit of Mortgagor* (1930) 5 Notre Dame L Rev 208, 208–209. An alternative to substitution is also discussed (in *CJS*, paras 21:120b and 55:21). It is stated that: 'If a creditor who has a lien on two funds, on one of which another creditor has a junior lien, elects to take his whole amount out of the fund on which the junior creditor has a lien, the latter will be entitled to have the prior lien assigned to him'. Although this would, no doubt, achieve the same result as substitution (q v the Scottish position discussed at n38) the assignment theory enjoys only minority support in the United States. In any case, it appears that marshalling will only be enforced by assignment where the security held by the junior creditor is, for one reason or another, defective: C S Buschmann, *Determination of Superior Equities in Cases of Marshaling and Subrogation* (1927) 2 Ind LJ 589, 592–593. This would make the assignment theory unworkable: a junior creditor, whose security has been rendered void under Chapter 1 of Part XII of the *Companies Act 1985* (UK) (as amended by Part IV of the *Companies Act 1989* (UK)), would have no standing to invoke the doctrine of marshalling.

[55]   [1988] 2 Ll Rep 398.

[56]   [1998] 1 BCLC 68.

coercion theory in a form that recognises that junior creditors may sometimes rest on their rights and that senior creditors may often act with alacrity.

In common with the original coercion theory, the hybrid model of marshalling **3.39** protects the junior creditor's security by eroding the rights of the senior creditor; the senior creditor will, if possible, be prevented from enforcing its security against that asset which is subject to the junior creditor's security. This version of marshalling thus does nothing to resolve the incongruity with English securities law that was manifest in the original coercion theory, *viz.* its interference with the senior creditor's pursuit of its legitimate rights.[57] The post-realisation theory, in contrast, enjoys the decisive advantage that it protects the junior security without infringing the rights of the senior creditor and, as such, is consistent with English securities law.

---

[57] Shalhoub, *Marshaling: Equitable Rights of Holders of Junior Interests*, 289–290, 290 and 292 argues that the coercion theory of marshalling is consistent with the legal rules of priority, in that marshalling permits the repayment in full of the senior debt but in a manner that avoids the exhaustion of the secured assets available to the junior creditor. The curtailment of the senior creditor's rights of enforcement is therefore a necessary extension of marshalling's priority-preservation *raison d'être*. See also *Am Jur*, para 53:3.

Part III

GENERAL PRINCIPLES—JURIDICAL NATURE OF MARSHALLING OF SECURITIES

4

MARSHALLING OF SECURITIES AND THE LAW OF SUBROGATION

Introduction	4.01	Marshalling and first six categories	4.24
		Marshalling and seventh category	4.27
Marshalling as a Redistributive Remedy	4.04	Marshalling is not an eighth category of	
		subrogation	4.32
Erosion of junior security by senior			
creditor	4.05	**Marshalling, Subrogation and Law**	
Marshalling and rectifying junior creditor's		**of Restitution**	
loss	4.06	Introduction	4.34
Marshalling and redistributing debtor's		No restitutionary analysis of marshalling	4.35
assets	4.07	Subrogation and law of restitution	4.38
		Marshalling and unjust enrichment:	
Marshalling as a Subrogation Remedy	**4.13**	deprivation of benefit	4.41
Lack of authority for classification of		who has been enriched?	4.43
marshalling as a subrogation remedy	4.14	has senior creditor been enriched?	4.44
Redistributive nature of subrogation		has the debtor been enriched?	4.48
categories	4.17	enrichment of unsecured creditors	4.51
		Restitutionary analysis of subrogation	
Comparison of Marshalling and		cannot be extended to marshalling	4.52
Subrogation	**4.20**	Marshalling is not a subrogation remedy	4.55
Established categories of subrogation	4.21		

A. Introduction

The purpose of this chapter is to consider the relationship between the equitable **4.01** doctrine of marshalling of securities and the law of subrogation. Any consideration of the nature of marshalling of securities necessarily raises the issue of whether marshalling can be characterised as a subrogation remedy or a new[1] category of subrogation.

The doctrine of marshalling achieves its objective of priority-preservation by plac- **4.02** ing the junior creditor in the position of the senior creditor to the extent of the latter's security rights against the debtor. This process of subrogation or substitution,

---

[1] As will be seen below, marshalling does not form one of the established categories of subrogation.

whereby the junior creditor is granted access to an asset of the debtor, to which the junior security does not extend, has the effect of redistributing the debtor's assets amongst those of its creditors, who remain after the discharge of the senior debt.

Marshalling is thus dependent upon subrogation (or an equivalent process[2]) for its efficacy. In addition, subrogation, by making available to one party the rights enjoyed by another party against an obligor, effects, like marshalling, a redistribution of the assets of the obligor.

4.03 Further, it is now accepted that the unifying principle for the disparate categories of subrogation is to be found in the law of restitution, *viz.* that all forms of subrogation have as their purpose the redress of unjust enrichment.[3] Both marshalling and subrogation, as noted above, effect a redistribution of assets by their substitution of one party to the rights of another. It is therefore arguable that marshalling is capable of being explained by the restitutionary principles that underlie subrogation and, consequently, being categorised as a subrogation remedy.

B. Marshalling of Securities as a Redistributive Remedy

4.04 Marshalling acts to preserve the priority-ranking of the security held by the junior creditor by effecting a redistribution of the debtor's assets.

Erosion of the junior security by the senior creditor

4.05 The recovery of the debt owed to the senior creditor out of an asset, which is subject to the junior creditor's security, erodes that security. Although the senior creditor's conduct does not affect the validity of the junior creditor's secured claim, it undermines the preferential status accorded by the junior security to the junior creditor's claim against the debtor. The junior creditor is relegated to a position no different from that of the debtor's unsecured creditors, to the extent that the asset subject to the junior security is not sufficient to discharge the junior creditor's claim, as a result of that asset having been utilised to satisfy the senior creditor's claim.

Marshalling and rectifying the junior creditor's loss

4.06 The doctrine of marshalling acts to redress this loss by placing the junior creditor in the position of the senior creditor, as against those assets that are encumbered by only the senior security. This has two immediate consequences:

---

[2] There is some support for a version of marshalling which employs assignment rather than subrogation. However, as noted in paragraphs 3.28 and 3.29, it is unlikely that assignment will displace subrogation or substitution as the preferred means of giving effect to the doctrine of marshalling.

[3] e g the recent decision of the House of Lords in *Banque Financière de la Cité v Parc (Battersea) Ltd* [1998] 1 All ER 737.

(1) The junior creditor is able to exchange its eroded security for an undiminished second security of equivalent priority-ranking *vis-à-vis* the remaining creditors of the debtor.

At the outset, the junior creditor conceded priority to only the senior creditor and, as such, ranked ahead of all the other creditors of the debtor (as regards the asset over which it holds security). It is only the particular manner in which the senior creditor has recovered its security that has derogated from the status of the junior creditor as the second-ranking creditor of the debtor. The doctrine of marshalling, by granting the junior creditor access to the senior creditor's security, permits the junior creditor to substitute the senior security for its own security. This has the effect of returning the junior creditor to its original priority-position as against the other creditors of the debtor.

(2) The unsecured portion of the junior debt is reconverted into a secured debt.

The conduct of the senior creditor has resulted in the junior creditor's claim against the debtor being relegated from the status of a wholly secured claim to that of a partially or wholly unsecured claim. The doctrine of marshalling rectifies this loss of priority by allowing the junior creditor to effectively discard its security and rely instead on the senior creditor's security; rather than having to claim under an eroded security, the junior creditor has had 'transferred' to it the benefit of the senior creditor's undiminished security. The junior creditor's claim against the debtor is thus, once more, a fully secured claim.

Marshalling and redistributing the debtor's assets

This substitution of the junior creditor to the security rights of the senior **4.07** creditor effects a redistribution of the debtor's assets. The recovery of the senior debt out of an asset that is subject to the junior security does not affect the quantum of the junior creditor's claim against the debtor; it does, however, undermine the priority-ranking of that claim and *reduce* the actual pay-out that the junior creditor will receive on the distribution of the debtor's assets amongst its creditors.

To the extent that its security has been eroded, the junior creditor will rank *pari* **4.08** *passu* with the unsecured creditors of the debtor. The doctrine of marshalling substitutes the intact senior security for the eroded junior security and converts the junior debt back into a secured debt. It *restores* the pay-out amount to the quantum the junior creditor would have received had the senior creditor recovered its debt in such a way that left the junior security intact (i e out of those assets which were encumbered by only the senior security).

4.09   However, the intervention of marshalling does not, in any way, affect the total amount of assets that the debtor has available to meet the claims of its creditors. Accordingly, the amount necessary to restore the junior creditor's pay-out amount can only come from the existing pool of the debtor's assets.

4.10   The doctrine of marshalling, once the senior debt has been discharged, reorganises the manner in which the assets of the debtor are to be employed in the satisfaction of the claims of its remaining creditors. It thus preserves the priority-ranking of the junior creditor by transferring to the junior creditor, in priority to the debtor's remaining creditors, an amount equivalent to the difference between:

   (i)   the amount that the junior creditor would have received had the senior creditor recouped its debt out of the asset or assets encumbered by only the senior security; and

   (ii) the lesser amount (if any) which the junior creditor would receive, on the enforcement of its security, as the result of the senior creditor having recouped its debt out of the asset encumbered by both the senior and junior securities.

4.11   As the total amount of the debtor's assets has not been altered, this transfer must necessarily be at the expense of the other remaining creditors of the debtor. The junior creditor, as a result of the senior creditor's conduct, has been relegated to the status of an unsecured creditor to the extent that the asset subject to the junior security is insufficient to satisfy the junior debt. Marshalling restores the junior creditor to its original position as a secured claimant in respect of the junior debt. The junior creditor, prior to the intervention of marshalling, was entitled to only the residual value (if any) of the asset subject to its security and an unsecured claim for the balance of its debt. After the application of marshalling, the junior creditor no longer has to claim for that part of its debt on an equal footing with unsecured creditors of the debtor; it is entitled once more to have the junior debt discharged ahead of them.[4]

4.12   The doctrine of marshalling therefore rectifies the loss sustained by the junior creditor out of assets which the junior creditor would otherwise have had to share equally with the debtor's other creditors. This is accomplished by conferring on the junior creditor the security rights of the senior creditor. That, in turn, effects a *redistribution*, from the unsecured creditors to the junior creditor, of the benefit of the debtor's assets (in an amount equivalent to the difference between (i) and (ii) above). Accordingly, the unsecured creditors of the debtor are required, by the doctrine of marshalling, to bear the burden of the preservation of the priority-ranking of the junior creditor's claim against the debtor.[5]

---

[4] Assuming that the asset to which it has permitted access *via* marshalling is sufficient to discharge the relevant balance of the junior debt.

[5] This is an important point in the context of the United States developments regarding the ability of unsecured creditors to prevent marshalling: see further Chapter 10.

C. Marshalling of Securities as a Subrogation Remedy

Marshalling makes good the loss suffered by the junior creditor at the hands of the **4.13** senior creditor (and by so doing preserves the priority-ranking of the former) by shifting that loss onto the unsecured creditors of the debtor. This redistribution of the debtor's assets is effected by placing the junior creditor in the position of the senior creditor *vis-à-vis* those assets of the debtor which are encumbered by only the senior security. The obvious inference to be drawn from marshalling's use of this substitutive process is that marshalling is a subrogation remedy.

Lack of authority for classification of marshalling as a subrogation remedy

Such a claim for marshalling is vitiated by the lack of supporting authority. This **4.14** particular issue has been the subject of comment in five Australian cases[6] and one New Zealand case,[7] but not in any English, Canadian or Irish cases on marshalling of securities. However, in none of these cases have the courts gone beyond bald assertions that marshalling is a form of subrogation.[8] Those comments, of themselves, provide little in the way of support for the classification of marshalling as a form of subrogation.[9]

---

[6] *Bank of NSW v City Mutual Life Assurance Society Ltd* [1969] VR 556; *Commonwealth Trading Bank v Colonial Mutual Life Assurance Society Ltd* (1970) 26 FLR 338; *Challenge Bank Ltd v Mailman* (unrep 14 May 1993, C of A (NSW)); *Sarge Pty Ltd v Cazihaven Homes Pty Ltd* (1994) 34 NSWLR 658; *Austin v Royal* (unrep 14 May 1998, Sup Ct of NSW).

[7] *National Bank of New Zealand Ltd v Caldesia Promotions Ltd and Jenkins Roberts & Associates Ltd* [1996] 3 NZLR 467.

[8] In *Bank of NSW v City Mutual Life Assurance Society Ltd* [1969] VR 556, 557, Gillard J. of the Supreme Court of Victoria stated: 'the doctrine of marshalling is closely allied to the doctrine of subrogation'. Similarly, in *Commonwealth Trading Bank v Colonial Mutual Life Assurance Society Ltd* (1970) 26 FLR 338, 350, Neasey J. of the Supreme Court of Tasmania observed that marshalling was a kind of subrogation. This was also the case with *Challenge Bank Ltd v Mailman* (unrep 14 May 1993, C of A (NSW)), where Mahoney J.A. of the New South Wales Court of Appeal noted: 'Their rights in respect of the mortgage and the proceeds of sale are based upon subrogation and the doctrines from which it is derived or with which it is associated, eg, marshalling, contribution and the like.' Again, in *National Bank of New Zealand Ltd v Caldesia Promotions Ltd and Jenkins Roberts & Associates Ltd* [1996] 3 NZLR 467, 474, Elias J. of the High Court stated that marshalling operated 'by a form of subrogation to place the junior creditor in the place of the senior creditor with recourse to the two securities'. Finally, in *Austin v Royal* (unrep 14 May 1998, Sup Ct of NSW), Giles C.J. of the Supreme Court of New South Wales stated: 'There is similarity between marshalling and subrogation as to securities, in that marshalling rests upon the principle that a creditor, having two funds to satisfy his debt, may not by the application of them to his demand defeat another creditor who may resort only to one of the funds'. C f *Sarge Pty Ltd v Cazihaven Homes Pty Ltd* (1994) 34 NSWLR 658 (which is discussed in n9).

[9] In *Sarge Pty Ltd v Cazihaven Homes Pty Ltd* (1994) 34 NSWLR 658, 662, Young J. observed that 'the right of a surety to have access to the principal's property to make good what the surety has paid' was a form of marshalling; q v the discussion of *Brown v Cork* [1985] BCLC 363 in paragraph 5.46.

4.15   Further, in all but two of the major texts on equity or securities law (from England and the other major common law jurisdictions), in which marshalling's use of subrogation has been considered, the doctrine of marshalling has been treated as if it were entirely independent of subrogation. This is not necessarily material to the issue, but is perhaps symptomatic of the following approach to subrogation noted by Mitchell:[10]

> It is commonly assumed in such works that subrogation has emerged and evolved independently in the particular fields in which they are concerned and hence that it may be safely treated in isolation from similar but unidentical manifestations of subrogation in other areas of law.

4.16   Of the two texts which consider marshalling as a form of subrogation, the first, Langdell's *A Brief Survey of Equity Jurisdiction*,[11] makes only fleeting mention of the doctrine of marshalling and then only to castigate it as an unwarranted application of the doctrine of subrogation.

Redistributive nature of the categories of subrogation

4.17   The second text, Meagher, Gummow & Lehane's *Equity Doctrines and Remedies*, addresses the issue in a more substantive fashion. This text explicitly identifies marshalling as one of a number of cases in which the doctrine of subrogation is available at law.[12]

The doctrine of marshalling, by allowing the junior creditor to take up the senior security, transfers the benefit of assets from unsecured creditors of the debtor to the junior creditor. Subrogation has a similar impact upon the assets of the party against whom the rights, that are the subject of the subrogation claim, are exercisable. Hence, the doctrine of subrogation, by permitting one party to take up the rights held by a second party against a third, also effectively transfers to the first

---

[10]   C Mitchell, *The Law of Subrogation* [1992] LMCLQ 483, 484. The sole reference to marshalling in C Mitchell, *The Law of Subrogation* (1994 Oxford) is on page 143, as part of his discussion of the situations in which a lender may wish to acquire a prior-ranking security *via* subrogation rather than relying on its own (e g because it is void or impaired). At no stage in his text does Mitchell consider marshalling to be one of the established categories of subrogation. Similarly, Goff & Jones' restitutionary analysis of the established categories of subrogation makes no mention of marshalling (Goff & Jones, *The Law of Restitution*, Chapter 31). See further the texts cited in nn17–23, which deal with subrogation, and e g J D Lipton, *Equitable Rights of Contribution and Subrogation: Recent Australian Judicial Approaches* (1995) 13 ABR 21; D McGill, *The Impact of Subrogation Rights upon Creditors' Management of Securities* (1997) 25 ABLR 118; M C Hemsworth, *Subrogation: The Problem of Competing Claims to Recovery Monies* [1998] JBL 111 where no mention is made of marshalling.

[11]   C C Langdell, *A Brief Survey of Equity Jurisdiction* (1908 Harvard), 15. cf. McGuinness, *The Law of Guarantee*, para 7.14 where it is considered that the surety's equitable right of subrogation to the security held by the creditor for the guaranteed debt is founded upon the doctrine of marshalling of securities. This assertion should perhaps be read subject to the subsequent statement (para 7.16) that the surety's subrogation rights are founded upon principles of equity similar to those underlying marshalling.

[12]   Meagher, Gummow & Lehane, *Equity Doctrines and Remedies*, paras 905 and 946.

party the benefit of assets that would otherwise have had to be shared with other parties with claims upon the third party.[13]

The redistributive nature of both marshalling and subrogation is borne out by the **4.18** analysis of Meagher, Gummow & Lehane. They argue that the several categories of subrogation—of which marshalling is one—are all redistributive in nature:[14]

> All instances of subrogation involve the adjustment of the interests of X, the claimant, to involvement in the legal relations between Y and Z. In cases of insurance Y, the insured or creditor, will recover twice unless the second recovery is for the benefit of X, the insurer or surety; as between X and Z it is equitable in cases of insurance and guarantee that the ultimate loss should rest upon Z as principal debtor or tortfeasor, not upon X as insurer or surety. With vendor's liens, unauthorised borrowings and *marshalling* there is no risk of double payment to Y, the vendor, the tradesman intra vires creditor, or double claimant. Rather the risk here is that, if there is no subrogation of X to Y's rights, Z will escape from his obligations to X, whether to give a mortgage as purchaser to secure borrowings from X, or to repay the unenforceable borrowings from X, or to *discharge the security already given to X over a fund insufficient to satisfy both X and Y* (emphasis added).

Nonetheless, this analysis of marshalling glosses over a crucial aspect of the man- **4.19** ner in which marshalling operates. It is not the ability of Z (the debtor) to discharge the security granted by it to X (the junior creditor) that X is concerned with; X's personal claim against Z continues without abatement. It is rather that Y (the senior creditor), by acting as it has, has prejudiced the priority-ranking conferred by that security upon X's claim against Z. It is this deterioration in priority which marshalling addresses. This does not, however, detract from the nature of marshalling and the instances of subrogation considered by Meagher, Gummow & Lehane as redistributive remedies.

D. A Comparison of Marshalling of Securities and the Established Categories of Subrogation

A comparison of marshalling with the established categories of subrogation **4.20** reveals that marshalling operates in a very different manner from subrogation and, as such, cannot comfortably be considered as a subrogation remedy or a new category of subrogation.[15]

---

[13] The first party by satisfying (though not in all cases extinguishing) the second party's claim against the third party will have increased the pool of assets available to the other creditors of the third party. Subrogation, by placing the first party in the shoes of the second party, in effect, transfers assets of a value equivalent to the quantum of that increase from those other creditors to the first party (this is because those assets to which they would otherwise have had a claim are no longer available to them).

[14] Meagher, Gummow & Lehane, *Equity Doctrines and Remedies*, para 951.

[15] Broadly speaking, one might accept that marshalling is a subrogation remedy purely in the sense that it operates by way of subrogation; that, however, is the full extent of its similarity to the established categories of subrogation.

Established categories of subrogation

4.21 The general consensus is that there are seven established categories of subrogation: (i) sureties; (ii) insurance; (iii) bills of exchange; (iv) trading trusts and receivers; (v) vendor's lien; (vi) prior securities; and (vii) *ultra vires* borrowings.[16]

4.22 Marshalling acts to preserve the priority-ranking of a junior creditor by substituting it to the security held by a senior creditor, where the senior creditor has, in recouping its prior-ranking debt, prejudiced the junior creditor's position. There are two key aspects of this process which need to be noted:

    (1) the junior creditor and the senior creditor, as evidenced by the common debtor rule, are generally creditors of the same debtor; and

    (2) the junior creditor's marshalling rights are not predicated upon consideration having passed from the junior creditor to the senior creditor.

4.23 An examination of the seven established categories of subrogation reveals that the above two attributes are unique to marshalling. Hence, if the doctrine of marshalling were to conform to the model of subrogation presented by these categories of subrogation, the common debtor rule would have no application and the right to marshall would be conditional upon the junior creditor having discharged the senior debt.

Marshalling of securities and the first six categories of subrogation

4.24 The disparity between marshalling and the established categories of subrogation may readily be ascertained in terms of the first six categories of subrogation:

    (i) *Sureties*—A surety, who has guaranteed the repayment of a debt owed by a debtor to a creditor, will, in the event that it repays the debt, be entitled to be subrogated to the creditor's rights against the debtor.[17]

    (ii) *Insurance*—An insurer, who has indemnified an insured against the happening of a certain event, will, in the event that it makes payment under the indemnity,

---

[16] As noted in paragraph 4.15, only Langdell, *A Brief Survey of Equity Jurisdiction* and Meagher, Gummow & Lehane, *Equity Doctrines and Remedies* consider that marshalling is a category of subrogation.

[17] See Marks & Moss, *Rowlatt on the Law of Principal and Surety*, 145–149; *Halsbury's*, Vol 20 ('*Guarantee and Indemnity*') (4th ed reissue 1993 Butterworths), para 228; Goff & Jones, *The Law of Restitution*, 602–604; Mitchell, *The Law of Subrogation*, 54–60. For the position in Australia, see: Meagher, Gummow & Lehane, *Equity Doctrines and Remedies*, paras 942–945; O'Donovan & Phillips, *The Modern Contract of Guarantee*, 653–683; J Glover, *Subrogation* in Parkinson (ed), *The Principles of Equity*, paras 1504–1505; S Christie, *Guarantor's Right of Subrogation* (1994) 10 BLB 21; McGill, *The Impact of Subrogation Rights upon Creditors' Management of Securities*. For the position in Canada, see: McGuinness, *The Law of Guarantee*, paras 7.11–7.20. To claim subrogation, it is not necessary for the surety to have paid the entire debt itself although it must have paid an amount in reduction of the debt: O'Donovan & Phillips, *The Modern Contract of Guarantee*, 657.

be entitled to be subrogated to any rights against third parties that may have accrued to the insured as a result of the occurrence of the event.[18]

(iii) *Bills of Exchange*—The drawer, or indorser, of a bill of exchange will, after making payment on the bill to the holder of the bill, be entitled to be subrogated to the holder's rights against the acceptor of the bill.[19]

(iv) *Trading Trusts and Receivers*—Where a trust or company in receivership (as the case may be) is being traded as a going concern, the creditors of the trust or company will be entitled to be subrogated to the right of indemnity that the trustee or receiver enjoys against the property of the trust or company.[20]

(v) *Vendor's Lien*—A vendor who has parted with possession of the property being sold enjoys a lien over that property until the purchase price has been paid. A third party will, in the event that it pays the purchase price, be entitled to be subrogated to the vendor's lien.[21]

(vi) *Prior Securities*—Where a creditor holds a security over the assets of a debtor, a third party will, in the event that it discharges the debt whose repayment is secured by that security, be entitled to be subrogated to the security.[22]

The above six categories of subrogation are diametrically opposed to marshalling **4.25** of securities. In all six categories, the right of subrogation is activated by payment having been made by, or consideration flowing from, the party seeking subrogation to the party, to whose rights subrogation is being sought. This is certainly not the case with marshalling, where there is no requirement that the junior creditor must have discharged the senior debt for it to be able to marshall the senior security.

---

[18] See Goff & Jones, *The Law of Restitution*, 606–619; Mitchell, *The Law of Subrogation*, 67–69 and 74–80; Hemsworth, *Subrogation: The Problem of Competing Claims to Recovery Monies*. For the position in Australia, see: Derham, *Subrogation in Insurance Law*; Meagher, Gummow & Lehane, *Equity Doctrines and Remedies*, paras 931–941; Glover, *Subrogation*, paras 1508–1509; in New Zealand, see: M Luey, *Proprietary Remedies in Insurance Subrogation* (1995) 25 VUWLR 449; and, in the United States, see: S L Kimball & D A Davis, *The Extension of Insurance Subrogation* (1962) 60 Mich L Rev 841.

[19] See A G Guest, *Chalmers and Guest on Bills of Exchange, Cheques and Promissory Notes* (14th ed 1991 Sweet & Maxwell), 448–449; Goff & Jones, *The Law of Restitution*, 605–606; Mitchell, *The Law of Subrogation*, 60–61 and 86–96; For the position in Australia, see: O'Donovan & Phillips, *The Modern Contract of Guarantee*, 661–665; Glover, *Subrogation*, paras 1506–1507; D Partlett, *The Right of Subrogation in Accommodation Bills of Exchange* (1979) 53 ALJ 694; J Glover, *Equity, Restitution and the Proprietary Recovery of Value* (1991) UNSWLJ 247, 263–264.

[20] See Goff & Jones, *The Law of Restitution*, 619–620. For the position in Australia, see: Meagher, Gummow & Lehane, *Equity Doctrines and Remedies*, paras 924–930 (the principle of subrogation to a receiver's indemnity, in contrast to subrogation to a trustee's indemnity, is limited to cases of *ultra vires* conduct on the part of the receiver); Glover, *Subrogation*, paras 1510–1511.

[21] See Goff & Jones, *The Law of Restitution*, 621–622. For the position in Australia, see: Meagher, Gummow & Lehane, *Equity Doctrines and Remedies*, paras 906–911; K Kanjian, *Subrogation to the Security Rights of the Unpaid Vendor and Mortgagee* (1980) 9 Syd LR 176.

[22] See Goff & Jones, *The Law of Restitution*, 621–622; Mitchell, *The Law of Subrogation*, 139–141. For the position in Australia, see: Meagher, Gummow & Lehane, *Equity Doctrines and Remedies*, paras 912–914; Glover, *Subrogation*, para 1513; Glover, *Equity, Restitution and the Proprietary Recovery of Value*, 264.

4.26 In addition, the common debtor rule, upon which the junior creditor's right to marshall is, as a general rule, predicated, is incompatible with the above categories of subrogation. In none of the six categories does the right of subrogation depend upon a pre-existing debtor-creditor or other relationship between the party seeking subrogation and the party against whom the rights, that the former is seeking to be subrogated to, are exercisable.

Marshalling of securities and the seventh category of subrogation

4.27 The position is more complex as regards the last of the established categories of subrogation:

> (vii) *Ultra Vires Borrowings*—Where a borrower, lacking the authority to do so, borrows funds from a lender and uses the funds to discharge its obligations to another party, the lender will be entitled to be subrogated to that party's rights against the borrower.[23]

4.28 This category of subrogation appears, at first glance, to be analogous to the doctrine of marshalling: in both instances, the party seeking subrogation, or seeking to exercise the right to marshall, and the party in respect of whose rights subrogation or marshalling is being sought appear to be creditors of a common debtor. This resemblance is, however, superficial.

4.29 First, the lender is not, in fact, a creditor of the borrower; the loan is considered to be void, as the borrower has acted *ultra vires* in obtaining funds from the lender.[24] Accordingly, there is no debt upon which a debtor-creditor relationship can be founded.

4.30 Secondly, the lender's subrogation rights are conditional upon the funds advanced by it having been utilised by the borrower to discharge the borrower's obligations to the third party, to whose rights against the borrower the lender is seeking to be subrogated.[25] The lender must therefore, in effect, have first made payment to a party to whom the borrower is obligated.

---

[23] *Barclays Bank plc v O'Brien* [1993] 4 All ER 417; *Castle Phillips Finance Ltd v Piddington* (unrep 7 Dec 1994, C of A). See Goff & Jones, *The Law of Restitution*, 622–638. For the position in Australia, see Meagher, Gummow & Lehane, *Equity Doctrines and Remedies*, paras 915–923; Glover, *Subrogation*, para 1512.

[24] *Re Cork and Youghal Railway* (1869) LR 4 Ch App 748; *Re National Permanent Benefit Building Society* (1869) LR 5 Ch App 309; *Blackburn Benefit Building Society v Cunliffe, Brooks & Co* (1882) 22 Ch D 61; *Baroness Wenlock v River Dee Co* (1887) 19 QB D 155; *Re Wrexham Mold and Connah's Quay Railway Co* [1899] 1 Ch 440; *Re Airedale Co-operative Worsted Manufacturing Society Ltd* [1933] Ch 639. As Goff & Jones, *The Law of Restitution*, 622n51 note, if the loan were valid, subrogation would be unnecessary. See also Meagher, Gummow & Lehane, *Equity Doctrines and Remedies*, para 917.

[25] *Blackburn Benefit Building Society v Cunliffe, Brooks & Co* (1882) 22 Ch D 61; *Baroness Wenlock v River Dee Co* (1887) 19 QB D 155; *Re Wrexham Mold and Connah's Quay Railway Co* [1899] 1 Ch 440; *Re Harris Calculating Machine Co* [1914] 1 Ch 920. See Goff & Jones, *The Law of Restitution*, 625–626 and 634–638; Meagher, Gummow & Lehane, *Equity Doctrines and Remedies*, para 918.

There is one further, crucial difference between category (vii) and marshalling of **4.31** securities: a lender, to whom subrogation is available, will, nonetheless, not be subrogated to any securities held by the party, to whom the obligations owed by the debtor have been discharged with the lender's funds.[26] The lender cannot, in contrast to marshalling, acquire the benefit of the priority-ranking of the party to whose rights it is being subrogated.[27]

Marshalling of securities is not an eighth category of subrogation

From the above analysis, it is obvious that the doctrine of marshalling of securities **4.32** operates in an entirely different manner from the established categories of subrogation. This precludes the recognition of marshalling as a new, eighth category of subrogation. The junior creditor—in contrast to the parties who are desirous of invoking the doctrine of subrogation—is not, in fact, seeking redress for something that it has transferred to the senior creditor. It is instead attempting to have rectified the loss suffered by it, as a result of the senior creditor having enforced its security against the asset over which the junior creditor also holds security.

Furthermore, the disparity between marshalling, on the one hand, and the estab- **4.33** lished categories of subrogation, on the other, lends credence to the view expressed by Langdell that marshalling is an anomalous doctrine in comparison with the other (in his view) categories of subrogation.

E. Marshalling of Securities, Subrogation and the Law of Restitution

Introduction

An alternative approach to explaining the nature of marshalling may be found in **4.34** the recent application of the law of restitution to subrogation.

It is generally accepted that the subrogation is a restitutionary remedy whose purpose is to redress unjust enrichment:[28] subrogation, by allowing one party to

---

[26] *Re Wrexham Mold and Connah's Quay Railway Co* [1899] 1 Ch 440; *Bannatyne v MacIver* [1906] 1 KB 103; *Re Harris Calculating Machine Co* [1914] 1 Ch 920. See Meagher, Gummow & Lehane, *Equity Doctrines and Remedies*, para 920.

[27] The lender acquires only the status of an unsecured creditor of the borrower. To permit the lender to obtain the benefit of the third party's security would place the lender in a better position than it would have been in had its loan been valid: see Goff & Jones, *The Law of Restitution*, 596.

[28] The status of subrogation as a restitutionary remedy has received unequivocal judicial sanction: e g the Court of Appeal's decision in *Boscawen v Bajwa* [1996] 1 WLR 328, 335 and that of the House of Lords in *Banque Financière de la Cité v Parc (Battersea) Ltd* [1998] 1 All ER 737, 740, 741, 744–745, 747, 748, 749 and 751 (discussed in C Mitchell, *Subrogation and Part Payments of Another's Debt* [1998] LMCLQ 14; D B Robertson, *Subrogation and the Law of Restitution* (1998) 9 JBFLP 146; P Watts, *Subrogation – A Step too far* (1998) 114 LQR 341; M G Bridge, *Failed*

substitute the rights held by another for its own, restores to the former a benefit of which it has been unjustly deprived. Marshalling achieves its objective of priority-preservation, by making use of subrogation (or an equivalent legal process).

On this basis, the restitutionary principles which underpin subrogation may also be capable of explaining marshalling. If that is the case, marshalling, by virtue of its adherence to those restitutionary principles, should properly be considered a subrogation remedy or a new category of subrogation.

No restitutionary analysis of marshalling

4.35 The claim that the restitutionary principles applicable to subrogation apply equally to marshalling is, again, hindered by the absence of supporting authority. The leading texts in which subrogation has been explained in terms of the law of restitution have all ignored the doctrine of marshalling.[29]

This lack of authority does not, of itself, render the restitutionary principles, on which subrogation is based, incapable of being extended to marshalling of securities.[30] The version of marshalling depicted by the post-realisation theory is redistributive in character; this is due to marshalling's use of subrogation (or an equivalent process) to grant a junior creditor access to the security held by the senior creditor. This absence of restitutionary analysis aside, marshalling does not rest comfortably with the restitutionary principles that have been advanced in the above texts.[31]

Contracts, Subrogation and Unjust Enrichment [1998] JBL 323). See also Mitchell, *The Law of Subrogation*, 8–15 and the recent decision of the Supreme Court of New South Wales in *Austin v Royal* (unrep 14 May 1998, Sup Ct of NSW).

[29] P Birks, *An Introduction to the Law of Restitution* (Revsd ed 1989 Oxford), 93–98; A Burrows, *The Law of Restitution* (1993 Butterworths), 76–93; Goff & Jones, *The Law of Restitution*, Chapter 31; Mitchell, *The Law of Subrogation*, 8–15 and Chapters 3, 5 and 6 (Mitchell considers marshalling on page 143, but see the comments in n10); A Tettenborn, *Law of Restitution in England and Ireland* (2nd ed 1996 Cavendish), paras 2–24–2–51. This is also the position in Canada: G H L Fridman & J G McLeod, *Restitution* (1982 Carswell), 392–394; G B Klippert, *Unjust Enrichment* (1983 Toronto), 205–215; P D Maddaugh & J D McCamus, *The Law of Restitution* (1990 Ontario), Chapter 8; and in the United States of America: *Restatement of the Law of Restitution, Quasi Contracts and Constructive Trusts* (1937 American Law Institute), paras 76g, 81I, 104 and 162; G E Palmer, *The Law of Restitution* (1978 Little, Brown & Co), paras 1.5(b) and 23.1 (as updated by M Eisenstein, *The Law of Restitution: 1994 Cumulative Supplement No. 1* (1994 Little, Brown & Co), para 23.1). C f (i) *Balkin v Peck* (unrep 24 July 1998, C of A (NSW)) in which Mason P. commented that marshalling was founded upon unjust enrichment; (ii) W M C Gummow, *Unjust Enrichment, Restitution and Proprietary Remedies* in P Finn (ed), *Essays on Restitution* (1990 Law Book Company), 69–70 in which it is argued that subrogation as well as marshalling and contribution are not readily accommodated within the framework of unjust enrichment.

[30] As will be seen below from the attempted application of the restitutionary analysis to marshalling, this could well be due to the fact that, in the context of marshalling, there is no identifiable enrichment of either (i) the party to whose security access is being sought (the senior creditor) or (ii) the party over whose assets the security in (i) is held (the debtor).

[31] For the awkwardness of the subrogation metaphor in the context of restitution, see Birks, *An Introduction to the Law of Restitution*, 21–22 and 95–98: the metaphor insists that negative

This may be illustrated by applying the following restitutionary analysis of subro- **4.36**
gation to marshalling:[32]

> The insurer, A, is subrogated to the rights of the assured, B, to prevent B's unjust
> enrichment . . . the surety, A, is subrogated to the rights of the creditor, C, to prevent
> the principal debtor's, B's, unjust enrichment. In insurance A is subrogated to B
> because A has agreed to indemnify B. In suretyship A is subrogated to C because A
> has agreed to indemnify C . . . What is critical is to recognise that subrogation is
> granted in each case to ensure that B disgorges the gain made at the expense of A, and
> that to achieve this A may be subrogated to either B or C.

The benefit, which is being restored to A, was originally transferred by A to the
party, whose rights A is being subrogated to (in the case of insurance) or to the
party against whom those rights are exercisable (in the case of suretyship). This
analysis asserts that the prevention of unjust enrichment *via* the medium of subrogation is predicated upon the party, who is asserting the right of subrogation,
having transferred something of value to the above parties. However, the doctrine
of marshalling, as noted in the previous section of this chapter, is not predicated
upon such a transfer from the junior creditor to a third party.

Nonetheless, support may be found in Langdell[33] and Meagher, Gummow & **4.37**
Lehane[34] for the proposition that marshalling is a category of subrogation,
although Langdell claims that such a classification is unwarranted. These two
texts accordingly render plausible the claim that the doctrine of marshalling, in
common with the established categories of subrogation, can be explained by reference to the principles of restitution.

Subrogation and the law of restitution

The restitutionary model of subrogation, put forward in the texts referred to **4.38**
above,[35] declares that subrogation, by permitting one party ('A') to substitute

---

assets – especially discharged debts and securities – should be treated in the same way as positive
assets. See also Mitchell, *The Law of Subrogation*, 29–32. C f *Banque Financière de la Cité v Parc
(Battersea) Ltd* [1998] 1 All ER 737, 749 where the conceptual difficulty faced by subrogation (and
marshalling) in the context of discharged securities was resolved. Lord Hoffmann stated: '. . . the
phrase "keeping the charge alive" needs to be handled with some care. It is not a literal truth but
rather a metaphor or analogy . . . In a case in which the whole of the secured debt is repaid, the charge
is not kept alive at all. It is discharged and ceases to exist . . . When judges say that the charge is "kept
alive" for the benefit of the plaintiff, what they mean is that his legal relations with a defendant who
would otherwise be unjustly enriched are regulated *as* if the benefit of the charge had been assigned
to him.' This avoids the argument that there is nothing to which the junior creditor may obtain
access on the repayment of the senior debt and the consequent discharge of the senior security. See
also the Australian case of *Austin v Royal* (unrep 14 May 1998, Sup Ct of NSW).

[32] Goff & Jones, *The Law of Restitution*, 592. See also Goff & Jones, *The Law of Restitution*, 601;
Tettenborn, *Law of Restitution in England and Ireland*, para 2–24.
[33] Langdell, *A Brief Survey of Equity Jurisdiction*, 15.
[34] Meagher, Gummow & Lehane, *Equity Doctrines and Remedies*, paras 905 and 946.
[35] q v n29.

another party's ('B') rights against a third party ('C') for its own rights against C, restores to A a benefit of which it has been unjustly deprived by either B, the party whose rights it is taking up, or C, the party against whom those rights are exercisable.[36]

4.39 There are three distinct elements upon which the restoration of the benefit to A, *via* subrogation, is predicated:[37]

(1) There must be some benefit of which A, the party seeking subrogation, has been deprived.

(2) Either B, whose rights A is seeking to be subrogated to, or C, a third party against whom the rights which A is seeking to substitute for its own are exercisable, has been enriched by the receipt of the benefit in (1). This enrichment must have occurred in one of the following two ways, depending upon the category of subrogation concerned:[38]

---

[36] Goff & Jones, *The Law of Restitution*, 591–594.

[37] Mitchell, *The Law of Subrogation*, 8–15; These three elements are common to all restitutionary doctrines/remedies: see Goff & Jones, *The Law of Restitution*, Chapter 1; Burrows, *The Law of Restitution*, 6–28. See also Tettenborn, *Law of Restitution in England and Ireland*, Chapter 1; G Virgo, *What is the Law of Restitution About?* in W R Cornish, R Nolan, J O'Sullivan & G Virgo (eds), *Restitution: Past, Present and Future* (1998 Hart Publishing); and A Burrows, *Understanding the Law of Obligations* (1998 Hart Publishing), 58–64; P Birks, *Modernising the Law of Restitution* (1993) 109 LQR 164; S Hedley, *Unjust Enrichment* (1995) 54 CLJ 578; J Bird, *Restitution's Uncertain Progress* [1995] LMCLQ 308; N J McBride & P McGrath, *The Nature of Restitution* (1995) 15 OJLS 33; L Ho, *The Nature of Restitution – A Reply* (1996) 16 OJLS 517; and A Burrows, *Restitution: where do we go from here?* [1997] CLP 95. For recent discussions of the law of restitution in (i) Australia, see K Mason & J W Carter, *Restitution Law in Australia* (1995 Butterworths); M McInnes (ed), *Restitution: Developments in Unjust Enrichment* (1996 Law Book Company); C Cato, *Restitution in Australia and New Zealand* (1997 Cavendish); A Burrows, *Understanding the Law of Restitution: A Map Through the Thicket* (1995) 18 UQLJ 149; P Birks, *Equity in the Modern Law: An Exercise in Taxonomy* (1996) 26 UWALR 1; (ii) New Zealand, see S Kos & P Watts, *Unjust Enrichment – the New Cause of Action* (1990 NZ Law Society); (iii) Canada, see B McLachlin, *Restitution in Canada* in Cornish, Nolan, O'Sullivan & Virgo (eds), *Restitution: Past, Present and Future*; L D Smith, *The Province of the Law of Restitution* (1992) 71 Can Bar Rev 672; J Beatson, *Proprietary Claims in the Law of Restitution* (1995) 25 CBLJ 66; and (iv) in the United States, see A Kull, *Rationalising Restitution* (1995) 83 Calif Law Rev 1191.

[38] This may be illustrated by reference to the established categories of subrogation: (i) *Sureties* – when the surety repays the debt owed to the creditor by the debtor, it discharges the creditor's claim against the debtor. The doctrine of subrogation, by reviving the creditor's rights for the benefit of the surety, prevents the debtor from being enriched by escaping its liability for the debt (criterion (2)(B)); (ii) *Insurance* – in contrast, the insurer, when it makes payment to the insured, does not extinguish the insured's rights against third parties. Subrogation, by allowing the insurer to take up the rights of the insured against the third parties, prevents the insured from being enriched by depriving it of the ability to recover twice from the insurer and the third parties (criterion (2)(A)); (iii) *Bills of Exchange, Trading Trusts and Receivers, Vendor's Lien, Prior Securities and Ultra Vires Borrowings* – these categories of subrogation all conform to the model depicted by criterion (2)(B). Subrogation prevents C, against whom the rights to which A is being subrogated are exercisable, from escaping the obligations incurred by C to B. See Goff & Jones, *The Law of Restitution*, 605–606, 619–620, 621–622 and 622–638; Mitchell, *The Law of Subrogation*, 487–492. For the position in Australia, see: Meagher, Gummow & Lehane, *Equity Doctrines and Remedies*, para 951; in Canada, see: Fridman & McLeod, *Restitution*, 393–394; and, in the United States, see: Palmer, *The Law of Restitution*, Chapter 23.

(A) B has been enriched. The transfer of the benefit from A to B has put B in the position of being able to recover twice in respect of the same claim; once from A and once from C;[39] or

(B) C has been enriched. The transfer of the benefit from A to B has allowed C to escape from having to perform its obligations to B.

(3) It is, however, insufficient for A to establish that it has been deprived from the benefit in (1) and that that benefit has enriched either B or C. It must also be established that the acquisition or retention (as the case may be) of the benefit by either B or C is unjust to A.[40]

Thus if the law of restitution, as it applies to subrogation, is capable of being extended to marshalling of securities, the above criteria must be satisfied by marshalling.   **4.40**

Marshalling and unjust enrichment—deprivation of benefit

The benefit of which the junior creditor, as the party who is claiming the right to marshall, has been deprived can readily be identified in terms of criterion (1).   **4.41**

The right to marshall, in terms of the post-realisation theory, is contingent upon the junior security being prejudiced by the actions of the senior creditor. Should that occur, the doctrine of marshalling will intervene to make good the loss

---

[39] q v n38 where it is considered that this criterion applies to the surety's rights of subrogation. Burrows, however, argues that the subrogation of the surety to the securities held by the creditor does not conform to the principles of restitution (in contrast to the surety's general right to be subrogated to the creditor's personal rights against the debtor): Burrows, *The Law of Restitution*, 82–83; Mitchell, *The Law of Subrogation*, 34. It is, Burrows submits, difficult to see how the conferral of a secured claim on the surety can be said to rectify the unjust enrichment of the debtor because, as a general rule, sureties do not intend that their common law right of indemnity against the debtor should be secured and, even more so, where the creditor's security post-dates the creation of the guarantee. In this latter case, subrogation effectively grants the surety the benefit of a thing of which it could not have been aware when it made its bargain to guarantee the debtor's indebtedness to the creditor (as the security did not then exist) (see also Tettenborn, *Law of Restitution in England and Ireland*, para 2–42). Accordingly, restitution should only permit subrogation to a creditor's securities in the limited circumstances where the surety intended that its own claim against the debtor (not the claim of the creditor to which it is seeking to be subrogated) – *viz.* its right of indemnity – would be secured and that such security was either not granted or was, for one reason or another, void. See further Burrows, *The Law of Restitution*, 85–87, 88 and 93 (c f Goff & Jones, *The Law of Restitution*, 603 where it is accepted that a surety who has discharged the principal debt is entitled to all the creditors' securities, including securities created after the contract of guarantee; Mitchell, *The Law of Subrogation*, 32–33). Birks, *An Introduction to the Law of Restitution*, 390 also questions why a plaintiff who did not originally have a claim *in rem* should be promoted to the rank of a secured creditor simply because the plaintiff's money was used to discharge a secured debt. See also Mitchell, *The Law of Subrogation*, 29–32.

[40] For the requisite injustice of the enrichment, see Birks, *An Introduction to the Law of Restitution*, 17–21, 22–25 and 40–44, and Chapter 4; J Beatson, *The Use and Abuse of Unjust Enrichment* (1991 Oxford), Chapter 2; Burrows, *The Law of Restitution*, 21–27; J Beatson, *Benefit Reliance and the Structure of Unjust Enrichment* [1987] CLP 71. See also, in Australia, V Annetta, *Priority Rights in Insolvency – the Doctrinal Basis for Equity's Intervention* (1992) 20 ABLR 311, 312–315.

suffered by the junior creditor by permitting the junior creditor to exchange its eroded security for the senior security, and, by so doing, will place the junior creditor in the position of the senior creditor as regards those assets encumbered by only the senior security.

4.42 Thus, the benefit, of which the junior creditor has been relieved as a result of the conduct of the senior creditor, is identifiable as the advantage over the other creditors of the debtor that the junior creditor derives from its security (or, more precisely, the priority-ranking conferred by that security). It may be quantified as the disparity between: (i) the amount that the junior creditor would have received had the senior creditor recouped its debt out of the asset or assets encumbered by only the senior security; and (ii) the amount (if any) which the junior creditor would receive on the enforcement of its depleted security.[41]

Marshalling and unjust enrichment—who has been enriched?

4.43 Having satisfied criterion (1) above, it is now necessary to ascertain, as required by criterion (2), which party (if any) has been enriched as a result of the junior creditor having been deprived of a benefit.[42]

Has the senior creditor been enriched?

4.44 Although the deprivation of benefit suffered by the junior creditor is due to the conduct of the senior creditor, the senior creditor will not, itself, have benefited from that particular consequence of its conduct.

4.45 The senior creditor's position, as the holder of paramount-ranking security, entitles it to realise the assets subject to the senior security in the order it sees fit.[43] In the absence of a contractual or other relationship between the senior and junior creditors, the fact that one of the assets subject to the senior security is also encumbered by the junior security will not constrain the senior creditor in freely electing between those assets.[44]

4.46 Thus, by acting in the manner that it is legally entitled to, the senior creditor will have deprived the junior creditor of the benefit of part or all of the junior security (in particular, the priority-ranking accorded by that security to the junior creditor's claim against the debtor). However, no benefit will have accrued to the senior creditor as a result of the erosion of the junior security; it has no bearing on the

---

[41] See paragraph 4.10.

[42] The relevant criterion is (2)(B). Criterion (2)(A) is not relevant, as the erosion of junior security obviously does not lead to a double-recovery by the senior creditor or the debtor (or any other party, for that matter).

[43] See further Chapter 3 regarding the version of marshalling depicted by the post-realisation theory.

[44] See the discussion of the limited duties imposed by law on the enforcement by a secured creditor of its security in paragraphs 3.07–3.17.

amount recoverable by the enforcement of the senior security nor has it otherwise enhanced the position of the senior creditor *vis-à-vis* the debtor.

Accordingly, the senior creditor—to whose security rights the junior creditor is **4.47** seeking to be substituted *via* marshalling—cannot be said to have been enriched by the erosion of the junior security. This is notwithstanding the fact that the deprivation of benefit suffered by the junior creditor is directly attributable to the manner in which the senior creditor has elected to enforce its security, and but for that election would not have occurred.

Has the debtor been enriched?

Nor has the debtor—as the party against whom the security rights that the junior **4.48** creditor is seeking to be substituted to are exercisable—been enriched by the erosion of the junior security. Marshalling is neutral in its impact upon the residue available to the debtor following the discharge of its creditors' claims.[45]

The manner in which the senior creditor has elected to recover the senior debt has **4.49** adversely affected the priority-ranking of the junior creditor's claim against the debtor, but has not, in any way, affected the validity of the claim itself. The junior creditor's claim against the debtor for the amount of the junior debt thus remains on foot although the junior creditor can no longer, as a result of the senior creditor's conduct, claim preferential status for the entire debt *qua* the debtor's other creditors.

Moreover, in terms of criterion (2)(B),[46] the junior creditor's marshalling rights **4.50** cannot be justified on the grounds that the erosion of the junior creditor has in some way relieved the debtor of its obligations to the senior creditor (being the party to whose security rights the junior creditor is seeking access); the junior creditor's right to marshall, as *per* the post-realisation theory, necessarily arises after the discharge of the senior debt.

Enrichment of the unsecured creditors

It is, instead, the unsecured creditors[47] of the debtor who have been enriched as a **4.51** result of the erosion of the junior security. This is because the junior creditor is no longer entitled to have the junior debt discharged ahead of the claims of the

---

[45]   q v paragraphs 4.07–4.12.
[46]   Criterion (2)(A) is clearly inapplicable: q v n42.
[47]   In the paradigmatic marshalling scenario, the debtor has only two secured creditors: the senior creditor and the junior creditor. The comments in this chapter concerning the enrichment of the debtor's unsecured creditors are equally applicable to all secured creditors who possess a lower priority-ranking than the junior creditor. The position of third party security holders is considered in more detail in Chapter 11.

unsecured creditors; to the extent that its security has been depleted, the junior creditor will rank *pari passu* with the unsecured creditors.[48]

The restitutionary analysis of subrogation cannot be extended to marshalling

4.52 The absence of the second criterion renders it unnecessary to consider whether or not the transfer of the benefit from the junior creditor to the unsecured creditors, and its continued retention by the unsecured creditors, is unjust *vis-à-vis* the junior creditor.[49] The junior creditor is not, in any case, seeking to marshall the unsecured creditors' rights against the debtor nor are the security rights, to which marshalling has granted the junior creditor access, exercisable against assets belonging to the unsecured creditors.

4.53 Further, in the circumstances in which marshalling will be made available to a junior creditor, neither the senior creditor (as the party to whose security the junior creditor is seeking to be substituted) nor the debtor (as the party against over whose asset that security is held) will have been enriched by the erosion of the junior security. The restitutionary principles that underpin the established categories of subrogation do not envisage that subrogation will be available where a party other than B—whose rights form the subject of the subrogation claim—or C—against whom those rights are exercisable—has been enriched.[50]

4.54 This disparity between marshalling and the restitutionary principles, upon which subrogation is based, renders it very difficult to accommodate marshalling within the restitutionary framework of subrogation:[51]

> Marshalling does not prejudice the first mortgagee, and is concerned to protect the position, not of the debtor-mortgagor, but of puisne mortgagees. This doctrine may be seen as an application of the principle that it should not lie in the choice of one creditor to determine whether or not other creditors are disappointed. It is not readily apparent how the operation of [the] doctrine readily, or helpfully, may be described as effecting restitution by a defendant to a plaintiff of a benefit derived 'at the expense' of a plaintiff.

---

[48] The unsecured creditors do not enjoy the full benefit of the depletion of the junior security as the junior debt has not been extinguished but has only been relegated from a secured debt to a partially or wholly unsecured one. See further paragraphs 4.10–4.12.

[49] Marshalling, by its substitution of the senior security for the eroded junior security, transfers this benefit back to the junior creditor: see paragraphs 4.10–4.12.

[50] This particular issue aside, it is also difficult to see how marshalling could be characterised as a restitutionary remedy whose purpose is to reverse the unjust enrichment of unsecured creditors (cf. *Balkin v Peck* (unrep 24 July 1998, C of A (NSW)). This is, again, due to the disjunction between marshalling's formal reorganisation of rights and the restoration of the relevant benefit effected by marshalling. The junior creditor is placed by marshalling in the position of the senior creditor so as to have the benefit of the senior creditor's security rights against the debtor. However, the parties who are being required to disgorge the benefit in question do not comprise either the party to whose rights the junior creditor is being substituted or the party against whom those rights are exercisable.

[51] Gummow, *Unjust Enrichment, Restitution and Proprietary Remedies*, 69.

Marshalling is not a subrogation remedy

The claim that marshalling, as a result of its use of subrogation or a process equiv- **4.55** alent to subrogation, is a subrogation remedy therefore cannot be sustained. Marshalling operates in an entirely different manner from the seven established categories of subrogation, and the restitutionary principles applicable to subrogation have no application to marshalling.

5

MARSHALLING OF SECURITIES AND OTHER EQUITABLE DOCTRINES AND REMEDIES

Marshalling of Securities and Consolidation of Mortgages		Marshalling and Contribution	
Introduction	5.02	Introduction	5.28
What is consolidation?	5.03	What is contribution?	5.29
Statutory curtailment of consolidation:		Contribution and:	
England and Ireland	5.05	secured debts	5.32
Australia and New Zealand	5.07	exoneration	5.33
Consolidation in North America	5.10	Marshalling is not a form of contribution	5.37
Ashburner's argument that marshalling is a form of consolidation	5.12	Further confusion about marshalling and contribution	5.44
Consolidation and assignments of:		**Marshalling and Specific Performance**	
equity of redemption	5.15	Introduction	5.49
only equity of redemption	5.18	Marshalling is not a form of specific performance	5.50
both equity of redemption and mortgage	5.20	Further confusion about marshalling and specific performance	5.55
Marshalling is not form of consolidation	5.22		

5.01 This chapter explores the relationship between marshalling of securities and consolidation of mortgages, contribution and specific performance.

Each of consolidation, contribution and specific performance has been claimed as the basis for the doctrine of marshalling. As such, the nature of marshalling would be explicable only by reference to its progenitor. Further, the claims made for consolidation and specific performance would, if correct, have serious consequences for the efficacy of marshalling.

A. Marshalling of Securities and Consolidation of Mortgages

Introduction

Ashburner contends, in his *Principles of Equity*,[1] that marshalling of securities is a **5.02** special instance of the application of the equitable doctrine of consolidation of mortgages. If Ashburner's argument can be sustained, a junior creditor's right to marshall would be subject to the same statutory constraints which have been imposed on consolidation in England, Ireland and Canada, and would arguably be unavailable in Australia and New Zealand where consolidation has been abolished by statute.

What is consolidation?

The equitable doctrine of consolidation represents a severe impediment to the **5.03** ability of a debtor to discharge individual mortgage debts.[2]

Where a creditor holds two or more *mortgages*,[3] and the mortgages have been granted over separate assets,[4] the creditor is entitled to 'consolidate' the mortgages

---

[1] Browne, *Ashburner's Principles of Equity*, 212–214.

[2] *Pelly v Wathen* (1849) 3 Hare 351; *Griffith v Pound* (1890) 40 Ch D 553. See Hanbury & Waldock, *The Law of Mortgages*, 169–170; Cousins, *The Law of Mortgages*, 427. Consolidation may also affect third parties. The Law Commission has observed: 'It can apply even when the equities of redemption have become vested in different mortgagors, and even if the mortgages were originally granted to different mortgagees. This makes the doctrine a trap for purchasers of property subject to a mortgage (in theory at least) since there is no way of establishing whether the vendor has created mortgages over other property which may be, or later become, vested in the mortgagee of the purchased property' (Law Commission, *Transfer of Land – Land Mortgages* (Law Com No 204, Nov 1991), para 6.44).

[3] The doctrine of consolidation is restricted to mortgages: *Crickmore v Freeston* (1870) 40 LJ Ch 137; *Cummins v Fletcher* (1880) 14 Ch D 699; *Re Raggett* (1880) 16 Ch D 117. See Keaton & Sheridan, *Equity*, 122. C f *Praed v Gardiner* (1788) 2 Cox Eq Cas 86, 89 where support may be found for the application of consolidation to pledges of bills, promissory notes, annuities and respondentia bonds. See also Ramsbotham, *Coote's Treatise on the Law of Mortgages*, 884; Tyler, *Fisher & Lightwood's Law of Mortgage*, 537.

[4] Consolidation does, however, encompass all types of mortgages, legal and equitable, over real or personal property: *Jones v Smith* (1794) 2 Ves Jun 372; *Watts v Symes* (1851) 1 De G M & G 240; *Farebrother v Wodehouse* (1856) 26 LJ Ch 81; *Tweedale v Tweedale* (1857) 23 Beav 341; *Spalding v Thompson* (1858) 26 Beav 637; *Tassell v Smith* (1858) 2 De G & J 713; *Selby v Pomfret* (1861) 7 Jur (NS) 835; *Cracknall v Janson* (1879) 11 Ch D 1; *Chesworth v Hunt* (1880) 5 CPD 266; *Griffith v Pound* (1890) 40 Ch D 553. See Ramsbotham, *Coote's Treatise on the Law of Mortgages*, 883; Hanbury & Waldock, *The Law of Mortgages*, 169; *Halsbury's*, Vol 32 ('*Mortgage*'), para 765; Marks & Moss, *Rowlatt on the Law of Principal and Surety*, 149; Keaton & Sheridan, *Equity*, 122; Baker & Langan, *Snell's Equity*, 399–400. See also Sykes & Walker, *The Law of Securities*, 610 where it is stated that consolidation is available in respect of mortgages over personalty except where an execution creditor has seized the chattels the subject of one of the mortgages. It also applies to sub-mortgages: *Silverthorn v Glazebrook* (1899) 30 OR 408.

i e the creditor has the power to refuse to allow the mortgagor to redeem one of the mortgages without also redeeming the others.[5]

5.04 However, a secured creditor will not, merely because it holds multiple mortgages, be entitled to consolidate them:

(1) The mortgages which are sought to be consolidated must be in existence when the right of consolidation is asserted.[6]

(2) The dates of redemption must have passed for all of the mortgages sought to be consolidated.[7]

(3) The mortgages sought to be consolidated must all have been granted by the same mortgagor.[8]

---

[5] See generally Webster, *Ashburner's Concise Treatise on Mortgages, Pledges and Liens*, 361–366; J A Strahan, *The Principles of the General Law of Mortgages* (3rd ed 1925 Sweet & Maxwell), 98–104; Ramsbotham, *Coote's Treatise on the Law of Mortgages*, 882–894; L B Tillard, *Wilshere's Principles of Equity* (2nd ed 1929 Sweet & Maxwell), 225–227; F W Maitland, *Equity* (1936 Cambridge), 200–201 and 287; R A Eastwood, *Strahan's Digest of Equity* (6th ed 1939 Butterworths), 397–399; Browne, *Ashburner's Principles of Equity*, 222–225; Hanbury & Waldock, *The Law of Mortgages*, 164–176; *Halsbury's*, Vol 32 ('*Mortgage*'), paras 761–762; Keaton & Sheridan, *Equity*, 103–104 and 119–122; Baker & Langan, *Snell's Equity*, 399–400; R E Megarry & H W R Wade, *The Law of Real Property* (5th ed 1984 Stevens & Sons), 955–960; Tyler, *Fisher & Lightwood's Law of Mortgage*, 534–538; Cousins, *The Law of Mortgages*, 427–434. For the position in Ireland, see Wylie, *Irish Land Law*, paras 13.069–13.074. For the position in Australia, see: Francis & Thomas, *Mortgages and Securities*, 361–365; W D Duncan & L Wilmott, *Mortgages Law in Australia* (1996 Federation Press), 83–84; R T J Stein & M A Stone, *Torrens Title* (1991 Butterworths), 193–194; Sykes & Walker, *The Law of Securities*, 179–182. For the position in Canada, see W B Rayner & R H McLaren, *Falconbridge on Mortgages* (4th ed 1977 Canada Law Book), 194. The origins of consolidation may be traced to *Marsh v Lee* (1670) 2 Ventris 337; *Lloyd v Cox* (1676–1677) 79 Selden Society 531; *Bacon v Vesey* (1677–1678) 79 Selden Society 660; *Margrave v Le Hooke* (1690) 2 Vern 207.

[6] *Brecon Corp v Seymour* (1859) 26 Beav 548; *Selby v Pomfret* (1861) 7 Jur (NS) 835; *Cracknall v Janson* (1879) 11 Ch D 1; *Re Raggett* (1880) 16 Ch D 117; *Re Gregson* (1887) 36 Ch D 223; *Griffith v Pound* (1880) 40 Ch D 553. See Strahan, *The Principles of the General Law of Mortgages*, 103–104; Ramsbotham, *Coote's Treatise on the Law of Mortgages*, 887; Hanbury & Waldock, *The Law of Mortgages*, 168–169; *Halsbury's*, Vol 32 ('*Mortgage*'), para 767; Tyler, *Fisher & Lightwood's Law of Mortgage*, 536; Cousins, *The Law of Mortgages*, 429–430.

[7] The right to consolidate is an equitable right and therefore cannot prevail over the mortgagor's legal right to discharge any one of the mortgages on the agreed-upon date for its redemption: *Cummins v Fletcher* (1880) 14 Ch D 699. See Webster, *Ashburner's Concise Treatise on Mortgages, Pledges and Liens*, 362; Strahan, *The Principles of the General Law of Mortgages*, 99–100; Ramsbotham, *Coote's Treatise on the Law of Mortgages*, 883; Tillard, *Wilshere's Principles of Equity*, 226; Eastwood, *Strahan's Digest of Equity*, 398; Baker & Langan, *Snell's Equity*, 399; Megarry & Wade, *The Law of Real Property*, 955–956; Cousins, *The Law of Mortgages*, 428–429.

[8] *Jones v Smith* (1794) 2 Ves Jun 372; *White v Hillacre* (1839) 3 Y & C Ex 597; *Aldworth v Robinson* (1840) 2 Beav 287; *Jones v Griffith* (1845) 2 Coll 207; *Higgins v Frankis* (1848) 15 LJ Ch 329; *Bowker v Bull* (1850) 1 Sim (NS) 29; *Thorneycroft v Crockett* (1848) 2 HLC 239; *Marcon v Bloxam* (1856) 11 Exch 586; *Lord Kensington v Bouverie* (1854) 19 Beav 39; *Cummins v Fletcher* (1880) 14 Ch D 699; *Re Raggett* (1880) 16 Ch D 117; *Sharp v Rickards* [1909] 1 Ch 109. See Webster, *Ashburner's Concise Treatise on Mortgages, Pledges and Liens*, 362; Strahan, *The Principles of the General Law of Mortgages*, 100–101; Ramsbotham, *Coote's Treatise on the Law of Mortgages*, 886–887 and 890–891; Eastwood, *Strahan's Digest of Equity*, 399; Hanbury & Waldock, *The Law of Mortgages*, 167; *Halsbury's*, Vol 32 ('*Mortgage*'), paras 764 and 768–769; Baker & Langan, *Snell's Equity*, 399; Megarry & Wade, *The Law of Real Property*, 956; Tyler, *Fisher & Lightwood's Law of*

(4) There must have been a time when all the mortgages were united in the same mortgagee and, contemporaneously, all the equities of redemption were united in the same mortgagor.[9] In contrast to condition (3), it is not necessary that the mortgages should have originally been granted to the same mortgagee.

Statutory curtailment of consolidation—England and Ireland

The ability of secured creditors to consolidate mortgages in England is governed **5.05** by section 93 of the *Law of Property Act 1925*, which provides:[10]

(1) A mortgagor seeking to redeem any one mortgage is entitled to do so without paying any money due under any separate mortgage made by him, or by any person through whom he claims, solely on property other than that comprised in the mortgage which he seeks to redeem.

This subsection applies only if and as far as a contrary intention is not expressed in the mortgage deeds or one of them.

(2) This section does not apply where all the mortgages were made before the first day of January, eighteen hundred and eighty-two.

(3) Save as aforesaid nothing in this Act, in reference to mortgages, affects any right of consolidation or renders inoperative a stipulation in relation to any mortgage made before or after the commencement of this Act reserving a right to consolidate.

Section 93(1) of this legislation expressly permits mortgagees and mortgagors to contract out of the statutory bar on consolidation.[11] Accordingly, a secured

---

Mortgage, 535–536; Cousins, *The Law of Mortgages*, 429. It is immaterial that, at the time the right to consolidate is asserted, the equities of redemption of the mortgages are held by parties other than the original mortgagor: see Webster, *Ashburner's Concise Treatise on Mortgages, Pledges and Liens*, 365; Ramsbotham, *Coote's Treatise on the Law of Mortgages*, 886. This is also the position in Australia: *Corozo Pty Ltd v Total Australia Ltd* [1987] 2 Qd R 11; Francis & Thomas, *Mortgages and Securities*, 362; Sykes & Walker, *The Law of Securities*, 179.

[9] *Margrave v Le Hooke* (1690) 2 Vern 207; *Re Breeds* (1841) 2 Mont D & De G 328; *Re Loosemore* (1843) 3 Mont D & De G 464; *Watts v Symes* (1851) 1 De G M & G 240; *Tweedale v Tweedale* (1857) 23 Beav 341; *Tassell v Smith* (1858) 2 De G & J 713; *Vint v Padget* (1858) 2 De G & J 611; *Selby v Pomfret* (1861) 7 Jur (NS) 835; *Neve v Pennell* (1863) 2 H & M 170; *Re Softley* (1875) LR 20 Eq 746; *Andrew v City Permanent Benefit BS* (1881) 44 LT 641; *Jennings v Jordan* (1881) 6 App Cas 698; *Pledge v White* [1896] AC 187; *Riley v Hall* (1898) 79 LT 244; *Re Salmon* [1903] 1 KB 149; *Hughes v Britannia Permanent Benefit BS* [1906] 2 Ch 607. See Webster, *Ashburner's Concise Treatise on Mortgages, Pledges and Liens*, 365–366; Strahan, *The Principles of the General Law of Mortgages*, 101; Hanbury & Waldock, *The Law of Mortgages*, 167–168; *Halsbury's*, Vol 32 ('*Mortgage*'), para 762; Baker & Langan, *Snell's Equity*, 399; Megarry & Wade, *The Law of Real Property*, 956; Tyler, *Fisher & Lightwood's Law of Mortgage*, 536–537. It is immaterial that, at the time the right to consolidate is asserted, the mortgages are held by a party other than the original mortgagee: see Webster, *Ashburner's Concise Treatise on Mortgages, Pledges and Liens*, 364; Ramsbotham, *Coote's Treatise on the Law of Mortgages*, 886–887 and 890–891. This is also the position in Australia: *In the Will of Underwood* (1889) 10 LR (NSW) Eq 227; Francis & Thomas, *Mortgages and Securities*, 262; Sykes & Walker, *The Law of Securities*, 179.

[10] This provision was reproduced from section 17 of the *Conveyancing Act 1881* (UK).

[11] See Webster, *Ashburner's Concise Treatise on Mortgages, Pledges and Liens*, 362; Ramsbotham, *Coote's Treatise on the Law of Mortgages*, 892–894; Tillard, *Wilshere's Principles of Equity*, 227; Eastwood, *Strahan's Digest of Equity*, 397–398; *Halsbury's*, Vol 32 ('*Mortgage*'), para 763; Cousins, *The Law of Mortgages*, 428; Sykes & Walker, *The Law of Securities*, 182. The Law Commission has

creditor will be unable to consolidate mortgages in England, unless expressly empowered to do so by the terms of the mortgages sought to be consolidated.

5.06   A similar situation prevails in Ireland.[12]

Statutory abolition of consolidation—Australia and New Zealand

5.07   The doctrine of consolidation has been abolished by statute in four of the Australian states: New South Wales, Queensland, Victoria and Western Australia.

Section 97 of the *Conveyancing Act 1919* (NSW) provides:

> (1) A mortgagor seeking to redeem any one mortgage made after the commencement of this Act shall by virtue of this Act be entitled to do so without paying any money due under any separate mortgage made whether before or after the commencement of this Act by him or by any person through whom he claims on property other than that comprised in the mortgage which he seeks to redeem.

> (2) This section applies notwithstanding any stipulation to the contrary.

Equivalent provisions have been enacted in Queensland,[13] Victoria[14] and Western Australia.[15] In contrast to the position in England and Ireland, the statutory bar on consolidation applies notwithstanding any stipulation to the contrary in the terms of a mortgage.

5.08   Although the other Australian states and territories have not enacted legislation affecting consolidation, there is considerable doubt whether the right of consolidation is capable of being asserted in any of those states or territories as regards mortgages over Torrens system land.[16]

---

recommended that the right to consolidate mortgages be abolished: 'It is not obvious why mortgagees still choose to retain the right to consolidate. Mortgagees who want to take several mortgages from the same mortgagor over different properties can (and do) achieve a similar result by charging each property with repayment of the total indebtedness. This leaves the mortgagee in as strong a position in relation to the mortgagor, and it has the considerable advantage over consolidation (from the point of view of everyone else) that it cannot trap third parties' (Law Commission, *Transfer of Land – Land Mortgages*, para 6.44).

[12] Section 17(1) of the *Conveyancing Act 1881*, which regulates consolidation of mortgages in Ireland, mirrors the provisions of section 93. See further Wylie, *Irish Land Law*, paras 13.069–13.074; Lyall, *Land Law in Ireland*, paras 23.6.1–23.6.5.

[13] Section 98 of the *Property Law Act 1974–1985* (Qld).

[14] Section 93 of the *Property Law Act 1958* (Vic). In contrast to New South Wales, Queensland and Western Australia, the doctrine has only been abolished in respect of old title land in Victoria. The comments in paragraph 5.08 apply equally to Victoria.

[15] Section 66 of the *Property Law Act 1969–1979* (WA).

[16] *Greig v Watson* (1881) 7 VLR (E) 79; *Browne v Cranfield* (1925) 25 SR (NSW) 443; *English Scottish and Australian Bank Ltd v Phillips* (1937) 57 CLR 302. See also Francis & Thomas, *Mortgages and Securities*, 364–365; Sykes & Walker, *The Law of Securities*, 321–322; Tyler, Young & Croft, *Fisher & Lightwood's Law of Mortgage*, para 31.11.

Consolidation has also been abolished by statute in New Zealand.[17]   **5.09**

Consolidation in North America

In Canada, the status of the doctrine of consolidation varies from province to   **5.10**
province. British Columbia has adopted the English approach, *viz.* consolidation
will be unavailable to a mortgagee unless a contrary intention is expressed in the
mortgage.[18]

The position is less certain in the other Canadian provinces, where consolidation has not specifically been the subject of legislation. In Ontario, it is considered that the statutory provision,[19] which deals with the enforcement of
registered charges by sale or foreclosure, has neither created a new statutory right
to consolidate nor extinguished any such right enjoyed by a mortgagee in
equity.[20] In Saskatchewan, however, the statutory provision dealing with a mortgagor's right to rectify a default before sale or foreclosure[21] has been held to have
extinguished a mortgagee's right to consolidate.[22] Finally, in the absence of cases
in point, it is not certain whether consolidation—where it has previously been
recognised[23]—has survived the enactment of similar provisions in the other
Canadian provinces.

The United States of America, in contrast to England and the other major com-   **5.11**
mon law jurisdictions, does not recognise the doctrine of consolidation.[24]

---

[17] Section 85 of the *Property Law Act 1952* (NZ). Further, it appears that consolidation was never available in New Zealand, in respect of Torrens system mortgages: *Wilkin v Deans* (1886) 6 NZLR 425. See also E C Adams, *Garrow's Law of Real Property* (1961 Butterworths), 558; Hinde, McMorland, Campbell & Grinlinton, *Butterworths Land Law in New Zealand*, para 8.049.

[18] Section 31 of the *Property Law Act, RSBC 1996*. See also *Richmond Savings Credit Union v Zilbershats* (1997) 35 BCLR (3d) 136.

[19] Section 97 of the *Land Titles Act, RSO 1990*.

[20] *Project Research Group Ltd v Acumen Investments Ltd* (1986) 43 RPR 50. C f *Credit Foncier Franco-Canadien v Walker* [1938] OWN 339 where it was held that the predecessor of section 97, by conferring upon a mortgagor a statutory, as opposed to an equitable, right to redeem had the effect of rendering consolidation unavailable in respect of statutory mortgages. It has likewise been suggested that this provision renders marshalling unavailable in respect of statutory mortgages: *Goodman v Parkhurst* [1980] 6 WWR 601. See also Rayner & McLaren, *Falconbridge on Mortgages*, 194 where it is considered that section 72 of the *Registry Act, RSO 1990*, which provides that no equitable interest affecting land is valid against a registered instrument, has extinguished an unreg-istered mortgagee's right to consolidate, in Ontario, as against a registered assignee of the equity of redemption. However, if the mortgages sought to be consolidated have been registered Falconbridge holds that consolidation will be available against a subsequent registered assignee.

[21] Section 44 of the *Queen's Bench Act, RSS 1978*.

[22] *Bank of Nova Scotia v Bartrop* [1983] 4 WWR 91; *Montreal Trust Co v Newberry Energy Ltd* (1983) 147 DLR (3d) 189.

[23] Manitoba (*Re Hamilton* (1895) 10 Man R 573); New Brunswick (*Maritime Warehousing & Dock Co v Nicholson* (1884) 24 NBR 170); Nova Scotia (*Slayter v Johnson* (1864) 5 NSR 502).

[24] Jones, *A Treatise on the Law of Mortgages of Real Property*, para 1083.

Ashburner's argument that marshalling is a form of consolidation

5.12 Ashburner considers that it is only by classifying marshalling as a form of consolidation, that the inferior position of marshalling rights *qua* third party transferees or disponees by way of security or purchase can be explained.[25] Support for this, in Ashburner's view, may be found in *Titley v Davies*.[26]

5.13 Ashburner's argument may be illustrated by reference to the paradigmatic marshalling situation where a senior creditor holds separate mortgages[27] over two assets of a debtor and a junior creditor holds a mortgage over one of those assets.

If, for one reason or another, the junior creditor[28] wishes to redeem the senior creditor's mortgage over the doubly-mortgaged asset, the senior creditor may apply the doctrine of consolidation against the junior creditor. The senior creditor has the power—since the senior debt is secured by separate mortgages over two distinct assets—to refuse to redeem that mortgage without the junior creditor also redeeming the mortgage over the other asset.

If the junior creditor complies with the senior creditor's demand, it will become entitled to the senior creditor's mortgages and will, in turn, be entitled to consolidate its original mortgage with the senior mortgages as against the debtor. However, until the junior creditor redeems the senior mortgages, it will have nothing more than a mere potentiality to succeed to the senior creditor's right of consolidation.

5.14 This potential right to consolidate is, however, vulnerable to subsequent dealings with the mortgaged assets by the debtor. If, before the junior creditor redeems the senior mortgages, the debtor grants a second mortgage over the singly-mortgaged asset or absolutely transfers the equity of redemption in it to a third party, that potential right will be extinguished.

Accordingly, a third party who acquires an interest in the equity of redemption of the singly-mortgaged asset before the junior creditor's right to consolidate arises, will be able to defeat any subsequent attempt at consolidation by the junior cred-

---

[25] See further Chapter 11.

[26] (1743) 2 Y & C Ch Cas 399. In this case, Jenyns granted a first-ranking mortgage over three assets to Shepheard, then granted a second mortgage over one of those assets to Titley, assigned the equity of redemption of a second asset to Peyton, and granted a second mortgage over the third asset to Davies. Lord Hardwicke held that, upon Titley purchasing Shepheard's mortgage, Titley was entitled to consolidate the first-ranking mortgage with his original mortgage; q v *Mutual Life Assurance Society v Langley* (1886) 32 Ch D 460 and Beddoes, *A Concise Treatise on the Law of Mortgages*, 105 where a similar view is taken of marshalling. It is of interest to note that there is no discussion of this case in Webster, *Ashburner's Concise Treatise on Mortgages, Pledges and Liens*.

[27] Consolidation is only available in respect of mortgages: q v nn3 and 4.

[28] The senior creditor's right to consolidate is, of course, also exercisable against the debtor. Ashburner is, however, only concerned with the initial exercise of that right against the junior creditor as he is seeking to relate it to the junior creditor's marshalling rights.

itor. This limitation, in Ashburner's opinion, applies, *mutatis mutandis*, to the doctrine of marshalling: a junior creditor's marshalling rights are liable to be controverted by a subsequent transfer or disposition, by the debtor, of the asset (which is encumbered by only the senior security) to a third party. It is this common ground between marshalling and consolidation that, in Ashburner's view, justifies the classification of marshalling as a form of consolidation.

Consolidation and assignments of the equity of redemption

The purpose of Ashburner's argument is to demonstrate that the constraints **5.15** imposed by third parties upon marshalling can be explained only by characterising marshalling as a form of consolidation. This necessitates a closer examination of the effect on consolidation of assignments of interests in the mortgaged assets.

It is implicit, in condition (4) above, that a mortgagee's right of consolidation is **5.16** capable of being asserted successfully against subsequent assignees of the equities of redemption (such as purchasers and *puisne* mortgagees).[29]

As a general rule, an assignee of the equity of redemption—whether the assign- **5.17** ment is absolute or by way of security—takes its interest subject only to those equities which existed against the mortgagor at the time of the assignment.[30] Thus, if a mortgagee is entitled to consolidate its mortgages against the original mortgagor, its right to consolidate will persist as against all assignees of the equity of redemption.[31] However, if the mortgagee does not enjoy the right to consolidate, as against the original mortgagor, it cannot later acquire that right as against an assignee of the equity of redemption from the mortgagor.[32]

Consolidation and assignments of only the equity of redemption

This may be illustrated by reference to the situation where two assets are mort- **5.18** gaged to the same mortgagee, either (i) contemporaneously to secure repayment

---

[29] *Hughes v Britannia Permanent Benefit BS* [1906] 2 Ch 607.

[30] *Harter v Colman* (1882) 19 Ch D 630; *Mutual Life Assurance Society v Langley* (1886) 32 Ch D 460.

[31] *Pope v Onslow* (1692) 2 Vern 286; *Willie v Lugg* (1761) 2 Eden 78; *Ex parte Carter* (1773) Amb 733; *Jones v Smith* (1794) 2 Ves Jun 372; *Watts v Symes* (1851) 1 De G M & G 240. See Webster, *Ashburner's Concise Treatise on Mortgages, Pledges and Liens*, 364–366; Strahan, *The Principles of the General Law of Mortgages*, 101–103; Tillard, *Wilshere's Principles of Equity*, 226–227; Browne, *Ashburner's Principles of Equity*, 222–223; Eastwood, *Strahan's Digest of Equity*, 398–399; Hanbury & Waldock, *The Law of Mortgages*, 171; *Halsbury's*, Vol 32 ('*Mortgage*'), paras 770–771.

[32] *Willie v Lugg* (1761) 2 Eden 78; *Selby v Pomfret* (1861) 7 Jur (NS) 835; *Cracknall v Janson* (1879) 11 Ch D 1; *Harris v Tubb* (1889) 42 Ch D 79; *Re Salmon* [1903] 1 KB 149. See Webster, *Ashburner's Concise Treatise on Mortgages, Pledges and Liens*, 364–366; Baker & Langan, *Snell's Equity*, 400; Tyler, *Fisher & Lightwood's Law of Mortgage*, 536–538. This is also the position in Australia: Francis & Thomas, *Mortgages and Securities*, 363; Sykes & Walker, *The Law of Securities*, 180.

of the same debt or (ii) at different times to secure the repayment of two distinct debts.

In both cases, when the second mortgage is granted, the equities of redemption will be united in the same party, the mortgagor, and the mortgages will be united in the same party, the mortgagee (as required by condition (4)). Thus an assignee of the equity of redemption, of either or both of the assets, will only ever acquire an interest which, at the time of the assignment, was subject to existing rights of consolidation.[33]

5.19 However, in the case of example (ii), if the equity of redemption of the asset subject to the first mortgage is assigned[34] before the grant of the second mortgage, the mortgagee will be unable to consolidate the two mortgages.[35] Nor will the mortgagee later be able to consolidate the mortgage, over the assigned asset as against that assignee or any subsequent assignee,[36] with the remaining mortgage.

Consolidation and assignments of both the equity of redemption and the mortgage

5.20 The same principles apply where two assets are mortgaged to different mortgagees, and the two mortgages subsequently vest in the hands of either one of the mortgagees or a third party. The eventual holder of the two mortgages will be able to consolidate the mortgages against the original mortgagor or an assignee of either or both of the equities of redemption, provided the mortgages were united in the same party prior to any assignment of the equity of redemption.[37]

5.21 However, if the same party takes an assignment of both equities of redemption prior to the mortgages becoming vested in one of the original mortgagees or a third party, the holder of the mortgages will be entitled to consolidate the mort-

---

[33] q v nn 30 and 31.

[34] It must be an absolute assignment otherwise the mortgagor's interest in the equity of redemption will continue. See Strahan, *The Principles of the General Law of Mortgages*, 102.

[35] *Barker v Gray* (1875) 1 Ch D 491; *Harter v Colman* (1882) 19 Ch D 630; *Mutual Life Assurance Society v Langley* (1886) 32 Ch D 460; *Minter v Carr* [1894] 3 Ch 498; *Andrew v City Permanent Benefit BS* (1881) 44 LT 641; *Jennings v Jordan* (1881) 6 App Cas 698; *Hughes v Britannia Permanent Benefit BS* [1906] 2 Ch 607. See Tyler, *Fisher & Lightwood's Law of Mortgage*, 536–538. This is also the position in Australia: Francis & Thomas, *Mortgages and Securities*, 362–363; Sykes & Walker, *The Law of Securities*, 180.

[36] q v n32.

[37] *White v Hillacre* (1839) 3 Y & C Ex 597; *Tweedale v Tweedale* (1857) 23 Beav 341; *Vint v Padget* (1858) 2 De G & J 611; *Selby v Pomfret* (1861) 7 Jur (NS) 835; *Jennings v Jordan* (1881) 6 App Cas 698; *Harter v Colman* (1882) 19 Ch D 630; *Minter v Carr* [1894] 3 Ch 498; *Pledge v White* [1896] AC 187. See Strahan, *The Principles of the General Law of Mortgages*, 102–103; Browne, *Ashburner's Principles of Equity*, 223; Baker & Langan, *Snell's Equity*, 400; Megarry & Wade, *The Law of Real Property*, 957–958.

gages against that party.[38] This exception is clearly inconsistent with the general rule that an assignee of the equity of redemption takes subject only to such equities as existed at the time of the assignment. Further, it leads to the entirely anomalous result that, if the equities of redemption were assigned at different times, the first assignment would have extinguished any right to consolidate but the second assignment, by reason only of the fact that there is a common assignee, would have revivified that right.

Marshalling is not a form of consolidation

Both the right to marshall securities and the right to consolidate mortgages are liable to be extinguished by subsequent assignments. However, this is not, on its own, sufficient to sustain Ashburner's argument that marshalling is a form of consolidation.[39]   **5.22**

First, the doctrine of marshalling is not limited in its application to mortgages, as the doctrine of consolidation is, with its insistence upon a separation of the equity of redemption from the other equitable interests in the asset over which the security has been granted.[40]   **5.23**

Secondly, the right to marshall is not dependent upon the expiration of the date of redemption for either or both of the senior and junior securities. The junior creditor's marshalling rights are predicated upon the enforcement of the senior security against an asset which is subject also to the junior security. Further, the senior creditor's rights of enforcement arise according to the terms of the senior security (and collateral) documentation; those terms would be unlikely to restrict enforcement to circumstances where the debtor has failed to discharge the senior debt by the date stipulated for the redemption of the senior security.   **5.24**

A third disparity between marshalling and consolidation is found in the latter's requirement that the mortgages sought to be consolidated must all have been the creation of the same mortgagor (*per* condition (3)). While this is generally   **5.25**

---

[38] *Bovey v Skipwith* (1671) 1 Ch Cas 201; *Tweedale v Tweedale* (1857) 23 Beav 341; *Vint v Padget* (1858) 2 De G & J 611; *Selby v Pomfret* (1861) 7 Jur (NS) 835; *Ex parte Hotchkin* (1875) LR 20 Eq 746; *Cummins v Fletcher* (1880) 14 Ch D 699; *Jennings v Jordan* (1881) 6 App Cas 698; *Harter v Colman* (1882) 19 Ch D 630; *Minter v Carr* [1894] 3 Ch 498; *Pledge v White* [1896] AC 187; c f *Beevor v Luck* (1867) LR 4 Eq 537. See Hanbury & Waldock, *The Law of Mortgages*, 171–173; Cousins, *The Law of Mortgages*, 432–433. This is also the position in Australia: Francis & Thomas, *Mortgages and Securities*, 363–364; Sykes & Walker, *The Law of Securities*, 181. In Australia and New Zealand – but not in England, Ireland or Canada – it is no longer necessary to challenge the wisdom of this exception.

[39] These doubts appear to be shared by the editor of the second edition of Ashburner's text: see Browne, *Ashburner's Principles of Equity*, 214 n2.

[40] See Robbins, *A Treatise on the Law of Mortgages, Pledges and Hypothecations*, 783; Ramsbotham, *Coote's Treatise on the Law of Mortgages*, 808 and 809. See further Chapter 9.

supported by the common debtor rule,[41] the doctrine of consolidation is far wider than the doctrine of marshalling in that it permits the consolidation of mortgages which have been created at different times to secure different debts. The doctrine of marshalling, in contrast, insists the senior security must grant to the senior creditor equal rights of recourse against each of the assets subject to the senior security, and those rights must secure repayment of the same debt.[42]

5.26 Fourthly, a mortgagee's right of consolidation can be exercised against the party in whose hands the equities of redemption have become united (assuming that the equities of redemption all relate to assets that were originally mortgaged by the same mortgagor). While there are no English (or Irish, Australian, Canadian or New Zealand) cases dealing with the ability of a junior creditor to marshall in equivalent circumstances,[43] there is no good reason why an assignee of the assets from the common debtor should be in any different position from the common debtor *qua* the junior creditor, in the event that the senior creditor recovers the senior debt out of the asset subject to both the senior and junior securities. Again, the disparity between the two doctrines lies in the scope of consolidation.[44] The ability to consolidate mortgages in such a situation does not depend upon those mortgages securing the same debt. However, marshalling, *per* the common debtor rule, is generally confined to situations where the assets, subject to the senior creditor's security, have been collateralised to secure the same debt.

5.27 Finally, there is no indication in any of the cases on marshalling of securities from England, Australia, Ireland and New Zealand that the right to marshall was in any way affected by the enactment of legislation restricting (or abolishing) consolidation of mortgages.[45]

---

[41] The senior and junior creditors must, as a general rule, be creditors of a common debtor and hold securities over that common debtor's assets: see further Chapters 7 and 8.

[42] See further Chapters 7 and 8.

[43] i e where both the asset subject to the senior and junior securities and the asset subject to only the junior security have become vested in a third party.

[44] It should be noted that a senior creditor cannot consolidate the senior security with a lower-ranking security to defeat the marshalling rights of a junior creditor who holds a security that ranks ahead of that lower-ranking security: *Ford v Tynte* (1872) 41 LJ Ch 758. See *Halsbury's*, Vol 32 ('*Mortgage*'), para 773.

[45] See further Chapter 2. In particular, Young J. in *Sarge Pty Ltd v Cazihaven Homes Pty Ltd* (1994) 34 NSWLR 658, 665 rejected any suggestion that marshalling was a form of consolidation (q v Hanbury & Waldock, *The Law of Mortgages*, 182). See also Meagher, Gummow & Lehane, *Equity Doctrines and Remedies*, para 1139.

B. Marshalling of Securities and Contribution

Introduction

A second basis for marshalling of securities is said to be the equitable doctrine of **5.28** contribution. Spence, in *The Equitable Jurisdiction of the Court of Chancery*,[46] claims that marshalling and contribution are derived from a common principle, *viz.* the fair distribution of liability amongst co-obligors. Support for this view of contribution may also be found in Story's *Commentaries on Equity Jurisprudence*.[47]

Spence states:[48]

> Contribution, if it differs from marshalling, does so *in specie* rather than generically, in form rather than in nature. Marshalling and Contribution are each of them between several persons of their rights respectively *inter se*, in respect of a charge or claim, which, affecting all of them, or properties belonging to all of them respectively, has been or may be enforced in a manner not unjust as far as the person is concerned by whom it was or may be enforced, but not just as between the persons or properties liable.

A similar view of contribution is expressed by Story:[49]

> . . . no one ought to profit by another man's loss where he himself has incurred a like responsibility. Any other rule would put it in the power of the creditor to select his own victim, and upon motives of mere caprice or favoritism to make a common burden a most gross personal oppression. It would be against equity for the creditor to exact or receive payment from one, and to permit, or by his conduct to cause the other debtors to be exempt from payment.

As marshalling effects a redistribution of a debtor's assets amongst its remaining creditors following the recoupment of the senior debt, Spence's claim of a common nature for marshalling and contribution appears plausible.

What is contribution?

The equitable doctrine of contribution provides that where two or more parties **5.29** are subject to a common liability,[50] then *prima facie* that liability should be borne

---

[46] *The Equitable Jurisdiction of the Court of Chancery*, 837.
[47] Bigelow, *Story's Commentaries on Equity Jurisprudence*, para 493.
[48] Spence, *The Equitable Jurisdiction of the Court of Chancery*, 837, quoting *Tombs v Roch* (1846) 2 Coll 490, 499–500. See also Meagher, Gummow & Lehane, *Equity Doctrines and Remedies*, paras 1004 and 1040 where *Tombs v Roch* is cited in support of this supposed affinity between the two doctrines.
[49] Bigelow, *Story's Commentaries on Equity Jurisprudence*, para 493. See also Story, para 633 where it is considered that marshalling is a 'near relation' of the doctrine of contribution.
[50] The parties must share a common obligation and be subject to a common demand: *Dering v Earl of Winchelsea* (1787) 1 Cox Eq Cas 318; *Pendlebury v Walker* (1841) 4 Y & C Ex 424. See O'Donovan & Phillips, *The Modern Contract of Guarantee*, 619–621.

equally by the parties.[51] The right of contribution is made available on the grounds that the party seeking contribution has paid money that its co-obligors are obliged to pay.[52] As such, a party can only claim contribution if it has paid an amount in excess of its share of the common liability.[53]

5.30 Accordingly, a co-debtor, who pays more than its rateable share of a common debt (for example, where the creditor has elected to proceed against that co-debtor, in preference to the other co-debtors, for the full amount of the common debt), will be entitled to recover the over-payment from its co-debtors.[54]

5.31 The doctrine of contribution provides only a presumptive rule for the distribution of a common liability; the co-debtors may agree between themselves that they should be liable for the common debt in unequal proportions.[55] Similarly, a co-debtor may agree with the creditor that it will not enforce any right of contribution against its co-debtors.[56]

---

[51] For a consideration of the equitable doctrine of contribution as it applies to common debts, see: Hanbury & Waldock, *The Law of Mortgages*, 117–119; Marks & Moss, *Rowlatt on the Law of Principal and Surety*, 152–161; Tyler, *Fisher & Lightwood's Law of Mortgage*, 526–527; Cousins, *The Law of Mortgages*, 284 and 438; Burrows, *The Law of Restitution*, 220–222; Goff & Jones, *The Law of Restitution*, generally at Chapter 13. See also the extensive discussion of contribution in the following Australian texts: Meagher, Gummow & Lehane, *Equity Doctrines and Remedies*, generally at Chapter 10; O'Donovan & Phillips, *The Modern Contract of Guarantee*, 614–653; J Glover, *Contribution* in P Parkinson (ed), *The Principles of Equity* (1996 Law Book Company).

[52] *Dering v Earl of Winchelsea* (1787) 1 Cox Eq Cas 318; *Ex parte Gifford* (1802) 6 Ves 805; *Craythorne v Swinburne* (1807) 14 Ves Jun 160; *Holmes v Williamson* (1817) 6 M & S 158; *Stirling v Forrester* (1821) 3 Bli 575; *Collins v Prosser* (1823) 1 B & C 682; *Davies v Humphreys* (1840) 6 M & W 153; *Duncan Fox & Co v North and South Wales Bank* (1880) 6 App Cas 1; *Ex parte Snowdon* (1881) 17 Ch D 44; *Ward v National Bank of New Zealand* (1883) 8 App Cas 755; *Ellesmere Brewery Co v Cooper* [1896] 1 QB 75; *Stirling v Burdett* [1911] 2 Ch 418; *Hay v Carter* [1935] Ch 397; *Wilson v Mitchell* [1939] 2 KB 869. See Meagher, Gummow & Lehane, *Equity Doctrines and Remedies*, paras 1004, 1006–1016 and 1020–1021.

[53] A co-debtor who pays less than its share of the common debt will not be permitted to claim contribution unless that payment becomes more than the co-debtor's due share as the result of a subsequent payment by that co-debtor or another co-debtor: *Davies v Humphreys* (1840) 6 M & W 153.

[54] Marks & Moss, *Rowlatt on the Law of Principal and Surety*, 158; O'Donovan & Phillips, *The Modern Contract of Guarantee*, 615–616 and 624–629; McGuinness, *The Law of Guarantee*, paras 9.2–9.9 and 9.14–9.16. See also P Bingham, *The Surety's Right to Contribution* (1984) 12 ABLR 394; J D Lipton, *Equitable Rights of Contribution and Subrogation: Recent Australian Judicial Approaches* (1995) 13 ABR 21.

[55] *Swain v Wall* (1641) 1 Rep Ch 149; *Dering v Earl of Winchelsea* (1787) 1 Cox Eq Cas 318; *Craythorne v Swinburne* (1807) 14 Ves Jun 160; *Coope v Twynam* (1823) Turn & R 426; *Pendlebury v Walker* (1841) 4 Y & C Ex 424; *Wisden v Wisden* (1854) 2 Sm & G 396; *Arcedeckne v Lord Howard* (1875) 45 LJ Ch 622; *Steel v Dixon* (1881) 17 Ch D 825; *Mackreth v Walmesley* (1884) 51 LT 19; *Re Ennis* [1893] 3 Ch 238; *Re Denton's Estate* [1904] 2 Ch 178; *In re Best* [1924] 1 Ch 42. See Marks & Moss, *Rowlatt on the Law of Principal and Surety*, 156–157; Meagher, Gummow & Lehane, *Equity Doctrines and Remedies*, paras 1004, 1017–1019 and 1022; O'Donovan & Phillips, *The Modern Contract of Guarantee*, 616–619; McGuinness, *The Law of Guarantee*, paras 9.5–9.6.

[56] See Meagher, Gummow & Lehane, *Equity Doctrines and Remedies*, paras 1023–1025; O'Donovan & Phillips, *The Modern Contract of Guarantee*, 616–617; McGuinness, *The Law of Guarantee*, para 9.8.

Contribution and secured debts

A co-debtor who is entitled to contribution from its co-debtors is also entitled to **5.32**
share in any security for the common debt granted by the co-debtors.[57]

Where two or more co-debtors have each made available an asset to a creditor as
security for the repayment of a common debt and the creditor recovers the debt
out of an asset of one of the co-debtors, that co-debtor may recover its over-
payment from the other co-debtors in proportion to the value of their assets.[58]
Further, the co-debtor will be entitled to be subrogated to the securities granted
by the other co-debtors to the creditor, to the extent of the over-payment.[59]

In this manner, contribution ensures that no co-debtor pays more than its due
share of the secured debt. The secured creditor is left free to enforce its security as
it sees fit, but contribution intervenes to prevent the creditor from imposing the
entire burden of the secured debt on the co-debtor out of whose asset the debt has
been recouped.

Contribution and exoneration

A co-debtor's right of contribution may, however, be superseded by a third party's **5.33**
rights of exoneration. If one of the co-debtors has granted security over two or

---

[57] See Marks & Moss, *Rowlatt on the Law of Principal and Surety*, 159 and 160; Meagher,
Gummow & Lehane, *Equity Doctrines and Remedies*, paras 1028–1030; O'Donovan & Phillips,
The Modern Contract of Guarantee, 651–652; McGuinness, *The Law of Guarantee*, para 9.19.

[58] *Aldrich v Cooper* (1803) 8 Ves Jun 382; *Collins v Prosser* (1823) 1 B & C 682; *Marquis of Bute
v Cunynghame* (1826) 2 Russ 275; *Hodgson v Hodgson* (1837) 2 Keen 704; *Davies v Humphreys*
(1840) 6 M & W 153; *Pendlebury v Walker* (1841) 4 Y & C Ex 424; *Johnson v Child* (1844) 4 Hare
87; *Kearsley v Cole* (1846) 16 M & W 153; *Middleton v Middleton* (1852) 15 Beav 450; *Hitchman v
Stewart* (1855) 3 Drewery 271; *Evans v Bremridge* (1855) 2 K & J 174; *Webb v Hewitt* (1857) 3
K & J 438; *Stringer v Harper* (1858) 26 Beav 33; *Lipscomb v Lipscomb* (1868) LR 7 Eq 501; *Dallas
v Walls* (1873) 29 LT 599; *Ellis v Emmanuel* (1876) 1 Ex D 157; *Trestrail v Mason* (1878) 7 Ch D
665; *Leonino v Leonino* (1879) 10 Ch D 460; *Steel v Dixon* (1881) 17 Ch D 825; *Re Dunlop* (1882)
21 Ch D 583; *Lowe v Dixon* (1885) 16 QB D 455; *Re Wolmershausen* (1890) 62 LT 541; *Ellesmere
Brewery Co v Cooper* [1896] 1 QB 75; *Re Denton's Estate* [1904] 2 Ch 178; *National Provincial Bank
v Brackenbury* (1906) 22 TLR 797; *American Surety Co of New York v Wrightson* (1910) 103 LT 663;
Smith v Wood [1929] 1 Ch 14; *In re Mainwaring* [1937] Ch 96; *Commercial Union Assurance Co Ltd
v Hayden* [1977] QB 804. See Tyler, *Fisher & Lightwood's Law of Mortgage*, 526–527; Goff & Jones,
The Law of Restitution, 321–322; O'Donovan & Phillips, *The Modern Contract of Guarantee*,
642–649.

[59] *Aldrich v Cooper* (1803) 8 Ves Jun 382; *Yonge v Reynell* (1852) 9 Hare 809; *Pearl v Deacon*
(1857) 24 Beav 186; *Goodwin v Gray* (1874) 22 WR 312; *Ward v National Bank of New Zealand*
(1883) 8 App Cas 755; *Re Arcedeckne* (1883) 24 Ch D 709; *Berridge v Berridge* (1890) 44 Ch D 168;
Smith v Wood [1929] 1 Ch 14; *Re Butlers Wharf Ltd* [1995] 2 BCLC 43. C f *Brown v Cork* [1985]
BCLC 363 where the Court of Appeal considered that this was an instance of marshalling (see the
discussion of this case in paragraph 5.46). This rule applies only to securities granted by the co-
debtors to the creditor, and not to securities granted by a third party to the creditor (*Chatterton v
Maclean* [1951] 1 All ER 761) or by a third party to one of the co-debtors (*Goodman v Keel* (1923)
4 DLR 468; c f *Sherwin v McWilliams* (1921) 17 Tas LR 16). See Meagher, Gummow & Lehane,
Equity Doctrines and Remedies, para 1029.

more of its assets to secure repayment of the common debt and subsequently transfers one of those assets to a third party, that asset will *prima facie* no longer be susceptible to the contribution claims of the other co-debtors.[60] Nor will the co-debtor, who transferred the asset, be entitled to claim contribution against the other co-debtors should the creditor recover the secured debt from the remaining assets of that co-debtor.[61]

5.34   However, if the creditor enforces its security against the transferred asset, the third party will be entitled to be exonerated out of the co-debtor's remaining assets for the amount appropriated by the creditor.[62] This right of exoneration is available to both purchasers for valuable consideration and volunteers.[63]

5.35   It is only where the transfer is on terms that expressly provide for the continued encumbrance of the asset by the original security, that the asset will remain susceptible to a contribution claim by the transferring co-debtor or one of its co-debtors. Nor will the third part enjoy any rights of exoneration.[64]

5.36   The position is more complex where all the assets subject to the security are transferred to third parties by the co-debtor: as a general rule, the assets will remain susceptible to contribution claims and none of the transferees will enjoy rights of exoneration.[65] There is one exception: a transferee for value, and on terms that expressly provide that the asset was being transferred free of the security, will be able to claim exoneration against transferees later in time and who (i) are volunteers or (ii) had, at the time of the transfer, notice of the security.[66]

---

[60]   *Waring v Ward* (1802) 7 Ves 332; *Lloyd v Johnes* (1804) 9 Ves 37; *Gee v Smart* (1857) 8 El & Bl 313; *Paget v Paget* (1898) 1 Ch 470; *Re Repington* [1904] 1 Ch 811; *Hall v Hall* [1911] 1 Ch 487; *Gee v Liddell* [1913] 2 Ch 62; *In re A Debtor* [1976] 1 WLR 952 (c f *Official Trustee in Bankruptcy v Citibank Savings Ltd* (1995) 38 NSWLR 116, 130 where it was doubted whether this case is an instance of exoneration); *Re Pittortou* [1985] 1 WLR 58. See Hanbury & Waldock, *The Law of Mortgages*, 118–119; *Halsbury's*, Vol 32 ('*Mortgage*'), para 920; Marks & Moss, *Rowlatt on the Law of Principal and Surety*, 207–208; Tyler, *Fisher & Lightwood's Law of Mortgage*, 527–530; Cousins, *The Law of Mortgages*, 438–439; Sykes & Walker, *The Law of Securities*, 185–186.

[61]   *In re Darby's Estate* [1907] 2 Ch 465.

[62]   *Rumbold v Rumbold* (1796) 3 Ves Jun 65; *In re Best* [1924] 1 Ch 42.

[63]   *Galton v Hancock* (1743) 2 Atk 428; *Kirkham v Smith* (1749) 1 Ves Sen 258; *Ker v Ker* (1869) 4 Ir R Eq 15; *Re Repington* [1904] 1 Ch 811.

[64]   *In re Mainwaring* [1937] Ch 96. The entire burden of the secured debt can, however, be thrown entirely on the transferee where the transferee has expressly agreed to indemnify the transferor for the whole of the secured debt: *Waring v Ward* (1802) 7 Ves 332. See Goff & Jones, *The Law of Restitution*, 321–322.

[65]   In the Australian case of *Chase Corporation (Australia) Pty Ltd v North Sydney Brick and Tile Co Ltd* (1994) 12 ACLC 997, 1,012, Cohen J. stated 'Difficulties arise where both properties have been assigned or . . . mortgaged. The general principle is that exoneration does not then apply because neither assignee is personally liable and accordingly the mortgage will be payable out of both properties'.

[66]   *Carter v Barnadiston* (1718) 1 P Wms 506; *Irvin v Ironmonger* (1831) 2 R & M 531; *Chappell v Rees* (1839) 9 LJ Ch 37; *Hughes v Williams* (1852) 3 Mac & G 683; *Finch v Shaw* (1854) 19 Beav 500; *Stronge v Hawkes* (1859) 4 De G & J 632; *In re Jones* [1893] 2 Ch 461; *Re Cook's Mortgage* [1896] 1 Ch 923. See also the extensive Irish case law on this point: *Averall v Wade* (1835) L & G

Marshalling is not a form of contribution

The views of Spence and Story on the nature of contribution and the marshalling **5.37**
of securities appear to be borne out by the above examination of contribution
(and the subsidiary doctrine of exoneration). Contribution as it applies to co-
debtors is, like marshalling, concerned with ensuring that a creditor cannot,
merely by reason of how it chooses to recover the debt owed to it, determine where
liability for that debt should fall.

Marshalling achieves this by granting a junior creditor access to the senior creditor's security. Likewise, contribution, to give effect to an over-paying co-debtor's
claim against its co-debtors, will allow the co-debtor access to the securities
granted to the common creditor by those co-debtors. Further, contribution
rights, in common with marshalling rights, may be defeated by a subsequent
transfer or disposition to a third party of an asset by a co-debtor.

On closer inspection, however, it becomes clear that the claim for marshalling **5.38**
made by Spence (and Story) is misconceived.

First, the doctrines of marshalling and contribution are concerned with the pro- **5.39**
tection of entirely different interests.[67] The presumptive rule of contribution is
that the burden of a common debt (whether secured or unsecured) owed to a creditor must be shared equally amongst the co-debtors. Marshalling, in contrast, acts
to protect the interest of a party, that is a stranger to the debtor-creditor relationship to which the first-ranking secured creditor is a party; marshalling protects the
priority-ranking of the holder of *mesne* security, not the interests of co-debtors of
the first-ranking secured creditor.

Secondly, marshalling and contribution are at variance as regards the actual dis- **5.40**
tribution of the burden of the relevant debt. Contribution requires equal sharing
of the common debt whereas marshalling imposes the entire burden of the senior
debt upon the unsecured creditors of the debtor.

---

temp Sugd 252; *Re Roddy's Estate* (1861) 11 Ir Ch R 369; *Ker v Ker* (1869) 4 IR Eq 15; *Re Roche's
Estate* (1890) 25 LR Ir 284; *McCarthy v M'Cartie (No 2)* [1904] 1 IR 100; *Tighe v Dolphin* [1906]
1 IR 305; *Ocean Accident & Guarantee Corp v Collum* [1913] 1 IR 337; *In re Chute's Estate* [1914]
1 IR 180.

[67] This is implicit in the comments of Isaacs J. of the High Court of Australia in *Ramsay v
Lowther* (1912) 16 CLR 1, 23, in which *Tombs v Roch* (1846) 2 Coll 490 was followed: 'Marshalling
regulates the order of different classes of assets and does not operate between assets of the same class.
As between the latter the question is, properly speaking, one of contribution'. See also *Re Denton's
Estate* [1904] 2 Ch 178; Meagher, Gummow & Lehane, *Equity Doctrines and Remedies*, paras
1032–1039; G E Dal Pont & D R C Chalmers, *Equity and Trusts in Australia and New Zealand*
(1996 Law Book Company), 266; Heydon & Loughlan, *Cases and Materials on Equity and Trusts*,
para 21.4.1.

5.41 Further, contribution (and exoneration), by adjusting the liability of one co-debtor to another, are in effect altering the quantum of the residue of assets available to each co-debtor upon the discharge of the common debt. Marshalling, on the other hand, is neutral in its impact upon the residue of a debtor's assets. It does not affect the aggregate liability of a debtor to its creditors, nor does it add to the debtor's pool of assets, but merely reorders the manner in which that liability is to be discharged following the recoupment of the senior debt.

5.42 An additional difference concerns the status of contribution rights *qua* marshalling rights: where the asset to which a co-debtor (or co-surety) is seeking access *via* contribution is the subject of a marshalling claim by a creditor, the co-debtor's contribution rights will be subordinated to the creditor's marshalling rights.[68]

5.43 Finally, it is relevant to note that both Spence and Story support the version of marshalling depicted by the coercion theory of marshalling.[69] It is therefore difficult to see how their comments on contribution can be taken as evidence that marshalling is a special case of a more general legal principle, to which contribution belongs. Marshalling, in their view, is a pre-emptive remedy; apart from the fact that it protects lower-ranking creditors from the caprice of the first-ranking creditor, it can have little in common with contribution which redistributes liability for a common debt.[70]

Further confusion about marshalling and contribution

5.44 The issue of the supposed affinity between marshalling of securities and contribution has been further confused by recent commentary on the Australian case of *Finance Corporation of Australia Ltd v Bentley*,[71] and comments concerning

---

[68] *Bartholomew v May* (1737) 1 Atk 487. See also Tyler, *Fisher & Lightwood's Law of Mortgage*, 527.

[69] Spence, *The Equitable Jurisdiction of the Court of Chancery*, 833–834; Bigelow, *Story's Commentaries on Equity Jurisprudence*, para 633.

[70] As a subsidiary point, the incidents of contribution were settled long before the advent of the post-realisation version of marshalling: *Anonymous* (1557) Cary 1; *Offley v Johnson* (1584) 2 Leon 166; *Harbert's Case* (1584) 3 Co Rep 11b; *Fleetwood v Charnock* (1629) Nelson 10; *Peter v Rich* (1629/1630) 1 Chan Rep 34; *Morgan v Seymour* (1637/1638) 1 Chan Rep 120; *Swain v Wall* (1641) 1 Rep Ch 149; *Hole v Harrison* (1673) 1 Ch Ca 246; *Herle v Harrison* (1674–1675) 73 Selden Society 138; *Cope v Cope* (circa 1710) 2 Salk 449; *Oneal v Mead* (1720) 1 P Wms 694; *Davis v Gardiner* (1723) 2 P Wms 187; *Godin v London Assurance Company* (1758) 1 Burr 489; *Newby v Reed* (1763) 1 W Bl 416; *Lawson v Wright* (1786) 1 Cox 275; *Dering v Earl of Winchelsea* (1787) 1 Cox Eq Cas 318; *Turner v Davies* (1796) 2 Esp 478. See O'Donovan & Phillips, *The Modern Contract of Guarantee*, 614–615. This is also the case with exoneration: *Huntington v Huntington* (1702) 2 Bro Parl Cas 1; *Pocock v Lee* (1707) 2 Vern 604; *Peirs v Peirs* (1750) 1 Ves Sen 521. Further, there are clear Roman law antecedents for contribution: D.46.1.17. See Marks & Moss, *Rowlatt on the Law of Principal and Surety*, 153.

[71] (1991) 5 BPR 97412.

marshalling in *Brown v Cork*[72] and the recent New Zealand case of *National Bank of NZ Ltd v Caldesia Promotions Ltd and Jenkins Roberts & Associates Ltd.*[73]

Fisher & Lightwood claim that the Australian case, *Finance Corporation of Australia* **5.45**
Ltd v Bentley,[74] is an example of the analogous natures of marshalling and contribution.[75] This is not, however, immediately obvious from a reading of this case. In the case, Mahoney J.A. in the New South Wales Court of Appeal merely noted counsel's submission that accounting for the proceeds of realisation of the security as between the mortgagee, mortgagor and surety should take place in an equitable manner.[76] It is difficult to see how this acknowledgement supports the view expressed in the above text.

In *Brown v Cork*,[77] Oliver L.J. stated:[78] **5.46**

> . . . where the principal debt is secured by security given by co-sureties, the co-surety who has paid more than his share of the principal debt is entitled to have the securities *marshalled* as between himself and his co-sureties (emphasis added).

This case concerned the ability of a co-surety to obtain access to securities held by a creditor. The Court of Appeal held that an over-paying co-surety was entitled to be subrogated to the creditor's securities, on repayment of the secured debt, to the extent of the co-surety's overpayment.[79] As seen from the above analysis of

---

[72] [1985] BCLC 363.

[73] [1996] 3 NZLR 467.

[74] (1991) 5 BPR 97412.

[75] E L G Tyler & R Oughton, *Fisher & Lightwood's Law of Mortgage: Supplement to Tenth Edition* (1994 Butterworths), A94. See also the Australian edition: Tyler, Young & Croft, *Fisher & Lightwood's Law of Mortgage*, para 30.2. The above comments apply equally to the two cases cited in support of this proposition: *Banner v Berridge* (1881) 18 Ch D 254 and *Finance & Investments Pty Ltd v Van Kempen* (1986) 6 NSWLR 305. Neither of these cases concerned marshalling or contribution, but instead dealt with the nature of accounting between first and second mortgagees following the enforcement of the first mortgage and the amount of interest recoverable by the former in the absence of an express provision in the mortgage.

[76] (1991) 5 BPR 97412, 11,839.

[77] [1985] BCLC 363.

[78] Ibid, 373. See also *Halsbury's*, Vol 20 ('*Guarantee and Indemnity*'), para 268 where it is stated: 'Marshalling of securities. As between co-guarantors who have given security for the payment of the principal debt, a guarantor who pays more than his share of the guaranteed liability is entitled to have the securities marshalled so as to ensure that each co-guarantor pays his due proportion and no more, without taking into account any rights of set-off that might otherwise exist as between the co-guarantors. This is so, even though one or more of the co-guarantors is insolvent'.

[79] The court applied *Smith v Wood* [1929] 1 Ch 14, a case in which similar comments had been made concerning the right of a co-surety to 'marshall' the securities granted by its co-sureties (21–22, 29 and 30–31). There is one important distinction between the use of the term 'marshalling' in *Brown v Cork* [1985] BCLC 363 and its use in *Smith v Wood*. In the latter case, the co-sureties were only severally liable for the principal debt whereas in the former case, they were jointly and severally liable. Russell L.J. in *Smith v Wood* (30) considered that, where the co-sureties were jointly liable, the principle by which a co-surety could obtain access to the securities was one of contribution, not marshalling. It was where the co-sureties were only severally liable, that the principle in question was one of marshalling. A surety's right to 'marshall' is considered in Chapter 8.

contribution, this is clearly an application of the fundamental principle of contribution that co-sureties, in the absence of agreement between themselves to the contrary, are rateably liable for the guaranteed debt. Moreover, Oliver L.J. expressly queried whether marshalling was the appropriate label for this principle.[80]

5.47 A similar issue has subsequently been considered in *Re Butlers Wharf Ltd.*[81] The High Court held that where a surety for part of a debt made payment of the full amount for which it was liable, it would be entitled to share rateably with the creditor in any security which had been given by the debtor for the whole debt. At no stage did the court consider that it was permitting the surety to marshal the securities held by the creditor.

5.48 Finally, in *National Bank of NZ Ltd v Caldesia Promotions Ltd and Jenkins Roberts & Associates Ltd,*[82] the High Court suggested that the apportionment principle[83] enunciated in *Barnes v Racster,*[84] *Bugden v Bignold*[85] *et al* was an instance of contribution, rather than marshalling.

This is by no means a novel claim. This claim was first made in an article by Derham,[86] where it was queried whether the apportionment principle could properly be characterised as an instance of marshalling, because it modified the rights of third parties, and thus infringed an apparent tenet of marshalling, *viz.* that marshalling is an equity which is enforced only against the mortgagor and its legal representatives and not against third parties.[87]

The relationship between a junior creditor's marshalling rights and third party rights is considered in Chapter 11. However, it suffices to note that marshalling, by its redistribution of the assets of the debtor, necessarily affects the rights of third

---

[80] [1985] BCLC 363, 374. A similar comment is made by *Halsbury's* in a note to the commentary cited in n78 (para 268n2).

[81] [1995] 2 BCLC 43. C f the United States equity text, Beach, Jr., *Commentaries on Modern Equity Jurisprudence,* in which para 790 calls the right of a co-surety to share in the securities granted to another co-surety by the debtor 'marshalling'.

[82] [1996] 3 NZLR 467, 475.

[83] This is the principle which applies where the asset, that is subject to the senior security sought to be marshalled, is encumbered by a security in favour of a third party: see further Chapter 11. C f the Australian case of *Sarge Pty Ltd v Cazihaven Homes Pty Ltd* (1994) 34 NSWLR 658, in which Young J. (662–663), when enumerating the various instances of marshalling, omitted to mention the apportionment principle although he did categorise as marshalling two principles not normally considered by Australian or English law to be instances of marshalling, *viz.* a surety's subrogation rights and the American inverse order rule.

[84] (1842) 1 Y & C Ch Cas 401.

[85] (1843) 2 Y & C Ch Cas 377.

[86] S R Derham, *Set-Off against an Assignee: the Relevance of Marshalling, Contribution and Subrogation* (1991) 107 LQR 126, 132–134. See also Meagher, Gummow & Lehane, *Equity Doctrines and Remedies,* para 1124 and MacDougall, *Marshalling and the Personal Property Security Acts: Doing Unto Others . . . ,* 93n10, where Derham's argument is noted.

[87] See further paragraphs 11.06–11.09.

parties such as unsecured creditors and, additionally, that the apportionment principle is one instance of the general principle that the right to marshall will prevail over all competing interests other than those arising by way of security or purchase. On this basis, the claim that the apportionment principle should be classified as a form of contribution cannot be sustained.[88]

C. Marshalling of Securities and Specific Performance

Introduction

The third of the claims about the nature of marshalling, contends that marshalling is based upon the equitable remedy of specific performance.[89] **5.49**

This is the view of marshalling that prevails in Ireland,[90] and may be attributed to the following statement of the Court of Appeal in *Ker v Ker*:[91]

> For what is the *rationale* of that doctrine? In my opinion, it is specific performance. When the owner of the incumbered estate sells, or settles for valuable consideration a parcel of it, and there is a covenant against incumbrances, or a declaration that the estate is free from incumbrances, or the nature of the dealing shows that the land is sold or settled *as if* free from incumbrances, equity, instead of leaving the purchaser to his action for damages, will specifically perform the covenant, be it express or implied, by making the lands retained by the grantor exonerate those he has sold or settled.

On this basis, marshalling is merely a procedural device,[92] whose efficacy is dependent upon a petition being made by the junior creditor to the court, and the grant of an order directing the senior creditor to enforce its security in a particular

---

[88] This would seem to have been conceded by Derham. Derham acknowledges that: '. . . the principle that the doctrine of marshalling is not enforced against third parties should be read with caution. For example, marshalling has the effect of reducing the assets of the mortgagor and so obviously it affects creditors of the mortgagor' ((1991) 107 LQR 126, 133n22) and 'Regardless, though of the label used to describe the right in question, there is authority for the view that the fundamental rule of marshalling applies, that the double claimant retains an unfettered right to realise his security in such a manner and order as he thinks fit' (133).

[89] See generally Meagher, Gummow & Lehane, *Equity Doctrines and Remedies*, Chapter 20; Spry, *The Principles of Equitable Remedies*, Chapter 3.

[90] *Ker v Ker* (1869) 4 IR Eq 15; *In re Lysaght's Estate* [1903] 1 IR 235, 244. C f *In re Chute's Estate* [1914] 1 IR 180, 187 where it was doubted whether the doctrine of marshalling could be said to rest on specific performance. However, beyond a comment to the effect that the view of marshalling in *Ker v Ker* was unsatisfactory, the court did not pursue the issue further.

[91] (1869) 4 IR Eq 15, 30–31. It is, however, difficult to see how this statement can be employed to argue that marshalling is based upon specific performance. The comments of the court are more appropriate to the doctrine of exoneration (q v the Australian case of *Chase Corp (Australia) Pty Ltd v North Sydney Brick and Tile Co Ltd* (1994) 12 ACLC 997, 1,012 which supports the classification of exoneration as a form of specific performance).

[92] Hanbury & Waldock, *The Law of Mortgages*, 181.

manner or substituting the senior security for the security held by the junior creditor.[93]

Marshalling is not a form of specific performance

5.50 The claim that marshalling is a form of specific performance is not persuasive under English (and Australian, Canadian and New Zealand) law.

5.51 The remedy of specific performance comprises two distinct remedies.[94] The first remedy is confined to executory contracts; it concerns the issuance of an order by a court compelling the execution *in specie* of a contract, which requires some further act to be done, so that the contracting parties may be placed in the position contemplated by them. The second remedy is far wider in scope; it encompasses all those situations in which equity will order the performance of existing contractual obligations because of the inadequacy of available common law remedies (e g damages).

5.52 To argue therefore that marshalling is a form of specific performance, is to hold that marshalling gives effect to the contractual obligations owed by one party to another. Marshalling, however, in no way depends upon a contractual or other relationship between the junior creditor and the senior creditor.

5.53 Further, the notion that marshalling is a form of specific performance is inconsistent with the manner in which equity gives effect to a junior creditor's marshalling rights.[95] Specific performance depends for its efficacy upon two contingencies: the petitioning of the court by the party seeking performance of a contractual obligation and the making of an order for the performance of that obligation. Marshalling, as noted above, is not only independent of such a contractual relationship but is automatically given effect to by equity. Once a senior creditor recoups its debt out of the asset, that is subject to both the senior and junior securities, the junior creditor will be entitled, without any further act on its part (or that of the senior creditor or debtor), to the benefit of the senior security over other assets of the debtor.[96]

---

[93] The issue as to whether marshalling coerces the senior creditor or only intervenes following the enforcement of the senior security remains undecided in Ireland: see further paragraph 3.26.

[94] *Blackett v Bates* (1865) LR 1 Ch 117; *Wolverhampton and Walsall Railway Co v London and NW Railway Co* (1873) LR 16 Eq 433. See Meagher, Gummow & Lehane, *Equity Doctrines and Remedies*, paras 2002–2003; Spry, *The Principles of Equitable Remedies*, 51–56.

[95] This is equally the case with the version of marshalling depicted by the coercion theory. The coercion of the senior creditor is effected by way of a mandatory injunction, which is, however, distinct from specific performance: see further paragraph 2.27.

[96] See the Australian case of *Westpac Banking Corporation v Daydream Island Pty Limited* [1985] 2 Qd R 330, 332. See further paragraphs 7.03 and 7.04.

In this regard, it is relevant to note the following comments of Fullagar J. of the **5.54**
Supreme Court of Victoria, in *Deta Nominees Pty Ltd v Discount Plastic Products
Pty Ltd*:[97]

> Take the case of A and B, each of whom is owed a separate debt by X. A's debt is
> secured by charges over two funds in the hands of X, but B's debt is secured only over
> the first and larger of the 2 funds. Suppose that B chooses to go against the first fund,
> leaving not enough for B. B can thus in equity compel A to make available to B his
> security . . . to assist B in recovering B's debt from X. Equity is in effect saying to A:
> 'You have received a benefit, and B has suffered a corresponding detriment, by your
> having your debt paid out of a fund which was charged to you both, and without
> exercising your right of security for the debt over the second fund; you are therefore
> bound in conscience to B to allow him to use that security of yours in order to recoup
> himself, and equity will enforce that obligation against you as if you were bound by
> some contract, for valuable consideration, to perform the obligation pointed out by
> conscience.'

This statement may be taken as supporting the view that, for a junior creditor to
marshall the senior security, it would need to petition the court for a remedy akin
to specific performance, *viz.* the coercion of performance on the part of the senior
creditor. However, marshalling, *per* the version adopted by the court in the above
case, does not depend upon the senior creditor's acquiescence for its efficacy.
Accordingly, the better view is that the court was merely stating that a senior creditor, having recouped the senior debt, could not in conscience deny the junior
creditor access to the senior security.

Further confusion about marshalling and specific performance—the apparent marshalling rights of volunteers

It has also been asserted that marshalling cannot be a form of specific performance **5.55**
because marshalling is available to volunteers.[98] An examination of the relevant
authorities reveals that this assertion does not, in fact, relate to the ability of a
volunteer to marshall the senior security;[99] it concerns, instead, the ability of a

---

[97] [1979] VR 167, 192.

[98] Hanbury & Waldock, *The Law of Mortgages*, 181 (which was cited with approval in the
Australian case of *Sarge Pty Ltd v Cazihaven Homes Pty Ltd* (1994) 34 NSWLR 658, 665). See also
Hewitt, *White & Tudor's Leading Cases in Equity*, 49–50 and 51–52; *Halsbury's*, Vol 16 ('*Equity*'),
para 877 and Vol 32 ('*Mortgage*'), para 916; Meagher, Gummow & Lehane, *Equity Doctrines and
Remedies*, para 1128.

[99] The original junior creditor will, invariably, not be a volunteer by reason of having provided
the debtor with secured credit. Marshalling will, however, be available to a creditor for value whose
security is voluntary: *Aldridge v Forbes* (1839) 9 LJ Ch 37; see also Robbins, *A Treatise on the Law of
Mortgages, Pledges and Hypothecations*, 783; Hewitt, *White & Tudor's Leading Cases in Equity*, 51. It
should also be noted: (i) *Boazman v Johnston* (1830) 3 Sim 377 is arguably authority for the proposition that volunteers cannot marshall; see also Robbins, *A Treatise on the Law of Mortgages, Pledges
and Hypothecations*, 784; Ramsbotham, *Coote's Treatise on the Law of Mortgages*, 808; c f *Lomas v
Wright* (1833) 2 My & K 769 which suggests that a voluntary creditor (i e a volunteer who is entitled to damages as a result of a failure to convey) can marshall; see also Hewitt, *White & Tudor's*

volunteer to whom an asset, the subject of the grant of a security by the transferor to a senior creditor, has been transferred to: (i) throw the liability for the senior debt onto the transferor; and/or (ii) resist the marshalling claims of a junior creditor of the transferor.[100]

Leading Cases in Equity, 41; *Halsbury's*, Vol 16 ('*Equity*'), para 877n4; and (ii) it is questionable whether a junior creditor can assign the right to marshall (as distinct from the junior security) to a third party for value or dispose of it to a volunteer: see Meagher, Gummow & Lehane, *Equity Doctrines and Remedies*, para 1129.

[100] *Carter v Barnadiston* (1718) 1 P Wms 506; *Galton v Hancock* (1743) 2 Atk 428; *King v Jones* (1814) 5 Taunt 518; *Hughes v Williams* (1852) 3 Mac & G 683; *Anstey v Newman* (1870) 39 LJ Ch 769; *Dolphin v Aylward* (1870) LR 4 E & I 486; *Farrington v Forrestor* [1893] 2 Ch 461; *Re Repington* [1904] 1 Ch 811. Q v the Irish cases of *Hales v Cox* (1863) 32 Beav 118; *In re Lysaght's Estate* [1903] 1 IR 235 and the New Zealand case of *Re Stephenson* (1911) 30 NZLR 145. See also Watson, *A Practical Compendium of Equity*, 38; Bigelow, *Story's Commentaries on Equity Jurisprudence*, para 633 n(b); Robbins, *A Treatise on the Law of Mortgages, Pledges and Hypothecations*, 783–784; Beddoes, *A Concise Treatise on the Law of Mortgages*, 104–105; Webster, *Ashburner's Concise Treatise on Mortgages, Pledges and Liens*, 466–467; Ramsbotham, *Coote's Treatise on the Law of Mortgages*, 808 and 811. C f *Mallot v Wilson* [1903] 2 Ch 494 where this ability of a volunteer was described as marshalling. See further Chapter 11.

6

THE RATIONALE FOR MARSHALLING OF SECURITIES

Introduction   6.01

Natural Justice Basis of Marshalling

Introduction   6.02
Protecting the junior creditor's legitimate
  expectation   6.03
Position of the unsecured creditors   6.05

Marshalling and Theories of Security

Introduction   6.06
'Secured debt puzzle'   6.08

**Functional and Private Property-Based
  Theories of Security**

Functional theory of security:
  introduction   6.12
  retrospective effect of new priority rules   6.14
  fallacy of parity between secured and
    unsecured creditors   6.15
  conclusion   6.16
Private property-based theory of security   6.17

**Monitoring and Informational Theories
  of Security**

Monitoring theory of security:
  introduction   6.18

post-contractual debtor misbehaviour   6.19
monitoring only secured assets   6.21
failure to explain negative pledges and
  floating charges   6.23
Free-rider theory of security—variation on
  monitoring theory   6.25
Relational theory of security—second variation
  on monitoring theory   6.28
Monitoring theory of security—conclusion   6.29
Informational theory of security:
  introduction   6.30
  security as pre-contractual, cost-minimisation
    device   6.31
  conclusion   6.32

**Marshalling and Conventional Theory of
  Security**

Introduction   6.34
Conventional theory of security—policy goals
  of security   6.35
Marshalling and policy goals of security   6.37
Competing theories of marshalling and
  policy goals of security   6.40
Conventional theory of security supports
  post-realisation theory of marshalling   6.43

A. Introduction

The equitable doctrine of marshalling of securities is an anomalous doctrine in the **6.01** sense that it is not readily susceptible to classification. It is not a subrogation remedy or a new category of subrogation, notwithstanding that it employs subrogation, or an equivalent legal process, to achieve its objective of priority-preservation. It resists restitutionary analysis, even though, in the very act of preserving priority, it redresses the loss sustained by a junior creditor at the hands of a senior creditor. Nor can it be accounted for in terms of the related equitable doctrines of consolidation, contribution and specific performance.

Nonetheless, the right of a junior creditor to marshall is capable of being explained by the principles of natural justice and the policy goals which underpin the concept of security itself.

B. Natural Justice Basis of Marshalling of Securities

Introduction

6.02 Keaton & Sheridan in *Equity*[1] and Story in *Commentaries on Equity Jurisprudence*[2] both advance the view that the doctrine of marshalling is mandated by the principles of natural justice.[3]

Keaton & Sheridan provide the following rationale for marshalling:[4]

> One of the doctrines of equity designed to relieve against accidents, marshalling is a process by which a person's interest in property is adjusted so as not to be adversely affected by the irrelevant acts of another person interested in the same property.

Similarly, Story speaks of the rationale for marshalling as follows:[5]

---

[1] Keaton & Sheridan, *Equity*, 303.

[2] Bigelow, *Story's Commentaries on Equity Jurisprudence*, para 633.

[3] Additional support for the natural justice basis for marshalling can be found in: (i) Wylie, *Irish Land Law*, para 3.055, which states that the limitations on marshalling are all premised on the equitable maxim that 'He who seeks equity, must do equity'. Support for this view can be found in the Australian case of *Chase Corp (Australia) Pty Ltd v North Sydney Brick and Tile Co Ltd* (1994) 12 ACLC 997, 1,010–1,011 where Cohen J. of the Supreme Court of New South Wales stated '. . . the authorities generally treat the principle of marshalling as requiring the parties to act equitably and that the role of the court has been, where necessary, to enforce that equitable conduct', and in the American equity text, Pomeroy Jr., *Equity Jurisprudence*, para 396. See also McDonald, *Marshalling* (1996), para 1602; McDonald, *Marshalling* (1997), para 24. A similar rationale has been proposed for consolidation: *Chesworth v Hunt* (1880) 5 CPD 266; Tillard, *Wilshere's Principles of Equity*, 225–226; *Halsbury's*, Vol 32 ('*Mortgage*'), para 761; Tyler, *Fisher & Lightwood's Law of Mortgage*, 534n(b); (ii) *McColl's Wholesale Pty Ltd v State Bank of NSW* [1984] 3 NSWLR 365, 378 where Powell J. of the Supreme Court of New South Wales stated 'Subrogation in favour of a surety . . . rests upon the same principles as those which support the doctrine of marshalling of securities, that is, that equity considers it against conscience that a creditor should use securities to the prejudice of a surety'; and (iii) *Sarge Pty Ltd v Cazihaven Homes Pty Ltd* (1994) 34 NSWLR 658, 665 where Young J. of the Supreme Court of New South Wales considered that marshalling rested on the principle of conscience.

[4] Keaton & Sheridan, *Equity*, 303.

[5] Bigelow, *Story's Commentaries on Equity Jurisprudence*, para 633. Similarly, J J S Wharton, *The Law Lexicon* (4th ed 1867 Stevens & Sons), 594 states that marshalling (as depicted by the post-realisation theory) is derived from the maxim, *sic utere tuo ut non alienum laedas* (one must enjoy one's property in such a manner as does not cause injury to another). H Broom, *Legal Maxims* (10th ed 1939 Sweet & Maxwell), 238 cites a related maxim, *expedit republicae ne sua re quis male utatur* (it is for the interest of the State that a person should not use his own property improperly) as the basis of marshalling. A further maxim quoted as the basis of marshalling is: *nemo exalterius*

The reason is obvious . . . it is the only way by which [the junior creditor] can receive payment. And natural justice requires that one man should not be permitted, from wantonness, or caprice, or rashness, to do an injury to another. In short we may here apply the common civil maxim, '*Sic utere tuo ut non alienum laedas*'; and still more emphatically the Christian maxim, 'Do unto others as you would they should do unto you'.

Protecting the junior creditor's legitimate expectation

A junior creditor has, by virtue of its bargain with the debtor, a legitimate expec- **6.03** tation that the debt owed to it will be repaid. The law is concerned with ensuring that that expectation is not defeated without due cause. To that end, the law will insulate a junior creditor from the consequences of the repayment of the senior debt. The mere act of repayment of the senior debt will not, on its own, be permitted to prejudice the recovery of the junior debt.

Although both the coercion and post-realisation theories have as their objective **6.04** the preservation of the junior creditor's priority-ranking, the version of marshalling depicted by the latter theory achieves that objective in a manner more consistent with the principles of natural justice identified by Keaton & Sheridan and Story. It redresses any harm to the priority-ranking of the junior creditor's claim against the assets of the debtor, without raising the possibility of countervailing injustice to the senior creditor.

The post-realisation theory, which portrays marshalling as a redistributive device, protects the security held by the junior creditor without impinging upon the rights conferred upon the senior creditor by its security. It thus ensures that the junior creditor is treated in a just and fair manner by the senior creditor but, unlike the coercion theory, ensures that that is not at the expense of injustice to the senior creditor. Accordingly, to the extent that the assets of the debtor permit, the legitimate expectation of the senior creditor is not interfered with and that of the junior creditor is protected.

The position of the unsecured creditors

The substitution of the junior creditor to the senior security and the consequent **6.05** redistribution of the debtor's assets, following the intervention of marshalling, do not *unfairly* prejudice the debtor's unsecured creditors. Marshalling does not deprive the unsecured creditors of anything to which they were legitimately entitled, prior to the enforcement of the senior security.

---

detrimento fieri debet locupletior (a person having two funds to satisfy his demands shall not by his election disappoint a party who has only one fund): J Indermaur & C Thwaites, *A Manual of the Principles of Equity* (1913 Barker), 176. See further M Emamzadeh, *Marshaling in Bankruptcy: Questioning the Recent Expansions to the Common Debtor Requirement* (1992) 30 Duquesne L Rev 309, 311; MacDougall, *Marshalling and the Personal Property Security Acts: Doing Unto Others . . .*, 92.

All the doctrine of marshalling accomplishes is the restoration of the junior creditor to the position it would have been in had the senior creditor enforced its security in a way that would have left the junior security intact. The unsecured creditors are therefore in no worse a position as a result of the junior creditor being permitted to marshall the senior security.[6]

Although the principles of natural justice explain why marshalling does not unfairly prejudice unsecured creditors, they call into question the denial of marshalling rights to unsecured creditors (who also have a legitimate expectation of repayment).[7]

C. Marshalling of Securities and Theories of Security

Introduction

6.06 While the principles of natural justice provide a coherent rationale for the operation of the doctrine of marshalling, those principles are unable to satisfactorily explain why the right to marshall should be confined to secured creditors.[8] The rationale of marshalling advanced by Keaton & Sheridan and Story is as applicable to unsecured creditors of a debtor as it is to a junior creditor of the debtor; all creditors, including unsecured creditors, have a legitimate expectation that the debts owed to them should be discharged.

6.07 The particular issue of why the law recognises such a device as security, and accords preferential treatment to the holders of security, has been the subject of considerable debate in the United States of America. This ontological inquiry into security (or the 'secured debt puzzle'[9] as it has been labelled) is relevant to the doc-

---

[6] C f Mosman, *The Proper Application of Marshaling on Behalf of Unsecured Creditors*, 654–655, who asserts that not only does the doctrine of marshalling prejudice the unsecured creditors but it also reduces the residue available to the debtor. See also F W Kroger & P Acconcia, *Marshaling: A Fourth Act Sequel to Commercial Tragedies?* (1989) 57 UMKCLR 205, 206–207, where it is stated that marshalling should be barred if it prejudices the unsecured creditors. Both these views are based on a misconception of the doctrine of marshalling. Marshalling rearranges the order of distribution of the debtor's assets subsequent to the enforcement of the senior security. In no way does it affect the total quantum of assets available for distribution to the creditors of the debtor. Mosman appears to suggest that the destruction of the *mesne* security is, in some way, accompanied by the extinction of the underlying personal claim for repayment of the junior debt; a claim which is apparently revived by the doctrine of marshalling. Moreover, by its very nature, marshalling always transfers funds from the unsecured creditors to the holder of *mesne* security. The opinions expressed by Mosman and Kroger & Acconcia have as their logical conclusion the abolition of the doctrine of marshalling: see further Chapter 10.

[7] See Chapter 10 for a discussion of the redundancy of marshalling by unsecured creditors.

[8] Unsecured creditors do not have standing to marshall: see further Chapter 10. See also Chapter 9 for a consideration of the apparent requirement of proprietary securities.

[9] The inquiry into the 'secured debt puzzle' has spawned a veritable genre, of which the more important articles are: T H Jackson & A T Kronman, *Secured Financing and Priorities Amongst Creditors* (1979) 88 Yale LJ 1143; J J White, *Public Policy Toward Bankruptcy: Me First and Other*

trine of marshalling of securities: a theory that is capable of explaining the phenomenon of security will be equally capable of explaining why marshalling differentiates between secured and unsecured creditors and affords protection to only members of the former class.

The 'secured debt puzzle'

The majority of theories that have been proposed to explain security have sought **6.08** to do so by justifying security as economically efficient.[10] These efficiency-based theories of security may be segregated into three broad categories:

Priority Rules (1980) 11 BJE 550; A Schwartz, *Security Interests and Bankruptcy Priorities: A Review of Current Theories* (1981) 10 J Legal Stud 1; S Levmore, *Monitors and Freeriders in Commercial and Corporate Settings* (1982) 92 Yale LJ 49; J J White, *Efficiency Justifications for Personal Property Security* (1984) 37 Vand L Rev 473; A Schwartz, *The Continuing Puzzle of Secured Debt* (1984) 37 Vand L Rev 1051; R M Stulz & H Johnson, *An Analysis of Secured Credit* (1985) 14 J Fin Econ 501; H Kripke, *Law and Economics: Measuring the Economic Efficiency of Commercial Law in a Vacuum of Fact* (1985) 133 U Pa L Rev 929; T H Jackson & A Schwartz, *Vacuum of Fact or Vacuous Theory: A Reply to Professor Kripke* (1985) 133 U Pa L Rev 987; F H Buckley, *The Bankruptcy Priority Puzzle* (1986) 72 Va L Rev 1393; R E Scott, *A Relational Theory of Secured Financing* (1986) 86 Colum L Rev 901; D G Carlson, *Rationality, Accident and Priority Under Article 9 of the UCC* (1986) 71 Minn L Rev 207; P Cellupcia, *The Insecure Place of Secured Debt in Corporate Finance Theory* (1988) 11 Harv J of Law & Public Pol 487; P M Shupack, *Solving the Puzzle of Secured Transactions* (1989) 41 Rutgers L Rev 1067; A Schwartz, *A Theory of Loan Priorities* (1989) 18 J Leg Stud 209; D G Baird & T H Jackson, *Bargaining After the Fall and the Contours of the Absolute Priority Rule* (1989) 55 U Chi L Rev 738; J W Bowers, *Whither What Hits the Fan?: Murphy's Law, Bankruptcy Theory, and the Elementary Economics of Loss Distribution* (1991) 26 Ga L Rev 27; J Drukarczyk, *Secured Debt Bankruptcy and the Creditor's Bargain Model* (1991) 11 Int Rev of Law & Eco 203; R C Picker, *Security Interests, Misbehaviour and Common Pools* (1992) 59 U Chi L Rev 645; G G Triantis, *Secured Debt under Conditions of Imperfect Information* (1992) 21 J Leg Stud 225; G G Triantis, *A Theory of the Regulation of Debtor-in-Possession Financing* (1993) 46 Vand L Rev 901; R L Barnes, *The Efficiency Justification for Secured Transactions: Foxes with Soxes and Other Fanciful Stuff* (1993) 42 Kan L Rev 13; B E Adler, *An Equity-Agency Solution to the Bankruptcy-Priority Puzzle* (1993) 22 J Leg Stud 73; L M LoPucki, *The Unsecured Creditor's Bargain* (1994) 80 Va L Rev 1887; S L Harris & C W Mooney Jr, *A Property-Based Theory of Security Interests: Taking Debtors' Choices Seriously* (1994) 80 Va L Rev 2021; H Kanda & S Levmore, *Explaining Creditor Priorities* (1994) 80 Va L Rev 2103; G G Triantis, *A Free-Cash-Flow Theory of Secured Debt and Creditor Priorities* (1994) 80 Va L Rev 2155; D G Carlson, *On the Efficiency of Secured Lending* (1994) 80 Va L Rev 2179; L A Bebchuk and J M Fried, *The Uneasy Case for the Priority of Secured Claims in Bankruptcy* (1996) 105 Yale LJ 857; R J Mann, *The First Shall be Last: A Contextual Argument for Abandoning Temporal Rules of Lien Priority* (1996) 75 Texas L Rev 11; B E Adler, *A Theory of Corporate Insolvency* (1997) 72 NYU L Rev 343; R J Mann, *Explaining the Pattern of Secured Debt* (1997) 110 Harv L Rev 625; L A Bebchuk & J M Fried, *The Uneasy Case for the Priority of Secured Claims in Bankruptcy: Further Thoughts and a Reply to Critics* (1997) 82 Cornell L Rev 1279; S L Harris & C W Mooney Jr, *Measuring the Social Costs and Benefits and Identifying the Victims of Subordinating Security Interests in Bankruptcy* (1997) 82 Cornell L Rev 1349; D G Baird, *The Importance of Priority* (1997) 82 Cornell L Rev 1420; R E Scott, *The Truth About Secured Financing* (1997) 82 Cornell L Rev 1436; S L Schwarcz, *The Easy Case for the Priority of Secured Claims in Bankruptcy* (1997) 47 Duke LJ 425. For an overview of this area, see J S Ziegel, *What can the Economic Analysis of Law teach Commercial and Consumer Law Scholars?* in R Cranston & R M Goode (eds), *Commercial and Consumer Law: National and International Dimensions* (1993 Oxford), 267–268 and B E Adler, *Secured Credit Contracts* in P Newman (ed), *New Palgrave Dictionary of Economics and the Law* (1998 Macmillan).

[10]   c f the functional and private property-based theories discussed below.

(i) the monitoring theory of security;

(ii) the informational theory of security; and

(iii) the conventional theory of security.

6.09   Although these theories are by no means in agreement as to the specific grounds for the existence of security, they have all predicated their analysis upon the *Kaldor-Hicks criteria* of efficiency.[11]

6.10   The model of security presented by the Kaldor-Hicks criteria is utilitarian in nature. It is considered that creditors will only take security over the assets of a debtor when it is efficient for them to do so; for the taking of security to be efficient, the aggregate utility gains of the creditor and debtor must exceed their aggregate disutility.[12] This presupposes that:[13]

(1) A debtor, who grants security to a creditor to secure the repayment of a debt, must be able to borrow either:

(A) an amount equivalent to what it would otherwise have been able to borrow (i e on an unsecured basis) but at a lower interest rate; or

(B) an amount greater than what it would otherwise have been able to borrow, at the same interest rate; and

(2) The transaction costs to the debtor of secured debt exceeds that of unsecured debt.[14] In (1), the extra cost of secured debt (e g establishment, commitment and drawdown fees, legal fees, registration fees, etc) is offset by the lower price or greater quantum of credit.

6.11   However, not all theories of security have sought to justify (or criticise) security on economic grounds. Before considering the monitoring, informational and

---

[11] The two seminal articles as regards the Kaldor-Hicks criteria are N Kaldor, *Welfare Propositions of Economics and Interpersonal Comparisons of Utility* (1939) 49 Econ J 549 and J R Hicks, *The Foundations of Welfare Economics* (1939) 49 Econ J 696. See also Shupack, *Solving the Puzzle of Secured Transactions*, 1070–1071n10; G G Triantis, *Debt Financing, Corporate Decision Making and Security Design* (1996) 26 CBLJ 93. The best introduction to efficiency analysis is R Posner, *The Economic Analysis of Law* (3rd ed 1986 Little, Brown & Co). C f Barnes, *The Efficiency Justification for Secured Transactions: Foxes with Soxes and Other Fanciful Stuff*, where it is argued that creating greater efficiency for only one of the participants in the loan transaction does not justify secured credit.

[12] There is one qualification, which should be taken into account. While the efficiency analysis of security may provide important insights into why the law treats security in a preferential manner, the motivations of secured creditors, on which the following theories are based, may be incapable of being reduced to a formula based solely on utility or efficiency maximisation. R M Goode, *Security: A Pragmatic Conceptualist's Approach* (1989) 15 Mon ULR 361, 363 makes the important point: '[t]he concept of transfer of ownership or other real rights as between transferor and transferee is not merely a logical one, it possesses independent justification . . . it responds to the psychological need of human beings to translate personal rights of acquisition into ownership. So long as their rights rest purely in contract they feel uneasy, they lack control and the ability to take pride in being an owner'. This psychological or irrational element is perhaps impossible to quantify.

[13] Jackson & Kronman, *Secured Financing and Priorities Amongst Creditors*, 1147–1149.

[14] It should be noted that this may not necessarily be the case for certain forms of unsecured financing, the best example of which is the negative pledge: q v n33.

conventional theories of security, mention should be made of the two major alternative approaches to security: the 'functional' and 'private property-based' theories of security.[15]

D. Functional and Private Property-Based Theories of Security

The functional theory of security—introduction

The functional theory of security is a misnomer for what is effectively an attack on **6.12** the very phenomenon of secured debt; the thrust of this theory is that security subsidises secured creditors (and debtors) at the expense of involuntary unsecured creditors and 'uninformed' or unsophisticated unsecured creditors.[16]

The functional theory argues that the preferential status accorded to secured creditors by the law is predicated on two false assumptions, *viz*: (i) unsecured creditors voluntarily subordinate their claims against a debtor to those of secured creditors; and (ii) unsecured creditors do so in the knowledge that their risk of non-payment is increased by the presence of security.[17]

---

[15] Other recent investigations into the secured debt puzzle have focused on the scope of the priority enjoyed by secured creditors rather than the actual rationale for security. For instance, Bebchuk and Fried, *The Uneasy Case for the Priority of Secured Claims in Bankruptcy* argue that according secured claims full priority over unsecured claims generates efficiency costs (for example, by permitting inefficient projects to be financed or allowing a borrower to continue in business when it should be liquidated). Bebchuk & Fried argue that these inefficiencies could be reduced by according only partial priority to secured claims. Much of this argument is restated in Bebchuk & Fried, *The Uneasy Case for the Priority of Secured Claims in Bankruptcy: Further Thoughts and a Reply to Critics*, 1293–1295, 1304–1309 and 1314–1321. The proposed partial priority options include permitting secured creditors priority only over those unsecured creditors who have consented to have their claims subordinated to those of the secured creditors. For this and other options, see Bebchuk & Fried, *The Uneasy Case for the Priority of Secured Claims in Bankruptcy*, 868–870 and 905–911 and Bebchuk & Fried, *The Uneasy Case for the Priority of Secured Claims in Bankruptcy: Further Thoughts and a Reply to Critics*, 1323–1328. Similarly, Mann, *The First Shall be Last: A Contextual Argument for Abandoning Temporal Rules of Lien Priority* argues that the 'first-in-time' rule of priority (under which the holder of a registered security interest is accorded priority over unregistered security interests and subsequent registered security interests) should be narrowed. Again, Mann does not dispute that secured creditors should enjoy priority but argues that the scope of a particular priority rule should be curtailed. For a defence of this priority rule, see Triantis, *A Theory of the Regulation of Debtor-in-Possession Financing*; Kanda & Levmore, *Explaining Creditor Priorities*; Triantis, *A Free-Cash-Flow Theory of Secured Debt and Creditor Priorities* where the first-in-time rule is argued for on the grounds that it prevents or impedes a debtor from subsequently raising debt in a manner which harms the first-in-time creditor by reducing the likelihood that that creditor will be repaid.

[16] The chief proponent of this analysis is LoPucki, *The Unsecured Creditor's Bargain*. See also S Knippenberg, *The Unsecured Creditor's Bargain: An Essay in Reply, Reprisal or Support?* (1994) 80 Va L Rev 1967 and Ponoroff & Knippenberg, *The Immovable Object Versus the Irresistible Force: Rethinking the Relationship between Secured Credit and Bankruptcy Policy*, 2258–2260 for an overview of LoPucki's arguments.

[17] LoPucki, *The Unsecured Creditor's Bargain*, 1892–1902 and 1916–1920.

6.13 Consequently, the priority rules should be radically overhauled to subordinate the claims of secured creditors to the claims of involuntary unsecured creditors[18] (in particular, the claims of victims of a tortfeasor debtor[19]). In the case of unsophisticated unsecured creditors, the preference accorded to secured creditors should be subjected to a 'reasonable person' test i e the claims of these unsecured creditors should be subordinated to a secured creditor's claims only to the extent that a reasonable person would have expected.[20]

The functional theory of security—retrospective effect of new priority rules

6.14 The functional theory of security is subject to a number of serious flaws. First, its proposals would, if implemented, operate retrospectively.[21] A prospective lender is able to obtain notice of legal proceedings currently on foot against a borrower by undertaking a search of the appropriate court registries. The lender would then be able to factor the impact of such proceedings into its decision to advance credit to the debtor. An equivalent process is not, of course, available to such a lender in respect of future legal proceedings. Nonetheless, under the functional theory of security, a secured creditor could, for instance, find itself subordinated to the claims of a victim of a tort subsequently committed by the debtor. Secured creditors may be forced to respond by taking a more active role in supervising the affairs of their debtors, which may lead to the imposition of shadow director liabilities and, consequently, an increase in the cost of credit to the debtor.

The functional theory of security—the fallacy of parity between secured and unsecured creditors

6.15 The subordination of security interests to the claims of unsecured creditors will not necessarily lead to parity between involuntary unsecured creditors (such as tort victims) and unsophisticated unsecured creditors (such as trade creditors), on the one hand, and banks and financial institutions, on the other. The latter are likely to look for substitutes for security that, whilst effective to protect their inter-

---

[18] LoPucki, *The Unsecured Creditor's Bargain*, 1907–1916. Another solution posited by LoPucki is for a regime of secured creditor insurance (akin to the mortgage insurance routinely taken by home mortgage lenders): LoPucki, *The Unsecured Creditor's Bargain*, 1906–1907.

[19] LoPucki focuses on tort victims but his comments are equally applicable to all involuntary unsecured creditors.

[20] LoPucki, *The Unsecured Creditor's Bargain*, 1947–1948. Support for this may also be found in Bebchuk & Fried, *The Uneasy Case for the Priority of Secured Claims in Bankruptcy*, 868–870 and Bebchuk & Fried, *The Uneasy Case for the Priority of Secured Claims in Bankruptcy: Further Thoughts and a Reply to Critics*, 1327–1328.

[21] S Block-Lieb, *The Unsecured Creditor's Bargain: A Reply* (1994) 80 Va L Rev 1989, 2003–2005.

ests, are likely to be less economically efficient than security and thus more costly to the debtor.[22]

The functional theory of security—conclusion

The functional theory of security is merely an exposition of the circumstances in   **6.16** which security should not confer priority, and does not concern itself with the more fundamental issue of why security exists.[23] Its flaws aside, it is of little utility in explaining why marshalling distinguishes between secured and unsecured creditors.

The private property-based theory of security

The private property-based theory of security argues that the law should facilitate   **6.17** the issuance of secured debt for two broad reasons.[24] First, the grant of security is often indistinguishable in its economic incidents from sales and the repayment of debts, something which the law freely permits. Secondly, a debtor, in granting security, is merely alienating its property and the law, again, accords (or should accord) persons the liberty to freely alienate property.

Again, this theory of security does not advance the investigation into the secured debt puzzle or the nature of marshalling of securities—the freedom to contract or alienate property may permit the creation of security but it is no explanation of why security exists.[25]

---

[22] J J White, *Work and Play in Revising Article 9* (1994) 80 Va L Rev 2089, 2101. The efficiency gains from adopting the reforms advocated by the functional theory of security are therefore doubtful. It may well be the case that the costs and inefficiencies of emasculating security would outweigh the costs and inefficiencies associated with the present system of priority for security. In addition, Schwarcz, *The Easy Case for the Priority of Secured Claims in Bankruptcy*, 484–485 notes that these proposed reforms may create incentives for sophisticated creditors to restructure financing transactions as sales transactions in a manner that mimics some of the economic incidents of security with a concomitant increase in transaction costs.

[23] The functional theory of security for all its preoccupation with the protection of involuntary creditors and voluntary but unsophisticated creditors fails to consider (i) the related issue of why the former category of creditors should have to share *pari passu* with the general body of unsecured creditors (who may include voluntary sophisticated creditors) and (ii) that voluntary unsecured creditors may protect themselves just as well by employing devices which while not securities enjoy the economic effects of securities (for example, retention of title clauses, flawed asset and set-off arrangements). The abolition or reduction of the priority-ranking of secured creditors is not necessarily the panacea envisaged by LoPucki and others. See further Baird, *The Importance of Priority*, 1424–1425 and 1429.

[24] Harris & Mooney, *A Property-Based Theory of Security Interests: Taking Debtors' Choices Seriously*, 2047–2066. See also Ponoroff & Knippenberg, *The Immovable Object Versus the Irresistible Force: Rethinking the Relationship between Secured Credit and Bankruptcy Policy*, 2260–2263 for an overview of Harris & Mooney's arguments.

[25] In addition, the property-based theory is flawed in its simplicity: the sales and debt repayment transactions quoted by Harris & Mooney typically affect only the parties to the transaction and, as such, are highly likely to make the parties to them better off – in efficiency terms – and no one else worse off. Security, in contrast, because of its priority-ranking always has an impact on third parties. See further A Schwartz, *Taking the Analysis of Security Seriously* (1994) 80 Va L Rev 2073, 2076–2086.

E. Monitoring and Informational Theories of Security

The monitoring theory of security—introduction

6.18 The monitoring theory of security argues that creditors take security for supervisory purposes, so as to minimise the risk of 'debtor misbehaviour'.[26]

This theory assumes that the price a creditor charges for a loan is a function of the creditor's assessment of the risk that the debtor will not repay the loan. However, having made the loan at a rate of interest based upon this perception, the creditor has no guarantee that the debtor will not act in a manner which undermines the assumptions on which the loan has been made.

The monitoring theory of security—post-contractual debtor misbehaviour

6.19 The monitoring theory asserts that the debtor has an incentive to 'misbehave' i e to act in a manner which increases the risk of loss to the creditor. Such conduct has the effect of reducing the real cost of the loan to the debtor, for, in acting in this way, the debtor is effectively able to obtain credit to finance a higher risk activity, at a cost reflecting the lower level of risk envisaged by the creditor at the time the loan was made.[27]

6.20 Faced with the risk of debtor misbehaviour, a creditor who is intending to advance credit to a debtor has two options: (i) it can simply demand a higher interest rate as compensation for bearing a greater risk; or (ii) it can attempt to reduce the risk of loss, consequent on such misbehaviour, by monitoring the conduct of the debtor after the loan has been made.

This second option may be implemented by requiring the debtor to provide the creditor with regular financial statements and similar information. However, the cost of this monitoring is likely to be passed onto the debtor, to the extent that the creditor perceives that the risk of misbehaviour cannot be eliminated by the mere fact of monitoring.[28]

The monitoring theory of security—monitoring only secured assets

6.21 Not all creditors are equally adept at monitoring the post-contractual conduct of a debtor. Nonetheless, the distinction drawn by the law between secured and

---

[26] See F Oditah, *Legal Aspects of Receivables Financing* (1990 Sweet & Maxwell), 15–17; Jackson & Kronman, *Secured Financing and Priorities Amongst Creditors*; Shupack, *Solving the Puzzle of Secured Transactions*, 1074–1079; M Gronow, *Secured Creditors of Insolvent Companies: Do They Get Too Good a Deal?* (1993) 1 ILJ 169, 172–177 and 179.

[27] Jackson & Kronman, *Secured Financing and Priorities Amongst Creditors*, 1149–1150.

[28] Jackson & Kronman, *Secured Financing and Priorities Amongst Creditors*, 1151–1152.

unsecured debts allows monitoring to be undertaken in an efficient manner.[29] A creditor with relatively high monitoring costs is likely to choose to lower those costs by taking security over certain assets of the debtor.

The reduction in costs is due to the fact that the level of monitoring required to ensure that the assets, over which security has been granted, remain undiminished in value is significantly less than that required for the supervision of the entire business of the debtor.[30] The creditor thus needs to supervise only what the debtor does with the assets that are subject to its security and is able to disregard the conduct of the debtor with respect to the remainder of its assets.

As a consequence, the creditor is able to charge a lower rate of interest for the secured debt. While the mere presence of security will not altogether eliminate the risk of debtor misbehaviour, so long as the assets, which secure the repayment of the debt, are kept intact the creditor will be insulated from the consequences of such misbehaviour.[31] Similarly, those creditors, who are relatively more 'talented' at monitoring will tend to remain unsecured. **6.22**

The monitoring theory of security—failure to explain negative pledges and floating charges

Although the monitoring theory is able to explain the presence of restrictive clauses and financial reporting covenants in standard form security documentation, it is unable to proffer any explanation for two important phenomena.[32] **6.23**

First, the monitoring theory fails to account for the fact that the documentation for an unsecured loan is likely to include far more onerous monitoring provisions than will usually be the case with a secured loan. The prime example of this is negative pledge lending.[33] Secondly, the security of first choice for most lenders is the floating charge, which invariably encompasses the entire business of the debtor. In both cases, it is difficult to see how security would assist a creditor in more efficiently monitoring the conduct of a debtor. **6.24**

---

[29] Drukarczyk, *Secured Debt Bankruptcy and the Creditor's Bargain Model*, 208.

[30] See further F H Easterbrook & D R Fischel, *Limited Liability and the Corporation* (1985) 52 U Chi L Rev 89, 99–101: secured credit may be a way of reducing the monitoring costs of both creditors and shareholders of a company, as creditors may possess a comparative advantage over shareholders in monitoring particular management decisions and the presence of security permits creditors to monitor the state of the security rather than the state of the whole enterprise.

[31] Jackson & Kronman, *Secured Financing and Priorities Amongst Creditors*, 1153.

[32] Oditah, *Legal Aspects of Receivables Financing*, 16–17.

[33] See D E Allan, *Negative Pledge Lending – Dead or Alive* in Cranston & Goode (eds), *Commercial and Consumer Law: National and International Dimensions*; J K Maxton, *Negative Pledges and Equitable Principles* [1993] JBL 458.

The free-rider theory of security—a variation on the monitoring theory

6.25   The free-rider theory of security is a variation on the monitoring theory. It contends that security permits creditors to avoid free-rider problems.[34]

Where there are several creditors, who share a common debtor, and at least one of them monitors the conduct of the debtor, it will be in the interest of the other creditors to free-ride on the efforts of that creditor. The free-riders are therefore able to benefit, at no cost to themselves, from that creditor's greater efficiency at monitoring.

6.26   Accordingly, the creation of security over the assets of the debtor is in the interests of both the monitoring creditor and the debtor.[35] The creditor is compensated for its monitoring efforts by being given priority over the other creditors of the debtor. The debtor, on the other hand, minimises its costs: the creditor doing the monitoring is likely, on the basis of this theory, to be the most efficient at monitoring (and consequently have the lowest monitoring costs); the grant of security, as compensation for the cost of monitoring, is therefore likely to ensure that those costs are not passed on to the debtor in the form of a higher interest rate.[36]

6.27   However, as is the case with the monitoring theory, the free-rider theory is only of limited utility. The free-rider theory fails to account for the converse of the situation on which it is based. As a general rule, the wider the security taken by the creditor, the greater will be its task of supervision. In the (likely) event that such a creditor obtains a floating charge, it will, in effect, be monitoring the entire business of the debtor. The mere fact that it holds security is unlikely, in this instance, to eliminate free-rider problems.

The relational theory of security—a second variation on the monitoring theory

6.28   A second variation on the monitoring theory is the relational theory of security, which contends that a creditor takes security because it and the debtor are effectively in a joint venture, and the security gives it leverage over the debtor.[37]

This theory is, however, limited to the circumstances of project finance, on which it was modelled. In conventional debt finance, in contrast to project finance, the creditor and debtor are not joint venturers. Such a relationship is likely to be the

---

[34] See Oditah, *Legal Aspects of Receivables Financing*, 16; Levmore, *Monitors and Freeriders in Commercial and Corporate Settings*; Shupack, *Solving the Puzzle of Secured Transactions*, 1077–1078.

[35] Levmore, *Monitors and Freeriders in Commercial and Corporate Settings*, 53–59 and 68.

[36] Because of that creditor's relative efficiency at monitoring, any increase in the interest rate is likely to be minimal.

[37] See Oditah, *Legal Aspects of Receivables Financing*, 16; Scott, *A Relational Theory of Secured Financing*; Shupack, *Solving the Puzzle of Secured Transactions*, 1080–1082.

last thing such a creditor would intend, given the much increased scope of its duties, as a joint venturer, to the debtor.[38] The relational theory is therefore unable to provide an explanation for the existence of security in general.

The monitoring theory of security—conclusion

The monitoring theory (and, in particular, the free-rider and relational variations **6.29** on this theory) is unable to provide a cogent rationale for the existence of security and why the law prefers creditors who hold security to those who do not. Consequently, it does not aid in an understanding of why marshalling evinces a similar preference for secured creditors.

The informational theory of security—introduction

In contrast to the monitoring theory (and the free-rider and relational theories), **6.30** the informational theory argues that the rationale for security may be ascertained from an examination of the pre-contractual position of the secured creditor *vis-à-vis* the debtor.[39]

The informational theory considers that it is difficult for a creditor to adequately assess the risk associated with making a loan to a debtor prior to the actual advance of the funds. The cost to the creditor of gathering the necessary information about the debtor will therefore be passed onto the debtor in the form of a higher price for the loan, namely a higher interest rate.

The informational theory of security—security as a pre-contractual cost-minimisation device

To minimise or eliminate this additional cost of obtaining credit, a debtor will **6.31** elect to grant security over its assets to a creditor. Not only does the grant of security benefit the debtor, in that it is able to obtain credit at a lower cost, but the provision of security is, of itself, evidence to the creditor that the debtor is a better credit-risk than other debtors, who are unable to provide matching security.[40]

---

[38] See D B Robertson, *The Lender-Borrower Relationship and the Subordination of Lenders' Claims – Part II* (1991) 2 JBFLP 147, 154–156; D B Robertson, *The Lender-Borrower Relationship and the Subordination of Lenders' Claims – Part III* (1991) 2 JBFLP 219, 220–221, 222–223 and 224.

[39] See Oditah, *Legal Aspects of Receivables Financing*, 15; Schwartz, *Security Interests and Bankruptcy Priorities: A Review of Current Theories*; White, *Efficiency Justifications for Personal Property Security*; Schwartz, *The Continuing Puzzle of Secured Debt*; Jackson & Schwartz, *Vacuum of Fact or Vacuous Theory: A Reply to Professor Kripke*; Schwartz, *A Theory of Loan Priorities*; Shupack, *Solving the Puzzle of Secured Transactions*, 1075–1077 and 1078–1079.

[40] White, *Efficiency Justifications for Personal Property Security*, 477 differs from Jackson and Schwartz on this last point. He argues that security does not function as a signal to the creditor of the debtor's better creditworthiness *vis-à-vis* other debtors.

The informational theory thus holds that the motivation for security is derived from the fact that secured creditors are able to charge lower interest rates while unsecured creditors must charge higher rates. The grant of security reduces the risk of loss to the secured creditor and, consequently, leads to a lower cost of credit to the debtor.

The informational theory of security—conclusion

6.32 The informational theory provides only an imperfect picture of security. It does not take into account the fact that a creditor is only likely to prefer the information proffered by the debtor about its own creditworthiness to information obtainable by the creditor from other sources where taking security is significantly cheaper than the latter alternative.

6.33 In addition, there is no guarantee that the provision of security by a debtor constitutes an accurate indication of its creditworthiness; the asset over which the security is granted may, unbeknownst to the creditor, be subject to a retention of title claim.

Again, the informational theory is of limited assistance in explaining the nature of marshalling.

F. Marshalling of Securities and the Conventional Theory of Security

Introduction

6.34 The conventional theory of theory rejects both the pre-contractual costs of assembling information and the post-contractual costs of supervision as the basis for security.[41]

The chief criticism of the monitoring and informational theories is that they 'operate in a world of academic reasoning reminiscent of the cloister and unfounded in any discussion of the factual world of commerce'.[42] It is, instead, asserted by the conventional theory that the law recognises security as a matter of public policy: the law recognises security because security makes credit more accessible.

---

[41] See Oditah, *Legal Aspects of Receivables Financing*, 17–18; Kripke, *Law and Economics: Measuring the Economic Efficiency of Commercial Law in a Vacuum of Fact*; Shupack, *Solving the Puzzle of Secured Transactions*, 1080.

[42] Kripke, *Law and Economics: Measuring the Economic Efficiency of Commercial Law in a Vacuum of Fact*, 931.

The conventional theory of security—the policy goals of security

In the absence of such a device as security, which gives secured creditors preferential rights of recourse to the assets of a debtor, many debtors would be either unable to obtain credit on an unsecured basis or would only be able to do so at relatively high rates of interest, because of the risk of loss to the creditor. **6.35**

Notwithstanding this, debtors usually possess assets which, if made available to a particular creditor ahead of other creditors, would allow them to obtain credit at more affordable rates from that creditor. Security reduces the risk of loss to creditors and, as a consequence, they are willing to lend funds at lower rates of interest.

Under the conventional theory, the law accords secured creditors priority over unsecured creditors because it recognises that security allows debtors access to credit which might not otherwise have been made available. Of the various theories put forward to explain the phenomenon of security, this is the simplest and most convincing. Security may well perform other functions, but principally it makes credit more readily available, and that justifies the privileged position of secured creditors. **6.36**

Marshalling of securities and the policy goals of security

As a corollary of the conventional theory of security, the law will do all it can to protect security and preserve the preferential status of secured claims, for by so doing it protects the supply of credit to debtors. It is this policy imperative which underpins the doctrine of marshalling of securities. **6.37**

The law takes the position that the secured claim of a junior creditor should not arbitrarily be placed in jeopardy merely because a senior creditor has, out of the various assets available to it, chosen to enforce its security against the very asset over which the junior creditor holds security.[43] Should that occur, marshalling will redress the loss sustained by the junior creditor by redistributing the assets of the debtor from the debtor's unsecured creditors to the junior creditor. **6.38**

Denying a junior creditor the right to marshall is thus likely to undermine the very purpose for which security has been taken. It will avail the junior creditor nothing to have obtained security if the efficacy of that security is a matter ultimately determinable by the senior creditor. The junior creditor will merely have provided credit to the debtor (on conditions more favourable than those on which it would have provided unsecured credit) in exchange for a preferential claim against the debtor's assets, the status of which claim can be eroded by the senior creditor. **6.39**

---

[43] q v the discussion above of the natural justice basis of marshalling.

The doctrine of marshalling obviates the need for junior creditors to pass on to debtors, in the form of higher interest rates for junior debt, the risk that their security will be jeopardised by the particular manner in which the senior security is enforced. By doing so, marshalling, in a manner consistent with the conventional theory of security, protects the supply of junior debt.

Competing theories of marshalling and the policy goals of security

6.40 According to the post-realisation theory of marshalling, the priority-position of junior creditors is preserved at the expense of a debtor's unsecured creditors and not the senior creditor.[44] By permitting a junior creditor to exchange its eroded security over one asset for the senior creditor's intact security over another, marshalling effectively 'redistributes' the loss sustained by the junior creditor to the unsecured creditors of the debtor.

Redistribution is not, however, the sole means by which the doctrine of marshalling can be given effect to.[45] The same objective—the preservation of the junior creditor's priority-ranking—can equally be achieved, under the coercion theory of marshalling, by directing the senior creditor to recover its debt out of the debtor's assets over which only it holds security.

6.41 A senior creditor will not necessarily know when its security rights are liable to be circumscribed by a lower-ranking creditor's marshalling rights. Generally, a senior creditor will possess little control over the creation of subsequent secured debt that does not purport to rank equally with, or above the senior debt.[46] The senior creditor, accordingly, will take its security subject to the risk that the debtor, by the subsequent creation of security that is both subordinate to, and narrower in scope than, the senior security will be able to diminish the senior creditor's security rights.

This restriction on a senior creditor's security rights, and the uncertainty as to when such a restriction may be imposed, render senior security less attractive to prospective lenders of senior debt. As a consequence, such lenders are likely to increase the interest rates for senior debt to compensate for the risk that they may be hindered, by the doctrine of marshalling, in the recovery of their debts.

6.42 Although the coercion theory of marshalling protects junior security and the supply of junior debt, it impacts adversely on the supply of senior debt. This runs

---

[44] See further paragraphs 4.10–4.12 and 4.51–4.54.

[45] As *per* the version of marshalling depicted by the original coercion theory of marshalling and the modern hybrid model of marshalling: see further Chapter 3.

[46] The restrictive clauses, which are found in security agreements, usually prohibit only the creation of subsequent securities that are designed to rank equally with or out-rank the senior creditor's security. Marshalling, however, is only available to junior creditors whose security ranks below the senior security.

counter to the policy basis of security advanced by the conventional theory of security. If the ultimate purpose of marshalling is the protection of the supply of junior debt, it is inconsistent with that purpose to give effect to marshalling in a manner that adversely affects the supply of senior debt.

The conventional theory of security supports the post-realisation theory of marshalling

Marshalling, as depicted by the post-realisation theory, does not protect the supply of junior debt at the expense of the supply of senior debt. This is because the priority-ranking of the junior security is not preserved at the expense of the senior security and, as such, senior security is not rendered less attractive to intending lenders. **6.43**

There is thus no need for senior creditors to factor the cost of a successful marshalling claim into the price charged for senior debt. The post-realisation theory of marshalling—in contrast to the coercion theory—therefore protects the supply of junior debt without causing a countervailing increase in the cost of senior debt (with a consequent negative impact upon the availability of senior debt). Accordingly, if security exists because it renders credit more accessible, marshalling cannot act in a coercive manner but must, instead, act in a manner that does not impinge on the rights of prior-ranking secured creditors, *viz.* as portrayed by the post-realisation theory. **6.44**

PART IV

PRE-REQUISITES OF MARSHALLING OF SECURITIES

7

MARSHALLING OF SECURITIES AND THE COMMON DEBTOR RULE

Introduction	7.01	Status of Assets Subject to Senior and	
Requirements of common debtor rule	7.02	Junior Securities	
Must the assets be subject to control of		Introduction	7.21
court?	7.03	Status of debtor's assets	7.22
Common debtor rule – other jurisdictions	7.05	Scope of junior security	7.24
Requirement of a Common Debtor		**Requirement of Equal Rights of Recourse**	
Introduction	7.06	**to Assets Subject to Senior Security**	
Several senior securities	7.08	Introduction	7.25
Common debtor and single senior debt	7.09	Senior creditor must not be bound to	
Requirement of common debtor and		have recourse to particular asset	7.27
redistributive nature of marshalling	7.17	Equal rights of recourse and efficacy of	
		marshalling	7.28
		Nature of senior security	7.32

A. Introduction

A junior creditor cannot marshall the security held by a senior creditor, simply **7.01** because its security ranks behind, and is narrower than, the senior security. Should the senior creditor enforce its security to the detriment of the junior creditor, the junior creditor will as a general rule only be entitled to marshall the senior creditor if the requirements of the 'common debtor rule' have been satisfied.[1]

Requirements of the common debtor rule

The common debtor rule prescribes the following four requirements, all of which **7.02** must be met in order for the junior creditor to be able to marshall the senior security, following the enforcement of the senior security against the asset over which the junior creditor holds security:[2]

---

[1] The apparent requirement of proprietary securities is examined in Chapter 9, and the recognised exceptions to the common debtor rule are considered in Chapter 8.

[2] Until the enforcement of the senior security, the junior creditor's right to marshall is a mere potentiality. See generally Hewitt, *White & Tudor's Leading Cases in Equity*, 41; Hanbury &

(1) the debts, whose repayment is secured by the securities held by the senior and junior creditors, must be owed to both creditors by the same or 'common' debtor;[3]

(2) the assets, over which both the senior and junior creditors hold security, must be owned by the common debtor;[4]

(3) the assets in (2) must be in existence at the time the junior creditor asserts its right to marshal the senior security;[5] and

(4) the senior creditor must have equal rights of recourse against each of the assets in (2).[6]

Must the assets be subject to the control of the court?

7.03 The following statement of Brett M.R. in *Webb v Smith* arguably imposes a further requirement upon the right to marshal, *viz.* the assets mentioned in (2) above must be subject to the control of the court:[7]

> [marshalling] applies when the funds are in Court and, when the Court can exercise a jurisdiction over them.

7.04 The better view, however, is that there is no such requirement. It is only where a court is petitioned to grant an order permitting a junior creditor to marshal the senior security, that the court will require the assets in question to be either in

---

Waldock, *The Law of Mortgages*, 177–178; *Halsbury's*, Vol 16 ('*Equity*'), para 877; Keaton & Sheridan, *Equity*, 304–305; Cousins, *The Law of Mortgages*, 436. It is irrelevant, to the availability of marshalling, whether or not the junior creditor had notice of the senior security: *Baldwin v Belcher* (1842) 3 Dr & War 173; *Hughes v Williams* (1852) 3 Mac & G 683; *Tidd v Lister* (1853) 3 De G M & G 857; *Heyman v Dubois* (1871) LR 13 Eq 158; *Ex parte Alston* (1868) 4 Ch App 168. See also Roberts, *Principles of Equity*, 177; Robbins, *A Treatise on the Law of Mortgages, Pledges and Hypothecations*, 782; Smith, *A Practical Exposition of the Principles of Equity*, 613–614; Ramsbotham, *Coote's Treatise on the Law of Mortgages*, 807. C f *Lanoy v Duke & Duchess of Athol* (1742) 2 Atk 444, 446; *Flint v Howard* [1893] 2 Ch 54, 72 and Thomson, *A Compendium of Modern Equity*, 420 where it is suggested that for the junior creditor to be able to marshal it must not have had notice of the senior security.

³ *Ex parte Kendall* (1811) 17 Ves 514; *Mason v Bogg* (1827) 2 My & Cr 443; *Thorpe v Jackson* (1837) 2 Y & C Ex 553; *Wallis v Woodyear* (1855) 2 Jur (NS) 179; *Dolphin v Aylward* (1870) LR 4 E & I 486; *Kendall v Hamilton* (1879) 4 App Cas 504; *Re Townley* [1922] 1 Ch 154.

⁴ *Ex parte Kendall* (1811) 17 Ves 514; *Thorpe v Jackson* (1837) 2 Y & C Ex 553; *Dolphin v Aylward* (1870) LR 4 E & I 486; *Kendall v Hamilton* (1879) 4 App Cas 504; *The 'Chioggia'* [1898] P 1. See also Hewitt, *White & Tudor's Leading Cases in Equity*, 41. C f *The 'Edward Oliver'* (1867) LR 1 A & E 379.

⁵ *Re The State Fire Insurance Company* (1863) 32 LJ Ch 300; *Re Professional Life Assurance Co* (1867) LR 3 Eq 668; *Re International Life Assurance Society* (1876) 2 Ch D 476. See also Hewitt, *White & Tudor's Leading Cases in Equity*, 41.

⁶ *The 'Priscilla'* (1859) Lush 1; *Dolphin v Aylward* (1870) LR 4 E & I 486; *Webb v Smith* (1885) 30 Ch D 192; *Re Townley* [1922] 1 Ch 154. C f *The 'Mary Ann'* (1845) 9 Jur 94; *The 'Edward Oliver'* (1867) LR 1 A & E 379.

⁷ (1885) 30 Ch D 192, 199. Q v *The 'Arab'* (1859) 5 Jur (NS) 417; Sykes & Walker, *The Law of Securities*, 184; McDonald, *Marshalling* (1996), para 1609; McDonald, *Marshalling* (1997), para 31.

court or held by a party to the proceedings.[8] Petitioning the court for an order to marshall is not an essential element of marshalling; a court may, in the absence of a specific petition, exercise its discretion to apply the doctrine of marshalling.[9] Nor is marshalling dependent upon a court order; a junior creditor's marshalling rights arise immediately upon a senior creditor recouping the senior debt out of the asset subject to the junior security.[10]

Common debtor rule—other jurisdictions

The common debtor rule, in the terms described above, is recognised in Australia,[11] Canada,[12] Ireland[13] and New Zealand.[14]   **7.05**

---

[8] *Lawrance v Galsworthy* (1857) 3 Jur (NS) 1049; *Ernst Brothers Co v Canadian Permanent Mortgage Corp* (1920) 57 DLR 500; *Commonwealth Trading Bank v Colonial Mutual Life Assurance Society Ltd* (1970) 26 FLR 338, 346. See also Meagher, Gummow & Lehane, *Equity Doctrines and Remedies*, para 1117; MacDougall, *Marshalling and the Personal Property Security Acts: Doing Unto Others . . .*, 114.

[9] *Gibbs v Ougier* (1806) 12 Ves 413; *Oamington Pty Ltd v Commissioner of Land Tax* (unrep 24 Nov 1997, Sup Ct of NSW). See also Beddoes, *A Concise Treatise on the Law of Mortgages*, 106; Hewitt, *White & Tudor's Leading Cases in Equity*, 41; *Halsbury's*, Vol 32 ('*Mortgage*'), para 915; Tyler, *Fisher & Lightwood's Law of Mortgage*, 533; Tyler & Oughton, *Fisher & Lightwood's Law of Mortgage: Supplement to Tenth Edition*, A94.

[10] *Westpac Banking Corporation v Daydream Island Pty Limited* [1985] 2 Qd R 330, 332.

[11] *In re W* (1901) 11 QLJ 108; *Re Holland* (1928) 28 SR (NSW) 369; *In re Wertheim* [1934] VLR 321; *Miles v Official Receiver* (1963) 109 CLR 501; *Re O'Leary* (1985) 61 ALR 674; *Finance Corporation of Australia Ltd v Bentley* (1991) 5 BPR 97412; *Australia and New Zealand Banking Group Ltd v Bendigo Building Society* (unrep 5 Oct 1992, Sup Ct of Vic); *Sarge Pty Ltd v Cazihaven Homes Pty Ltd* (1994) 34 NSWLR 658. See also Francis & Thomas, *Mortgages and Securities*, 370; Sykes & Walker, *The Law of Securities*, 183; Meagher, Gummow & Lehane, *Equity Doctrines and Remedies*, paras 1108–1109 and 1111–1113; O'Donovan & Phillips, *The Modern Contract of Guarantee*, 679–680; McDonald, *Marshalling* (1996), paras 1605–1607; McDonald, *Marshalling* (1997), paras 26, 28 and 29.

[12] *Re Hamilton* (1895) 10 Man R 573; *Dominion Lumber v Gelfand* (1916) 34 WLR 624; *Re Steacy* (1917) 39 OLR 548; *Ernst Brothers Co v Canadian Permanent Mortgage Corp* (1920) 57 DLR 500; *Royal Bank of Canada v Izen* [1921] 2 WWR 929; *G Ruso Construction Ltd v Laviola* (1976) 27 Chitty's LJ 136; *Bank of British Columbia v Tamavi Holdings Ltd* (1978) 29 CBR (NS) 111; *Invesco Holdings Ltd v Kendall* [1979] 4 WWR 571; *Farm Credit Corp v McLane* (1983) 30 Sask R 320; *Montmor Investments Ltd v Montreal Trust Co* (1984) 53 BCLR 275; *Canada v French* (unrep 15 Jan 1985, Ont HCJ); *Brown v Canadian Imperial Bank of Commerce* (1985) 50 OR (2d) 420; *Westcoast Savings Credit Union v P E DeVito & Associates Ltd* (unrep 24 Feb 1986, BCSC); *Toronto-Dominion Bank v Whitaker* (unrep 4 July 1986, Alta QB); *Canadian Trustco Mortgage Co v Wenngatz Construction & Holdings Ltd* (1986) 1 BCLR (2d) 302; *Montreal Trust Co v Montreal Trust Co of Canada* (1988) 24 BCLR (2d) 238; *Fiatallis North America Inc v Pigott Construction Ltd* (1992) 3 PPSAC (2d) 30; *Ontario Inc v Allison* (1995) CBR (3d) 144; *Granville Savings & Mortgage Corp v Bob B Co Holdings Ltd* (1996) 24 BCLR (3d) 348; *Richmond Savings Credit Union v Zilbershats* (1997) 35 BCLR (3d) 136; *Re Allison* (1998) 38 OR (3d) 337.

[13] *Lombard & Ulster Banking Limited v Murray & Murray* [1987] ILRM 522.

[14] *Re Taylor* [1934] NZLR 117; *Re Manawatu Transport Ltd* (1984) 2 NZCLC 99,084. See also Hinde, McMorland, Campbell & Grinlinton, *Butterworths Land Law in New Zealand*, para 8.148; Schumacher, *Marshalling*, 90–91; Cleaver, *Marshalling*, 284–285.

B. Requirement of a Common Debtor

Introduction

7.06 The common debtor rule stipulates that the senior and junior creditors must be secured creditors of a common debtor and, further, that the assets, subject to the senior and junior securities, must be the property of the common debtor (*per* requirements (1) and (2) of the common debtor rule).

7.07 This can be illustrated by the following example where the senior creditor holds senior security over assets A and B, and the junior creditor holds security over asset B. Under the common debtor rule assets A and B must be owned by the same party, and the senior and junior securities must secure the repayment of debts owed to the senior and junior creditors respectively by that party.

Several senior securities

7.08 It is not necessary that the security rights which the senior creditor enjoys in respect of assets A and B must be derived from a single security.[15] Thus, the fact that repayment of the senior debt is secured by a senior security (SC1) over asset A and a separate senior security (SC2) over asset B will not, of itself, prevent the junior creditor from marshalling the senior security. However, SC1 must confer upon the senior creditor rights of recourse to asset A that are equal to the rights of recourse conferred by SC2 against asset B.[16]

A common debtor and a single senior debt

7.09 Cousins, in *The Law of Mortgages*, states:[17]

> It is *not* necessary for the securities to have been created at the same time, or to have been given in respect of the *same debt*. But if two securities are given, one in respect of each of *two debts*, marshalling is not permitted unless the debts are those of the same person (emphasis added).

7.10 Marshalling, as noted above, is not limited to circumstances where the repayment of the senior debt is secured by a single security. However, in contrast to the view expressed by Cousins, the doctrine of marshalling is only available where the

---

[15] *Gwynne v Edwards* (1825) 2 Russ 289n. See also Robbins, *A Treatise on the Law of Mortgages, Pledges and Hypothecations*, 783; Ramsbotham, *Coote's Treatise on the Law of Mortgages*, 808; *Halsbury's*, Vol 32 ('*Mortgage*'), para 915; Cousins, *The Law of Mortgages*, 436.

[16] The junior creditor's ability to marshall SC2 will not be affected by the fact that repayment of the senior debt is secured by a third senior security (SC3) over a further asset (C) of the debtor, and that the rights of recourse conferred upon the senior creditor by SC3 against C are not equal to the senior creditor's rights of recourse against A or B. The junior creditor would, however, be unable to marshall SC3.

[17] Cousins, *The Law of Mortgages*, 436.

senior security or securities (as the case may be) secures the repayment of a single senior debt owed to the senior creditor by the common debtor.[18]

Moreover, permitting a junior creditor to marshall the senior security, in the circumstances envisaged by Cousins, is inconsistent with the manner in which marshalling acts to preserve the priority-ranking of the junior security.[19] This may be demonstrated by reference to the situation in which the debtor owes distinct debts, D1 and D2, to the senior creditor and the repayment of D1 is secured by senior security over asset A and the repayment of D2 is secured by senior security over asset B. **7.11**

According to Cousins the junior creditor would be entitled to marshall the senior security over asset B where the senior creditor has enforced its security against asset A, and recouped senior debt D1 out of that asset (and the residue of asset A is insufficient to discharge the junior debt). The senior creditor, however, is still owed senior debt D2, whose repayment is secured over asset B. The junior creditor, whose security does not extend to asset B, cannot use marshalling to displace a security which does.[20] The repayment of the junior debt out of asset B will therefore be postponed until the discharge of senior debt D2.[21] Only then would the junior creditor be entitled to step into the position of the senior creditor as regards the senior security over asset B. **7.12**

Permitting the junior creditor to marshall the senior security over asset B has, however, the effect of subjecting that asset to a secured claim in excess of that originally bargained for by the debtor. Instead of being subject to a secured claim for the amount of D2, asset B is now subject to a secured claim of potentially twice the amount of D2. This latter claim comprises senior debt D2 and an amount equal to the least of: **7.13**

---

[18] q v n15. This is also the position in Australia: Meagher, Gummow & Lehane, *Equity Doctrines and Remedies*, para 1110; New Zealand: Cleaver, *Marshalling*, 284 and Canada: MacDougall, *Marshalling and the Personal Property Security Acts: Doing Unto Others . . .*, 102. There is a single exception to the requirement of a single senior debt, derived from *Barnes v Racster* (1842) 1 Y & C Ch Cas 401: this requirement will be taken to have been satisfied where one of the two or more assets subject to the senior security secures the repayment of one debt and the other asset (or assets) secures repayment of that debt and another debt.

[19] See Schumacher, *Marshalling*, 90–91.

[20] See further Chapter 11.

[21] It may be thought that the senior security should be rateably apportioned between the senior and junior creditors. This situation is, however, very different from the circumstances in which marshalling by apportionment will apply where, typically, the senior creditor holds security over assets A and B, and the junior creditor holds a second-ranking security over asset A while a third party holds a second-ranking security over asset B. In those circumstances the junior creditor enjoys rights equivalent to those possessed by the third party. Here, the junior creditor is competing with the senior creditor for the benefit of asset B, and the senior creditor clearly outranks the competing interest of the junior creditor. See further Chapter 11.

(i) the amount required to discharge the junior debt (or the balance thereof);[22]

(ii) senior debt D2;[23] and

(iii) the residual value of asset B.[24]

7.14 This would not be the case if assets A and B were subject to a single senior debt (say D*), rather than two distinct debts D1 and D2 respectively. In this situation, the maximum potential exposure of asset B to the secured claim of the senior creditor plus the marshalling claim of the junior creditor would be an amount equal to D* (if the senior creditor recouped D* out of asset A, asset B would only be susceptible to a marshalling claim of up to D*).

7.15 Instead, asset B has been made subject to both a secured claim of D2 and a marshalling claim potentially equivalent to D2. The doctrine of marshalling does not create security where none previously existed; it only permits access to existing securities. Yet this is what Cousins's formulation of marshalling entails. Asset B, because marshalling has been permitted in circumstances where the senior security secures the repayment of two distinct debts, has been subjected to two secured claims: the senior creditor's original secured claim and an additional secured claim conferred on the junior creditor by the doctrine of marshalling.

7.16 Cousins's expansion of marshalling to circumstances where the senior security secures the repayment of multiple senior debts (albeit all owed to the senior creditor by the same debtor) cannot be sustained. Marshalling accomplishes its objective of priority-preservation by permitting the junior creditor to substitute an existing, intact senior security, over some other asset of the debtor, for its own eroded security, not by creating an entirely new security for the benefit of the junior creditor. Accordingly, the senior security over the asset encumbered by the junior security and the senior security sought to be marshalled must secure the repayment of a single senior debt.[25]

The requirement of a common debtor and the redistributive nature of marshalling

7.17 The requirement of a common debtor is consistent with the redistributive nature of marshalling. This may be illustrated by the following example where, *ceteris*

---

[22] Marshalling only acts to preserve the original priority-ranking of the junior creditor's claim against the debtor; it does not improve the position of the junior creditor by conferring upon it the benefit of a secured claim greater than its original secured claim against asset A; q v Goff & Jones, *The Law of Restitution*, 596.

[23] The senior security over asset B, that the junior creditor is seeking to marshal, secures the repayment of a maximum amount equal to D2.

[24] The senior security cannot confer upon the junior creditor a secured claim against the debtor in excess of the residue of asset B, following the discharge of senior debt D2.

[25] q v n18. C f *Halsbury's*, Vol 20 ('*Guarantee and Indemnity*'), para 226 where it is considered that a surety is entitled to marshall where a senior creditor enjoys a right of consolidation in respect of several senior securities for distinct senior debts: see further paragraphs 8.29–8.32.

paribus, an asset (A) that is subject to the senior and junior securities is owned by the debtor, and an asset (B) that is subject to only the senior security is owned by a third party.[26] If the senior creditor recoups the senior debt by enforcing its security over asset A, then according to the common debtor rule the junior creditor will not be able to marshall the senior security over asset B.[27]

The purpose of the above requirement is to prevent a junior creditor from marshalling the senior security to the detriment of parties, who are strangers to the debtor-creditor relationship between the debtor and the junior creditor.[28]

In the above scenario, the senior security sought to be marshalled encumbers asset **7.18** B, which is owned by a party other than the debtor. Moreover, liability for repayment of the junior debt rests solely with the debtor, and has not been assumed by the third party who owns asset B. Permitting the junior creditor to gain access to the senior security over asset B would have the effect of imposing the burden of the junior debt (or such part of that debt as asset B is able to meet) upon a party who was not originally liable for that debt.[29]

Further, marshalling, if applied, would permit the junior creditor to substitute a **7.19** first-ranking security over asset B for its eroded second-ranking security over asset A. This would not lead to the restoration of the junior creditor to its original priority-position against the debtor but would, instead, confer upon the junior

---

[26] The right to marshall is, as a general rule, not capable of being successfully asserted in respect of assets which from the outset are owned by different parties. However, the fact that assets have subsequently become vested in different parties will not, of itself, prevent the junior creditor from marshalling the senior security: see further paragraph 8.20 and Chapter 11. The junior creditor's ability to marshall will persist in the face of a transfer or disposition of the asset encumbered by only the senior security to a third party who takes that asset subject to the senior security, where the transfer or disposition post-dates the creation of the junior security: see paragraphs 11.50–11.54. The principles underlying this persistence of marshalling rights (as enunciated in paragraphs 11.57–11.60) cannot, however, be extended to situations where the above asset was held by the third party from the outset or acquired from the common debtor prior to the creation of the junior security: see paragraphs 11.47–11.48.

[27] c f the converse situation (i e the junior creditor is a creditor of the third party and holds security over the third party's asset) where the surety exception to the common debtor rule will permit marshalling *provided that*, as between the debtor and the third party, the debtor is required to bear the burden of the senior debt: *Halsbury's*, Vol 16 (*'Equity'*), para 877; Meagher, Gummow & Lehane, *Equity Doctrines and Remedies*, para 1109. See further Chapter 8. The application of the surety exception can, however, be ousted by arrangements between the debtor, senior creditor and third party that infringe requirement (4) of the common debtor rule (for instance where the third party has agreed to make B available only on the basis that A is insufficient to discharge the senior debt).

[28] See Cavanagh, *The Law of Money Securities*, 550–551; Meagher, Gummow & Lehane, *Equity Doctrines and Remedies*, para 1108. See also Cousins, *The Law of Mortgages*, 436 where it is considered that marshalling would be available where two distinct secured debts are owed by the debtor to the senior creditor but not where one of the debts is owed by the debtor and the other by a third party (c f the exception discussed in n18).

[29] This is also likely to prejudice the position of other creditors of the third party and, consequently, have negative consequences for the supply of credit to parties (such as the third party) who have provided collateral security for the repayment of senior debt.

creditor the benefit of a secured claim against a party, in respect of which it did not previously enjoy such a claim. Thus, marshalling, were it to grant the junior creditor the benefit of the senior security over asset B, would not be acting to preserve the secured status of the junior creditor *qua* the debtor; rather it would have effectively created a new security, where none previously existed, in favour of the junior creditor over an asset of a stranger.[30]

7.20 Nor can it be said that, by granting the junior creditor access to the security held by the senior creditor over B, the doctrine of marshalling is effecting a redistribution of the debtor's assets amongst its remaining creditors. Allowing the junior creditor to marshall the senior security over an asset owned by a party who is not indebted to the junior creditor is thus incompatible with the redistributive nature of marshalling.

C. Status of Assets Subject to Senior and Junior Securities

Introduction

7.21 The assets, over which the senior and junior creditors hold security, must be in existence when the junior creditor seeks to marshall the senior security (*per* requirement (3) of the common debtor rule).[31]

Status of the debtor's assets

7.22 The above requirement is straightforward. First, the doctrine of marshalling applies following the enforcement by the senior creditor of the senior security against an asset over which the junior creditor also holds security. Obviously, there must be an asset in existence (and to which the senior security has attached), against which the senior creditor can enforce its security.

7.23 Secondly, the asset, subject to the senior security sought to be marshalled, must also be in existence. There must be something against which the junior creditor

---

[30] The third party by making asset B available to the senior creditor as security for repayment of the senior debt will be presumed to be a surety of the senior debt: *Re Conley* [1938] 2 All ER 127. This is irrespective of whether the third party is personally liable for the senior debt: O'Donovan & Phillips, *The Modern Contract of Guarantee*, 9–10. Where the senior debt is discharged by the senior creditor enforcing its security over asset A, the third party will be released from liability for the senior debt: O'Donovan & Phillips, *The Modern Contract of Guarantee*, 299–300 and 312–314; McGuinness, *The Law of Guarantee*, paras 6.75–6.76. The release of the senior security over asset B means that marshalling would only be able to grant the junior creditor access to that asset by effectively creating a fresh security for the junior creditor's benefit.

[31] q v n5. This is also the position in Australia: Gummow, *Marshalling and Protected Assets*, 121; New Zealand: Cleaver, *Marshalling*, 283; and Canada: MacDougall, *Marshalling and the Personal Property Security Acts: Doing Unto Others . . .*, 101.

can assert the senior creditor's security rights; otherwise the ability to substitute the senior security for its own would avail the junior creditor nothing.

Scope of the junior security

The junior security must be narrower in scope than the senior security. If the **7.24** senior creditor holds senior security over assets A and B, the junior creditor will be unable to marshal the senior security if it also holds security over those assets.[32] However, the mere fact that the junior creditor holds security over more than one asset will not of itself disqualify the junior creditor from marshalling the senior security. If the senior creditor holds security over assets A, B and C, and the junior creditor holds security over assets A and B, the junior creditor will still be able to marshal the senior security over asset C.[33]

D. Requirement of Equal Rights of Recourse to Assets Subject to Senior Security

Introduction

The senior creditor must have 'equal rights of recourse'[34] to (i) the asset subject to **7.25** both the senior and junior securities (asset A in the above scenario) and (ii) the asset subject to the senior security, that the junior creditor is seeking to marshal (asset B) (*per* requirement (4) of the common debtor rule).[35]

---

[32] See the Canadian cases of *Montmor Investments Ltd v Montreal Trust Co* (1984) 53 BCLR 275; *Farm Credit Corp v McLane* (1983) 30 Sask R 320; *Toronto-Dominion Bank v Whitaker* (unrep 4 July 1986, Alta QB).

[33] See the Canadian case of *Canadian Trustco Mortgage Co v Wenngatz Construction & Holdings Ltd* (1986) 1 BCLR (2d) 302.

[34] This requirement of 'equal rights' is sometimes taken to refer to the securities held by the senior and junior creditors respectively: e g MacDougall, *Marshalling and the Personal Property Security Acts: Doing Unto Others . . .*, 109 where it is stated: 'Having equal rights, therefore, appears to mean that the two creditors should have interests of the same nature though of different priority . . . Being of the same nature does not mean the claimants necessarily have to have the same status'. The inappropriateness of this usage is pointed out by Meagher, Gummow & Lehane, *Equity Doctrines and Remedies*, para 1119: the rights of the senior and junior creditors cannot be 'equal' because, as regards the doubly-secured asset, the senior creditor's security is obviously superior to that of the junior creditor. In addition, there is no requirement that the senior and junior creditors must hold securities of the same type or nature although *Webb v Smith* (1885) 30 Ch D 192 purportedly restricts marshalling to securities of a proprietary nature: see further Chapter 9.

[35] q v n6. See also Robbins, *A Treatise on the Law of Mortgages, Pledges and Hypothecations*, 788; Webster, *Ashburner's Concise Treatise on Mortgages, Pledges and Liens*, 465; Hewitt, *White & Tudor's Leading Cases in Equity*, 58; Ramsbotham, *Coote's Treatise on the Law of Mortgages*, 812; Derham, *Set-Off*, 593–594. This is also the position in Australia: *Re Holland* (1928) 28 SR (NSW) 369; *Miles v Official Receiver* (1963) 109 CLR 501; Meagher, Gummow & Lehane, *Equity Doctrines and Remedies*, para 1111; Gummow, *Marshalling and Protected Assets*, 121; and New Zealand: Cleaver, *Marshalling*, 283.

7.26   The leading authority for this particular requirement is *Webb v Smith*, where Brett M.R. stated:[36]

> I cannot think that the doctrine of marshalling applies where there are different funds as to which *different* rights exist (emphasis added);

Lindley L.J. further stated that marshalling would be denied where:[37]

> there were not two funds to which the [senior creditor] could resort, that is, two funds standing upon an *equal* footing (emphasis added).

Senior creditor must not be bound to have recourse to a particular asset

7.27   The junior creditor will be unable to marshall the senior security if the senior creditor is bound, under the terms of an agreement or arrangement with the debtor, to look to asset A or asset B in preference to the other.[38]

From the junior creditor's perspective, such an agreement or arrangement will generally only be relevant where the senior creditor is bound to have recourse to asset A first.[39] In these circumstances, the senior creditor will only be entitled to enforce the senior security against asset B if the proceeds of realisation of asset A are insufficient to discharge the senior debt. Should the proceeds of asset A prove insufficient, the junior creditor will find that not only has its security been rendered worthless but, because of requirement (4) of the common debtor rule, it will be unable to recover its secured status by marshalling the senior security over asset B.[40]

---

[36]   (1885) 30 Ch D 192, 199.

[37]   Ibid, 202.

[38]   See the Australian cases of *Re Holland* (1928) 28 SR (NSW) 369 and *Miles v Official Receiver* (1963) 109 CLR 501. See further Meagher, Gummow & Lehane, *Equity Doctrines and Remedies*, para 1111; Tyler, Young & Croft, *Fisher & Lightwood's Law of Mortgage*, para 30.8. This is also the position in New Zealand: Schumacher, *Marshalling*, 91. Meagher, Gummow & Lehane, *Equity Doctrines and Remedies*, para 1111 argues that requirement (4) also mandates equal treatment of the proceeds of realisation: if the senior creditor is bound to apply the proceeds of realisation of A to discharge its security over B, the doctrine of marshalling will not apply. This is equivalent to a stipulation that the senior creditor must look to A first and will only be entitled to have recourse to B if the proceeds of A are inadequate to discharge the senior debt.

[39]   c f Sykes & Walker, *The Law of Securities*, 183 where it is stated: 'To permit the marshalling principle to operate the creditor must have a genuine option to resort to one property or the other; the creditor must *not be bound to resort to the property over which he or she has the sole security*' (emphasis added). However, the right to marshall will generally be irrelevant where the senior creditor is bound to look first to the asset encumbered by only the senior security. Moreover, the above statement may be contrasted with the equivalent passage from E I Sykes, *The Law of Securities* (4th ed 1986 Law Book Company), 177 where it was stated: 'To permit the marshalling principle the creditor taking steps to get his debt paid must have a genuine option to resort to one property or the other; he must not be bound to resort to the property over which he has the *two securities*' (emphasis added).

[40]   See Keaton & Sheridan, *Equity*, 304–305; Meagher, Gummow & Lehane, *Equity Doctrines and Remedies*, para 1112.

Equal rights of recourse and the efficacy of marshalling

The common debtor rule, in effect, requires the security rights enjoyed by the senior creditor over asset A to be interchangeable with its security rights over asset B, i e the rights possessed by the senior creditor over the first asset must be equivalent to its rights in respect of the other. **7.28**

The notion of 'equal rights of recourse' means equality of access, i e the senior creditor is not constrained in its election as to which of the various assets encumbered by the senior security should be employed in discharging the senior debt.[41] Once the election has been made and the senior security enforced, the asset in question should be capable of being employed to its fullest extent to discharge the senior debt. **7.29**

Thus, if the senior creditor enforces its security against asset A and discharges its debt out of the proceeds of asset A, there must be some security which the junior creditor can exchange for its own; failing that, the doctrine of marshalling will be unable to restore the junior creditor's claim against the debtor to its original priority-ranking. **7.30**

The doctrine of marshalling will be unable to rectify the loss of priority suffered by the junior creditor, where the senior creditor possesses unequal rights of recourse to the assets subject to the senior security. The absence of equal rights of recourse will, as noted above, usually only be of concern to the junior creditor where the senior creditor is bound to recover its debt out of asset A first.

In that situation, the senior creditor's rights of recourse against asset B will be subject to a contingency, *viz.* that the proceeds derived from the enforcement of the senior security against asset A are insufficient to discharge the senior debt. Should the senior creditor—as it is bound to—recover the entire amount of the senior debt out of asset A that contingency will never eventuate. There will therefore be nothing to which the junior creditor can be substituted, *qua* asset B, to make good the loss sustained by it as a result of the senior creditor recovering its debt out of asset A.[42] **7.31**

Thus, if the senior creditor does not have the freedom to choose which of the assets, subject to the senior security, should be utilised to discharge the senior debt, the junior creditor will be unable to marshall the senior security.

---

[41] See O'Donovan & Phillips, *The Modern Contract of Guarantee*, 679n702.

[42] It is uncertain whether marshalling would be permitted if the contingency has been satisfied at the time the junior creditor seeks to marshall the senior security (i e the proceeds of A are insufficient to discharge the senior debt).

Nature of the senior security

7.32   *Webb v Smith*[43] has been taken as establishing the rule that the doctrine of marshalling is applicable to only *proprietary securities* i e the securities held by the
senior and junior creditors must confer upon them proprietary interests in the
various assets that encumbered by those securities. This issue forms the subject of
Chapter 9.

7.33   However, it suffices to note here that the doctrine of marshalling will not be
excluded merely because the senior creditor holds a non-proprietary security over
either or both of assets A and B. Where the senior creditor holds different types of
security for the senior debt, the fact that the rights conferred by those securities are
not identical is not relevant provided that the senior creditor enjoys equal rights of
access to the encumbered assets.

---

[43] (1885) 30 Ch D 192.

8

EXCEPTIONS TO THE COMMON DEBTOR RULE

Introduction	**8.01**	New Zealand Loan etc. v Loach:	
Surety Exception to Common Debtor Rule		facts	8.37
		judgment	8.38
Introduction	8.05	Re Manawatu Transport Ltd	8.42
Debtor must be obligated to third party	8.07	Narrow scope of surety exception under	
Limitation of junior creditor's marshalling		New Zealand law	8.43
rights	8.09	Fallacious priority consent	8.45
Converse situation—junior creditor holds			
security over debtor's asset	8.11	**Piercing Corporate Veil and Marshalling**	
Surety exception:		Introduction	8.49
other jurisdictions	8.13	Permitting marshalling by piercing	
and third party's right of exoneration	8.18	corporate veil—USA	8.51
and redistributive nature of		Piercing corporate veil under English law	8.53
marshalling	8.21	Capital contribution and:	
Confusion about marshalling and rights		marshalling	8.55
of sureties	8.26	policy goals of security	8.57
Covenants against marshalling in context		Comparison of surety exception and	
of guarantees	8.33	corporate veil exception	8.59
Questioning Efficacy of Surety Exception		Differing approaches of English and US	
		courts to waiving requirements of	
Introduction	8.35	common debtor rule	8.62

A. Introduction

This chapter is concerned with the sole situation in which it is recognised that **8.01** English law will not insist upon strict compliance with the requirements of the common debtor rule, *viz.* where the assets subject to the senior security are separately owned by the debtor and a surety of the senior debt.[1] This is the 'surety exception' to the common debtor rule.

---

[1] A second exception – although not recognised as such by the authorities – effectively applies in the case of certain transfers or dispositions to third parties of the asset subject to only the senior security. This issue is considered in detail in Chapter 11. A further exception to the common debtor rule is suggested by *Halsbury's*, Vol 32 ('*Mortgage*'), para 916, where it is stated: 'Where an agent has pledged property, on which his principal has a lien, with property of his own as security for his own

8.02   The surety exception has not, however, been unconditionally accepted by the common law jurisdictions surveyed in this text. The New Zealand courts have questioned the efficacy of the surety exception. In *New Zealand Loan & Mercantile Agency Co Ltd v Loach*[2] and *Re Manawatu Transport Ltd,*[3] it was considered that the surety exception was founded upon a misapprehension as to the status of the junior creditor's marshalling rights *vis-à-vis* the surety's subrogation rights.

8.03   Nor is the surety exception, as applied in England, accepted in the United States of America. The United States courts have developed an alternative exception to the common debtor rule: the requirements of the common debtor rule will be deemed to have been complied with, where it would be inequitable to treat the assets owned by the debtor and the surety as being subject to separate ownership.

8.04   Accordingly, a comparative review of the nature of the exceptions to the common debtor rule in New Zealand and the United States will also be undertaken.

B. Surety Exception to the Common Debtor Rule

Introduction

8.05   The surety exception permits marshalling in the absence of compliance with requirements (1) and (2) of the common debtor rule,[4] *viz.* where the senior and junior creditors do not have a common debtor and the assets, over which the senior and junior creditors hold securities, are not owned by the same party.

8.06   The operation of the surety exception may be demonstrated as follows. Assume that a debtor who owns asset A has granted a first-ranking security to a senior creditor, and a third party who owns asset B has granted a first-ranking security to the senior creditor and a second-ranking security to a junior creditor. If the third party has:

> (a) guaranteed repayment of the senior debt and granted the security over asset B to the senior creditor in support of that guarantee; or

---

debt, the principal is entitled to have the debt thrown on the agent's property'. However, the principal does not require an exemption from the requirements of the common debtor rule, in order to marshall the senior security: here, the senior creditor holds a pledge over two or more assets of the agent whilst the principal holds a non-possessory lien over one of those assets. See *Broadbent v Barlow* (1861) 3 De G F & J 570; *Ex parte Alston* (1868) 4 Ch App 168; *Re Burge, Woodall & Co* [1912] 1 KB 393. See also Hewitt, *White & Tudor's Leading Cases in Equity*, 56–57; Ramsbotham, *Coote's Treatise on the Law of Mortgages*, 1483; Meagher, Gummow & Lehane, *Equity Doctrines and Remedies*, para 1118.

  [2] (1912) 31 NZLR 292.
  [3] (1984) 2 NZCLC 99,084.
  [4] See further Chapter 7.

(b) made asset B available to secure repayment of the senior debt, without assuming personal liability for the senior debt,

the junior creditor, should the senior creditor recover the senior debt by enforcing its security against asset B, *may*[5] be entitled to marshall the senior security over asset A.[6]

The debtor must be obligated to the third party

The mere fact that the senior and junior debts are owed, and the assets subject to the senior and junior securities are owned, by different parties is not sufficient for the purposes of the surety exception. There must be an obligation upon the debtor who owns the asset (A) subject only to the senior security to bear the burden of the senior debt, as between it and the third party who owns the asset (B) subject to the senior and junior securities[7] i e the third party must have a right of indemnity against the debtor entitling the third party to recover from the debtor any payments made by it in reduction of the senior debt[8] (or some other right enabling the third party to shift the senior debt on to the debtor).

8.07

This requirement has been expressed in the following terms:[9]

> It is often stated that marshalling does not apply unless the creditors in the language of Lord Eldon [in *Ex parte Kendall*], 'both are creditors of the same person'. While, however, the ordinary case for the application of the doctrine is that of two creditors and a common debtor, it is sufficient that as between the persons interested the two debts ought to be paid by the same person even though he may not be directly liable to the creditor for the two debts.

---

[5] There is a further requirement which must be satisfied: see paragraphs 8.07–8.08.

[6] See Roberts, *Principles of Equity*, 177; P H Winfield, *Jenks' English Civil Law* (8th ed 1947 Butterworths), para 1396; Keaton & Sheridan, *Equity*, 306–307; *Halsbury's*, Vol 16 ('*Equity*'), para 877.

[7] *Ex parte Kendall* (1811) 17 Ves 514. See also Chitty, *Index to All the Reported Cases Decided in the Several Courts of Equity and Bankruptcy in England and Ireland*, 4048 and 4051. It is unclear, in the absence of cases on point, whether a right of contribution would be sufficient to found a right to marshall. A co-debtor who pays more than its due portion of a common debt is entitled to recover that over-payment *via* contribution from its co-debtor and to that end may be subrogated to the creditor's rights (including any securities) against the latter to the extent of the over-payment: see paragraphs 5.29–5.32. It may be argued that a junior creditor of the third party should be entitled to rely on the third party's right of contribution against the debtor (as a co-debtor) to marshall the senior security over A, albeit only to the extent of the over-payment (q v paragraphs 8.09–8.10).

[8] In the absence of an express right of indemnity, a right of indemnity will be implied between the parties provided the third party had made asset B available as security for the repayment of the senior debt at the request of the debtor: see O'Donovan & Phillips, *The Modern Contract of Guarantee*, 586–587.

[9] Rayner & McLaren, *Falconbridge on Mortgages*, 315. See also the Australian case of *Sarge Pty Ltd v Cazihaven Homes Pty Ltd* (1994) 34 NSWLR 658, 660–662; Meagher, Gummow & Lehane, *Equity Doctrines and Remedies*, para 1109; O'Donovan & Phillips, *The Modern Contract of Guarantee*, 544. Cf. Cleaver, *Marshalling*, 287n51.

8.08 In addition, as the doctrine of marshalling is an equitable doctrine, the requisite obligation between the debtor and the third party must be one that is recognised by equity.[10]

Limitation of junior creditor's marshalling rights

8.09 A junior creditor will be unable to employ the surety exception to recover from the debtor a greater amount than that recoverable by the third party as a surety of the senior debt. Although there are no English (or Irish, Australian, Canadian or New Zealand) marshalling cases on point, it would be inconsistent with the nature of marshalling if a creditor of the third party could, *via* marshalling, place itself in a better position than the third party itself *vis-à-vis* the debtor.

8.10 This limitation is relevant where the third party has guaranteed the repayment of only part of the senior debt. The third party, upon the discharge of the full amount for which it was surety, will be entitled to share rateably with the senior creditor in the security given by the debtor for the entire debt.[11] The junior creditor will, by marshalling the senior security, be unable to recover more than the third party's rateable share of that security.

Converse situation—junior creditor holds security over the debtor's asset

8.11 Marshalling will not, however, be available in the converse situation, *viz.* where the debtor who owns asset A has granted a first-ranking security over A to a senior creditor and a second-ranking security to a junior creditor, and a third party who owns asset B, has granted a first-ranking security over B to the senior creditor. This is the case, whether or not the third party is a surety of the senior debt.[12]

8.12 The rationale for denying the junior creditor access to the senior security over the third party's asset is that the third party is a stranger to the debtor–creditor relationship between the debtor and the junior creditor:[13]

---

[10] *Ex parte Kendall* (1811) 17 Ves 514, 520. See also Meagher, Gummow & Lehane, *Equity Doctrines and Remedies*, para 1109; O'Donovan & Phillips, *The Modern Contract of Guarantee*, 544.

[11] It appears that the surety can only exercise this right following the discharge of the entire debt owed to the creditor: Marks & Moss, *Rowlatt on the Law of Principal and Surety*, 151; Goff & Jones, *The Law of Restitution*, 604; Mitchell, *The Law of Subrogation*, 42; Meagher, Gummow & Lehane, *Equity Doctrines and Remedies*, para 945. C f *Re Butlers Wharf Ltd* [1995] 2 BCLC 43, 50 where it is considered that this right may arise while the balance of the creditor's debt (unsupported by the guarantee) is outstanding.

[12] See the New Zealand case of *Re Manawatu Transport Ltd* (1984) 2 NZCLC 99,084 and the Canadian cases of *Ernst Brothers Co v Canadian Permanent Mortgage Corp* (1920) 47 OLR 362 (affirmed on appeal in (1920) 57 DLR 500) and *Fiatallis North America Inc v Pigott Construction Ltd* (1992) 3 PPSAC (2d) 30. See also Pomeroy Jr., *A Treatise on Equitable Remedies*, para 868; O'Donovan & Phillips, *The Modern Contract of Guarantee*, 680–681; Cleaver, *Marshalling*, 286–287.

[13] Orde J. of the Ontario Supreme Court in *Ernst Brothers Co v Canadian Permanent Mortgage Corp* (1920) 47 OLR 362, 371. See the discussion of requirements (1) and (2) of the common debtor rule in paragraphs 7.17–7.20.

It would be inequitable to permit the securities to be marshalled if in the result one who was not under any obligation to pay both debts should suffer. But, where the owner of the equity of redemption in both funds is the one who ought ultimately to pay both debts, there is clearly a case for marshalling.

Surety exception—other jurisdictions

The surety exception, in the terms described above, is recognised in Australia.[14]   **8.13**

In Canada, the position is less clear. The majority of cases on the point support the   **8.14**
surety exception;[15] there is, however, case law that denies a junior creditor of a
surety the right to marshal the security held by the senior creditor over an asset of
the debtor.[16]

There are no reported cases concerning the surety exception in Ireland.   **8.15**

The treatment of the surety exception in New Zealand forms the topic of the next   **8.16**
section of this chapter.

In terms of the United States of America, the surety exception was initially   **8.17**
accepted[17] but, due to the perceived superiority of the competing rights of the
surety, is no longer applied.[18]

Surety exception and the third party's right of exoneration

The Canadian courts have also permitted marshalling where the debtor and third   **8.18**
party are not principal and surety as regards the senior debt, but the third party
enjoys a right of exoneration against the debtor in respect of the senior debt.

In *Ernst Brothers Co v Canadian Permanent Mortgage Corp*,[19] the debtor had   **8.19**
granted senior security over an asset to Canadian Permanent Mortgage Corp
('CPMC'), and the third party had granted senior and junior securities over an

---

[14] *Sarge Pty Ltd v Cazihaven Homes Pty Ltd* (1994) 34 NSWLR 658. See also Francis & Thomas, *Mortgages and Securities*, 371; Meagher, Gummow & Lehane, *Equity Doctrines and Remedies*, para 1109; O'Donovan & Phillips, *The Modern Contract of Guarantee*, 544–545 and 680–681; McDonald, *Marshalling* (1996), para 1605.

[15] *Quay v Sculthorpe* (1869) 16 Gr 449; *G Ruso Construction Ltd v Laviola* (1976) 27 Chitty's LJ 136; *Brown v Canadian Imperial Bank of Commerce* (1985) 50 OR (2d) 420; *Re Allison* (1998) 38 OR (3d) 337. See also Rayner & McLaren, *Falconbridge on Mortgages*, 315; MacDougall, *Marshalling and the Personal Property Security Acts: Doing Unto Others . . .*, 106–108.

[16] *Bank of British Columbia v Tamavi Holdings Ltd* (1978) 29 CBR (NS) 111.

[17] *Ayres v Husted* 15 Conn 504 (1843); *Neff v Miller* 8 Pa (Barr) 347 (1848); *Newsom v McLendon* 6 Ga 392 (1849); *House v Thompson* 3 Head 512 (1859); *Carter v Tanners' Leather Co* 81 NE 902 (1907); *Savings & Loan Corp v Bear* 154 SE 587 (1930). See also Bigelow, *Story's Commentaries on Equity Jurisprudence*, paras 643–645 where the English position regarding the surety exception is adopted.

[18] q v nn 85 and 86.

[19] (1920) 57 DLR 500. See also Rayner & McLaren, *Falconbridge on Mortgages*, 315; Meagher, Gummow & Lehane, *Equity Doctrines and Remedies*, para 1109; O'Donovan & Phillips, *The Modern Contract of Guarantee*, 544–545.

asset to CPMC and Ernst Brothers Co ('Ernst') respectively. The third party subsequently disposed of its asset to the debtor subject to the senior and junior securities. The Appellate Division of the Ontario Supreme Court held that, as between the debtor and the third party, the third party was entitled to be exonerated by the debtor for liability in respect of the senior debt. Accordingly, upon CPMC recouping the senior debt out of the asset encumbered by the junior security, Ernst was entitled to marshall CPMC's security over the other asset.

8.20 It is unlikely that such an application of the surety exception would be recognised by English law. This may be illustrated by the following example. Assume that an asset (B) subject to the senior and junior securities is transferred to a third party, and an asset (A) subject to only the senior security is retained by the debtor. If the senior debt is recouped by enforcing the senior security against asset B, the cases on contribution and exoneration discussed in Chapter 5 would deny the transferee a right of exoneration against asset A for the amount of the senior debt,[20] with the consequence that the junior creditor would be unable to marshall the senior security over asset A.[21]

Surety exception and the redistributive nature of marshalling

8.21 The purpose of requirements (1) and (2) of the common debtor rule is to prevent a junior creditor from marshalling the senior security over an asset of a party who is a stranger to the debtor-creditor relationship between the debtor and the junior creditor. Were marshalling to be permitted, the burden of the junior debt would be imposed upon this party and, moreover, marshalling, by conferring a secured claim upon the junior creditor against that party's asset, would effectively have created a fresh security in favour of the junior creditor.

8.22 In the case of the surety exception, the debtor is also a stranger to the debtor–creditor relationship between the third party and the junior creditor. The junior creditor is a creditor of only the third party and it is the third party, not the debtor, who has made its asset available as security for repayment of the junior debt. However, the distinguishing *indicium* is that the debtor, as between it and the third party, is obligated to bear the burden of the senior debt.[22]

8.23 The doctrine of marshalling, when it applies by reason of the surety exception, permits the junior creditor as a creditor of the third party to shift the burden of the

---

[20] *In re Mainwaring* [1937] Ch 96. See further paragraph 5.35.

[21] The absence of a right of exoneration will not be fatal to the junior creditor's ability to marshall the senior security over A provided that there is some other obligation recognised by equity on the part of the debtor to bear the burden of the senior debt: see paragraphs 8.07–8.08. This may be contrasted with the situation where A is transferred to the third party subject to the senior security and B is retained by the debtor. If the senior debt is recouped out of B, it is likely that the junior creditor will be entitled to marshall the senior security over A: see further Chapter 11.

[22] See paragraphs 8.07–8.08.

senior debt on to the debtor (by making use of the third party's right to do so).[23]
This is accomplished by allowing the junior creditor to substitute the senior security over the debtor's asset for its eroded security over the third party's asset. This
has the effect of conferring upon the junior creditor the benefit of a secured claim
against a party, against whom it did not previously enjoy such a claim.
Additionally, it is not the case that the status of the junior creditor's claim *vis-à-vis*
the third party has been preserved; the junior creditor has, instead, been able to
exchange a secured claim against one party for a secured claim against another.

This exceptional result is, however, capable of being justified on the basis that the **8.24**
junior creditor's assumption of the senior creditor's security rights against the
debtor flows from equity's enforcement of the debtor's obligation, as between it
and the third party, to bear the burden of the senior debt.[24] Upon the senior creditor recouping the senior debt out of the third party's asset, the third party will be
entitled to shift the burden of that debt back on to the debtor. The surety exception permits the junior creditor, as a secured creditor of the third party, to obtain
the benefit of this redistribution of the senior debt and, by so doing, preserves the
secured status of the junior creditor's claim.

Moreover, the debtor, as the party primarily liable for the senior debt, is in no **8.25**
worse a position as a result of the imposition upon it of the burden of the senior
debt. Thus it cannot be said that the position of other creditors of the debtor has
been jeopardised by the application of the surety exception. The surety exception,
by preserving the secured status of the junior creditor's claim without adversely
affecting the other creditors of the debtor, is therefore also consistent with the policy goals of security identified by the conventional theory of security.

Confusion about marshalling and the rights of sureties

The surety exception to the common debtor rule is concerned with the ability of **8.26**
a creditor of a surety to marshall the senior security held over an asset of the

---

[23] *Ex parte Kendall* (1811) 17 Ves 514, 520. See also Meagher, Gummow & Lehane, *Equity Doctrines and Remedies*, para 1109; O'Donovan & Phillips, *The Modern Contract of Guarantee*, 544.

[24] The third party's right of indemnity – which entitles it to recover amounts paid by it in reduction of the senior debt – is enforced by subrogating the third party to the senior creditor's rights
(including the senior security) against the debtor: see Marks & Moss, *Rowlatt on the Law of Principal
and Surety*, 150; O'Donovan & Phillips, *The Modern Contract of Guarantee*, 653. This right of subrogation is subordinate to the junior creditor's right to marshall the senior security, thus entitling
the junior creditor to the benefit of the redistribution of the senior debt in priority to the third party:
see paragraphs 8.46–8.48. In the absence of such an indemnity, a junior creditor of the third party
may be unable to marshall the senior security (see paragraphs 8.07–8.08). It is not certain whether
a right of contribution would suffice (see paragraph 8.07). In the absence, however, of either a right
of indemnity or a right of contribution, the third party will have no rights of subrogation
(O'Donovan & Phillips, *The Modern Contract of Guarantee*, 657n539); there will thus be no right
of the third party which the junior creditor can utilise to gain access to the senior security over the
debtor's asset.

debtor; it is not concerned with the 'special' ability of sureties to marshall. There are, however, a number of authorities that have confused the surety's right to be subrogated to a creditor's security with marshalling.[25]

8.27 A recent example is Young J.'s categorisation of 'the right of a surety to have access to the principal's property to make good what the surety has paid' as an instance of marshalling in the Australian case of *Sarge Pty Ltd v Cazihaven Homes Pty Ltd.*[26] A surety's right to be subrogated to the security granted by a debtor to a creditor in respect of the guaranteed debt, is not a marshalling right.[27]

8.28 A review of the relevant authorities reveals two further applications of the term 'marshalling' to sureties. The first concerns the right of a surety, whose right of indemnity against a debtor has been secured over an asset of the debtor, to marshall prior-ranking security over another asset of the debtor. This is not a special case of marshalling. Assume a debtor who owns assets A and B has granted a first-ranking security over both of those assets to a senior creditor, and a second-ranking security over asset A to a surety of the senior debt to secure the surety's right of indemnity against the debtor. If the senior creditor recoups the senior debt out of asset A, the surety will—as a junior creditor of the debtor—be entitled to marshall the senior security over asset B.[28]

8.29 The second usage of marshalling regarding sureties is more problematic. It is considered that:[29]

---

[25] *Ex parte Salting* (1883) 25 Ch D 148; *New Zealand Loan & Mercantile Agency Co Ltd v Loach* (1912) 31 NZLR 292; *Finance Corp of Australia Ltd v Bentley* (1991) 5 BPR 97412; *Sarge Pty Ltd v Cazihaven Homes Pty Ltd* (1994) 34 NSWLR 658.

[26] Ibid, 662. *Heyman v Dubois* (1871) LR 13 Eq 158 is cited in support of this proposition. Similar claims for *Heyman v Dubois* are made by *New Zealand Loan & Mercantile Agency Co Ltd v Loach* (1912) 31 NZLR 292, 296 and *Finance Corp of Australia Ltd v Bentley* (1991) 5 BPR 97412, 11,842–11,843, and in the following texts: Robbins, *A Treatise on the Law of Mortgages, Pledges and Hypothecations*, 784; Beddoes, *A Concise Treatise on the Law of Mortgages*, 103; Ramsbotham, *Coote's Treatise on the Law of Mortgages*, 808 and 812; Keaton & Sheridan, *Equity*, 306; Tyler, *Fisher & Lightwood's Law of Mortgage*, 532; and O'Donovan & Phillips, *The Modern Contract of Guarantee*, 541.

[27] A similar misconception is to be found in *Ex parte Salting* (1883) 25 Ch D 148, 152 (q v Ramsbotham, *Coote's Treatise on the Law of Mortgages*, 127 where *Ex parte Salting, Heyman v Dubois* (1871) LR 13 Eq 158 and *South v Bloxam* (1865) 2 H & M 457 are cited in support of the surety's right to marshall the senior security so as to obtain repayment of the guaranteed debt). This misconception is exposed in Meagher, Gummow & Lehane, *Equity Doctrines and Remedies*, para 1134; Evans, *Outline of Equity and Trusts*, para 11.8. See also the discussion of the established categories of subrogation in paragraphs 4.24 and 4.27.

[28] See Bigelow, *Story's Commentaries on Equity Jurisprudence*, para 639; O'Donovan & Phillips, *The Modern Contact of Guarantee*, 682. C f *Halsbury's*, Vol 20 ('*Guarantee and Indemnity*'), para 226, where it is considered that the surety can marshall the senior security by compelling the senior creditor to recover the senior debt out of asset B. This coercive view of marshalling is, however, unlikely to be persuasive: see further Chapter 3.

[29] *Halsbury's*, Vol 20 ('*Guarantee and Indemnity*'), para 226. See also Hewitt, *White & Tudor's Leading Cases in Equity*, 55–56; Marks & Moss, *Rowlatt on the Law of Principal and Surety*, 148; McGuinness, *The Law of Guarantee*, paras 7.19–7.20.

Where the creditor has security for a different debt from that guaranteed by the guarantor, and can consolidate that security with another held by him for the guaranteed debt, the guarantor may have the securities marshalled in his favour; thus, after the creditor has been paid in full the guarantor has a right to be reimbursed, not only out of the security for the guaranteed debt, but also, in case of any deficiency, out of the other security, and to insist, where the latter security is sufficient to cover both debts, upon having the guaranteed debt liquidated out of it.

Thus, where a debtor has granted separate securities over assets A and B to a senior **8.30** creditor to secure the repayment of senior debts D1 and D2 respectively, a surety of senior debt D1 will be entitled to 'marshall' the senior security over asset B if the senior creditor is entitled to consolidate its securities.[30] Further, the surety will also be able to 'marshall' the securities so as to compel the senior creditor to recoup both D1 and D2 out of asset B.

This, however, is not an instance of marshalling of securities, as is obvious from a **8.31** review of the chief authority for the statement quoted in paragraph 8.29.[31] In *Heyman v Dubois*,[32] a debtor had granted multiple securities to a creditor in respect of distinct debts. Bacon V.C. held that a surety of one of the debts, upon discharging that debt, was entitled to 'marshall' the securities so as to recover its payment out of the balance of the proceeds of enforcement of the securities, following the creditor's consolidation of the securities. The surety was an unsecured creditor of the debtor. Moreover, the facts of this case do not satisfy the requirements of the common debtor rule or the surety exception. Thus, despite the use of the term 'marshalling' by Bacon V.C., it is clear that this case is not concerned with marshalling of securities.[33] In addition, it is doubtful whether a surety can coerce the senior creditor in the manner depicted above.[34]

---

[30] Absent the right of consolidation, the surety will only be entitled to be subrogated to the senior security over A on the discharge of D1: *Re Butlers Wharf Ltd* [1995] 2 BCLC 43. See also Mitchell, *The Law of Subrogation*, 42.

[31] *Heyman v Dubois* (1871) LR 13 Eq 158.

[32] Ibid. This is also the case with *Praed v Gardiner* (1788) 2 Cox Eq Cas 86 (cited by *Halsbury's*, Vol 20 ('*Guarantee and Indemnity*'), para 226n2). See further Meagher, Gummow & Lehane, *Equity Doctrines and Remedies*, para 1132; O'Donovan & Phillips, *The Modern Contact of Guarantee*, 682.

[33] It is difficult to see how the other cases, cited by *Halsbury's*, Vol 20 ('*Guarantee and Indemnity*'), para 226n2, support either a surety's right to the separate securities held by a creditor for the guaranteed debt and other debts of the debtor, or the description of that right as a form of marshalling: *Wright v Morley* (1805) 11 Ves Jun 12; *Drew v Lockett* (1863) 32 Beav 499; *Ex parte Alston* (1868) 4 Ch App 168; *Ex parte Salting* (1883) 25 Ch D 148. This is similarly the case with *Spalding v Rudding* (1846) 15 LJ Ch 374 and *Kemp v Falk* (1882) 52 LJ Ch 167 (cited by Hewitt, *White & Tudor's Leading Cases in Equity*, 55–56; q v *Halsbury's*, Vol 32 ('*Mortgage*'), para 916n7).

[34] This apparent right of coercion appears to be based upon *Aldrich v Cooper* (1803) 8 Ves Jun 382, 388–389 (which depicts marshalling of securities as a coercive remedy) and *Newton v Chorlton* (1853) 10 Hare 646, 652 (where it is considered that a surety can compel a creditor to seek satisfaction of the guaranteed debt from the debtor). The better view is that a surety cannot compel the creditor but may, following the enforcement by the creditor of its security against the assets of the debtor and surety, insist that the creditor treat itself as satisfied out of the proceeds of the debtor's

8.32 Also, in *Farebrother v Wodehouse*,[35] the Master of the Rolls held that a surety's right to the benefit of the several securities held by a creditor, for the guaranteed debt and other debts of the debtor, was subordinate to the creditor's right to consolidate its securities. Thus, the creditor's securities could only be made available to the surety following the discharge of the secured debts.

Covenants against marshalling in the context of guarantees

8.33 This confusion concerning the 'marshalling' rights of sureties may go some way towards explaining the presence of covenants against marshalling in guarantee documentation. These covenants typically contain an undertaking by the surety, in favour of the creditor, not to marshall the creditor's securities.

8.34 A covenant expressed in the above terms is superfluous. First, a surety, unless it holds security over the assets of the debtor, will be unable to marshall the creditor's security. Secondly, assuming that the surety holds such a security, its right to marshall will only arise following the recoupment by the creditor of its debt *via* the enforcement of its security. It is difficult to see what interest the creditor would have in denying the surety access to its security once the creditor's debt has been discharged.

C. Questioning the Efficacy of the Surety Exception

Introduction

8.35 Whilst the New Zealand courts have accepted the validity of the surety exception to the common debtor rule, they have raised serious doubts about the ability of a junior creditor to marshall senior security by making use of that exception.

8.36 In *New Zealand Loan & Mercantile Agency Co Ltd v Loach*[36] and *Re Manawatu Transport Ltd*,[37] it was considered that a junior creditor's marshalling rights would generally be subordinate to the subrogation rights of a surety. The junior creditor

---

asset in priority to the proceeds of the surety's asset: *In re Westzinthus* (1833) 5 B & Ad 817; *In re A Debtor* [1976] 1 WLR 952. See also Marks & Moss, *Rowlatt on the Law of Principal and Surety*, 207–209; q v n28.

[35] (1856) 26 LJ Ch 81. C f (i) *Bowker v Bull* (1850) 1 Sim (NS) 29, which is arguably authority for the reverse position, *viz.* a creditor's consolidation rights are subordinate to a surety's subrogation rights (however, in this case, the creditor was unable to consolidate because the mortgages in question had not all been granted by the same mortgagor) and (ii) *Re Butlers Wharf Ltd* [1995] 2 BCLC 43, 51 where it was doubted whether *Farebrother v Wodehouse* 'was ever good law'; and Marks & Moss, *Rowlatt on the Law of Principal and Surety*, 149 where it was considered that *Farebrother v Wodehouse* is limited to circumstances where the surety had notice that separate securities were to be granted for the debts.

[36] (1912) 31 NZLR 292.

[37] (1984) 2 NZCLC 99,084. See Hinde, McMorland, Campbell & Grinlinton, *Butterworths Land Law in New Zealand*, para 8.148.

would, in those circumstances, be unable to avail itself of the surety exception. The surety exception, as applied in New Zealand, is thus far less efficacious than the version recognised in England, Australia and Canada.

New Zealand Loan & Mercantile Agency Co Ltd v Loach—the facts

The facts of this case are straightforward. The senior creditor held first-ranking **8.37** security over an asset (A) of the debtor, and an asset (B) of the surety of the senior debt, to secure the repayment of the senior debt. The debtor subsequently granted a second-ranking security over asset A to secure repayment of the debt to the junior creditor, New Zealand Loan & Mercantile Agency Co Ltd. The junior creditor sought to marshall the senior security over asset B.

New Zealand Loan & Mercantile Agency Co Ltd v Loach—the judgment

Denniston J. in the Supreme Court held that the junior creditor's right to marshall **8.38** the senior security was subordinate to the surety's competing rights in respect of that security.[38] As such, the surety's right to shift the burden of the senior debt on to asset A prevailed over the junior creditor's right to obtain access *via* marshalling to asset B. The reasoning of Denniston J. is set out in more detail below.

Denniston J. stated that a surety was entitled, on the basis of *Heyman v Dubois*,[39] to **8.39** 'marshall' the security held by a creditor over the surety's asset and an asset of the debtor, so as to ensure that the guaranteed debt was discharged out of the debtor's asset in preference to the surety's asset.[40] This right of marshalling was coercive:[41]

> The object of marshalling is to compel resort to his securities in a certain order, or make the [senior creditor], if he sells in a different order, a trustee for the surety as to the proceeds in that order.

There was therefore a conflict between the junior creditor's right to marshall the **8.40** senior security and the right of the surety, itself, to 'marshall' the senior security. Denniston J. noted that *South v Bloxam*[42] had been taken as establishing the proposition that a surety's right to the security held by a creditor was inferior to the right of a *puisne* secured creditor to marshall that security.[43] He considered,

---

[38] See Cleaver, *Marshalling*, 285–286.
[39] (1871) LR 13 Eq 158.
[40] *New Zealand Loan & Mercantile Agency Co Ltd v Loach* (1912) 31 NZLR 292, 296 and 302.
[41] Ibid, 303.
[42] (1865) 2 H & M 457.
[43] Denniston J. noted (296–297) that this view had been taken by Coote (see Ramsbotham, *Coote's Treatise on the Law of Mortgage*, 812). This is also the view taken by Bigelow, *Story's Commentaries on Equity Jurisprudence*, para 633n(b); Robbins, *A Treatise on the Law of Mortgages, Pledges and Hypothecations*, 788; Beddoes, *A Concise Treatise on the Law of Mortgages*, 103; Hewitt, *White & Tudor's Leading Cases in Equity*, 56; Marks & Moss, *Rowlatt on the Law of Principal and Surety*, 149–150; Tyler, *Fisher & Lightwood's Law of Mortgage*, 532; Meagher, Gummow & Lehane, *Equity Doctrines and Remedies*, para 1133; Mitchell, *The Law of Subrogation*, 59.

however, that this proposition was based upon a misreading of *South v Bloxam*[44] and that the case had only decided that 'the surety was not entitled to tack to his security as against a second mortgagee costs incurred in resisting the creditor's claim, except so far as they were properly incurred for the benefit of the estate'.[45]

8.41   Thus the contest between the junior creditor and the surety would be determined in accordance with the general rule of priorities as between competing equities: *qui prior est tempore potior est jure*.[46] Denniston J. held that:[47]

> As to the equities: as against a security out of the property of the surety, *the right of the surety to compel recourse for his benefit in the first instance to the property of the principal debtor ought surely to be superior in effect, as it is prior in time, to a similar right on the part of a puisne encumbrancer* who claims to get the benefit, to the prejudice of the surety, of something for which he has given no consideration, and from which the surety has received no benefit (emphasis added).

Re Manawatu Transport Ltd

8.42   The facts of this case were substantially the same as those of *New Zealand Loan & Mercantile Agency Co Ltd v Loach*,[48] in that a junior creditor of the debtor was seeking to marshall the senior security over an asset of the surety. The High Court held that the surety exception did not apply to situations where the party seeking to marshall was a creditor of the debtor, rather than a creditor of the surety.[49] However, the High Court also held, following *New Zealand Loan & Mercantile Agency Co Ltd v Loach*,[50] that the junior creditor would be unable to marshall as its marshalling rights were inferior to the competing rights of the surety, the guarantee granted by the surety having preceded the grant of the junior security.[51]

---

[44]   (1865) 2 H & M 457.

[45]   *Dixon v Steel* [1901] 2 Ch 602, 607 (explaining the decision in *South v Bloxam* (1865) 2 H & M 457). Denniston J., in *New Zealand Loan & Mercantile Agency Co Ltd v Loach* (1912) 31 NZLR 292, adopted this interpretation (300–302). Denniston J.'s approach has been approved of in the Australian cases of *Commonwealth Trading Bank v Colonial Mutual Life Assurance Society Ltd* (1970) 26 FLR 338, 349–350 and *Sarge Pty Ltd v Cazihaven Homes Pty Ltd* (1994) 34 NSWLR 658, 664.

[46]   See generally Meagher, Gummow & Lehane, *Equity Doctrines and Remedies*, paras 803–805; Sykes & Walker, *The Law of Securities*, 402–405, 407–408 and 801–802.

[47]   *New Zealand Loan & Mercantile Agency Co Ltd v Loach* (1912) 31 NZLR 292, 304. Denniston J. also referred to the principle, expressed in *The 'Chioggia'* [1898] P 1, that marshalling would not be applied to the prejudice of third parties; Denniston J. held (298) that the surety could defeat the junior creditor's claim to marshall the senior security as the surety was such a third party: see the discussion of this apparent principle in paragraphs 11.06–11.09.

[48]   (1912) 31 NZLR 292.

[49]   *Re Manawatu Transport Ltd* (1984) 2 NZCLC 99,084, 99,088.

[50]   (1912) 31 NZLR 292.

[51]   (1984) 2 NZCLC 99,084, 99,089–99,090.

Narrow scope of the surety exception under New Zealand law

If the view, taken by the New Zealand courts, of the status of a junior creditor's **8.43** marshalling rights *qua* the subrogation rights of a surety of the senior debt is correct, the surety exception will only be available to the junior creditor where the grant of the junior security precedes the grant of the guarantee.[52] Since the guarantee in question concerns the repayment of the senior debt, it will invariably have been granted contemporaneously with, or prior to, the grant of the senior security (since that security secures performance of the guarantee). Sureties will thus, generally, be in a position to gainsay junior creditors' claims to marshall the senior security.[53]

The better view, however, is that the reasoning of the New Zealand courts cannot **8.44** be sustained. Both cases are correct, to the extent that they can be said to support the proposition that the surety exception has no application where the secured creditor who is seeking to marshall the senior security is a creditor of the debtor, not a creditor of the surety.[54] Indeed, there was little need for Denniston J. in *New Zealand Loan & Mercantile Agency Co Ltd v Loach*[55] to look beyond *Ex parte Kendall.*[56]

Fallacious priority contest

The decision of Denniston J. in *New Zealand Loan & Mercantile Agency Co Ltd v* **8.45** *Loach*[57] is, moreover, predicated upon, first, a misconception as to the nature of a surety's rights *qua* the creditor of the guaranteed debt and, secondly, a fallacious priority contest between the junior creditor and the surety. As considered in paragraph 8.31, it is doubtful whether *Heyman v Dubois*[58] is authority for the right of a surety *via* 'marshalling' to compel a creditor to look first to the debtor for recovery of the guaranteed debt.

Absent this 'marshalling' right, the surety's claim against the creditor's security **8.46** is solely a subrogation claim, i e if the surety makes a payment in respect of the guaranteed debt, the surety will upon that debt being discharged be entitled to be

---

[52] Absent an event which postpones the 'priority position' of the surety to that of the junior creditor.

[53] See Schumacher, *Marshalling*, 91.

[54] This is the case with *Re Manawatu Transport Ltd* (1984) 2 NZCLC 99,084 but is arguably not the case with *New Zealand Loan & Mercantile Agency Co Ltd v Loach* (1912) 31 NZLR 292: Eichelbaum J., in the former case, queried whether the latter case was to be 'regarded as an affirmation of the common debtor rule, or as turning solely on the competing equities as between a surety and a person claiming to marshall' (99,090).

[55] (1912) 31 NZLR 292.

[56] (1811) 17 Ves 514. See Meagher, Gummow & Lehane, *Equity Doctrines and Remedies*, para 1133.

[57] (1912) 31 NZLR 292.

[58] (1865) 2 H & M 457.

subrogated to all securities held by the creditor for the debt.[59] Accordingly, any priority contest between the junior creditor and surety must concern the status of the former's marshalling rights *vis-à-vis* the latter's subrogation rights. The fallacious nature of such a contest is immediately apparent: the junior creditor's right to marshall the senior security is contingent upon the senior creditor recouping the senior debt out of the asset subject also to the junior security, *viz.* the debtor's asset. However, in the event that the senior debt is discharged out of the debtor's asset, the surety will have no right—and no need—to be subrogated to the senior security over the debtor's asset. Conversely, should the senior creditor recoup the senior debt out of the surety's asset, the surety will be entitled to be subrogated to the senior security over the debtor's asset but the junior creditor will have no right to marshall the senior security over the surety's asset. The 'competing' rights of the junior creditor and the surety, in the circumstances envisaged by *New Zealand Loan & Mercantile Agency Co Ltd v Loach*[60] and *Re Manawatu Transport Ltd*,[61] are never coterminous.

8.47   A priority contest between a junior creditor and a surety is only comprehensible where the junior creditor holds *mesne* security over an asset of the surety, and is seeking to marshall the senior security over an asset of the debtor (*viz.* the very circumstances contemplated by the surety exception). The surety exception effectively subordinates the surety's right of subrogation to the senior security to the junior creditor's right to marshall that security.[62] Thus, by its very nature, the surety exception is pre-emptive of the priority contest articulated in *New Zealand Loan & Mercantile Agency Co Ltd v Loach*.[63] Nonetheless, marshalling—in common with the surety's right of subrogation—imposes the burden of the senior debt on the debtor as the party primarily liable for the senior debt (and, by so doing, preserves the secured nature of the junior creditor's claim).

8.48   Further, the surety, *via* subrogation, is entitled to stand in the place of the senior creditor and have the benefit of every security held by the senior creditor for the guaranteed debt. The surety will, as a result of subrogation, be in no better position than the senior creditor as regards the senior creditor's security and other rights.[64] Thus, where the senior security is subject to a marshalling claim, a claim that cannot be denied by the senior creditor, it would be difficult to justify the

---

[59]   The surety must have paid an amount in reduction of the guaranteed debt, although it need not, itself, have repaid the entire debt; its right to be subrogated to the creditor's securities arises only after the entire debt has been discharged: see Mitchell, *The Law of Subrogation*, 41–42 and 60; Meagher, Gummow & Lehane, *Equity Doctrines and Remedies*, para 945.

[60]   (1912) 31 NZLR 292.

[61]   (1984) 2 NZCLC 99,084.

[62]   See Mitchell, *The Law of Subrogation*, 59. C f Cleaver, *Marshalling*, 286, where it is argued that, upon the discharge of the senior debt out of the surety's asset, the surety should be subrogated to the senior security ahead of the junior creditor.

[63]   (1912) 31 NZLR 292.

[64]   See Meagher, Gummow & Lehane, *Equity Doctrines and Remedies*, para 944.

abrogation of that claim by the party seeking to be substituted to the position of the senior creditor.[65]

D. Piercing the Corporate Veil and Marshalling of Securities

Introduction

The law of the United States, in common with English, Australian, Canadian, **8.49** Irish and New Zealand law, recognises the common debtor rule.[66] Moreover, the United States courts have also considered the requirement of common ownership of the assets encumbered by the senior security capable of being waived. Accordingly, under United States law, the fact that the relevant assets are severally owned by the debtor and a third party will not necessarily bar the junior creditor from marshalling the senior security.

However, the waiver of the requirements of the common debtor rule is accom- **8.50** plished under United States law by piercing the corporate veil, which separates the debtor from the third party and grants to each the status of a distinct legal entity. The transgression of the separate legal identities of the debtor and the third party results in the effective imputation of common ownership of the assets subject to the senior security. In contrast to English law, the junior creditor's ability to marshall the senior security does not flow automatically from the relationship between the debtor and the third party.[67]

Permitting marshalling by piercing the corporate veil—the United States of America

The United States courts have stated their preparedness to pierce the corporate **8.51** veil where the debtor and/or third party has engaged in 'inequitable conduct' towards the junior creditor.[68] Piercing the corporate veil allows the court to treat the debtor and the third party, as indistinguishable from one another, for the purposes of the common debtor rule. The requirements of the common debtor rule,

---

[65] Ibid, para 1133.

[66] *Meyer v United States* 375 US 233 (1963); *Farmers & Merchants Bank v Gibson* 7 BR 437 (1980). See also Bigelow, *Story's Commentaries on Equity Jurisprudence*, paras 633n(b) and 642; Beach Jr., *Commentaries on Modern Equity Jurisprudence*, para 783; Pomeroy Jr., *Equity Jurisprudence*, para 1414; Pomeroy Jr., *A Treatise on Equitable Remedies*, para 868; McCoy, *Bispham's Principles of Equity*, para 317; *Am Jur*, para 53:13; Emamzadeh, *Marshaling in Bankruptcy: Questioning the Recent Expansions to the Common Debtor Requirement*, 312–316.

[67] c f in Canada, where the court in *Montmor Investments Ltd v Montreal Trust Co* (1984) 53 BCLR 275 considered that the common debtor rule could be satisfied by piercing the corporate veil, but declined to do so.

[68] See Kroger & Acconcia, *Marshaling: A Fourth Act Sequel to Commercial Tragedies?* 210–211; Emamzadeh, *Marshaling in Bankruptcy: Questioning the Recent Expansions to the Common Debtor Requirement*, 324–325 and 327.

having been satisfied in this manner, the junior creditor may marshall the senior security.

8.52 Thus, a junior creditor is permitted to assert its marshalling rights where it would be inequitable for the assets of the third party not to be regarded as susceptible to the claims of the debtor's creditors, in the same manner as the debtor's assets. This concept of inequitable conduct embraces a wide gamut of dealings, ranging from inadequate capitalisation of the debtor to overt fraud on the part of the debtor or third party.[69] Thus a junior creditor may marshall the senior security where neither the debtor nor the third party is guilty of fraudulent conduct towards the junior creditor.[70]

Piercing the corporate veil under English law

8.53 The English courts, in contrast to the United States courts, have demonstrated considerable reluctance to disregard the corporate veil that separates a company from its shareholders.[71] It is only in the following circumstances, that an English court will be prepared to pierce the corporate veil so as to identify one distinct legal entity with another:

---

[69] Inequitable conduct is 'conduct which may be lawful, yet shocks one's good conscience. It means, *inter alia*, a secret or open fraud, lack of faith or guardianship by a fiduciary; an unjust enrichment, not enrichment by bon chance, astuteness or business acumen, but enrichment through another's loss brought about by one's own unconscionable, unjust, unfair, close or double dealing or foul conduct' (*In re Harvest Milling Co* 221 F Supp 836 (1963), 838). See also *In re Tampa Chain Co, Inc* 53 BR 772 (1985). For an overview, and economic analysis, of the circumstances in which United States courts have allowed creditors to pierce the corporate veil and reach the assets of shareholders, see Easterbrook & Fischel, *Limited Liability and the Corporation*, 109–113.

[70] *In re Jack Green's Fashions for Men – Big & Tall, Inc* 507 F 2d 130 (1979); *Farmers & Merchants Bank v Gibson* 7 BR 437 (1980); *In re AEI Corp* 11 BR 97 (1981); *In re United Medical Research, Inc* 12 BR 941 (1981); *In re Multiple Services Industries, Inc* 18 BR 635 (1982); *In re Plad, Inc* 24 BR 676 (1982); *In re Computer Room, Inc* 24 BR 732 (1982); *DuPage Lumber & Home Improvement Center Co., Inc v Georgia-Pacific Corp* 34 BR 737 (1983); *In re Rich Supply House, Inc* 43 BR 68 (1984); *In re Tampa Chain Co, Inc* 53 BR 772 (1985); *In re Dealer Support Services International, Inc* 73 BR 763 (1987); *In re Vermont Toy Works, Inc* 82 BR 258 (1987). See I D Labovitz, *Marshaling Under the UCC: the State of the Doctrine* (1982) 99 Banking LJ 440; B Weintraub & A N Resnick, *Compelling a Senior Lienor to Pursue Remedies Against a Guarantor – A Misapplication of the Marshaling Doctrine* (1985) 18 UCCLJ 178, 180–181; M Lachman, *Marshaling Assets in Bankruptcy: Recent Innovations in the Doctrine* (1985) 6 Cardozo LR 671, 682–683; Karasik & Kolodney, *The Doctrine of Marshaling Under the Bankruptcy Code*, 103–104; Kroger & Acconcia, *Marshaling: A Fourth Act Sequel to Commercial Tragedies?* 210–211.

[71] See R R Pennington, *Company Law* (6th ed 1990 Butterworths), 8–52; P L Davies, *Gower's Principles of Modern Company Law* (6th ed 1997 Sweet & Maxwell), 77–83 and 148–177; *Palmer's Company Law* (1997 Service Sweet & Maxwell), paras 2.1519–2.1522; *British Company Law and Practice* (1998 Service CCH), paras 2–100 and 2–150.

(1) where the piercing of the corporate veil is expressly sanctioned by legislation, as in the case of companies,[72] insolvency,[73] competition[74] and revenue[75] legislation;[76] and

(2) where, in the absence of empowering legislation, the court considers that the company has been incorporated to avoid an existing legal obligation of its shareholders or to perpetrate a fraud.[77]

However, in neither (1) nor (2) is a broad power conferred upon the courts to pool the assets of the company and its shareholders for the purposes of discharging the claims of a creditor of the company.[78]

A case can therefore be made out for permitting marshalling under English law, **8.54** where to insist upon strict compliance with the common debtor rule would enable the debtor and/or third party to fraudulently avoid their obligations to a junior creditor. However, it is doubtful whether an English court would be

---

[72] e g (i) where the number of shareholders of a company falls below the statutory minimum, the shareholders may be liable for the debts of the company (section 24 of the *Companies Act 1985* (UK)) and (ii) where a parent company must produce group accounts for all companies in the group (section 227 of the *Companies Act 1985* (UK)).

[73] e g a controlling shareholder may be liable as a 'shadow director' for wrongful trading under section 214(7) of the *Insolvency Act 1986* (UK). See Pennington, Company Law, 44–46; Davies, *Gower's Principles of Modern Company Law*, 151–155; R M Goode, *Principles of Corporate Insolvency Law* (2nd ed 1997 Sweet & Maxwell), 466.

[74] e g under EC competition law (as contained in Articles 85 and 86 of the EC Treaty), a holding company and its subsidiary may be treated as a single economic unit.

[75] e g the provisions of the *Income and Corporation Taxes Act 1988* (UK) regarding 'close companies'.

[76] See generally *Palmer's Company Law*, paras 2.1520–2.1522; *British Company Law and Practice*, para 2–100. This category of legislation should be differentiated from legislation which, whilst it permits a claimant against one legal entity access to the assets of another, does not deny their separate legal identities: *The Albazero* [1977] AC 774; *Bank of Tokyo v Karoon* [1986] 3 All ER 468; *Adams v Cape Industry plc* [1990] 2 WLR 657. See further L Gallagher & P Ziegler, *Lifting the Corporate Veil in Pursuit of Justice* [1990] JBL 292, 309–312.

[77] *Jones v Lipman* [1962] 1 WLR 832; *Merchandise Transport Ltd v British Transport Commission* [1962] 2 QB 173; *Re A Company* (1985) 1 BCC 99, 421; *Re Polly Peck International plc* [1996] BCC 486. See Pennington, *Company Law*, 47–48; *Palmer's Company Law*, para 2.1522; *British Company Law and Practice*, para 2–150; Gallagher & Ziegler, *Lifting the Corporate Veil in Pursuit of Justice*, 302–307. There are a number of other situations in which the courts will, in the absence of empowering legislation, render the shareholders of a company liable for the debts of the company (e g where the company and its principal or controlling shareholder are in a relationship of agency and the debts of the company were incurred within the scope of that agency: *Re FG (Films) Ltd* [1953] 1 WLR 483; *Firestone Tyre and Rubber Co Ltd v Lewellin* [1957] 1 WLR 464). However, the liability of the shareholder, in those situations, arises as a consequence of the legal relationship between it and the company, not because the courts have chosen to disregard their separate legal identities.

[78] See Goode, *Principles of Corporate Insolvency Law*, 130–140. While a liquidator or other administrator of an insolvent company or the trustee in bankruptcy may obtain access to assets, that are ostensibly held by parties other than the insolvent/bankrupt, that will be achieved by castigating the means by which such parties obtained those assets as voidable transactions or preferences (*per* Part VI, and Chapter V of Part IX, of the *Insolvency Act 1986* (UK)). The overturning of the means of acquisition is not equivalent to the abolition of the separate legal identities of the insolvent and the third parties.

prepared to waive the requirements of the common debtor rule where the conduct of the debtor and third party, though opprobrious, falls short of fraud.

Capital contribution and marshalling of securities

8.55   The ability of the United States courts to order pooling of the assets of a debtor and its related parties for the benefit of the debtor's creditors is of particular relevance to marshalling. Where a debtor is considered to be inadequately capitalised, the assets of related parties (such as its holding company or controlling shareholder[79]) may be deemed to be a contribution to the debtor's capital.[80]

8.56   The rationale for the application of marshalling, on the grounds of inadequate capitalisation, where the assets subject to the senior security are owned by the principal debtor and a related party has been expressed in the following terms:[81]

> Several courts have held that when a guarantor who is also a controlling shareholder provides the lender with the primary collateral needed to obtain a working capital loan to either initiate or continue the operation of the debtor corporation, the 'common debtor' requirement is satisfied and the equitable remedy of marshalling is available . . . Under such circumstances, the collateral pledged by the guarantor/shareholder is held, by those courts permitting marshalling, to be the equivalent of a capital contribution to the corporation . . . which a court in equity should consider as a fund for the corporation itself, so that there is a 'common debtor'.

Capital contribution and the policy goals of security

8.57   The concept of capital contribution recognises the manner in which corporate groups conduct their economic activities:[82]

---

[79]   The mere fact that control over a subsidiary is exercised by a holding company is not sufficient under English law to warrant the piercing of the corporate veil which segregates the subsidiary from the holding company: *Re Southard & Co Ltd* [1979] 1 WLR 1198; *Multinational Gas & Petroleum Co v Multinational Gas & Petroleum Services Ltd* [1983] 3 WLR 492; *Adams v Cape Industries plc* [1990] 2 WLR 657; *Re Polly Peck International plc* [1996] BCC 486. See *Palmer's Company Law*, para 2.1522; *British Company Law and Practice*, para 2–150.

[80]   *Farmers & Merchants Bank v Gibson* 7 BR 437 (1980); *In re United Medical Research, Inc* 12 BR 941 (1981); *In re Multiple Services Industries, Inc* 18 BR 635 (1982); *In re Computer Room, Inc* 24 BR 732 (1982); *In re Tampa Chain Co, Inc* 53 BR 772 (1985). See also *Am Jur*, para 53:13; Mosman, *The Proper Application of Marshaling on Behalf of Unsecured Creditors*, 651–654; Lachman, *Marshaling Assets in Bankruptcy: Recent Innovations in the Doctrine*, 679–682; Kroger & Acconcia, *Marshaling: A Fourth Act Sequel to Commercial Tragedies?* 210–211; Emamzadeh, *Marshaling in Bankruptcy: Questioning the Recent Expansions to the Common Debtor Requirement*, 322–324 and 326–327.

[81]   *In re Tampa Chain Co, Inc* 53 BR 772 (1985), 794–795.

[82]   A Nolan, *The Position of Unsecured Creditors of Corporate Groups: Towards a Group Responsibility Solution which gives Fairness and Equity a Role* (1993) 11 C&SLJ 461, 484–485. There is a considerable body of literature in England dealing with the piercing of the corporate veil in relation to members of the same corporate group: e g D D Prentice, *Some Comments on the Law Relating to Corporate Groups* in J McCahery, S Picciotto & C Scott (eds), *Corporate Control and Accountability* (1993 Oxford); F G Rixon, *Lifting the Veil Between Holding and Subsidiary*

[A]ssociated corporations engaged in related businesses often pool their assets and trading activities to conduct their businesses as a single enterprise. Because the rationale is to maximise the profit of the enterprise as a whole rather than the profit of the individual constituent parts, a common feature of enterprise management is that the interests of individual group members are 'sacrificed' in the interests of the enterprise.

The fact that a related party of the debtor has made available its assets as security for the senior debt is likely to have influenced other creditors of the debtor in their decision to extend credit to the debtor. These creditors would have considered that their risk of loss has been reduced by the extension of the senior security beyond the assets of the debtor to those of a related party.

The assets of the related party subject to the senior security should consequently **8.58** be treated as being no different from the assets of the debtor *qua* the debtor's creditors, as a strict insistence on the separate legal identities of the debtor and the related party would be in derogation of the legitimate expectations of the creditors of the debtor.[83] The concept of capital contribution, by bringing the assets owned by a related party of the debtor within the ambit of marshalling, acts to assure the supply of credit and, as such, is consistent with the policy goals of security identified by the conventional theory of security.[84]

Comparison of the surety exception and the corporate veil exception

The facilitation of marshalling, by piercing the corporate veil between the debtor **8.59** and the third party, is not materially different from the surety exception recognised by English law. This 'corporate veil' exception operates in substantially the same circumstances as the surety exception, *viz.* it is only relevant where the assets, subject to the senior security, are severally owned by the debtor and a third party surety of the senior debt.

Companies (1986) 102 LQR 415; H Collins, *Ascription of Legal Responsibility to Groups in Complex Patterns of Economic Integration* (1990) 53 MLR 731; G P Stapledon, *A Parent Company's Liability for Debts of an Insolvent Subsidiary* (1995) 16 Co Lawyer 152; E Ferran, *Lifting the veil* [1996] All ER Annual Review 47; C Nakajima, *Lifting the Veil* (1996) 17 Co Lawyer 187; R Schulte, *Corporate Groups and the Equitable Subordination of Claims on Insolvency* (1997) 18 Co Lawyer 2.

[83] J M Landers, *A Unified Approach to Parent, Subsidiary and Affiliate Questions in Bankruptcy* (1975) 42 U Chi L Rev 589 advocates pooling of group assets on the basis that the moral hazard created by limited liability operates as an incentive for shareholders to transfer the costs of risky business activities to creditors. Landers argues that pooling should be permitted where: (a) individual companies within the group are operated with a view to the overall profitability of the group; (b) creditors perceive individual companies as members of the group and expect payment from the group; and (c) the fact that one group company has substantially more assets relative to other members is either simply fortuitous or the result of an attempt to prefer the creditors of that company to creditors of other group companies. See further P I Blumberg, *The American Law of Corporate Groups* in McCahery, Picciotto & Scott (eds), *Corporate Control and Accountability*; A Posner, *The Rights of Creditors of Affiliated Corporations* (1976) 43 U Chi L Rev 499; E J Wes Jr, *Substantive Consolidations in Bankruptcy: A Flow of Assets Approach* (1977) 65 Cal LR 720.

[84] See further Chapter 6.

8.60 However, the mere fact that the relationship between the debtor and the third party is one of debtor and surety is, under United States law, insufficient grounds for the piercing of the corporate veil. It must also be shown that the surrounding circumstances warrant the transgression of the separate legal identities of the debtor and the surety. The United States courts have stated that they will only permit marshalling where there has been inequitable conduct (which includes inadequate capitalisation) on the part of the debtor and/or the surety.

8.61 This is in marked contrast to the surety exception. The very fact that the assets, subject to the senior security, are owned by the debtor and a party who has guaranteed repayment of the senior debt will, of itself, sustain the junior creditor's right to marshal the senior security.

Differing approaches of the English and United States courts to waiving the requirements of the common debtor rule

8.62 The disparate nature of the exceptions to the common debtor rule recognised by English and United States law is due to the particular view taken in each jurisdiction of the status of the surety's rights of subrogation *vis-à-vis* the junior creditor's marshalling rights. The United States courts, in contrast to the English courts, have consistently refused to allow a junior creditor to marshal the senior security in the face of the competing subrogation rights of a surety.[85]

8.63 The rationale for this approach is that the surety is considered to enjoy rights that are, of themselves, superior to those of the junior creditor. This is well illustrated by the following statement from *Mason v Hull*:[86]

> [I]f [the surety] should be compelled to pay [the senior debt], he would be entitled to be subrogated to the rights of the [senior] creditor, and enforce the . . . lien against the property of the principal, and to all the benefits of that lien, which, being superior to [the junior creditor's] mortgages, would at last appropriate the fund in question in preference to the mortgages held by [the junior creditor].

The United States authorities are thus far more disparaging of the status of the junior creditor's marshalling rights, relative to the surety's rights of subrogation,

---

[85] *Mason v Hull* 45 NE 632 (1896); *Jenkins v Smith* 48 NYS 126 (1897); *Hall v Hyer* 37 SE 594 (1900); *Swift & Co v Kortrecht* 112 F 709 (1902); *Speer v Home Bank* 206 SW 405 (1918); *Meyer v United States* 375 US 233 (1963); *In re Wilson Dairy Co* 30 BR 67 (1983); *In re Ludwig Honold Manufacturing* 33 BR 724 (1983); *In re Weiss* 34 BR 346 (1983); *DuPage Lumber & Home Improvement Center Co., Inc v Georgia-Pacific Corp* 34 BR 737 (1983); *Enloe v Franklin Bank & Trust Co* 445 NE 2d 1005 (1983); *In re Maimone* 41 BR 974 (1984); *In re Childers* 44 BR 23 (1984). See also *Am Jur*, para 52:28 where it is stated: 'Where a fund is held by a surety or guarantor, marshaling is barred because the debtor does not hold the funds which are in the hands of the surety or guarantor and, therefore, are not assets subject to marshalling.'
[86] 45 NE 632 (1896), 633. See also *CJS*, paras 21:112b and 55:6; Mosman, *The Proper Application of Marshaling on Behalf of Unsecured Creditors*, 652–653; Lachman, *Marshaling Assets in Bankruptcy: Recent Innovations in the Doctrine*, 678; C H Averch & J P Prostok, *The Doctrine of Marshaling: an Anachronistic Concept Under the Bankruptcy Code* (1990) 22 UCCLJ 224, 229–230.

than the New Zealand authorities noted above. The New Zealand cases, *New Zealand Loan & Mercantile Agency Co Ltd v Loach*[87] and *Re Manawatu Transport Ltd*,[88] leave open the possibility, albeit a slender one, that the junior creditor will be able to defeat the surety in a priority contest and consequently marshall the senior security. That is not the case in the United States.

The surety's ability to frustrate the marshalling rights of the junior creditor was not, however, considered in those United States cases which established the corporate veil exception to the common debtor rule.[89] The decision to permit marshalling, in those cases, was not predicated upon a reappraisal of the status of the junior creditor's marshalling rights *vis-à-vis* the subrogation rights of the surety; it was, instead, simply considered that marshalling was possible as the common debtor rule had been satisfied by the piercing of the corporate veil between the debtor and the surety. **8.64**

However, any doubts concerning the efficacy of the junior marshalling rights have been dispelled by subsequent United States cases on the corporate veil exception.[90] The courts in those cases have held that the circumstances, which warrant the piercing of the corporate veil for the purpose of satisfying the common debtor rule, also provide justifiable grounds for subordinating the surety's subrogation rights to the junior creditor's marshalling rights. **8.65**

---

[87] (1912) 31 NZLR 292.

[88] (1984) 2 NZCLC 99,084.

[89] *In re Jack Green's Fashions for Men – Big & Tall, Inc* 507 F 2d 130 (1979); *Farmers & Merchants Bank v Gibson* 7 BR 437 (1980); *In re AEI Corp* 11 BR 97 (1981); *In re Multiple Services Industries* 18 BR 635 (1982); *In re Plad, Inc* 24 BR 676 (1982); *In re Computer Room, Inc* 24 BR 732 (1982); *DuPage Lumber & Home Improvement Center Co., Inc v Georgia-Pacific Corp* 34 BR 737 (1983); *In re Dealer Support Services International, Inc* 73 BR 763 (1987). See also Emamzadeh, *Marshaling in Bankruptcy: Questioning the Recent Expansions to the Common Debtor Requirement,* 325 and 327–328.

[90] *In re United Medical Research, Inc* 12 BR 941 (1981); *In re Rich Supply House, Inc* 43 BR 68 (1984); *In re Tampa Chain Co, Inc* 53 BR 772 (1985); *In re Vermont Toy Works, Inc* 82 BR 258 (1987). See Weintraub & Resnick, *Compelling a Senior Lienor to Pursue Remedies Against a Guarantor – A Misapplication of the Marshaling Doctrine,* 181; B Weintraub & A N Resnick, *Subordination of the Guarantor's Subrogation Rights – the Marshaling Doctrine Revisited* (1986) 18 UCCLJ 364, 367–369.

9

MARSHALLING OF SECURITIES AND THE REQUIREMENT OF PROPRIETARY SECURITIES

Introduction	9.01	judgment	9.18
Proprietary and Non-Proprietary Securities		Requirement of proprietary securities is without foundation	9.22
Introduction	9.02	Restricting marshalling to real property mortgages in Canada	9.25
Proprietary versus non-proprietary securities	9.04	**Extension of Marshalling to Non-Security Rights**	
Mortgages	9.06		
Fixed equitable charges	9.07	Smit Tak and expansion of marshalling rights	9.26
Uncrystallised floating charges	9.08		
Pledges	9.09	Unwarranted expansion of scope of marshalling	9.30
Possessory liens	9.10		
Non-possessory liens	9.11	Conclusion	9.34
Availability of marshalling and triumph of form over substance	9.12	**Marshalling of Securities and Quasi-Securities**	
Special case of floating charges	9.14	Introduction	9.35
Webb v Smith and Requirement of Proprietary Securities		Set-off and marshalling	9.36
		Title retention devices and marshalling	9.37
Introduction	9.15	Negative pledges and marshalling	9.38
Webb v Smith:		Indiscriminate expansion of marshalling rights	9.39
facts	9.17		

A. Introduction

9.01 This chapter is concerned with the nature of interests that are required for a marshalling claim and that may be the subject of such a claim.

Two cases, in particular, are relevant to a determination of these issues. The first, *Webb v Smith*,[1] is said to establish the requirement that, in order for marshalling to be available, both the senior and junior creditors must hold securities which confer upon them proprietary interests in the common debtor's assets.

---

[1] (1885) 30 Ch D 192.

The second case, *Smit Tak International Zeesleepin Bergingsbedrijf BV v Selco Salvage Ltd*,[2] claims, in contrast, that marshalling is available in respect of all rights held by a senior creditor against a debtor, provided that those rights confer upon the senior creditor equal rights of recourse as between: (i) the asset subject to the junior security; and (ii) the asset the subject of the right sought to be marshalled.

B. Proprietary and Non-Proprietary Securities

Introduction

Prior to *Webb v Smith*,[3] a junior creditor who wished to marshall the senior creditor's security upon the prejudicial recovery of the senior debt had only to satisfy the requirements of the common debtor rule.[4] The nature of the particular securities held by the senior and junior creditors made no difference to the availability of marshalling; it was sufficient that the debts owed to the senior and junior creditors were secured over assets of a common debtor, and that the senior security conferred on the senior creditor equal rights of access to the assets subject to the senior security. **9.02**

This state of affairs has apparently been altered by *Webb v Smith*.[5] It is considered that, as a result of this case, the doctrine of marshalling now undertakes an inquiry into the nature of the senior and junior securities.[6] Those securities must confer upon the senior and junior creditors proprietary interests in the assets the subject of the securities. If neither the junior nor the senior security does so, the junior creditor will be unable to marshall the senior security following its enforcement, notwithstanding that the common debtor rule has been complied with. **9.03**

Proprietary versus non-proprietary securities

On the basis of *Webb v Smith*,[7] the particular *form* taken by the senior and junior securities is critical to the success of any claim by the junior creditor to marshall the senior security. Only the holder of a proprietary security is entitled to the protection of the doctrine of marshalling, and only a proprietary security may be the subject of a marshalling claim. **9.04**

---

[2] [1988] 2 Ll Rep 398.

[3] (1885) 30 Ch D 192.

[4] See further Chapters 7 and 8.

[5] (1885) 30 Ch D 192.

[6] Keaton & Sheridan, *Equity*, 304; Tyler, *Fisher & Lightwood's Law of Mortgage*, 531n(q); McDonald, *Marshalling* (1996), para 1608. C f Hanbury & Waldock, *The Law of Mortgages*, 178; P R Wood, *English and International Set-Off* (1989 Sweet & Maxwell), para 16–165; Meagher, Gummow & Lehane, *Equity Doctrines and Remedies*, paras 1114–1119; Derham, *Set-Off Against an Assignee: the Relevance of Marshalling, Contribution and Subrogation* 136–138.

[7] (1885) 30 Ch D 192.

9.05 One means of classifying securities[8] is by reference to the proprietary/non-proprietary dichotomy.[9] Proprietary securities encompass those securities where the performance of an obligation is *secured* by the grant to the obligee of a *proprietary interest*[10] in an asset or assets belonging to the security provider.[11] Non-proprietary securities, on the other hand, involve arrangements whereby the performance of an obligation is secured over assets, without the transfer of proprietary interests in those assets to the obligee.

Mortgages

9.06 English law recognises two types of mortgages: the legal mortgage and the equitable mortgage.[12] Both legal and equitable mortgages are proprietary securities.

The legal mortgage comprises a transfer of ownership of the mortgaged asset from the mortgagor to the mortgagee, subject to the mortgagor's equity of redemption (*viz.* the mortgagor's right to demand a reconveyance of ownership upon performance of the secured obligation).[13] There are two sub-categories of equitable mortgage: (i) agreements to grant a legal mortgage; and (ii) mortgages over equitable, as opposed to legal, interests. In both cases, the mortgagor retains ownership of the

---

[8] Absolute title arrangements – such as chattel leases, hire purchase agreements, conditional sales and retention of title or Romalpa clauses – known as 'reverse securities' (because the creditor, not the debtor, has reserved a proprietary interest in certain assets as security for the repayment of a debt), are not generally recognised as securities proper by English law. See Sykes & Walker, *The Law of Securities*, 660–674.

[9] This classification corresponds, as a general rule, to the distinction drawn by English law between possessory and non-possessory securities (the sole exception is the floating charge). A possessory security entails the transfer of possession of an asset from the debtor to the creditor without the transfer of any proprietary rights in that asset. The prime examples of this are the pledge and possessory lien. A non-possessory security, on the other hand, involves the transfer of proprietary rights (but not possession), in the asset over which the security has been granted, from the debtor to the creditor. This type of security is exemplified by the mortgage and the fixed charge. See R M Goode, *Legal Problems of Credit and Security* (2nd ed 1988 Sweet & Maxwell), Chapter 1.

[10] Sykes & Walker, *The Law of Securities*, 7 states: 'The concept of 'proprietary' involves a certain relationship between a person and a thing by virtue of which the person has certain rights which he or she may exercise over the thing . . . Such rights may be spoken of as in re, that is, exercisable in, to and over the thing . . . When a person has ownership of a res he or she has a collection or aggregation of rights in re, such as the rights of possession and of enjoyment and the right of transfer or disposal of the res'. Proprietary rights range from special or qualified property to ownership. The latter comprises the greatest possible interest that a party may have in a thing (A M Honore, *Ownership* in A G Guest (ed), *Oxford Essays in Jurisprudence* (1961 Oxford)). Special property comprises any right or combination of rights in a *res* that falls short of ownership.

[11] Sykes & Walker, *The Law of Securities*, 6–10 and 14 argue that 'all securities presuppose some proprietary right'. If that is correct, the distinction allegedly drawn by *Webb v Smith* (1885) 30 Ch D 192 is redundant.

[12] c f a statutory mortgage over Torrens system land in Australia and New Zealand which is equivalent to an equitable charge, rather than a legal or equitable mortgage: Sykes & Walker, *The Law of Securities*, 227–228.

[13] Sykes & Walker, *The Law of Securities*, 39–66 and 605–606.

mortgaged asset while the mortgagee obtains an equitable interest in that asset.[14]

Fixed equitable charges

A fixed equitable charge comprises an 'appropriation of real or personal property **9.07** for the discharge of a debt or other obligation'.[15] In contrast to the mortgage, there is, strictly speaking, no transfer of proprietary interests in the asset subject to the charge from the chargor to the chargee. The chargee, instead, obtains from the chargor certain equitable rights which entitle it to realise the charged asset upon the default of the chargor.

Thus, although there is no transfer of pre-existing proprietary rights in the charged asset from the chargor to the chargee, the charge—as an encumbrance on that asset—qualifies the chargor's proprietary rights. The charge is considered a proprietary security as there has been a *transfer by subtraction* from the debtor's bundle of proprietary rights in the asset.[16]

Uncrystallised floating charges

The nature of the floating charge remains controversial. The majority view[17] is **9.08** that a floating charge merely hovers over the assets of the debtor and does not grant to the creditor any equitable interest in the assets of the debtor until such time as crystallisation occurs (on crystallisation, the floating charge is converted into a fixed equitable charge).[18]

---

[14] Ibid., 148–156, 610–615 and 616–617.

[15] Tyler, *Fisher & Lightwood's Law of Mortgage*, 4.

[16] Sykes & Walker, *The Law of Securities*, 197–198, 616–617 and 748–749; E Ferran, *Floating Charges – the Nature of the Security* [1988] CLJ 213, 213–214. See further R M Goode, *Charges Over Book Debts: A Missed Opportunity* (1994) 110 LQR 592; M G Bridge, *Fixed Charges and Freedom of Contract* (1994) 110 LQR 340; A Berg, *Charges Over Book Debts: A Reply* [1995] JBL 433; S Worthington, *Fixed Charges over Book Debts and other Receivables* (1997) 113 LQR 562; A Bidin, *Re Coslett: Equitable Interests and the Nature of Fixed and Specific Charges* (1997) 18 Co Lawyer 25; R Gregory & P Walton, *Fixed Charges Over Changing Assets—The Possession and Control Heresy* (1998) 2 CfiLR 68.

[17] Goode, *Legal Problems of Credit and Security*, 47–51; Sykes & Walker, *The Law of Securities*, 958–959; W J Gough, *Company Charges* (2nd ed 1996 Butterworths), 97–101 and 332–373; S Worthington, *Proprietary Interests in Commercial Transactions* (1996 Oxford), 72–79; J C Nkala, *Some Aspects of the Jurisprudence of the Floating Charge* (1993) 11 C&SLJ 301; J Naser, *The Juridical Basis of the Floating Charge* (1994) 15 Co Lawyer 11; R Grantham, *Refloating a Floating Charge* (1997) 1 CfiLR 53; C H Tan, *Automatic Crystallisation, De-crystallisation and Convertibility of Charges* (1998) 2 CfiLR 41.

[18] c f J H Farrar, *World Economic Stagnation Puts the Floating Charge on Trial* (1980) 1 Co Lawyer 83 and Ferran, *Floating Charges – the Nature of the Security* who argue that both fixed and floating charges confer equitable interests in the charged assets upon the creditor from the time of their inception. They are therefore both proprietary securities. C f D Everett, *The Nature of Fixed and Floating Charges as Security Devices* (1988 Monash) who argues that neither the fixed charge nor the floating charge confers upon the creditor any equitable interests. On this basis, neither charge would qualify as a proprietary security.

Accordingly, an uncrystallised floating charge is a non-proprietary security.

Pledges

9.09   In the case of a pledge, possession of an asset is transferred from the pledgor to the pledgee as security for the performance of an obligation owed to the pledgee.[19]

The status of the pledge is ambiguous as the pledgee enjoys a 'special property' in the pledged asset that allows it to sell the asset on non-performance of the secured obligation and to assign its security, by way of sub-pledge, to third parties.[20] It has been argued that, as a consequence of this special property held by the pledgee, the pledge is a proprietary security.[21]

The better view, however, is that the pledge is, in fact, a non-proprietary security.[22] Unlike the mortgage or the charge, the pledgee cannot trace its security into the hands of third parties; the pledgee cannot recover possession of the pledged assets (as can a mortgagee or chargee) but is entitled to only a claim for damages in tort for trespass or conversion. Thus, the secured claim the pledgee enjoyed in respect for the pledged asset has been converted by its loss of possession into an unsecured claim.

Possessory liens

9.10   The possessory or common law lien arises *via* operation of law and permits a obligee who is lawfully in possession of assets belonging to a obligor to retain possession of those assets, until the obligor repays either a debt associated with those assets (called a 'particular lien') or its entire indebtedness to the obligee (called a 'general lien').[23]

While the possessory lien is similar in nature to the pledge (in each case the security holder may withhold possession until performance of the secured obligation), it is a much clearer case of a non-proprietary security; the lienor has neither the right to sell the asset nor may it assign its security over the asset.[24]

---

[19]   Sykes & Walker, *The Law of Securities*, 732–733.
[20]   Ibid.
[21]   Ibid, 732.
[22]   *Donald v Suckling* (1866) LR 1 QB 585, 594 where the pledge was defined as: 'a real right or jus in re, *inferior to property*, which vests in the holder a power over the subject, to retain it in security of the debt for which it is pledged, and qualifies so far and retains the right of property in the pledger or owner'. See further N Palmer & A Hudson, *Pledge* in N Palmer & E McKendrick (eds), *Interests in Goods* (2nd ed 1998 LLP).
[23]   Sykes & Walker, *The Law of Securities*, 739–740.
[24]   Ibid, 737–738.

Non-possessory liens

Non-possessory liens (or equitable liens) are proprietary securities. There is, in **9.11** essence, no difference between a non-possessory lien and an equitable charge, save that the former arises by operation of law while the latter is created by agreement between the chargor and chargee.[25]

Availability of marshalling and the triumph of form over substance

Webb v Smith[26] poses no problems for a junior creditor seeking to marshall where **9.12** it and the senior creditor hold mortgages, charges or non-possessory liens over the assets of the common debtor. This, however, is not the case where either one or both of the junior and senior securities is a pledge, uncrystallised floating charge or possessory lien. Should either the junior creditor or the senior creditor hold one of these securities, the junior creditor will, on the basis of *Webb v Smith*,[27] be unable to marshall the senior security.

This case thus represents a triumph of form over substance, producing anomalous **9.13** results. Where a junior creditor holds a proprietary security, but a senior creditor holds a pledge, uncrystallised floating charge or possessory lien, the senior security will be beyond the reach of marshalling with the consequence that marshalling will be unable to preserve the priority-ranking of a proprietary security.

The special case of floating charges

The potential difficulties that an uncrystallised floating charge may pose for a **9.14** junior creditor intending to marshall are, however, largely illusory.[28]

The enforcement of the senior security by the senior creditor, upon which marshalling is predicated, necessarily requires that that security, if it is a floating charge, must have first crystallised, in which case it is no different from a fixed charge.

Again, a junior creditor who holds a floating charge will be unable to marshall the senior security until that charge has crystallised. Most modern floating charge documentation includes cross-default clauses the effect of which are to cause a

---

[25] Ibid, 199 and 750–752.

[26] (1885) 30 Ch D 192.

[27] Ibid.

[28] c f it has been queried, in Australia, as to whether subrogation – and perhaps marshalling – is available in respect of floating charges: *O'Day v Commercial Bank of Australia* (1933) 50 CLR 200. However, subrogation to floating charges has subsequently been permitted in Australia in *Australia and New Zealand Banking Group Ltd v Carnegie* (unrep 16 June 1987, Sup Ct of Vic); *Re Selvas Pty Ltd* (1989) 52 SASR 449. This is also the position in New Zealand: *National Bank of New Zealand Ltd v Chapman* [1975] 1 NZLR 480; and Canada: *Roynat Ltd v Denis* (1982) 139 DLR (3d) 265. See further O'Donovan & Phillips, *The Modern Contract of Guarantee*, 673–674.

floating charge to crystallise, among other things, on the enforcement of security by any other creditor of the debtor.

C. *Webb v Smith* and the Requirement of Proprietary Securities

Introduction

9.15 The requirement of proprietary securities, that is said to be have been introduced by *Webb v Smith*,[29] is inconsistent with the line of English cases in which marshalling has been applied to pledges[30] and possessory liens.[31] Admittedly, there was no discussion in those cases of the nature of the securities to which marshalling applied; it was assumed that they were, simply by virtue of being securities, susceptible to the doctrine of marshalling.[32]

9.16 An examination of *Webb v Smith*,[33] however, demonstrates that there is no inconsistency between it and the cases supporting the application of marshalling to pledges and liens. *Webb v Smith*[34] does not therefore impose on marshalling the requirement of proprietary securities claimed for it.[35]

Webb v Smith—the facts

9.17 The defendants ('Smith') were auctioneers who had sold a brewery and furniture on behalf of a customer and were liable to account to the customer for the sale proceeds. The customer, in turn, owed Smith auction fees for the sale of the brewery

---

[29] (1885) 30 Ch D 192.

[30] *Broadbent v Barlow* (1861) 3 De G F & J 570; *Ex parte Alston* (1868) 4 Ch App 168; *Re Burge, Woodall & Co* [1912] 1 KB 393. See *Halsbury's*, Vol 32 ('*Mortgage*') para 916; Tyler, *Fisher & Lightwood's Law of Mortgage*, 531n(q); Meagher, Gummow & Lehane, *Equity Doctrines and Remedies*, para 1118.

[31] *Trimmer v Bayne* (1803) 9 Ves 209; *Sproule v Prior* (1826) 8 Sim 189. See Tyler, *Fisher & Lightwood's Law of Mortgage*, 531. Marshalling of possessory liens has also been permitted in Ireland: *Buckley v Buckley* (1887) 19 LR Ir 544. The cases in which marshalling has been permitted in respect of bottomry bonds are not relevant. Although bottomry bonds are often referred to as maritime liens, that terminology is a misnomer; they are, in fact, equitable charges rather than liens: see Sykes & Walker, *The Law of Securities*, 749–750 (q v Davies & Dickey, *Shipping Law*, 132 and 135 where it is noted that while a bottomry bond takes priority over all ship mortgages without exception, it, as a general rule, concedes priority to any maritime lien: *Cargo ex Galam* (1863) Br & Lush 167). For a discussion of the application of marshalling to bottomry bonds, see Robbins, *A Treatise on the Law of Mortgages, Pledges and Hypothecations*, 789; Smith, *A Practical Exposition of the Principles of Equity*, 614; Hewitt, *White & Tudor's Leading Cases in Equity*, 59; Ramsbotham, *Coote's Treatise on the Law of Mortgages*, 1510; and, more recently, the Australian case of *Patrick Stevedores No 2 Pty Ltd v MV Skulptor Konenkov* (1996) 136 ALR 211, 226.

[32] e g Hanbury & Waldock, *The Law of Mortgages*, 178 where it is stated that marshalling applies to mortgages, charges and liens. However, no mention is made of pledges and the reference to liens might have been intended to encompass only non-possessory liens.

[33] (1885) 30 Ch D 192.

[34] Ibid.

[35] q v n6.

and furniture. The proceeds of the sale of the brewery, but not the proceeds of sale of the furniture, were subject to a lien in favour of Smith, as security for Smith's auction fees. Smith thus had a right of lien over one set of proceeds but only a right of set-off against the other.

The customer charged his interest in the proceeds of the brewery sale to Webb, pursuant to an assignment by way of security (to secure the repayment of a debt owed by the customer to Webb). Notice of the assignment was duly given by the customer to Smith. However, prior to remitting the brewery sale proceeds to Webb and the furniture sale proceeds to the customer, Smith deducted from the former proceeds the auction fees owed.

Webb v Smith—the judgment

9.18 Webb claimed that the doctrine of marshalling was available to protect his interest in the brewery sale proceeds; *viz.*, Smith should have satisfied the claim for auction fees out of the furniture sale proceeds. Webb claimed further that, as Smith had, instead, elected to look to the brewery sale proceeds for the satisfaction of the claim, Webb was entitled to the benefit of Smith's right of set-off against the furniture sale proceeds.

9.19 The Court of Appeal rejected Webb's claims, with Cotton L.J. holding that:[36]

> It is true that apparently there were two funds: but the Defendants [Smith] had no claim against or lien over the fund produced by the sale of the furniture: they could only have a set-off as to it, and the doctrine of marshalling applies only where there are claims or charges upon both funds. Therefore there could be no marshalling.

9.20 Furthermore, the rights of Smith to both funds were required to be on 'an equal footing'. Lindley L.J stated:[37]

> The vice of the argument for the Plaintiff [Webb] is that in truth there were not two funds to which the Defendants [Smith] could resort, that is, two funds standing upon an equal footing. The Defendants had a superior right of lien as to the fund produced by the sale of the brewery.

9.21 Accordingly, marshalling would not be available 'where there are different funds as to which different rights exist'.[38] Smith had different rights of recourse to the

---

[36] *Webb v Smith* (1885) 30 Ch D 192, 200.

[37] Ibid, 202.

[38] Ibid, 199. C f *Moxon v The Berkeley Mutual Benefit Building Society* (1890) 59 LJ Ch 524. The senior creditor, in this case, held a mortgage over an asset of the debtor and a right of set-off against a fund of the debtor. The debtor subsequently granted a second mortgage over the asset to a junior creditor and assigned the fund by way of security (subject to the right of set-off) to a third party. On the enforcement of the mortgage, Kay J. (as he then was) applied marshalling by apportionment (see further Chapter 11). However, the authority of this case as regards the nature of the rights of recourse required to be held by the senior creditor is weakened by the fact that *Webb v Smith* was not considered by Kay J., a fact that was acknowledged by Warner J. in *Smit Tak International Zeesleepin Bergingsbedrijf BV v Selco Salvage Ltd* [1988] 2 Ll Rep 398, 406.

two funds: a lien over the brewery sale proceeds and a right of set-off against the furniture sale proceeds. Webb therefore could not avail himself of the protection of the doctrine of marshalling, following the recoupment by Smith of the debt owed by the customer out of the proceeds subsequently charged to Webb.

Requirement of proprietary securities is without foundation

9.22 It is difficult to see how *Webb v Smith*[39] constitutes authority for the proposition that marshalling requires both the junior and senior creditors to hold proprietary securities.

9.23 The Court of Appeal refused to permit Webb to marshall Smith's right of set-off on the grounds that Smith had *unequal* rights of recourse to the two sets of proceeds that were subject to Smith's claim for auction fees.[40] This case thus only decides that, in order for marshalling to be available, the security held by the senior creditor must confer upon it equal rights of recourse to the asset, subject to the junior security, and the asset, subject to the senior security in respect of which marshalling is being sought.[41]

9.24 Marshalling was therefore denied on the grounds that the requirements of the common debtor rule had not been satisfied, not because Smith did not hold proprietary securities over the two sets of proceeds. This leaves open the question as to whether Webb may have been able to invoke the doctrine of marshalling had Smith possessed liens over both sets of proceeds or only rights of set-off (*per* the requirement of 'claims or charges').[42] But in raising this question, the case firmly resolves the earlier question as to the requirement of proprietary securities: neither the lien (which was clearly possessory in nature) nor the right of set-off[43] held by Smith constitutes a proprietary security.

---

[39] (1885) 30 Ch D 192.

[40] See also Hewitt, *White & Tudor's Leading Cases in Equity*, 58; Meagher, Gummow & Lehane, *Equity Doctrines and Remedies*, para 1114; Gummow, *Marshalling and Protected Assets*; Derham, *Set-Off Against an Assignee: the Relevance of Marshalling, Contribution and Subrogation*, 137.

[41] This is the fourth element of the common debtor rule: see further Chapter 7.

[42] q v Wood, *English and International Set-Off*, para 16–165 where it is observed: '[T]he case suggests that if the rights had been equal, marshalling might have applied'. C f the Australian case of *Commonwealth Trading Bank v Colonial Mutual Life Assurance Society Ltd* (1970) 26 FLR 338, 345 where Neasey J. described *Webb v Smith* (1885) 30 Ch D 192 as follows: '... because the defendants had a security over one fund only and not over the other, the doctrine of marshalling did not apply'.

[43] P R Wood, *Title Finance, Derivatives, Securitisations, Set-Off and Netting* (1995 Sweet & Maxwell), para 6–3 states: '[T]he main effect of set-off is that a debtor with a set-off is in substance 'secured' in that the debtor's cross-claim can be paid or discharged by setting it off against the creditor's claim ... However, set-off is not security proper in that the creditor does not grant the debtor a security interest over the creditor's property in the debt owed to the creditor to secure the cross-claim owed by the creditor to the debtor'. Q v M B Hapgood, *Set-Off Under the Laws of England* in F W Neate (ed) *Set-Off as Security* (1990 IBA), 37, where it is stated: 'A right of set-off is not per se security in the strict sense. The essential difference between set-off and security is that set-off is a procedure by which a *debtor* reduces or extinguishes his own liability by the application of property

There is, accordingly, no good reason why marshalling should be limited to proprietary securities.

Restricting marshalling to real property mortgages in Canada

There is, in addition, in Canada a line of authority that suggests that marshalling **9.25** is restricted to real property mortgages. In *Steinbach Credit Union Ltd v Manitoba Agricultural Credit Corp*,[44] the Manitoba Court of Queen's Bench stated: '. . . the third loan of the applicant is not secured by a real property mortgage, and the doctrine of marshalling would not, in my opinion, apply to this loan'. These comments were interpreted by the Saskatchewan Court of Queen's Bench in *National Bank of Canada v Makin Metals Ltd*[45] to mean that a real property mortgage was a pre-requisite for marshalling.

On appeal, this point was left undecided although the Saskatchewan Court of Appeal noted the substantial body of case law in Canada and the United States to the contrary[46] and, in particular, the Canadian case of *Re Bread Man Inc*[47] where marshalling with respect to chattel securities was permitted. Given the number of cases under English law where marshalling has been permitted in respect of securities other than real property mortgages,[48] it is unlikely that the courts would require both the senior and junior securities to be real property mortgages in order for marshalling to be available.[49]

D. Extension of Marshalling to Non-Security Rights

Smit Tak and the expansion of marshalling rights

The soundness of the proposition that marshalling is only available where **9.26** both the senior and junior creditors hold proprietary securities has recently been

---

to which he is beneficially entitled (his claim against the other party); whereas the realisation of security is a process by which a *creditor* reduces or extinguishes the secured liability by the application of property in which the creditor has the limited interest of a mortgagee or a chargee'. See also S McCracken, *The Banker's Remedy of Set-Off* (1993 Butterworths), 165–167 and 174–185; Derham, *Set-Off*, 559–566.

[44] (1991) 72 Man R (2d) 161, 168.
[45] [1993] 3 WWR 318, 328.
[46] *National Bank of Canada v Makin Metals Ltd* (1994) 116 Sask R 236, 240.
[47] (1979) 89 DLR (3d) 599. C f *Royal Trust Company v H A Roberts Group Limited* [1995] 4 WWR 305, where it was considered that *National Bank of Canada v Makin Metals Ltd* was authority for the proposition that the doctrine of marshalling has no application to securities over personal property encompassed by the Canadian Personal Property Securities Acts.
[48] See the cases noted in nn30 and 31 where marshalling has been permitted in relation to pledges and liens. See also *Re Fry* [1912] 2 Ch 86 where marshalling was first applied to equitable charges.
[49] See further Tyler, Young & Croft, *Fisher & Lightwood's Law of Mortgage*, para 30.8; MacDougall, *Marshalling and the Personal Property Security Acts: Doing Unto Others . . .*, 94–96.

questioned in *Smit Tak International Zeesleepin Bergingsbedrijf BV v Selco Salvage Ltd.*[50]

Warner J. considered that there was nothing in the decision in *Webb v Smith*[51] to suggest that marshalling should be limited in its application to proprietary securities.[52] Warner J. took the view that *Webb v Smith*[53] was only authority for the proposition that a junior creditor would not be able to marshall where the senior creditor did not possess equal rights of recourse to the assets that were available for the repayment of the senior debt.[54]

9.27 Accordingly, Warner J. found himself able to resolve the second question left open by *Webb v Smith*:[55] a junior creditor would be entitled to avail itself of the doctrine of marshalling where the senior creditor held, not security, but equal rights of set-off against two or more of the assets of the debtor. Warner J. stated:[56]

> Bearing in mind that equity is concerned to achieve fairness rather than to give effect to technicalities, I can see no reason why, where the first claimant is liable to the debtor or his assigns in respect of two debts, as against which he is entitled to exercise a right of set-off, those debts should not be regarded, for the purposes of the equitable doctrine of marshalling, as funds to which the first claimant is entitled to resort ... *Webb v Smith* is not however authority for the proposition that there can never be marshalling where the first claimant has only rights of set-off.

9.28 In this case, Smit Tak had rights of set-off against debts owed by it to Selco Salvage. Selco Salvage had assigned a number of those debts to three banks. Warner J. considered that, in the event that Smit Tak chose to enforce its right of set-off against the assigned debts, the banks would be entitled to marshall Smit Tak's set-off rights against the debts retained by Selco Salvage. Marshalling was available as Smit Tak's set-off rights conferred upon it equal rights of recourse against the assigned debts and the debts remaining with Selco Salvage.[57]

9.29 A right of set-off held by one party against a debt owed by it to another party does not, however, confer upon the first party any proprietary interest in the debt owed to the second party.[58] Nor does it constitute a non-proprietary security over that

---

[50] [1988] 2 Ll Rep 398.
[51] (1885) 30 Ch D 192.
[52] [1988] 2 Ll Rep 398, 406.
[53] (1885) 30 Ch D 192.
[54] [1988] 2 Ll Rep 398, 406.
[55] (1885) 30 Ch D 192.
[56] [1988] 2 Ll Rep 398, 406.
[57] Similarly, if Selco Salvage had assigned all the debts to different assignees, Smit Tak's set-off rights would be apportioned rateably between the two assignees in a manner analogous to the principle in *Barnes v Racster* (1842) 1 Y & C Ch Cas 401. Knight Bruce V.C. stated (405): 'where each of two funds has been assigned or charged by the debtor to a different subsequent claimant, equity interposes so as to secure that the claim of the first claimant is borne by the two funds rateably'.
[58] q v n43. See also R A Ladbury, *Rights of Set-Off as Security* in Neate, *Set-Off As Security*, 69 where it is stated: '[A] right of set-off does not create any equitable security interest or right in rem. It follows from this view that a right of set-off is a personal right only'.

debt.[59] Thus, the decision in *Smit Tak*[60] not only applies the doctrine of marshalling to non-proprietary securities but also brings non-security rights, such as set-off, within the embrace of the doctrine.

Unwarranted expansion of the scope of marshalling

It is unlikely that the expansion of marshalling contemplated by *Smit Tak*[61] is **9.30** capable of being sustained. The major weakness of the case lies in the court's treatment of set-off.

The right of set-off against a debt, such as the right that Smit Tak was entitled to **9.31** assert, is a procedural defence to any action which the creditor to whom that debt is owed may undertake for the recovery of the debt.[62] The liability of the creditor to the debtor (*viz.* the cross-debt supporting the right of set-off) can be employed to reduce or extinguish the debtor's liability to the creditor. The debt owed to the creditor and the cross-debt owed to the debtor would therefore be discharged, by setting one off against the other, to the extent of the lesser liability.

Accordingly, it is conceptually difficult to see how a party might utilise, *via* the **9.32** doctrine of marshalling, another party's right of set-off, after that right of set-off has been asserted by the latter party to partially or wholly discharge its indebtedness to a third party. Once a right of set-off has been exercised, there remains nothing to which a party seeking to marshall that right can be substituted.[63]

This, however, is exactly what the decision in *Smit Tak*[64] entails: the three banks **9.33** were considered entitled to Smit Tak's right of set-off against the debt owed to

---

[59] The House of Lords in *Re Bank of Credit and Commerce International SA (No 8)* [1998] 1 BCLC 68 has overruled *Re Charge Card Services Ltd* [1986] 3 WLR 697, holding that a party may acquire a valid proprietary interest by way of charge over its own indebtedness. Accordingly, the first party would be able to validly charge back the cross-debt owed to it by the second party to secure the repayment of the debt owed by it to the second party. See McCracken, *The Banker's Remedy of Set-Off*, 178–182; Derham, *Set-Off*, 551–559; R M Goode, *Charge-Backs and Legal Fictions* (1998) 114 LQR 178; G McCormack, *Charge Backs and Commercial Certainty in the House of Lords* (1998) 2 CfiLR 111.

[60] [1988] 2 Ll Rep 398.

[61] Ibid.

[62] Wood, *English and International Set-Off*, para 19.01[1]; Derham, *Set-Off*, 20–27. See also, in Australia: F Jordan, *Chapters on Equity in New South Wales* (6th ed 1945 Sydney), 156–158; Meagher, Gummow & Lehane, *Equity Doctrines and Remedies*, paras 3701 and 3704.

[63] *Smit Tak International Zeesleepin Bergingsbedrijf BV v Selco Salvage Ltd* [1988] 2 Ll Rep 398 also supports a hybrid model of marshalling: see further Chapter 3. As regards the extinguishment of set-off rights once exercised, see Derham, *Set-Off Against an Assignee: the Relevance of Marshalling, Contribution and Subrogation*, 137. Meagher, Gummow & Lehane, *Equity Doctrines and Remedies*, para 1115 adopt Derham's views on this issue: '[I]t makes no sense to speak of [the junior creditor] as subrogated to a defence available to the debtor in another action brought by another party'. It is thus unlikely that the 'reviving' subrogation articulated by the House of Lords in *Banque Financière de la Cité v Parc (Battersea) Ltd* [1998] 1 All ER 737 would be of application here: see further paragraphs 4.34 and 4.35.

[64] [1988] 2 Ll Rep 398.

Selco Salvage, after that right of set-off had been exercised against the debt assigned to the banks.

Conclusion

9.34 It can therefore be concluded that the doctrine of marshalling of securities applies to, and is available in respect of, all securities, be they proprietary or non-proprietary in nature. *Webb v Smith*[65] does not have the effect of requiring both the senior and junior creditors to hold proprietary securities while *Smit Tak*[66] does not render marshalling available in respect of non-securities.

E. Marshalling of Securities and Quasi-Securities

Introduction

9.35 Quasi-securities are devices that perform the economic function of security, but without the legal indicia of security, *viz*. devices that confer on their holder a preferential claim against the assets of the debtor but defy classification as a mortgage, charge, pledge or lien.

The principal examples of quasi-securities are rights of set-off, title retention devices and the negative pledge.[67]

Set-off and marshalling of securities

9.36 On the basis of the above examination of *Smit Tak*,[68] a junior creditor would not be able to marshall rights of set-off held by a senior creditor. Nor would a junior creditor whose only rights against the debtor were those of set-off be able to use this case to support its right to marshall the security held by a senior creditor.[69]

---

[65] (1885) 30 Ch D 192.

[66] [1988] 2 Ll Rep 398.

[67] A *guarantee* is not a quasi-security; it only provides a creditor with an additional party – the surety – against whom recourse may be had should the debtor fail to discharge its indebtedness to the creditor. The creditor's claim under the guarantee is no different from the claims of the surety's unsecured creditors. Nor can a *subordination of debt* be properly considered a quasi-security. A subordination effects a rearrangement of the relative priority ranking of one class of creditors *qua* another. The subordination does not, of itself, create rights against the debtor in addition to the rights already possessed by the creditors who are parties to the subordination (although the subordination may constitute a security over the assets of the subordinated creditors). Thus where an unsecured creditor is a beneficiary of a subordination, as is typically the case, there is no question of its status as an unsecured creditor having been altered. What the subordination does is to defer the claims of those creditors, who would otherwise rank ahead of or *pari passu* with the unsecured creditor, to that unsecured creditor's claim against the debtor. See generally P R Wood, *The Law of Subordinated Debt* (1990 Sweet & Maxwell); P R Wood, *Project Finance, Subordinated Debt and State Loans* (1995 Sweet & Maxwell), Chapter 8.

[68] [1988] 2 Ll Rep 398.

[69] A creditor whose only rights against a debtor are those of set-off is an unsecured creditor.

Title retention devices and marshalling of securities

Title retention devices (such as chattel leases, hire purchase agreements, condi- **9.37**
tional sales and Romalpa clauses) purport to 'secure' the repayment of the debt
owed to a creditor by a debtor, by reserving ownership of chattels in the possession
of the debtor to the creditor until that debt has been discharged.[70]

A junior creditor will not be able to use the doctrine of marshalling to obtain the
benefit of an asset that is subject to a title retention device in favour of the senior
creditor (or a third party[71]). In this situation, the junior creditor will be unable to
satisfy the requirements of the common debtor rule as the asset to which access *via*
marshalling is being sought is owned by a party other than the common debtor.[72]

Negative pledges and marshalling of securities

A negative pledge is, in its simplest form, a covenant by the debtor in favour of a **9.38**
creditor not to create security over its assets. By means of this device, the creditor
ensures that it will rank at least *pari passu* with the other creditors of the debtor. A
negative pledge is thus no more than a contractual obligation to refrain from certain acts and, despite its appellation, does not constitute a security.[73]

A senior creditor who is the beneficiary of a negative pledge possesses no rights
against specific assets of the debtor to which a junior creditor can obtain access *via*
marshalling. Moreover, the issue of marshalling rights will be irrelevant if the negative pledge is efficacious; the senior and junior creditors will, in that situation,
rank *pari passu* as between themselves.

Indiscriminate expansion of marshalling rights

The indiscriminate extension of the right to marshall to the holders of non- **9.39**
security and quasi-security interests is inexplicable when considered in the context of the redistributive character of marshalling.

---

[70] The line between quasi-security and security is a particularly fine one in the case of Romalpa
clauses that purport to reserve ownership in assets other than the chattels supplied by the creditor
(e g products manufactured using those chattels) or the proceeds of sale of the chattels. See generally G McCormack, *Reservation of Title* (2nd ed 1995 Sweet & Maxwell); Worthington, *Proprietary
Interests in Commercial Transactions*, Chapter 2; G McCormack, *Title Retention and the Company
Charge Registration System* in Palmer & McKendrick (eds), *Interests in Goods*.

[71] See further paragraph 10.12.

[72] Nor can the junior creditor rely on the surety exception (the asset in question certainly does
not secure a guarantee of the senior debt).

[73] See the Australian case of *Pullen v Abalcheck* (1990) 20 NSWLR 732. Similarly, the majority
of United States cases have denied the status of security to negative pledges: *Tahoe National Bank v
Phillips* 480 P 2d 320 (1971); *Weaver v TriCity Credit Bureau* 557 P 2d 1072 (1976); *Equitable
Trust Co v Imbesi* 412 A 2d 96 (1980); *Chase Manhattan Bank v Gems-by-Gordon Inc* 649 F 2d 710
(1981); c f *Coast Bank v Minderhout* 392 P 2d 265 (1964). See further Allan, *Negative Pledge
Lending – Dead or Alive*.

The doctrine of marshalling has as its objective the preservation of the priority-ranking of the junior creditor's claim against the debtor. This is accomplished by a redistribution of the debtor's assets amongst its remaining creditors, once the senior debt has been discharged, for the benefit of the junior creditor.

9.40 The preservation of priority by means of such a redistribution necessarily presupposes a hierarchy of claims against the debtor, with these claims being segregated between those which are protected by marshalling and those which are not. The preferential status of the class of protected claimants is maintained *via* the transfer to them of the benefit of assets away from the latter class, should the members of the former class be prejudiced by the enforcement of the security held by the paramount-ranking creditor.

Absent such a hierarchy, the concept of redistribution, and with it that of marshalling, becomes otiose. In the absence of a hierarchy of claims, marshalling will be unable to effect anything more than a reshuffling of the benefit of assets amongst creditors with equal ranking claims to those assets. Each creditor who invokes the doctrine of marshalling would be permitted to exchange its claim against an asset for a claim of equivalent priority-ranking against another asset. The asset swap, and the doctrine under whose auspices the swap has been effected, would thus be entirely meaningless.[74]

---

[74] Extending marshalling rights to unsecured creditors in the presence of the secured/unsecured hierarchy is equally meaningless: see further Chapter 10.

PART V

LIMITATIONS ON MARSHALLING OF SECURITIES

10

MARSHALLING OF SECURITIES AND THE RIGHTS OF UNSECURED CREDITORS

Introduction   10.01
Extension of Marshalling Rights to Unsecured
  Creditors

Introduction   10.04
Marshalling on behalf of unsecured
  creditors   10.05
Special position of trustees in bankruptcy
  under US law   10.06

Redundancy of judicial lien marshalling   10.08
Unsecured Creditors and Extinguishment of
  Marshalling Rights

Introduction   10.11
Death knell of marshalling   10.13

A. Introduction

Under English law, unsecured creditors do not have the right to marshall: a creditor who is seeking access to the security held by a senior creditor of a debtor must, itself, be a secured creditor of that debtor.[1]   **10.01**

---

[1] *Finch v Winchelsea* (1718) 1 P Wms 399n (an earlier case, *Burgh v Francis* (1673) Cas temp Finch 28 was incorrectly cited in *Averall v Wade* (1835) L & G temp Sugd 252 as supporting this position); *Anstey v Newman* (1870) 39 LJ Ch 769. See also Webster, *Ashburner's Concise Treatise on Mortgages, Pledges and Liens*, 467; *Halsbury's*, Vol 32 ('*Mortgage*'), para 916; Tyler, *Fisher & Lightwood's Law of Mortgage*, 532; Cousins, *The Law of Mortgages*, 435. This is also the position in Ireland: *Averall v Wade* (1835) L & G temp Sugd 252; Australia: *DM & BP Wiskich Pty Ltd v Saadi* (unrep 16 Feb 1996, Sup Ct of NSW); Sykes & Walker, *The Law of Securities*, 183; New Zealand: *Re Watkins* [1938] NZLR 847; and Canada: *Williamson v Loonstra* (1973) 34 DLR (3d) 275; *Nova Scotia Savings & Loan Co v O'Hara* (1979) 7 RPR 281; *Re Bread Man Inc* (1979) 89 DLR (3d) 599; *Bank of Nova Scotia v Adriatic Development Ltd* [1985] 2 WWR 627; *Ontario Inc v Allison* (1995) CBR (3d) 144. C f (i) *Lomas v Wright* (1833) 2 My & K 769 which suggests that a voluntary creditor – whose claim is inferior to those of unsecured creditors for value – can marshall; (ii) the Australian case of *In re Crothers* [1930] VLR 49 in which marshalling by apportionment was applied in favour of unsecured creditors (the soundness of this case has been questioned in subsequent Australian (*Re Wood* [1949] St R Qd 17) and New Zealand (*Re Tremain* [1934] NZLR 369) cases).

10.02 Similarly, it is accepted by English law that unsecured creditors do not form one of the classes of third parties who can defeat a junior creditor's right to marshall.[2]

10.03 Recent developments in the United States of America have attacked the validity of these two principles. The trustee in bankruptcy of the common debtor has been permitted in the United States to marshall the senior security on behalf of unsecured creditors. In addition, the United States courts have permitted unsecured creditors to prevent a junior creditor from marshalling the senior security on the grounds that marshalling would prejudice them.

This chapter considers whether these United States developments are capable of being sustained under English law.

B. Extension of Marshalling Rights to Unsecured Creditors

Introduction

10.04 In common with English law, the law of the United States has consistently refused to permit unsecured creditors of a debtor to marshall the security held over the debtor's assets by a senior creditor.[3] This is well illustrated by the following statement in *American Jurisprudence*:[4]

---

[2] *Lanoy v Duke & Duchess of Athol* (1742) 2 Atk 444; *Hamilton v Royse* (1804) 2 Sch & Lef 315; *Re Tristram* (1825) 1 Dec 288; *Barnes v Racster* (1842) 1 Y & C Ch Cas 401; *Baldwin v Belcher* (1842) 2 Dr & War 173; *Haynes v Forshaw* (1853) 11 Hare 93; *Gibson v Seagrim* (1855) 20 Beav 614; *Re Stephenson* (1866) 3 De G M & G 969; *Ex parte Alston* (1868) 4 Ch App 168; *Dolphin v Aylward* (1870) LR 4 E & I 486; *Flint v Howard* [1893] 2 Ch 54; *Gray v Stone & Funnell* (1893) 69 LT 282. See Jenks, *English Civil Law*, para 1396; Hanbury & Waldock, *The Law of Mortgages*, 179; *Halsbury's*, Vol 32 ('*Mortgage*'), para 917; Tyler, *Fisher & Lightwood's Law of Mortgage*, 532–533; Cousins, *The Law of Mortgages*, 436; Strahan, *The Marshalling of Mortgages*, 308. This is also the position in Ireland: *In re Scott's Estate* (1862) 14 Ir Ch R 63; *Hales v Cox* (1863) 32 Beav 118; *Re Lynch's Estate* (1867) 1 Ir R Eq 396; and Canada: *Williamson v Loonstra* (1973) 34 DLR (3d) 275; *Re Bread Man Inc* (1979) 89 DLR (3d) 599 (c f MacDougall, *Marshalling and the Personal Property Security Acts: Doing Unto Others . . .*, 114 where it stated that there should be no absolute bar on the ability of unsecured creditors to prevent marshalling). See further Chapter 11.

[3] *Union Bank v Laird* 15 US 390 (1817); *Lewis v United States* 92 US 618 (1875); *The 'Edith'* 94 US 518 (1876); *Schraff v Meyer* 35 SW 858 (1896); *Merrill v National Bank* 173 US 131 (1899); *Stickel v Atwood* 56 A 687 (1903); *First National Bank of Boston v Proctor* 40 F 2d 841 (1930); *Wenatchee Production Credit Association v Pacific Fruit & Produce Co* 92 P 2d 883 (1939); *Greenwich Trust Co v Tyson* 27 A 2d 166 (1942); *In re Careful Laundry, Inc* 104 A 2d 813 (1954); *Johnson v Lentini* 169 A 2d 208 (1961); *In re Computer Room, Inc* 24 BR 732 (1982); *In re McElwaney* 40 BR 66 (1984); *In re Mesa Intercontinental, Inc* 79 BR 669 (1987); *In re Gibson Group, Inc* 151 BR 133 (1993). See also *CJS*, paras 21:118 and 55:17; *Am Jur*, para 53:18; Mosman, *The Proper Application of Marshaling on Behalf of Unsecured Creditors*, 641–642; Lachman, *Marshaling Assets in Bankruptcy: Recent Innovations in the Doctrine*, 675–676; Emamzadeh, *Marshaling in Bankruptcy: Questioning the Recent Expansions to the Common Debtor Requirement*, 316–319. C f *In re Hale* 141 BR 225 (1992) in which unsecured creditors were permitted to marshall.

[4] *Am Jur*, para 53:18.

An unsecured creditor generally does not have standing to assert the right or equity to have assets marshaled since the doctrine is basically a protection for junior secured creditors.

Marshalling on behalf of unsecured creditors

Notwithstanding the weight of United States authority to the contrary, it was decided in *In re Jack Green's Fashions for Men—Big & Tall, Inc*[5] that the trustee in bankruptcy could marshall the senior security over the bankrupt debtor's assets, on behalf of the debtor's unsecured creditors.

10.05

This radical departure from the established authorities was explained as follows:[6]

> Federal courts of bankruptcy are courts of equity and may apply the doctrine of marshalling in proper cases . . . In this case it would be in the highest degree inequitable to allow the [senior creditor] to exhaust the business assets of the corporate bankrupt without first looking to the real estate mortgaged to it. To permit such a course would leave the [unsecured] creditors of the business with nothing.

The trustee in bankruptcy was thus permitted to compel the senior creditor to recoup the senior debt out of the debtor's real estate assets, in preference to the debtor's business assets.[7] This extension of marshalling has since been affirmed in a number of other United States cases.[8]

The special position of the trustee in bankruptcy under United States law

In re Jack Green's Fashions for Men—Big & Tall, Inc[9] is not, however, authority for the general proposition that an unsecured creditor of a debtor is entitled to marshall the senior security in the same manner as a junior creditor. It is only the trustee in bankruptcy who is considered eligible to marshall the senior security, albeit on behalf of the unsecured creditors. Accordingly, until such time as the debtor is declared bankrupt and a trustee appointed over its assets, the unsecured creditors will be unable to marshall the senior security.

10.06

This is said to be due to the special position of the trustee in bankruptcy under United States federal insolvency legislation. Section 544(a)(1) of the *Bankruptcy*

10.07

---

[5] 507 F 2d 130 (1979).

[6] 507 F 2d 130 (1979), 133. It is difficult to see how the mere fact that a secured creditor might choose to recover its debt out of one asset as opposed to another would prejudice the interests of the unsecured creditors. See also Emamzadeh, *Marshaling in Bankruptcy: Questioning the Recent Expansions to the Common Debtor Requirement*, 321–322 and 326.

[7] The doctrine of marshalling, as it applies in the United States, is a pre-emptive remedy: see further Chapter 3.

[8] *Shedoudy v Beverly Surgical Supply Co* 161 Cal Rptr 164 (1980); *In re AEI Corp* 11 BR 97 (1981); *In re Ludwig Honold Manufacturing* 33 BR 724 (1983); *In re Liberty Outdoors, Inc* 204 BR 746 (1997).

[9] 507 F 2d 130 (1979).

Reform Act 1978 (USA) accords the trustee in bankruptcy the status of a 'judicial lien creditor':[10]

(a) The trustee shall have, as of the commencement of the case, and without regard to any knowledge of the trustee or of any creditor, *the rights and powers of,* or may avoid any transfer of property of the debtor or any obligation incurred by the debtor that is avoidable by—

(1) a creditor that extends credit to the debtor at the time of the commencement of the case, and that obtains, at such time and with respect to such credit, a *judicial lien* on all property on which a creditor on a simple contract could have obtained such a judicial lien, whether or not such a creditor exists (emphasis added).

Under section 544(a)(1), the trustee in bankruptcy is deemed to be a secured creditor of the debtor, with a priority-ranking inferior to that of the debtor's existing secured creditors.[11] This section introduces a new secured creditor but does not otherwise affect the order of priorities as between the debtor's secured creditors and unsecured creditors or within the class of secured creditors. It is on the basis of this provision that trustees in bankruptcy are considered able to marshall senior security.[12]

Redundancy of judicial lien marshalling

10.08 It is difficult to see how conferring on the trustee in bankruptcy a right to marshall on behalf of the unsecured creditors, improves the position of the unsecured creditors.[13]

---

[10] There is no equivalent provision in the bankruptcy or corporate insolvency legislation of the United Kingdom, Ireland, Australia or New Zealand.

[11] See Lachman, *Marshaling Assets in Bankruptcy: Recent Innovations in the Doctrine,* 676–677 and 687.

[12] *In re Jack Green's Fashions for Men – Big & Tall, Inc* 507 F 2d 130 (1979) and the cases cited in n8. C f the United States courts which remain divided as to whether the trustee in bankruptcy, by virtue of its status as a judicial lien creditor, can marshall on behalf of unsecured creditors: *Am Jur,* para 53:18; Emamzadeh, *Marshaling in Bankruptcy: Questioning the Recent Expansions to the Common Debtor Requirement,* 318. See *In re McElwaney* 40 BR 66 (1984), 70–71 where the court stated that section 544's purpose was to protect the bankrupt's estate from secret liens, rather than conferring on the trustee the power to marshall. See also *In re Dig It, Inc* 129 BR 65 (1991); *In re El Paso Truck Center, Inc* 129 BR 109 (1991); *In re Borges* 184 BR 874 (1995) which denied the trustee in bankruptcy the right to marshall.

[13] Mosman's objections (*The Proper Application of Marshaling on Behalf of Unsecured Creditors,* 643–645) to *In re Jack Green's Fashions for Men – Big & Tall, Inc* 507 F 2d 130 (1979) are unconvincing. He criticises this case on three grounds: (i) it is inconsistent with the senior creditor's right to freely elect amongst the remedies available to it; (ii) where a senior creditor releases any part of its security over the asset which is encumbered by only the senior security, its security over the other assets of the debtor will be reduced proportionately; and (iii) the doctrine of marshalling should not be interfered with as the courts should 'let sleeping dogs lie'. In terms of (i), it is difficult to see how the trustee's right to marshall would be any more of an infringement of the senior creditor's freedom of action than a junior creditor's right to marshall. Point (ii) appears to assume that the extension of marshalling rights to the trustee in bankruptcy in some way involves a reduction in the scope of the senior security.

Unsecured creditors are the lowest-ranking creditors of a debtor; they rank behind the senior creditor and any other secured creditors. The status of the trustee as a judicial lien creditor does not derogate from the priority-position of existing secured creditors. Accordingly, the conferral of that status upon the trustee in bankruptcy will not improve the position of the unsecured creditors *vis-à-vis* the debtor (or the debtor's creditors).

10.09 Nor will the assertion of marshalling rights by the trustee in bankruptcy place the unsecured creditors in any better position.[14] Should the senior creditor be compelled (this being the manner in which marshalling is principally applied in the United States) to recoup its debt out of a particular asset, the unsecured creditors will continue to rank last as regards the residue of the debtor's assets. Likewise, permitting the trustee in bankruptcy to exchange its judicial lien for the senior security following the discharge of the senior debt will not improve the position of the unsecured creditors. While the unsecured creditors would in this manner obtain the benefit of a secured claim, the trustee will only be permitted access to the senior security following the discharge, or in the absence, of any competing secured claims.[15]

10.10 Further, permitting unsecured creditors, or another party on their behalf, to exercise marshalling rights makes little sense in the context of the redistributive nature of marshalling.

Marshalling preserves the priority-ranking of the junior creditor by permitting it to substitute the senior security for its own; the junior creditor is thus able to exchange its security over a diminished asset for the senior creditor's security over a different, and intact, asset. This exchange of securities redresses the loss sustained by the junior creditor by transferring to it the benefit of an asset that would otherwise have been available to the unsecured creditors (and any secured creditors ranking behind the junior creditor).

Such a redistribution of the debtor's assets is otiose when it is the unsecured creditors who are seeking to marshal the senior security. Again, the right to marshal will only be available when the senior debt, and all other superior claims, have

---

[14] There is a further problem with the supposed marshalling rights of the trustee in bankruptcy. The judicial lien conferred upon the trustee by section 544(a)(1) appears, from the wording of that section, to encompass all of the debtor's assets, and it will therefore be at least equivalent in scope to the senior security. Marshalling is unlikely to be available (and would, in any event, be superfluous) where the junior security encompasses the same assets as, or greater assets than, the senior security: see the Canadian cases of *Farm Credit Corp v McLane* (1983) 30 Sask R 320; *Montmor Investments Ltd v Montreal Trust Co* (1984) 53 BCLR 275.

[15] The trustee in bankruptcy, as a judicial lien creditor, ranks behind the debtor's existing secured creditors: q v n11. United States law does not recognise any principle of, or analogous to, marshalling by apportionment; hence, marshalling is not available in the presence of equal or superior competing claims: see further paragraph 11.27.

been satisfied.[16] Thus, all marshalling will achieve is a redistribution, if it can be termed that, of the residue of the debtor's assets amongst the only parties entitled to those assets and whose claims rank *pari passu* with one another.[17]

C. Unsecured Creditors and Extinguishment of Marshalling Rights

Introduction

10.11 Of greater concern is a second innovation of the United States courts. In *In re Spectra Prism Industries, Inc,*[18] *In re Center Wholesale, Inc*[19] and *In re West Coast Optical Instruments, Inc*[20] it was decided that a junior creditor would be prevented from marshalling the senior security if the application of marshalling would prejudice the unsecured creditors of the debtor.

10.12 This development runs counter to established principles of English and American law. It is the position in England[21] and the United States[22] that a junior creditor's marshalling rights prevail over the debtor and all parties claiming under the debtor, other than purchasers or security holders. Accordingly, neither the unsecured creditors nor any party acting on their behalf should be able to interfere with the junior creditor's exercise of its marshalling rights.[23]

---

[16] A junior creditor cannot marshall the security of a senior creditor, under the law of the United States, where some third party enjoys rights *equal or superior* in equity to those of the junior creditor *qua* the asset, over which the security sought to be marshalled is held: see further paragraph 11.27.

[17] Marshalling preserves, but does not improve, the original priority-position of a junior creditor: see further Chapter 3. Accordingly, marshalling (assuming it is available) will not promote an unsecured creditor ahead of the other unsecured creditors.

[18] 28 BR 397 (1983).

[19] 759 F 2d 1440 (1985).

[20] 177 BR 720 (1992).

[21] q v n2. See further Chapter 11.

[22] *Ingersoll v Somers Land Co* 89 A 288 (1913); *Anderson v Engwall* 149 NW 611 (1914); *Langdel v Moore* 168 NE 57 (1929); *James Stewart & Co v National Shawmut Bank of Boston* 196 NE 169 (1935); *Sanborn, McDuffee Co v Keefe* 187 A 97 (1936). See *CJS*, paras 21:111c and 55:5; *Am Jur*, para 53:18 and, in particular, 53:18n29 where it is stated: 'The depletion of funds otherwise available to unsecured creditors does not constitute legal prejudice in the marshalling context'. C f Langdell, *A Brief Survey of Equity Jurisdiction*, 16 where it is asserted that equity, when confronted with a contest between a junior creditor and unsecured creditors, in the context of marshalling, should resolve any imbalance in favour of the latter. A junior creditor would thus only be able to marshall where the only creditors of the debtor were the senior creditor, itself (and other secured creditors).

[23] There are a number of contractual devices, to which an unsecured creditor can resort, that would have the effect of depriving the junior creditor of the ability to marshall. For instance, assets supplied under a Romalpa or retention of title clause will not be susceptible to marshalling claims, for so long as the purchase price remains outstanding those assets will not be subject to the senior security. See generally McCormack, *Reservation of Title*; Worthington, *Proprietary Interests in Commercial Transactions*, Chapter 2; McCormack, *Title Retention and the Company Charge*

The death knell of marshalling

Accepting the constraints imposed upon the right to marshall by *In re Spectra* **10.13**
Prism Industries, Inc.,[24] *In re Center Wholesale, Inc*[25] and *In re West Coast Optical*
Instruments, Inc[26] would result in the effective abolition of the doctrine of mar-
shalling.[27]

In *In re Spectra Prism Industries, Inc.*,[28] it was held that the trustee in bankruptcy of **10.14**
a debtor could prevent a junior creditor from marshalling the senior security on
the basis that marshalling would adversely affect the claims of the unsecured creditors.[29] It was considered that the trustee, as a judicial lien creditor under section
544(a)(1), enjoyed standing equivalent to that of a third party security holder. It
was therefore open to the trustee to deny the junior creditor the right to marshall
in circumstances where the trustee was of the opinion that marshalling would
prejudice the ability of the unsecured creditors to recover the debts owed to them
by the debtor.

Adopting *In re Spectra Prism Industries, Inc*[30] would prevent junior creditors **10.15**
from ever marshalling the senior security. Under English law, marshalling preserves the priority-ranking of a junior creditor by effecting a redistribution of the
benefit of assets from the debtor's unsecured creditors to the junior creditor. This
preservation of priority is accomplished at the expense of the unsecured creditors
and, as such, necessarily prejudices the ability of those creditors to recover their
debts.

Registration System. In addition to the Romalpa clause, other absolute-title devices, such as chattel
leases, hire purchase agreements and conditional sales, will perform the same function: see I Davies,
Absolute Title Financing in Commercial Transactions (1985) Anglo-Am L Rev 71.

[24] 28 BR 397 (1983).

[25] 759 F 2d 1440 (1985).

[26] 177 BR 720 (1992).

[27] See B Weintraub & A N Resnick, *Marshaling of Assets in Bankruptcy Cases: the Spectre of
Constance v Harvey Appears Again* (1984) 16 UCCLJ 384; Lachman, *Marshaling Assets in
Bankruptcy: Recent Innovations in the Doctrine*, 686–688; Averch & Prostock, *The Doctrine of
Marshaling: an Anachronistic Concept Under the Bankruptcy Code*, 240–241; MacDougall,
Marshalling and the Personal Property Security Acts: Doing Unto Others . . ., 112–113.

[28] 28 BR 397 (1983).

[29] This is supported by Kroger & Acconcia, *Marshaling: A Fourth Sequel Act to Commercial
Tragedies*, 206–207. An alternative rationale for limiting the junior creditor's right to marshall is
proposed by Kroger & Acconcia (208), utilising *Meyer v United States* 375 US 233 (1963), 237
where the court stated that the purpose of marshalling 'is to prevent the arbitrary action of the senior
lienor from destroying the rights of a junior lienor or a *creditor having less security*' (emphasis in article). Kroger & Acconcia argue that the unsecured creditors should be placed in this category of protected parties. However, having *less* security (than the junior creditor) is not equivalent to having *no*
security.

[30] 28 BR 397 (1983).

10.16 The decisions in *In re Center Wholesale, Inc*[31] and *In re West Coast Optical Instruments, Inc*[32] are even less explicable. In each case, the junior creditor was denied the right to marshall on the grounds that marshalling would prejudice the debtor by reducing the assets available to the debtor and its unsecured creditors.[33]

The redistribution of the debtor's assets effected by the doctrine of marshalling following the discharge of the senior debt does not, in any way, affect the quantum of the debtor's assets. Marshalling only alters the manner in which the debtor's assets are to be applied in meeting the claims of its remaining creditors. The two cases are thus founded upon a misconception of the nature of marshalling and, accordingly, are of little persuasive value.

---

[31] 759 F 2d 1440 (1985).
[32] 177 BR 720 (1992).
[33] This is also the contention of Mosman, *The Proper Application of Marshaling on Behalf of Unsecured Creditors*, 654–655.

11

MARSHALLING OF SECURITIES AND THIRD PARTIES

Introduction	11.01	general rule	11.22
		notice of junior security	11.25
Marshalling in Presence of Third Party		exceptions to the general rule	11.27
Rights	11.05	other jurisdictions	11.28
Will prejudice to third parties prevent		and redistributive nature of marshalling	11.30
marshalling?	11.06	and policy goals of security	11.37
Privileged status of third party security			
holders and transferees/disponees	11.10	**Third Party Transferees or Disponees and**	
Junior creditor's inchoate equity and		**Exclusion of Marshalling Rights**	
persistence of marshalling rights	11.12	Introduction	11.41
Disparate treatment of third party security		Exclusion of marshalling rights:	
holders and transferees/disponees	11.15	general rule	11.42
		time of transfer or disposition	11.45
Third Party Security Holders and Marshalling		identity of third party	11.49
by Apportionment		notice of junior security	11.50
Introduction	11.18	other jurisdictions	11.55
Sharing benefit of senior security	11.20	Marshalling, transfers and dispositions to	
Marshalling by apportionment:		third parties and policy goals of security	11.57

A. Introduction

As a general rule, under English law, a junior creditor's right to marshall the senior **11.01** security is capable of being enforced not only against the debtor[1] but also against the majority of third parties claiming under the debtor.

---

[1] *Ex parte Kendall* (1811) 17 Ves 514; *Haynes v Forshaw* (1853) 11 Hare 93; *Moxon v The Berkeley Mutual Benefit Building Society* (1890) 59 LJ Ch 524. See Robbins, *A Treatise on the Law of Mortgages, Pledges and Hypothecations,* 777; Webster, *Ashburner's Concise Treatise on Mortgages, Pledges and Liens,* 465; Hewitt, *White & Tudor's Leading Cases in Equity,* 40; Ramsbotham, *Coote's Treatise on the Law of Mortgages,* 802; Baker & Langan, *Snell's Equity,* 421–422; Tyler, *Fisher & Lightwood's Law of Mortgage,* 531; Cousins, *The Law of Mortgages,* 436; O'Donovan & Phillips, *The Modern Contract of Guarantee,* 680. This is also the position in New Zealand: *Re Tremain* [1934] NZLR 369; and Canada: *Granville Savings & Mortgage Corp v Bob B Co Holdings Ltd* (1996) 24 BCLR (3d) 348. C f the Australian case of *In re Crothers* [1930] VLR 49 in which the court considered that a debtor could, as a result of statutory intervention, defeat a junior creditor's right to marshall (it is, however, unclear what detriment a debtor would suffer from the exercise by the junior

11.02   The junior creditor's marshalling rights will prevail over secured creditors who rank behind the junior creditor[2] and all unsecured creditors.[3] Those rights will also prevail over the trustee in bankruptcy, receiver or liquidator of the debtor[4] and the debtor's real and personal representatives.[5]

11.03   It is only where the asset, over which the security the junior creditor is seeking to marshall is held, has been transferred to a third party, by way of security or absolute transfer, that the junior creditor's ability to marshall will be adversely affected. The position of the junior creditor *qua* third parties has been explained by Kay L.J. in *Flint v Howard* in the following terms:[6]

> The right of a subsequent mortgagee of one of the estates to marshall—that is, to throw the prior charge on both estates upon that which is not mortgaged to him—is an equity which is not enforced against third parties, that is, against anyone except the mortgagor and his legal representatives claiming as volunteers under him. It is not enforced against a mortgagee or purchaser of the other estate. If both estates are subject to separate second mortgage[s] the Court apportions the first mortgage between them;[7]

and similarly by Saunders J. of the Ontario Supreme Court in *Re Bread Man Inc*:[8]

> It seems to me that third parties who may not be prejudiced by the application of the doctrine do not include unsecured creditors of the debtor. It is logical that *bona fide* subsequent purchasers and mortgagees of the property without notice should be protected for their interest in the property would be seriously affected by the application of the doctrine. In most cases they would have no way to anticipate the possible exposure to marshalling . . . It is also logical that unsecured credits [sic] of debtors should

---

creditor of its marshalling rights). The court in *Re Tremain* declined to follow *In re Crothers* on this point: see further Chapter 10.

[2]   q v n32.

[3]   See further Chapter 10.

[4]   *Re Tristram* (1825) 1 Deac 288; *Baldwin v Belcher* (1842) 3 Dr & War 173; *Ex parte Alston* (1868) 4 Ch App 168. See Robbins, *A Treatise on the Law of Mortgages, Pledges and Hypothecations*, 780; Webster, *Ashburner's Concise Treatise on Mortgages, Pledges and Liens*, 465; Hewitt, *White & Tudor's Leading Cases in Equity*, 54; Ramsbotham, *Coote's Treatise on the Law of Mortgages*, 805; *Halsbury's*, Vol 32 ('Mortgage'), para 917; Tyler, *Fisher & Lightwood's Law of Mortgage*, 531; Cousins, *The Law of Mortgages*, 436.

[5]   *Lanoy v Duke & Duchess of Athol* (1742) 2 Atk 444; *Flint v Howard* [1893] 2 Ch 54. See *Halsbury's*, Vol 32 ('*Mortgage*'), para 917; Cousins, *The Law of Mortgages*, 436.

[6]   [1893] 2 Ch 54, 73.

[7]   A novel defence to marshalling relying on this principle was raised in the Australian case of *Commonwealth Trading Bank v Colonial Mutual Life Assurance Society Ltd* (1970) 26 FLR 338, 348–349; the defendant argued that the right to marshall could not be exercised against the first mortgagee, as the first mortgagee was such a third party. This was rejected by Neasey J. on the basis that the rule applied to subsequent mortgagees and purchasers, not prior mortgagees. What Neasey J. did not say was that to accept the defendant's argument would be to effectively extinguish the right of junior creditors to marshall. See also *Moxon v The Berkeley Mutual Benefit Building Society* (1890) 59 LJ Ch 524, in which Kay J. (as he then was) held that the senior creditor could not interfere with the junior creditor's right to marshall.

[8]   (1979) 89 DLR (3d) 599, 602. See also *Victor Investment Corporation v Fidelity Trust Company* (1973) 41 DLR (3d) 65.

not be protected for in the absence of a statutory provision, they should have no better right to the fund than the debtor himself.

Accordingly, a junior creditor will be entitled to obtain access *via* marshalling to the asset subject to only the senior security, in priority to the residual rights of the debtor in that asset and the competing rights of third parties to that asset (except for those third parties whose rights have been acquired by way of security or absolute transfer or disposition). **11.04**

This chapter will examine the complex rules that have been developed in England and the other major common law jurisdictions, to resolve conflicts between the marshalling claims of junior creditors and third party security holders and transferees or disponees.

B. Marshalling in the Presence of Third Party Rights

The propositions put forward in this chapter, concerning the persistence of marshalling in the face of competing third party rights, differ markedly from more traditional treatments of marshalling's limits. **11.05**

Will prejudice to third parties prevent marshalling?

Several commentators have stated, as a matter of general principle, that marshalling cannot be applied to the prejudice of third parties.[9] If sustained, this principle would substantially weaken the scope of marshalling, for marshalling by its very nature preserves the priority position of the junior creditor at the expense of other claimants against the debtor. **11.06**

It is claimed that support for this principle is to be found in the comments of the English courts in *Aldrich v Cooper*,[10] *Dolphin v Aylward*,[11] *Webb v Smith*[12] and *The 'Chioggia'*.[13] **11.07**

---

[9] See Smith, *A Practical Exposition of the Principles of Equity*, 614; Hewitt, *White & Tudor's Leading Cases in Equity*, 41 and 47; *Halsbury's*, Vol 16 ('*Equity*'), paras 877 and 878; Derham, *Set-Off against an Assignee: The Relevance of Marshalling, Contribution and Subrogation*, 132–134. This is also the case with the following Australian (McDonald, *Marshalling* (1997), para 32) and American (Bigelow, *Story's Commentaries on Equity Jurisprudence*, para 633n(b); Pomeroy Jr., *Equity Jurisprudence*, para 1414; Pomeroy Jr., *A Treatise on Equitable Remedies*, para 867) texts.

[10] (1803) 8 Ves Jun 382, 391 where Lord Eldon considered that marshalling would only be applied 'if no third persons are concerned'.

[11] (1870) LR 4 E & I 486, 502 where Lord Hatherley stated 'the doctrine of marshalling shall not be applied to prejudice third parties'.

[12] (1885) Ch D 192, 202 where Lindley L.J. stated 'assets shall not be marshalled where by so doing another man's rights would be prejudiced'.

[13] [1898] P 1, 6 where Gorell Barnes J. stated 'marshalling cannot be permitted to the prejudice of third persons'.

11.08 Those cases are not, however, inconsistent with the limits of marshalling stated in this chapter; the cases can be explained on one of the two following grounds. First, there are the cases in which marshalling was refused because there had never been compliance with the common debtor rule, and thus permitting marshalling would prejudice the third party owner of the asset to which the junior creditor was seeking access.[14] Secondly, the remaining cases concern situations in which a third party transferee or disponee was able to resist the claim of the junior creditor to the transferred asset.[15]

11.09 Accordingly, a more accurate statement of the principle is that, assuming the common debtor rule (or the surety exception[16]) has been satisfied, the junior creditor's marshalling rights will prevail over all third parties except those with whom the second category of cases is concerned and third party security holders.[17]

The privileged status of third party security holders and transferees/disponees

11.10 Other commentators have been content to merely articulate the privileged status of third party security holders and transferees or disponees *vis-à-vis* junior creditors. These accounts are not entirely satisfactory in that they do not explain why these two categories of third parties should prevail over junior creditors whereas other third parties do not.[18]

11.11 Nor do they explain the disparate treatment of third party security holders, on the one hand, and third party transferees or disponees, on the other.[19] A third party, to whom the asset that the junior creditor is seeking to obtain access to *via* marshalling has been transferred or disposed of, can prevent the junior creditor from marshalling the security over that asset. Third party security holders, in contrast,

---

[14] *Webb v Smith* (1885) Ch D 192; *The 'Chioggia'* [1898] P 1. See further paragraphs 7.17–7.20.

[15] *Aldrich v Cooper* (1803) 8 Ves Jun 382; *Dolphin v Aylward* (1870) LR 4 E & I 486. The Irish case, *Averall v Wade* (1835) L & G temp Sugd 252, which has been cited in support of this apparent principle can also be explained on this basis. These cases are also capable of being explained in terms of non-compliance with the common debtor rule: see further paragraphs 11.47, 11.48, 11.50 and 11.53.

[16] c f n44.

[17] Support for this interpretation of the authorities may be found in Ramsbotham, *Coote's Treatise on the Law of Mortgages*, 811 and the Australian case of *Commonwealth Trading Bank v Colonial Mutual Life Assurance Society Ltd* (1970) 26 FLR 338, 348.

[18] See Cavanagh, *The Law of Money Securities*, 550–551; Keaton & Sheridan, *Equity*, 305–306; Baker & Langan, *Snell's Equity*, 421–422; Tyler, *Fisher & Lightwood's Law of Mortgage*, 531–533; Cousins, *The Law of Mortgages*, 437–438; Strahan, *The Marshalling of Mortgages*, pp. 308–309. This is also the case with the following Australian texts: Francis & Thomas, *Mortgages and Securities*, 370–371; Sykes & Walker, *The Law of Securities*, 183–184. C f Hanbury & Waldock, *The Law of Mortgages*, 179–181; in Australia: Meagher, Gummow & Lehane, *Equity Doctrines and Remedies*, paras 1122–1130; and in New Zealand: Cleaver, *Marshalling*, 292–294.

[19] The rules outlined here are fully described further below.

can do no such thing; their presence may at most lead to the modification of the junior creditor's marshalling rights.[20]

Junior creditor's inchoate equity and the persistence of marshalling rights

The persistence of the junior creditor's marshalling rights is, in part, capable of being explained in terms of the nature of the interest conferred upon the junior creditor by the doctrine of marshalling.   **11.12**

The doctrine of marshalling, following the prejudicial recovery of the senior debt, confers upon the junior creditor what may be best described as an 'inchoate equity'[21] (which whilst falling short of an equitable interest or estate[22] is superior to a 'mere equity'[23]) in the asset subject to the senior security sought to be marshalled. This equity is binding upon the debtor, and also places the junior   **11.13**

---

[20] This is on the assumption that no priority or other arrangements are in place between the third party and the senior creditor: see further Chapter 12.

[21] The nature of the interest enjoyed by the junior creditor is *sui generis*. It resists classification under English law as either an equitable interest or a mere equity. For a discussion of this two-fold division of 'equities', see V T H Delany, *Equitable Interests and 'Mere Equities'* (1957) 21 Conv (NS) 195; A R Everton, *'Equitable Interests' and 'Equities' – in Search of a Pattern* (1976) 40 Conv (NS) 209. Australian law, in contrast, employs a tripartite distinction between equitable interests, mere equities and personal equities: see generally M Neave & M Weinberg, *The Nature and Function of Equities* (1979) 6 U Tas LR 24 and 115; D Wright, *The Continued Relevance of Divisions in Equitable Interests in Real Property* (1995) 3 APLJ 163. A personal equity under Australian law corresponds to the mere equity recognised by English law, being a personal right to seek an equitable remedy: see Meagher, Gummow & Lehane, *Equity Doctrines and Remedies*, para 428. The inchoate equity constituted by marshalling under English law corresponds to a mere equity under Australian law: see O'Donovan & Phillips, *The Modern Contract of Guarantee*, 681n710. C f McDonald, *Marshalling* (1996), para 1603; McDonald, *Marshalling* (1997), para 25 where it considered that marshalling constitutes a personal equity under Australian law.

[22] See the Australian cases of *Commonwealth Trading Bank v Colonial Mutual Life Assurance Society Ltd* (1970) 26 FLR 338; *Sarge Pty Ltd v Cazihaven Homes Pty Ltd* (1994) 34 NSWLR 658; *Chase Corporation (Australia) Pty Ltd v North Sydney Brick and Tile Co Ltd* (1994) 12 ACLC 997; and *Austin v Royal* (unrep 14 May 1998, Sup Ct of NSW) which deny that marshalling confers upon the junior creditor an equitable or proprietary interest in the asset subject to the senior security sought to be marshalled. See further paragraphs 3.08 and 3.23. C f the United States case of *Cheesebrough v Millard* (1815) 1 Johns Chan 408 and Meagher, Gummow & Lehane, *Equity Doctrines and Remedies*, paras 1122, 1123, 1129 and 1130 where it is considered that the junior creditor obtains a limited proprietary interest.

[23] Pomeroy Jr., *A Treatise on Equitable Remedies*, paras 867 and 870 considers that marshalling confers only a mere equity upon the junior creditor. A mere equity *strictu sensu* is not an equitable interest or estate but is a personal right of action, the assertion of which may at the court's discretion limit or qualify such an interest or estate: Baker & Langan, *Snell's Equity*, 25; Delany, *Equitable Interests and 'Mere Equities'*, 199 and 201; Everton, *'Equitable Interests' and 'Equities' – in Search of a Pattern*, 210. Marshalling lacks this discretionary element; it is available 'automatically' to the junior creditor following the recovery of the senior debt out of the asset subject to the senior and junior securities (assuming that the common debtor or the surety exception has been satisfied): see paragraphs 7.03–7.04. On the other hand, it is difficult to see how marshalling could be taken as conferring an equitable interest upon the junior creditor (q v n22) in the face of doubts about the ability of a junior creditor to assign its marshalling rights (as distinct from its security): see Meagher, Gummow & Lehane, *Equity Doctrines and Remedies*, para 1129. This is a characteristic which marshalling appears to share with mere equities: see Baker & Langan, *Snell's Equity*, 25.

creditor in a position superior to that of all third parties other than third party security holders or transferees/disponees. As such, this equity explains:

(1) why marshalling prevails as against the debtor and all parties standing in the position of the debtor *vis-à-vis* the junior creditor (such as the trustee in bankruptcy, receiver, liquidator or real or personal representative of the debtor); and

(2) why marshalling prevails as against third parties (i) who enjoy only a personal claim against the debtor (such as unsecured creditors) or (ii) whose secured claims against the debtor do not extend to the asset in question and rank below that of the junior security.[24]

11.14 The third parties encompassed by category (2) do not, however, include third party security holders and transferees or disponees. As regards these two sub-categories of third parties, it is important to note that the junior creditor's equity does not arise until the senior creditor recovers the senior debt through the enforcement of the senior security against the asset subject to both the senior and junior securities. Until that time, the junior creditor has only a potential equity, or a mere potentiality to marshall. Thus, notwithstanding the junior creditor's prior compliance with the common debtor rule (or the surety exception), this potential equity is susceptible to being qualified or prevented from ever arising by subsequent dealings by the debtor with its interest in the asset encumbered by only the senior security. This qualification or displacement of the potential equity goes some way towards explaining the privileged position of third party security holders and transferees or disponees *vis-à-vis* the junior creditor.[25]

The disparate treatment of third party security holders and transferees/disponees

11.15 Drawing upon the above analysis, the disparate treatment of third party security holders, on the one hand, and third party transferees or disponees, on the other, can be explained as follows.

11.16 A third party transferee or disponee who takes the relevant asset free of the senior security will forestall the conversion of the junior creditor's potential equity into a marshalling right capable of granting it access to that asset.[26] Following the enforcement of the senior security, there will be nothing to which the junior creditor's marshalling right can attach; marshalling does not create securities, it merely confers upon the junior creditor the benefit of an existing security. Moreover, at the time at which the junior creditor seeks to rely upon the doctrine of mar-

---

[24] q v n32.

[25] For an analysis of third party security holders and transferees/disponees in light of the redistributive nature of marshalling and the policy goals of security, see paragraphs 11.30–11.40 and 11.57–11.63 respectively.

[26] The persistence of the junior creditor's marshalling rights where the third party has taken the asset in question subject to the senior security is considered in paragraphs 11.50–11.54.

shalling, the requirements of the common debtor rule will clearly not be satisfied (notwithstanding that they may have previously been satisfied).

In contrast, the presence of a third party security holder will not controvert the **11.17** junior creditor's compliance with the common debtor rule. Instead, the debtor, by granting a security over the relevant asset to a third party, will have placed that third party in a position equivalent to that of the junior creditor; each of the junior creditor and the third party has a potential equity in respect of the asset subject to the other's security. Which of their potential equities is converted into a right to marshall depends upon the asset against which the senior creditor elects to enforce its security. Just as marshalling will act to protect the junior creditor from the adverse consequences of the senior creditor's election, so too will it endeavour to ensure that the preservation of the junior creditor's priority position is not achieved at the expense of a party in an equivalent position to the junior creditor *qua* the senior creditor[27] (a party who, had the senior creditor made a different election, would in the same manner as the junior creditor be entitled to seek the redress of marshalling).[28]

C. Third Party Security Holders and Marshalling by Apportionment

Introduction

Where the asset that is subject to the senior security which a junior creditor is seek- **11.18** ing to marshall is also encumbered by a second-ranking security held by a third party, a modified form of marshalling known as 'marshalling by apportionment' will apply. The law relating to marshalling by apportionment has remained unchanged since it was settled in the nineteenth century in the cases of *Barnes v Racster*[29] and *Bugden v Bignold.*[30]

However, whilst the junior creditor continues to enjoy the right to marshall the **11.19** senior security in the face of a competing third party security, the principle of marshalling by apportionment represents a substantial derogation from the junior

---

[27] q v paragraph 11.21.

[28] The junior creditor's inchoate equity also explains the junior creditor's entitlement to the residue of the asset encumbered by the third party's security ahead of the debtor: see further paragraph 11.23.

[29] (1842) 1 Y & C Ch Cas 401. There are *dicta* in one Australian case, *Mir Bros Projects Pty Ltd v Lyons* [1977] 2 NSWLR 192, 196 which deny that the principle of apportionment, as established in *Barnes v Racster*, is related to marshalling. The Supreme Court of New South Wales, however, gave no reasons for this view. See further Sykes & Walker, *The Law of Securities*, 185. See also the discussion in paragraph 5.48 of the proposition that the apportionment principle is a form of contribution.

[30] (1843) 2 Y & C Ch Cas 377.

creditor's usual marshalling rights. The junior creditor will be unable *via* marshalling to obtain the full benefit of the senior security. The exchange of securities effected by marshalling will not result in the conferral upon the junior creditor of a first-ranking claim to the intact asset to the full extent of the junior debt (as would have been the case in the absence of the third party's security):[31]

> [T]here can be no marshalling if the rights of third parties would be thereby interfered with; hence, if a debtor charge two funds, F1 and F2, in favour of A, and subsequently charge F1 in favour of B, and F2 in favour of C, B cannot require A to satisfy himself out of F2, because to do so would work an injustice to C.

Sharing the benefit of the senior security

11.20　The impact of the third party security upon the junior creditor's marshalling rights may be demonstrated by reference to the following example. Assume that a debtor who owns assets A and B has granted a first-ranking security over assets A and B to a senior creditor, a second-ranking security over asset A to a junior creditor, and a second-ranking security over asset B to a third party.[32]

In this situation, the junior creditor will not enjoy exclusive access to the senior security should the senior creditor recover the senior debt out of asset A, but will be required to share the benefit of the senior security with the third party. The junior creditor will thus be prevented from marshalling the senior security in an unmitigated fashion to the prejudice of the third party. The doctrine of marshalling will, instead, attempt to preserve the priority-ranking of the securities held by both the junior creditor and the third party, irrespective of whose security has been actually eroded by the enforcement of the senior security.[33]

This is accomplished by a *notional* redistribution of the burden of the senior debt between assets A and B in proportion to the value of each asset (again, irrespective

---

[31] Cavanagh, *The Law of Money Securites*, 551.

[32] Marshalling by apportionment will not apply – but the unqualified form of marshalling will – where the third party holds a third-ranking security over A instead of a second-ranking security over B, or otherwise concedes priority to the junior creditor: *Re Mower's Trusts* (1869) LR 8 Eq 110. Neither form of marshalling will apply where the third party has acquired the senior security: *Bovey v Skipwith* (1671) 1 Ch Cas 201. See also Robbins, *A Treatise on the Law of Mortgages, Pledges and Hypothecations*, 787; Beddoes, *A Concise Treatise on the Law of Mortgages*, 104; Webster, *Ashburner's Concise Treatise on Mortgages, Pledges and Liens*, 467; Hewitt, *White & Tudor's Leading Cases in Equity*, 49; Ramsbotham, *Coote's Treatise on the Law of Mortgages*, 811 and 812. Marshalling by apportionment is only available, as a general rule, where the same owner of two properties grants a second-ranking security on each of the properties in favour of two different secured creditors: see the Canadian case of *Richmond Savings Credit Union v Zilbershats* (1997) 35 BCLR (3d) 136.

[33] Marshalling by apportionment does not interfere with the ability of the senior creditor to recover the senior debt as it sees fit. In *Moxon v The Berkeley Mutual Benefit Building Society* (1890) 59 LJ Ch 524, 526 Kay J. (as he then was) stated: 'The right is quite independent of [the senior creditor]. It does not interfere with him, but if he chooses to pay himself out of one estate, then, to the extent of the proportion of that estate as between the two separate assigns, it must be paid out of the other estate'.

of whether the senior security was enforced against asset A or asset B).[34] As a consequence, neither the junior creditor nor the third party will receive, on marshalling the senior security, the full benefit of an intact senior security but rather the benefit of only a rateable proportion of the senior security.[35]

The rationale for this notional redistribution has been expressed by Neasey J. in **11.21** the following terms:[36]

> . . . the rule is clear that where Blackacre and Whiteacre are mortgaged to A, and afterwards Blackacre is mortgaged to B and Whiteacre mortgaged to C, marshalling will not be applied so as to prejudice either B or C. In such a case their rights are to require that A's debt shall be satisfied rateably out of the two estates so as to leave a proper proportion thereof respectively to satisfy the claims of B and C, the ultimate surplus arising from both estates being payable to the mortgagor or those claiming under him.

Marshalling by apportionment—the general rule

If the senior creditor were to recoup the senior debt out of A, the junior creditor **11.22** would be entitled to be substituted to the senior security over asset B, *to the extent of that proportion of the senior debt which is rateably apportionable to asset B*. It is only *after* this amount has been recovered by the junior creditor that the third party will be permitted to recoup the debt owed to it out of asset B.[37]

---

[34] *Shalcross v Dixon* (1838) 7 LJ (NS) 180; *Barnes v Racster* (1842) 1 Y & C Ch Cas 401; *Bugden v Bignold* (1843) 2 Y & C Ch Cas 377; *Gibson v Seagrim* (1855) 20 Beav 614; *Re Mower's Trusts* (1869) LR 8 Eq 110; *Wellesley v Lord Mornington* (1869) 17 WR 355; *Ford v Tynte* (1872) 41 LJ Ch 758; *Liverpool Marine Credit Co v Wilson* (1872) 7 Ch App 507; *Trumper v Trumper* (1872) LR 14 Eq 295; *Cracknall v Janson* (1879) 11 Ch D 1; *Flint v Howard* [1893] 2 Ch 54; *Moxon v The Berkeley Mutual Benefit Building Society* (1890) 59 LJ Ch 524; *Wood v West* (1895) 40 Sol Jo 114; *Baglioni v Cavalli* (1900) 83 LT 500. See Spence, *The Equitable Jurisdiction of the Court of Chancery*, 834–836; Cavanagh, *The Law of Money Securities*, 550–551; Robbins, *A Treatise on the Law of Mortgages, Pledges and Hypothecations*, 787 and 788–789; Thomson, *A Compendium of Modern Equity*, 420; Beddoes, *A Concise Treatise on the Law of Mortgages*, 103–104; Webster, *Ashburner's Concise Treatise on Mortgages, Pledges and Liens*, 466; Hewitt, *White & Tudor's Leading Cases in Equity*, 47–49; Ramsbotham, *Coote's Treatise on the Law of Mortgages*, 811 and 812–813; Browne, *Ashburner's Principles of Equity*, 214; Hanbury & Waldock, *The Law of Mortgages*, 179–181; Keaton & Sheridan, *Equity*, 305–306; Baker & Langan, *Snell's Equity*, 422; *Halsbury's*, Vol 16 ('Equity'), para 878 and Vol 32 ('Mortgage'), para 918; Tyler, *Fisher & Lightwood's Law of Mortgage*, 531–532; Cousins, *The Law of Mortgages*, 437–438; Derham, *Set-Off*, 592–593; Strahan, *The Marshalling of Mortgages*, 308–309; Derham, *Set-Off against an Assignee: The Relevance of Marshalling, Contribution and Subrogation*, 132–134. C f the Australian case of *In re Crothers* [1930] VLR 49 in which marshalling by apportionment was applied in favour of unsecured creditors: see further Chapter 10.

[35] Francis & Thomas, *Mortgages and Securities*, 370; Gummow, *Marshalling and Protected Assets*, 131.

[36] *Commonwealth Trading Bank v Colonial Mutual Life Assurance Society Ltd* (1970) 26 FLR 338, 346–347. See also the Australian case of *Chase Corporation (Australia) Pty Ltd v North Sydney Brick and Tile Co Ltd* (1994) 12 ACLC 997, 1,009 where Cohen J. stated that the rationale for marshalling by apportionment was to ensure that neither subsequent securityholder lost an opportunity to satisfy part or all of its debt.

[37] Under Scots law, the sharing of the senior security is effected by way of assignment; if the senior creditor recovers the senior debt out of A, the junior creditor will be entitled to a rateable assignment of the senior security over B. See Lord Kames, *Principles of Equity*, 80.

11.23 However, the debtor (and its other creditors) will not be entitled to any residue of asset B that remains following the discharge of the junior creditor's share of the senior security, and the third party's debt. Instead, the junior creditor will have a superior claim to the residue, to the extent that the junior debt remains outstanding after the application of the junior creditor's share of the senior security and any residue of asset A.[38] This entitlement of the junior creditor to the residue of asset B is due to the fact that, once the third party's debt has been discharged, the junior creditor's marshalling rights will revert to their original, unabated status.[39]

11.24 The order of priorities will be converted from:

A	B
Senior Creditor	Senior Creditor
Junior Creditor	Third Party
to:	

A	B
(1) Senior Creditor	(2) Junior Creditor (to rateable proportion of senior security)[40]
(2) Junior Creditor (as regards any residue)	(3) Third Party
	(4) Junior Creditor for any balance outstanding

Marshalling by apportionment—notice of junior security

11.25 The fact that the third party had notice of the junior security, when it took security over asset B, is, as a general rule, irrelevant.[41] Accordingly, the debtor can by

---

[38] *Moxon v The Berkeley Mutual Benefit Building Society* (1890) 59 LJ Ch 524. See Hanbury & Waldock, *The Law of Mortgages*, 180; Francis & Thomas, *Mortgages and Securities*, 370; Meagher, Gummow & Lehane, *Equity Doctrines and Remedies*, para 1126.

[39] Francis & Thomas, *Mortgages and Securities*, 370.

[40] The junior creditor is entitled to only the lesser of this rateable proportion and the balance of the junior debt outstanding following the recovery of the senior debt out of A: q v paragraph 7.13.

[41] This refers to notice of the junior creditor's security, not notice of any equity conferred by marshalling; prior to the enforcement of the senior security, the junior creditor's potential equity is simply that, a mere potentiality. See *Shalcross v Dixon* (1838) 7 LJ (NS) 180; *Webb v Smith* (1885) 30 Ch D 192; *Flint v Howard* [1893] 2 Ch 54; *Baglioni v Cavalli* (1900) 83 LT 500. See Robbins, *A Treatise on the Law of Mortgages, Pledges and Hypothecations*, 787; Webster, *Ashburner's Concise Treatise on Mortgages, Pledges and Liens*, 466; Ramsbotham, *Coote's Treatise on the Law of Mortgages*, 811; Hanbury & Waldock, *The Law of Mortgages*, 179; Tyler, *Fisher & Lightwood's Law of Mortgage*, 531; Cousins, *The Law of Mortgages*, 437. This is also the position in Ireland: *Averall v Wade* (1835) L & G temp Sugd 252; *Smyth v Toms* [1918] 1 IR 338; and Australia: *Commonwealth Trading Bank v Colonial Mutual Life Assurance Society Ltd* (1970) 26 FLR 338; Meagher, Gummow & Lehane,

granting a second security to a third party modify the junior creditor's marshalling rights, and the fact that the third party had notice of the earlier security will not of itself render the third party's security subject to the junior security (by permitting the junior creditor to marshall the senior security as if the subsequent security did not exist).

Notice of the junior security will, however, be relevant[42] where the junior creditor **11.26** has taken the junior security in the mistaken belief that it was a first-ranking rather than a second-ranking security over asset A, and the third party had notice of that fact when it acquired its security over asset B.[43]

Marshalling by apportionment—exceptions to the general rule

The principle of marshalling by apportionment is a presumptive rule that may be **11.27** contracted out of:[44]

Equity Doctrines and Remedies, para 1125; Gummow, *Marshalling and Protected Assets*, 131n60. C f the Irish case of *In re Archer's Estate* [1914] 1 IR 285, where Wylie J. held that a debtor could not prejudice a junior creditor's right to marshall by creating a later security. This decision, if correct, would mean that a junior creditor's potential equity is inviolate. See the discussion of this case in n49.

[42] The issue of notice is also relevant where the security held by the third party was created subsequent to the enforcement of the senior security against the asset subject to both the senior and junior securities. If the third party took its security with notice of the junior security, it is arguable that the junior creditor should be entitled to marshall the senior security without reference to the third party's security. Notice of the junior security over one asset may not be taken to equate to notice of the junior creditor's equity as regards the other but, at the very least, marshalling by apportionment will apply. However, in the converse situation, the absence of notice on the part of the third party should not prevent marshalling by apportionment from applying. This is demonstrative of the *sui generis* nature of the equity conferred by marshalling. As a general rule, a party who acquires the equitable estate (such as an assignee by way of security or a *puisne* mortgagee) for value and without notice will take free of any existing *mere equities*. Baker & Langan, *Snell's Equity*, 50. That is not the case with marshalling. It would be strange if a third party, whose security was created while the equity was a mere potentiality could only qualify the junior creditor's ability to marshall, whilst a third party who took its security after that equity had come into existence could defeat the junior creditor's marshalling rights.

[43] *Stronge v Hawkes* (1859) 4 De G & J 632 and the Irish case of *Tighe v Dolphin* [1906] 1 IR 305. See Hanbury & Waldock, *The Law of Mortgages*, 180; Cousins, *The Law of Mortgages*, 437; Francis & Thomas, *Mortgages and Securities*, 370–371; Gummow, *Marshalling and Protected Assets*, 132n61. The junior creditor's marshalling rights will, in this situation, apply to their fullest extent.

[44] A further exception arguably applies in the case of the surety exception. Assume that asset A is owned by a debtor who has granted a first-ranking security over it to a senior creditor and a second-ranking security to a third party, and that asset B is owned by a surety for the senior debt who has granted a first-ranking security over that asset to the senior creditor and a second-ranking security to a junior creditor. The junior creditor and third party are not in an equivalent position *qua* one another. The junior creditor, on the basis of the surety exception, would be entitled to marshall the senior security over asset A. Conversely, the third party would have no marshalling rights in respect of the senior security over asset B: see paragraphs 7.17–7.20 and 8.11–8.12. On this basis, if the senior creditor recovers the senior debt out of asset B, the junior creditor should arguably be entitled to marshall the senior security over asset A in a manner unqualified by the presence of the third party's security. This exceptional result, in the absence of case law on point, is a corollary of the arguments detailed in paragraphs 8.21–8.25.

(1) Marshalling by apportionment will not apply where the third party security is subordinate to the senior and junior securities i e the third party has agreed that the debt owed to it should only be repaid once the senior and junior debts have been discharged. In this situation, the junior creditor will be entitled to exercise its marshalling rights to their fullest extent.[45]

(2) Marshalling by apportionment will not apply where the junior creditor and the third party have agreed that the junior creditor's ability to marshall is not to be impaired by the presence of the third party security. Again, the junior creditor's marshalling rights will be exercisable to the fullest extent.[46]

Marshalling by apportionment—other jurisdictions

11.28 Marshalling by apportionment, in the terms described above, is recognised in Australia,[47] Canada,[48] Ireland[49] and New Zealand.[50]

---

[45] *Aldridge v Forbes* (1839) 9 LJ Ch 37; *Re Mower's Trusts* (1869) LR 8 Eq 110. See Cavanagh, *The Law of Money Securities*, 551; Robbins, *A Treatise on the Law of Mortgages, Pledges and Hypothecations*, 787–788; Beddoes, *A Concise Treatise on the Law of Mortgages*, 104; Webster, *Ashburner's Concise Treatise on Mortgages, Pledges and Liens*, 467; Ramsbotham, *Coote's Treatise on the Law of Mortgages*, 812; Hanbury & Waldock, *The Law of Mortgages*, 180; Robb, *Nokes' Outline of the Law of Mortgages and Receiverships*, 85; Keaton & Sheridan, *Equity*, 306; Baker & Langan, *Snell's Equity*, 422; *Halsbury's*, Vol 16 ('*Equity*'), para 878 and Vol 32 ('*Mortgage*'), para 918; Tyler, *Fisher & Lightwood's Law of Mortgage*, 532; Cousins, *The Law of Mortgages*, 437. This is also the position in Australia: *White v London Chartered Bank of Australia* (1877) 3 VLR 33. See Francis & Thomas, *Mortgages and Securities*, 370; Meagher, Gummow & Lehane, *Equity Doctrines and Remedies*, para 1124; Gummow, *Marshalling and Protected Assets*, 131–132.

[46] *Lipscomb v Lipscomb* (1869) LR 7 Eq 501; *De Rochefort v Dawes* (1871) LR 12 Eq 540. See Baker & Langan, *Snell's Equity*, 422.

[47] *White v London Chartered Bank of Australia* (1877) 3 VLR 33; *Commonwealth Trading Bank v Colonial Mutual Life Assurance Society Ltd* (1970) 26 FLR 338; *Mir Bros Projects Pty Ltd v Lyons* [1977] 2 NSWLR 192; *Mir Bros Projects Pty Ltd v Lyons* [1978] 2 NSWLR 505; *Chase Corp (Australia) Pty Ltd v North Sydney Brick and Tile Co Ltd* (1994) 12 ACLC 997. See Francis & Thomas, *Mortgages and Securities*, 370–371; Meagher, Gummow & Lehane, *Equity Doctrines and Remedies*, paras 1124–1126; Sykes & Walker, *The Law of Securites*, 183–184; McDonald, *Marshalling* (1996), para 1611; McDonald, *Marshalling* (1997), para 33; Gummow, *Marshalling and Protected Assets*, 131–132 (the cases cited in nn47–50 are authority for the general principle of marshalling by apportionment; the position in other jurisdictions concerning the issue of notice and the exceptions to the general principle are cited in the notes to paragraphs 11.26 and 11.27).

[48] *Adams v Keers* (1919) 51 DLR 514; *Seel Investments Ltd v Greater Canadian Securities Corp Ltd* (1967) 65 DLR (2d) 45; *Victoria & Grey Trust Co v Brewer* (1971) 14 DLR (3d) 28; *Victor Investment Corporation v Fidelity Trust Company* (1973) 41 DLR (3d) 65; *Richmond Savings Credit Union v Zilbershats* (1997) 35 BCLR (3d) 136.

[49] *Re Lawder's Estate* (1861) 11 Ir Ch R 346; *Re Roddy's Estate* (1861) 11 Ir Ch R 369; *Re Roche's Estate* (1890) 25 LR Ir 284; *Smyth v Toms* [1918] 1 IR 338. See Wylie, *Irish Land Law* at paras 13.079 and [13].080 (sic); Lyall, *Land Law in Ireland*, para 23.7.3(a). C f *In re Archer's Estate* [1914] 1 IR 285 (this case is of doubtful authority following the comments by Ross J. in *Smyth v Toms* (at 346) that *In re Archer's Estate* was in 'direct conflict' with the established precedents; see further Tyler, *Fisher & Lightwood's Law of Mortgage*, 532n(x)). Ramsbotham, *Coote's Treatise on the Law of Mortgages*, 803–804 argues that the two cases can be reconciled: *Smyth v Toms* sets out the general principle of marshalling by apportionment, whereas *In re Archer's Estate* covers the special situation where the senior creditor holds first-ranking security over assets A and B, second-ranking security over A and third-ranking security over B, the junior creditor holds second-ranking security over B

In contrast, the law of the United States does not recognise marshalling by appor-   **11.29**
tionment or any analogous principle. Instead, a general rule that a junior creditor
cannot marshall in the presence of equal or superior competing rights is applied.[51]
Accordingly, a junior creditor will be only entitled to marshall the senior security
where it has priority over the third party security and, in those circumstances, its
marshalling rights will be unimpaired by the presence of the third party security.[52]

Marshalling by apportionment and the redistributive nature of marshalling

The doctrine of marshalling, *via* the redistribution of the debtor's assets once the   **11.30**
senior debt has been discharged, endeavours to ensure that the junior creditor is
not prejudiced by the particular order in which the senior creditor has chosen to
realise the assets subject to its security. This redistribution is effected by granting
the junior creditor access to the senior security over that asset of the debtor, in
respect of which the senior creditor is the sole encumbrancer.

However, when marshalling by apportionment applies, the asset which is subject   **11.31**
to the security that the junior creditor is seeking to marshall, is also subject to a
security held by a third party. If the junior creditor were to be permitted to marshall the senior security in a completely unmitigated manner, it would in effect be
able to transfer the entire burden of the senior debt onto the third party. In doing
so, the junior creditor would be eroding the third party's security and, as a consequence, jeopardising the third party's ability to recover the debt owed to it.

The junior creditor would therefore be inflicting upon the third party the very   **11.32**
thing that provides the impetus for the intervention of the doctrine of marshalling
on the junior creditor's behalf. The erosion of the junior security would, in these

and the third party holds third-ranking security over A. Here, the junior creditor would be entitled
to marshall unabated the senior securities over A.

[50]   *Olivier v Colonial Bank* (1887) 5 NZLR 239; *National Bank of NZ Ltd v Caldesia Promotions
Ltd and Jenkins Roberts & Associates Ltd* [1996] 3 NZLR 467. See Hinde, McMorland, Campbell &
Grinlinton, *Butterworths Land Law in New Zealand*, para 8.149.

[51]   See *Am Jur*, para 53:15 where it is stated: 'The right or equity to have assets marshaled, however, will not overcome or impair a superior, or even an equal, equity of another person'. See also
Pomeroy Jr., *A Treatise on Equitable Remedies*, para 867; McCoy, *Bispham's Principles of Equity*, para
317; *CJS*, paras 21:111 and 55:5. C f Bigelow, *Story's Commentaries on Equity Jurisprudence*, para
634a where the English position regarding marshalling by apportionment is adopted (Story, however, suggests (para 634a) that for marshalling by apportionment to apply, (i) the junior creditor and
the third party must each have had notice of the senior security and (ii) the third party must have
had notice of the junior security when it took its security over B).

[52]   A number of United States cases have asserted that the junior creditor enjoys priority for the
purposes of marshalling where the third party security over the asset, subject to the senior security
that the junior creditor is seeking to marshall, was created *subsequent* to the junior security: *Ingersoll
v Somers Land Co* 89 A 288 (1913); *Sanborn, McDuffee Co v Keefe* 187 A 97 (1936); *Equitable
Savings & Loan Association v 20th Avenue Corp* 235 NYS 2d 394 (1962); *Meyer v United States* 375
US 233 (1963). It is, however, difficult to see how a junior creditor could (in the absence of a priority arrangement) assert priority over a third party where the junior creditor's security does not
extend to the asset over which the third party holds security.

circumstances, be rectified by the erosion of the third party's security. Moreover, the conferral on the junior creditor of the benefit of the *entire* senior security, over an asset that is also subject to the third party's security, would effectively grant the junior creditor priority over the third party *vis-à-vis* that asset. The junior creditor who does not hold a security over this asset would have conferred upon it, by operation of the doctrine of marshalling, priority over a creditor who holds such a security.

11.33 The iniquity of allowing the junior creditor an unmodified right to marshall becomes obvious when it is realised that the third party is in an equivalent position to the junior creditor *qua* the senior creditor. If the senior creditor had recovered its debt out of the asset over which the third party held security, it would have been the third party who would be seeking to gain access *via* marshalling to the asset subject to the junior creditor's security.

11.34 The apportionment of the senior security between the junior creditor and the third party is designed to overcome the problems associated with allowing one secured creditor an unfettered right to marshall the senior security over an asset, in respect of which another creditor holds *mesne* security. The apportionment principle recognises that the junior creditor and the third party are in an equivalent position *qua* one another.[53] Assuming that the requirements of the common debtor rule have been satisfied,[54] both parties have a potential equity as regards the asset encumbered by the other's security. The creditor who is ultimately able to invoke the doctrine of marshalling is determined by the particular asset against which the senior creditor elects to enforce its security.

11.35 Accordingly, marshalling by apportionment prevents the entire burden of the senior debt from falling upon any one of the creditors, who holds second-ranking security over assets subject to the senior security. The junior creditor, if it enjoyed an unfettered right to marshall, would be able to shift the entire burden of the senior debt onto the third party. Similarly, if the junior creditor were denied the right to marshall, the senior creditor could, by its conduct, cause the entire burden of the senior debt to fall on the junior creditor.

11.36 Marshalling by apportionment acts, as best it can, to preserve the priority-ranking of the securities held by the junior creditor and the third party while minimising the loss sustained by each of them as a result of the modification of their mar-

---

[53] The third party security holder is not in an equivalent position to the junior creditor in the case of the exceptions to marshalling by apportionment (see paragraph 11.27). Should the senior creditor recoup its debt out of the asset that is subject to the junior security, in the circumstances encompassed by those exceptions, the junior creditor will be entitled to make up any shortfall out of the asset that is encumbered by the third party's security, in priority to the claims of the third party.

[54] It is unlikely that marshalling by apportionment would be available where the surety exception applies: q v n44.

shalling rights.[55] This is accomplished by imposing upon each creditor a share of the senior debt that is in proportion to the value of the asset over which it holds security.[56]

Marshalling by apportionment and the policy goals of security

The parity of treatment of the junior and third party securities, mandated by marshalling by apportionment, is consistent with the conventional theory of security examined in Chapter 6. **11.37**

The apportionment of the senior security between the junior creditor and the third party ensures that, as far as possible, the original priority-ranking of each party's secured claim against the debtor is preserved in proportion to the value of the asset over which it holds security. As a result of the application of this principle, each party is in a position better than that in which it would have been had the other party been permitted to throw the entire burden of the senior debt onto the asset subject to the former party's security. **11.38**

Marshalling by apportionment recognises that the claims of the junior creditor and the third party are of equal merit (the junior creditor holds a second-ranking security over one asset and the third party holds a second-ranking security over another) and that there is no objective means of determining which of the claims should be preferred to the other. Accordingly, this qualification of marshalling means that the priority-ranking of one party is not preserved by sacrificing the interest of the other. **11.39**

The provision of credit is, on this basis, not jeopardised by the extension to a creditor of a qualified right to marshall where the asset to which it is seeking access *via* marshalling is encumbered by a security in favour of another creditor. **11.40**

D. Third Party Transferees or Disponees and Exclusion of Marshalling Rights

Introduction

Whilst a third party security holder is only able to modify a junior creditor's marshalling rights, a third party transferee or disponee can prevent those rights from **11.41**

---

[55] q v paragraph 11.21.

[56] The senior security is not divided equally amongst the junior creditor and the third party *per se*. Each creditor is, instead, given a share of the senior security that is in proportion to the value of the asset over which it holds security. The share of the senior security that the junior creditor receives is equivalent to (senior debt) multiplied by ((value of A)/(aggregate value of A + B)). Similarly, the third party will receive a benefit equivalent to (senior debt) multiplied by ((value of B)/(aggregate value of A + B)). In this manner, the burden of the senior debt is distributed amongst the junior creditor and the third party in proportion to the value of the asset over which the other party holds security.

arising. A debtor is able by effecting a transfer or disposition to a third party of an asset, the subject of the grant of security to a senior creditor, to place that asset beyond the reach of marshalling.

Exclusion of marshalling rights—the general rule

11.42 The exclusion of the junior creditor's marshalling rights may be demonstrated by reference to the following example. Assume that a debtor who owns assets A and B has granted a first-ranking security over those assets to a senior creditor and a second-ranking security over asset A to a junior creditor, and, subsequent to the grant of the securities, has transferred or disposed of asset B to a third party.[57]

11.43 Where the terms of the transfer or disposition expressly provide that the asset is being transferred free of the security,[58] the cases are agreed that the junior creditor will be unable to have recourse to the doctrine of marshalling in the event that the senior creditor recovers the senior debt through the enforcement of the senior security over asset A.[59] The junior creditor's ability to marshall will be abrogated, irrespective of whether the third party is a purchaser for value or a volunteer.[60]

11.44 This is because the transfer or disposition of asset B to the third party delivers unencumbered title to asset B into the hands of the third party. The doctrine of

---

[57] Chapter 11 is concerned only with the transfer or disposition of the asset encumbered by only the senior security i e the issue of how a debtor may, without reference to the junior creditor, abrogate a junior creditor's ability to marshall. For a discussion of the position regarding the transfer or disposition of the asset subject to both the senior and junior securities, see paragraphs 8.18–8.20.

[58] The co-operation of the senior creditor will be required if B is to be transferred to the third party free of the senior security, unless the security is a floating charge; otherwise the general rule will not apply, and the junior creditor's marshalling rights will arguably persist: see the discussion in paragraphs 11.50–11.54 on the issue of notice. If the senior security is a mortgage, fixed equitable charge or non-possessory lien, it will follow B into the hands of the third party unless released by the senior creditor; similarly, in the case of a pledge or possessory lien, the senior creditor would have to relinquish possession of B for B to be released from the senior security. In contrast, a floating charge enables the debtor to transfer B, without the need to seek the consent of the senior creditor, unless the transfer or disposition is prohibited by the terms of the floating charge (e g a transfer or disposition outside the ordinary course of the debtor's business), in which case it will cause the floating charge to crystallise into a fixed charge. See further Chapter 9 on the nature of securities.

[59] *Hartley v O'Flaherty* (1813–1830) Beat 61; *Chappell v Rees* (1839) 9 LJ Ch 37; *Mallott v Wilson* [1903] 2 Ch 494; *In re Darby's Estate* [1907] 2 Ch 465; *Re Burge, Woodall & Co* [1912] 1 KB 393; *In re Best* [1924] 1 Ch 42; *In re Mainwaring* [1937] Ch 96. See Cavanagh, *The Law of Money Securities*, 551; Robbins, *A Treatise on the Law of Mortgages, Pledges and Hypothecations*, 787; Beddoes, *A Concise Treatise on the Law of Mortgages*, 104–105; Webster, *Ashburner's Concise Treatise on Mortgages, Pledges and Liens*, 466 and 467; Hewitt, *White & Tudor's Leading Cases in Equity*, 53–54; Ramsbotham, *Coote's Treatise on the Law of Mortgages*, 806; Hanbury & Waldock, *The Law of Mortgages*, 179; *Halsbury's*, Vol 32 ('*Mortgage*'), para 916; Baker & Langan, *Snell's Equity*, 421–422.

[60] *Hughes v Williams* (1852) 3 Mac & G 683; *Hales v Cox* (1863) 32 Beav 118; *Anstey v Newman* (1870) 39 LJ Ch 769; *Dolphin v Aylward* (1870) LR 4 E & I 486; *Mallott v Wilson* [1903] 2 Ch 494. Strictly speaking, it is not the case that a volunteer can defeat a junior creditor's marshalling rights but rather that, the common debtor rule not being satisfied, the disposition has prevented those rights from arising: c f O'Donovan & Phillips, *The Modern Contract of Guarantee*, 681n710.

marshalling does not preserve the priority-ranking of the junior debt by granting a new security to the junior creditor. It operates by granting the junior creditor access to an existing security, *viz.* the senior security over asset B. Once the transfer or disposition to the third party has been completed, the senior security will cease to subsist over asset B, thus negating any prior compliance with the requirements of the common debtor rule. As a consequence, there will be nothing in respect of asset B against which the junior creditor can assert its right to marshall.

Exclusion of marshalling rights—time of transfer or disposition

The cases on the point are all concerned with situations where the transfer or disposition to the third party *post-dates* the creation of the junior security. This gap in the case law is, nonetheless, capable of being resolved.[61]   **11.45**

Until such time as the senior debt is prejudicially recovered by the senior creditor out of asset A, the junior creditor possesses merely a potential equity that is capable of being excluded by an intervening transfer or disposition of asset B to a third party. This potential to marshall implies, in the context of this inquiry, that the relevant transfer or disposition post-dates the creation of the junior security. Where the transfer or disposition of asset B pre-dates the creation of the junior security, that potentiality never arises, irrespective of whether the third party takes asset B subject to the senior security.   **11.46**

Where the third party takes asset B free of the senior security there will be no question of the junior creditor ever having complied with the requirements of the common debtor rule. Following the enforcement of the senior security against asset A, there will be nothing against which the junior creditor can assert the right to marshall.   **11.47**

---

[61] The time of transfer/disposition *qua* the time of enforcement of the senior security is also material. The junior creditor's equity arises automatically following the recovery of the senior debt out of asset A. A third party purchaser of the legal estate in asset B for value without notice will take free of the junior creditor's equity: see Meagher, Gummow & Lehane, *Equity Doctrines and Remedies*, paras 846 and 848–860. The position is less certain where the third party purchases only the equitable estate or interest in asset B: such a purchaser will be bound by prior equitable interests, but not mere equities, of which it had no notice: Baker & Langan, *Snell's Equity*, 50; R E Megarry, *Mere Equities, the Bona Fide Purchaser and the Deserted Wife* (1955) 71 LQR 480, 482; Delany, *Equitable Interests and 'Mere Equities'*, 199. It is unclear, in the absence of case law on the point, how the inchoate equity constituted by marshalling would fare in such a priority contest. The junior creditor is, however, on stronger ground in the case of purchasers of the equitable estate with notice of the equity (again it is not certain whether notice of the junior security over asset A would necessarily be taken to equate to notice of the junior creditor's equity as regards asset B: q v n42) and volunteers: c f Meagher, Gummow & Lehane, *Equity Doctrines and Remedies*, para 1123 where it considered that a volunteer without notice of the junior security would take free of the junior creditor's 'interest' in asset B. There is no good reason why, following the recoupment of the senior debt, a third party would take asset B subject to the senior security (it is relevant to note that the right to marshall is contingent upon the debt secured by the senior security over assets A and B having been discharged: see Cleaver, *Marshalling*, 293–294).

11.48 Even if the third party were to take asset B subject to the senior security, the junior creditor will be unable to marshall the senior security over that asset as again the requirements of the common debtor rule will at no stage have ever been satisfied.[62]

Exclusion of marshalling rights—identity of the third party

11.49 The issue of the persistence of the junior creditor's marshalling rights in the face of a transfer or disposition to a third party is only relevant where the third party is a party other than the junior creditor. If the equity of redemption—or any other residual interest retained by the debtor in asset B following the grant of the senior security over that asset[63]—were to be assigned to the junior creditor, the junior creditor would be unable to marshall the senior security.[64]

Exclusion of marshalling rights—notice of the junior security

11.50 The position as regards the junior creditor's ability to marshall the senior security is less certain where the third party has not contracted to take asset B free of the senior security.[65]

11.51 There is a line of authority which supports the proposition that the transfer or disposition will only prevent the junior creditor from marshalling the senior security if the third party did not have notice of the junior security when it acquired asset B.[66]

---

[62] Nor will the surety exception be available to the junior creditor, even though the third party transferee/disponee may, by taking subject to the senior security, be considered a surety of the senior debt: see further paragraphs 7.17–7.20, 8.11 and 8.12.

[63] Similarly, if the junior creditor took an assignment of the senior security over B, it would be equally redundant for the junior creditor to seek recourse to the doctrine of marshalling: see the Australian case of *Porter v Associated Securities Ltd* (1976) 1 BPR 97027 and Tyler, Young & Croft, *Fisher & Lightwood's Law of Mortgage*, para 30.10. The senior creditor could abrogate the junior creditor's ability to marshall by assigning its security over asset B to a third party, thus abrogating any prior compliance with the common debtor rule. If, however, the senior creditor were to assign its security or securities over assets A and B to a third party, the junior creditor's marshalling rights would be unaffected. C f Cousins, *The Law of Mortgages*, 436 where it is stated: 'The right [to marshall] is not lost by reason of the two funds or securities later becoming vested in different persons'.

[64] This would be the case irrespective of whether the assignment of the residual interest was absolute or by way of security: *Re Stephenson* (1866) 3 De G M & G 969. Marshalling requires the junior security to be narrower in scope than the senior security: see paragraph 7.24.

[65] The authorities cited in paragraphs 11.51–11.52 are capable of being reconciled with the principles underlying the common debtor rule (as enunciated in paragraphs 7.17–7.20) by reference to the timing of the transfer/disposition relative to the time of creation of the junior security. Where the transfer/disposition pre-dates the creation of the junior security, the junior creditor will be unable to marshall the senior security due to non-compliance with the common debtor rule, prior compliance being irrelevant: see paragraphs 11.46–11.48. However, where the transfer/disposition post-dates the creation of the junior security, the above authorities contemplate the persistence of marshalling rights.

[66] *Aldridge v Forbes* (1839) 9 LJ Ch 37; *Hughes v Williams* (1852) 3 Mac & G 683; *Rooke v Lord Kensington* (1856) 21 Beav 470; *Anstey v Newman* (1870) 39 LJ Ch 769; *Dolphin v Aylward* (1870)

The opposing line of authority maintains that notice is irrelevant: the third party, **11.52** as an incident of its acquisition of asset B subject to the senior security, bears the risk that that security may at some later date be the subject of a marshalling claim.[67]

The better view is represented by the latter line of authority.[68] The third party has **11.53** not bargained for an unencumbered asset. All that the transfer or disposition has accomplished—which is all that the third party has, in fact, agreed to—is to place the third party in the position of the debtor in respect of the transferred asset. As the asset acquired by the third party continues to be subject to the senior security, the third party cannot expect, merely by reason of a change of ownership, to be in a better position than was the debtor *qua* the junior creditor. Accordingly, the third party takes the asset subject to the risk that, should the senior creditor enforce its security over the asset retained by the debtor in preference to its security over the third party's asset, a lower-ranking creditor of the debtor (*viz.* the junior creditor) may be entitled to marshall that security.

Further, according to the former line of authority, the transfer or disposition to **11.54** the third party will not abrogate the junior creditor's ability to marshall if the third party had notice of the junior security over asset A at the time of the transfer or disposition. However, until such time as the senior creditor enforces the senior

---

LR 4 E & I 486; *Re Walhampton Estate* (1884) 26 Ch D 391. See Robbins, *A Treatise on the Law of Mortgages, Pledges and Hypothecations*, 781; Hewitt, *White & Tudor's Leading Cases in Equity*, 51; Ramsbotham, *Coote's Treatise on the Law of Mortgages*, 811–812. Tyler, *Fisher & Lightwood's Law of Mortgage*, 533 states, in the course of discussing the extinguishment of marshalling rights by rights of exoneration, that marshalling will not be available against a third party purchaser or volunteer, unless the asset in question has been transferred with a right of exoneration against the senior security. This necessarily implies that the transferred asset remains subject to the senior security. However, if the senior creditor recoups the senior debt out of the asset retained by the debtor and the junior creditor marshalls the senior security over the transferred asset, the third party's right of exoneration is likely to be rendered illusory. Presumably, what Fisher & Lightwood mean is that, if the senior creditor recoups the senior debt out of the transferred asset the third party will be entitled to be exonerated out of the asset retained by the debtor in priority to the junior creditor, and the junior creditor will have no right to marshall the senior security. This is, however, inconsistent with the cases on contribution and exoneration discussed in paragraphs 5.33–5.36.

[67] *Gwynne v Edwards* (1825) 2 Russ 289n; *Finch v Shaw* (1854) 19 Beav 500; *Haynes v Forshaw* (1853) 11 Hare 93 (c f Tyler, *Fisher & Lightwood's Law of Mortgage*, 533n(q) where it is considered that these two cases are inconsistent with the cases on marshalling by apportionment as they suggest that the asset transferred necessarily remains subject to a junior creditor's marshalling rights); *In re Jones* [1893] 2 Ch 461; *Re Cook's Mortgage* [1896] 1 Ch 923; *Mallott v Wilson* [1903] 2 Ch 494; *In re Darby's Estate* [1907] 2 Ch 465; *Re Burge, Woodall & Co* [1912] 1 KB 393; *In re Best* [1924] 1 Ch 42.

[68] The two opposing lines of authority effectively operate as exceptions to the common debtor rule, although they are not expressly recognised as such by the commentators and the cases. While the junior creditor may have previously satisfied the requirements of the common debtor rule, the transfer or disposition to the third party of the asset encumbered by only the senior security abrogates that compliance. Permitting the junior creditor recourse to the doctrine of marshalling upon the enforcement of the senior security against the asset retained by the debtor controverts requirements (1) and (2) of the common debtor rule.

security against asset A, the most that the junior creditor will have is a potential equity to marshall. It is difficult to see how notice of a security over asset A translates into notice of a potential equity in respect of asset B, as distinct from an existing equity that would be capable of binding third party transferees or disponees with notice of that equity.[69]

Exclusion of marshalling rights—other jurisdictions

11.55   The exclusion of a junior creditor's marshalling rights—where the asset in question has been transferred or disposed of on terms that expressly provide that the asset is being transferred free of the senior security—is recognised in Canada,[70] Ireland[71] and New Zealand.[72] It is also likely that this principle is recognised in Australia.[73]

11.56   Where, however, the various jurisdictions differ is in relation to transfers or dispositions to a third party on terms that do not provide that the asset is being transferred free of the security. The position in Canada is clearly that the third party will prevail over the junior creditor unless it had notice of the junior security at the time of the transfer or disposition.[74] This would also appear to be the position in Australia.[75] In contrast, the position in Ireland is that notice is irrelevant.[76] It is not certain how a New Zealand court would decide this issue.

Marshalling, transfers and dispositions to third parties and the policy goals of security

11.57   The proposition that marshalling should not differentiate between the debtor and a third party transferee or disponee who takes the asset encumbered by the senior

---

[69]   For a discussion of the rules of priority as they affect equitable interests and mere equities, see Baker & Langan, *Snell's Equity*, 50; Megarry, *Mere Equities, the Bona Fide Purchaser and the Deserted Wife*, 482; Delany, *Equitable Interests and 'Mere Equities'*, 199.

[70]   *Ernst Brothers Co v Canadian Permanent Mortgage Corp* (1920) 57 DLR 500; *Johal v Sahota* (1986) 2 BCLR (2d) 218. See also Rayner & McLaren, *Falconbridge on Mortgages*, 316–317.

[71]   *Averall v Wade* (1835) L & G temp Sugd 252; *Hales v Cox* (1863) 32 Beav 118; *Ker v Ker* (1869) 4 IR Eq 15; *In re Lysaght's Estate* [1903] 1 IR 235; *McCarthy v M'Cartie (No 2)* [1904] 1 IR 100; *Ocean Accident & Guarantee Corp Ltd and Hewitt v Collum* [1913] 1 IR 337; *Hollinshead v Devane* (1914) 49 ILT 87.

[72]   *Re Stephenson* (1911) 30 NZLR 145.

[73]   q v n75.

[74]   *Jones v Beck* (1871) 18 Gr 671; *Clark v Bogart* (1880) 27 Gr 450; *Pierce v Canavan* (1882) 7 OAR 187; *Renwick v Berryman* (1886) 3 Man R 387; *Fraser v Nagle* (1888) 16 OR 241.

[75]   In *Chase Corp (Australia) Pty Ltd v North Sydney Brick and Tile Co Ltd* (1994) 12 ACLC 997, 1,014 Cohen J. suggested that a junior creditor would be entitled to marshall despite an assignment to a third party, if unconscionability, lack of good faith or notice of the junior security on the part of the assignee could be established. See also Meagher, Gummow & Lehane, *Equity Doctrines and Remedies*, para 1123 where it is considered that the third party assignee, even if a volunteer, will prevail over the junior creditor in the absence of notice of the junior security.

[76]   *Hales v Cox* (1863) 32 Beav 118; *In re Rorke's Estate* (1865) 15 Ir Ch R 316; *In re Lysaght's Estate* [1903] 1 IR 235; *McCarthy v M'Cartie (No 2)* [1904] 1 IR 100. C f Lyall, *Land Law in Ireland*, para 23.7.3(b) where the opposing position is supported.

security subject to that security is consistent with the conventional theory of security.

The circumstances to which this proposition relates involve the transfer or disposition of the above asset subsequent to the grant by the debtor of the security in favour of the junior creditor.[77] The third party, by taking the asset subject to the senior security, has not only agreed that that asset should be potentially liable for the senior debt but has also assumed the risk that another creditor of the debtor may obtain access to the asset *via* marshalling.[78] The third party would, however, be in no worse a position by reason of the junior creditor being permitted to marshall the senior security (as opposed to the senior creditor recouping the senior debt by enforcing that security).[79]

In contrast, barring the junior creditor from marshalling, in these circumstances, **11.58** is likely to have adverse consequences for the supply of credit by the holders of *mesne* security. All that the transfer or disposition has effected is a change of ownership of the assets subject to the senior security. The actual assets which, after the transfer or disposition, are subject to the senior security are no different from those that were encumbered by it at the time the junior creditor acquired its security.[80]

The junior creditor is likely to have relied on the fact that at the time it took secu- **11.59** rity the senior security encompassed assets in addition to that over which it was taking security. The wider scope of the senior security increases the likelihood of the senior debt and, as a consequence, the junior debt being repaid. Accordingly, this lower risk of non-payment should be reflected in a lower cost of credit to the debtor.

Denying the junior creditor the right to marshall would undermine these assump- **11.60** tions and, as such would be inconsistent with the policy goals of security.[81] The junior creditor would face the risk unmitigated by the potentiality of marshalling that the senior creditor could impose upon it the entire burden of the senior debt, by choosing to recover that debt out of the asset retained by the debtor. It is likely that prospective lenders would seek to address this uncertainty by increasing the cost of credit, a move that would render credit less accessible to borrowers.

---

[77] q v n68.

[78] Implicit in this assumption of the risk of marshalling is that the transfer/disposition post-dates the creation of the junior security. c f paragraphs 7.17–7.20.

[79] Even if the balance of the junior debt were to exceed the senior debt, the junior creditor would only be able to recover an amount up to senior debt out of the third party's asset.

[80] c f paragraphs 11.46–11.48 concerning the junior creditor's inability to marshall where the relevant transfer or disposition pre-dates the grant of the junior security.

[81] This is not to argue that the junior creditor's potential equity should be inviolate: see paragraphs 11.61–11.63.

11.61　The exclusion of marshalling rights where an asset is transferred or disposed of free from the senior security can also be reconciled with the policy goals of security.

11.62　Save where the senior security is a floating charge, the consent of the senior creditor will be required for an asset subject to the senior security to be transferred or disposed of to the third party free of that security.[82] This is likely, in the ordinary course, to involve a partial repayment of the senior debt in exchange for the release of the asset. This reduction in the senior debt would also address the increased risk of loss to the junior creditor, as a result of the diminution in the assets subject to the senior security.

11.63　In the case of a floating charge, the consent of the senior creditor will not be required where the transfer or disposition is permitted by the terms of the floating charge.[83] It is therefore likely that the debtor will receive consideration for the transfer or disposition, as dispositions to volunteers would not normally be permitted by the terms of a floating charge. The debtor would have thus exchanged one asset for another (e g receivables or proceeds), and this latter asset will, on its acquisition by the debtor, be subject to the senior creditor's floating charge. Again, this 'asset exchange' should address the issue of risk of loss to the junior creditor flowing from the transfer or disposition of an asset subject to the senior security.[84]

---

[82] q v n58.

[83] Ibid.

[84] In addition, the junior creditor, as the holder of the second-ranking security over an asset, should be cognisant of the nature of the prior security. If the prior security is a floating charge, the junior creditor would be aware of the debtor's licence to transfer or dispose of assets in accordance with the terms of the floating charge and, consequently, should have factored this into the cost of credit provided by it to the debtor.

12

COVENANTS AGAINST MARSHALLING AND OTHER CONTRACTUAL CONSTRAINTS

Introduction	12.01	Conclusion	12.12
Covenants Against Marshalling	12.03	Purchase Money Security Arrangements Between Debtor and Third Parties	12.13
Covenant (1)	12.05		
Covenant (2)	12.06		
Covenant (3)	12.07	Priority-position of purchase money securities	12.15
Conclusion	12.08		
		Conclusion	12.18
Priority Arrangements Between Senior Creditor and Third Parties	12.09		
Priority arrangements	12.11		

A. Introduction

The terms on which a senior creditor provides finance to a debtor are likely to include, as a 'boilerplate' clause, a covenant that purports to oust the right of other creditors to marshall the senior security. Such covenants are, however, based on a misconception as to how marshalling operates under English law. **12.01**

Two other contractual devices pose, on the other hand, a more serious threat to a junior creditor's ability to marshall the senior security. Voluntary arrangements between the senior creditor and a third party security holder that controvert the presumptive rules of priority may abrogate the junior creditor's marshalling rights. Similarly, arrangements between the debtor and a third party security holder which cause an existing senior creditor to relinquish its priority-ranking to the third party, may also preclude the junior creditor from marshalling the senior security. **12.02**

This chapter considers the impact on marshalling rights of covenants against marshalling, priority arrangements between the senior creditor and third parties, and purchase money security arrangements between the debtor and third parties.

B. Covenants Against Marshalling

12.03 Cleaver notes that there are two types of 'covenant against marshalling' which may be employed by a senior creditor to prevent a junior creditor from marshalling the senior security:[1]

(1) The debtor covenants with the senior creditor not to create subsequent securities over any of the assets subject to the senior security, without obtaining a waiver of the right to marshall from the holder of the subsequent security.[2]

(2) The senior security is structured in a manner which ensures that the senior creditor at no stage enjoys equal rights of recourse to the various assets subject to the senior security.[3]

12.04 A third type of covenant is also encountered:

(3) The debtor agrees that the senior creditor will be under no obligation to marshall the senior security.

Covenant (1)

12.05 It is entirely possible for a junior creditor to waive existing or future marshalling rights.[4] However, it is difficult to see what incentive the junior creditor has to execute such a waiver[5] or how the waiver is of benefit to the senior creditor.

The junior creditor's right to marshall, if available, only arises following the recovery of the senior debt *via* the enforcement of the senior security; it thus does not carry with it any adverse consequences for the efficacy of the senior security. Given this, there would seem to be little point in attempting to convince a prospective lender of junior debt of the merits of conceding the protection afforded it by marshalling.

---

[1] Cleaver, *Marshalling*, 296–299. For covenants preventing a surety from exercising its apparent marshalling rights, see paragraphs 8.33 and 8.34.

[2] Cleaver, *Marshalling*, 296 and 298. The simplest means of achieving this would be for the senior creditor to enter into an agreement with junior creditors. However, this would require constant monitoring of the debtor by the senior creditor. Given the additional cost of such monitoring, it is likely to be more efficient for the senior creditor to impose the burden of abrogating marshalling rights upon the debtor.

[3] Cleaver, *Marshalling*, 296–297; Meagher, Gummow & Lehane, *Equity Doctrines and Remedies*, para 1120.

[4] q v a surety may waive its right of subrogation expressly (*Re Fernandes* (1844) 6 H & N 717; *Midland Banking Co v Chambers* (1869) 4 Ch App 398) or impliedly (*Allen v De Lisle* (1857) 5 WR 158; *Brandon v Brandon* (1859) 28 LJ Ch 147). See Marks & Moss, *Rowlatt on the Law of Principal and Surety*, 151–152; Mitchell, *The Law of Subrogation*, 48; Meagher, Gummow & Lehane, *Equity Doctrines and Remedies*, para 945.

[5] As an added incentive to perform, the arrangements between the senior creditor and the debtor may stipulate that non-compliance by the debtor will constitute an event of default permitting the acceleration of the loan and enforcement of the senior security.

Covenant (2)

This second type of covenant precludes a junior creditor from satisfying the **12.06**
fourth requirement of the common debtor rule which calls for parity of recourse
by the senior creditor to the assets subject to the senior security.[6]

The junior creditor is thus denied access to the senior security whilst the problems
faced by covenant (1) are avoided. The efficacy of the ouster of marshalling rights
does not depend upon the future conduct of the debtor and the junior creditor; it,
instead, takes effect automatically in accordance with the terms of the financing
arrangements between the senior creditor and the debtor.

Again, it is not clear what a senior creditor intends to achieve—other than the
derogation of its own security position—by taking comparatively inferior rights
over some of the assets encompassed by the senior security, since the doctrine of
marshalling does not interfere with its right to enforce the senior security.

Covenant (3)

Covenant (3) is similarly unmeritorious. Putting aside the difficulties with bind- **12.07**
ing a junior creditor to forgo its marshalling rights, this type of covenant seems to
be based on the fallacious assumption that marshalling impacts upon the quantum of the debtor's assets. Further, it is again unclear what the senior creditor
intends to achieve by denying the junior creditor the right to marshall once the
senior debt has been satisfied.

Conclusion

In short, covenants against marshalling are superfluous.[7] Such covenants appear **12.08**
to be based upon the misconception that the exercise of marshalling rights by a
junior creditor is, in some way, injurious to the senior creditor.[8] The version of
marshalling that prevails in England, Australia, Canada and New Zealand is one
which does not detract from the freedom of the senior creditor to enforce its security as it sees fit.[9]

---

[6] See further Chapter 7.

[7] This may not be the case when it is not the version of marshalling depicted by the coercion
theory that concerns a creditor, but rather the application of marshalling by apportionment e g
where a junior creditor requires a covenant against marshalling by third parties. The efficacy of such
a covenant would, again, depend upon compliance by the debtor and the third party.

[8] See Schumacher, *Marshalling*, 92.

[9] It has been stated (Cleaver, *Marshalling*, 297) that covenants against marshalling do, in limited
circumstances, perform a useful function: '[t]his covenant against marshalling is really only of use to
a [senior creditor] in cases where it has an interest in protecting the surplus security of the [debtor]'.
The examples given are all cases where the senior creditor is an associated party of the debtor
(Cleaver, *Marshalling*, 298). Again, this proposition is premised upon the misconception that marshalling in some way reduces the residue available to the debtor.

C. Priority Arrangements Between a Senior Creditor and Third Parties

12.09 In contrast to covenants against marshalling, in favour of the senior creditor, there may be significant benefits flowing to a third party security holder from the abrogation of a junior creditor's marshalling rights.

12.10 Where, for example, the senior security encompasses two assets, A and B, and the junior creditor and third party hold second-ranking security over assets A and B respectively, neither the junior creditor nor the third party will be able to invoke the doctrine of marshalling so as to throw the entire burden of the senior debt onto the asset over which the other holds security.[10] Instead, a modified form of marshalling will apply with the senior security being rateably apportioned between them.[11]

Priority arrangements

12.11 If the third party is able to abrogate the junior creditor's right to marshal, it will obviate the risk that its ability to recoup the debt owed to it out of the asset subject to its security, will be constrained by the presence of a second-ranking security over some other asset of the debtor. A prime means of achieving this is by way of a priority arrangement[12] between the senior creditor and the third party, under which the senior creditor agrees to postpone the priority-ranking of its security over asset B to that held by the third party.[13]

The senior creditor will, under this priority arrangement, continue to enjoy priority over the junior creditor but the priority positions of the senior creditor and the third party will be exchanged. The senior creditor will retain its position of

---

[10] If the third party security were held over A and the third party ranked behind the junior creditor, the junior creditor's marshalling rights would be unaffected. See further paragraphs 11.03 and 11.18.

[11] This modified form of marshalling by apportionment may also be contracted out of: see paragraph 11.25.

[12] It should be noted that priority arrangements between secured creditors are distinct from subordinations of debt, which typically encompass the postponement of the claims of one or more unsecured creditors to the claims of other unsecured creditors. Further, priority arrangements, in contrast to subordinations of debt, do not alter the right of either the senior creditor or the third party to repayment of its debt; all they provide for is a reordering of the relative priorities of the secured claims held by the contracting parties. See generally Wood, *The Law of Subordinated Debt*; Wood, *Project Finance, Subordinated Debt and State Loans*, Chapter 8. Debt subordinations are not considered as unsecured creditors do not have standing to marshal: see further Chapter 10.

[13] This raises the issue of what benefit the senior creditor derives from the priority arrangement. It may be the case that: (i) in the absence of such an arrangement, the debtor would be unable to raise additional finance, thus affecting its ability to repay the senior debt (the senior creditor has conceded priority in respect of only one of the assets subject to the senior security); or (ii) the senior creditor is a related party of the debtor or the third party.

first-ranking creditor *vis-à-vis* asset A while the third party will be promoted to that position in respect of asset B.

Conclusion

In the event that the senior creditor recovers its debt out of asset A,[14] the junior cred- **12.12**
itor will be unable to marshall the senior security over asset B, as the rights the third
party possesses in relation to asset B are clearly superior to any rights which the doctrine of marshalling may confer upon the junior creditor.[15] Thus, the third party,
rather than having to share the benefit of the senior security with the junior creditor,
will be able to recoup its indebtedness out of asset B ahead of the junior creditor.

D. Purchase Money Security Arrangements Between a Debtor and Third Parties

As a general rule, a security granted to a third party after the creation of the senior **12.13**
and junior securities will, at best, only modify the junior creditor's marshalling
rights.

If, however, the third party's security is a purchase money security, the junior cred- **12.14**
itor's marshalling rights will not merely be modified but will, instead, be placed in
abeyance until the debt owed to the third party has been discharged. The purchase
money security will rank ahead of the senior security and, as such, endow the third
party with rights superior to the junior creditor's right to marshall.

The priority-position of purchase money securities

A purchase money security is a security taken by a creditor over an asset of a **12.15**
debtor, to secure the repayment of funds that have been advanced by the creditor
to the debtor for the specific purpose of acquiring that asset.[16]

Where, for example, the senior security[17] encompasses two assets, A and B, and
the junior creditor holds security over asset A and a third party holds a purchase

---

[14] Given that the senior creditor holds a first-ranking security over A and a second-ranking security for the same debt over B it will, *ceteris paribus*, clearly prefer to enforce its security against A first.
Alternatively, the senior creditor and the third party could agree that the senior creditor will only
look to B to the extent that A is insufficient to discharge the senior debt. The junior creditor will be
unable to marshall since the senior creditor will no longer enjoy equal rights of recourse to A and B,
as required by the common debtor rule: see further Chapters 7 and 9.

[15] See further Chapter 11.

[16] Goode, *Legal Problems of Credit and Security*, 98.

[17] The security held by the senior creditor must be either (i) a mortgage/fixed charge that extends
to future assets or (ii) a floating charge (with an effective restrictive clause prohibiting the grant of
subsequent security in priority to the floating charge): B will otherwise fall outside the scope of the
senior security or concede priority to the third party's security. The junior creditor will be unable to
obtain, *via* marshalling, the benefit of B. See Goode, *Legal Problems of Credit and Security*, 32–37;
Gough, *Company Charges*, 431–439.

money security over asset B, the availability of marshalling will depend on the outcome of the priority contest between the senior creditor and the third party.

12.16 Prior to the decision of the House of Lords in *Abbey National Building Society v Cann*,[18] there were two possible outcomes to this dispute:

(1) at the time the debtor acquires asset B there will be a split instance in time (*scintilla temporis*), in which the debtor will be the absolute owner of asset B, before the securities held by the senior creditor and the third party encompass that asset. The senior creditor will, in these circumstances, enjoy priority over the third party;[19] and

(2) the debtor's interest in asset B will be encumbered from the time of the acquisition of that asset by the third party security. The third party will thus enjoy priority over the senior creditor.

Should (1) be the correct outcome, the third party's security will be no different from any other second-ranking security over B, and the principle of marshalling by apportionment will apply.

12.17 The House of Lords adopted outcome (2) and expressly overruled the authorities that supported outcome (1). An asset acquired with funds advanced by a third party for that purpose, with the asset as the subject of the security for the advance, will never, even for a *scintilla temporis*, be the unencumbered property of the debtor.[20] The third party security will attach *eo instanti* when the debtor acquires asset B and, as such, will rank ahead of even a senior security which pre-dates it.

Conclusion

12.18 The purchase money security thus confers on the third party rights to asset B that are superior to the junior creditor's marshalling rights. Accordingly, if the senior creditor recoups the senior debt out of asset A, the junior creditor will be unable to marshal the senior security over asset B, until the debt secured by the purchase money security has been discharged.

12.19 As regards the position of the junior creditor, purchase money security arrangements between the debtor and a third party have the same consequences as priority arrangements between the senior creditor and a third party. In both instances,

---

[18] [1991] AC 56.

[19] q v n17.

[20] See Goode, *Legal Problems of Credit and Security*, 98–100; G Goldberg, *Vivat ac vivat scintilla temporis* (1992) 108 LQR 380; J Jeremie, *Gone in an Instant – The Death of 'Scintilla Temporis' and the Growth of a Purchase Money Security Interest in Real Property* [1994] JBL 363. This is also the position in Australia: *Composite Buyers Limited v State Bank of New South Wales* (1990) 3 ACSR 196; and in New Zealand: *Australian Guarantee Corporation (NZ) Limited v Nicholson* (1995) 7 NZCLC 260,932. For the position in Canada, see: R C C Cuming, *Floating Charges and Fixed Charges of After-Acquired Property* (1988) 67 Can Bar Rev 506; L J Lysaght & G R Stewart, *Priority between Competing Secured Creditors: Exploring the Borderlands between Personal Property Securities Rules and the Common Law* (1995) 74 Can Bar Rev 50.

the senior creditor concedes priority to the third party in relation to the asset that is subject to the senior security sought to be marshalled by the junior creditor. The only distinction is that the extinguishment of marshalling rights in the latter case is due to the senior creditor's voluntary relinquishment of its priority-ranking, whereas in the former case the postponement of priority is involuntary.

Chapter 11 reveals that a debtor, by subsequent dealings with the assets subject to the senior security, can modify or abrogate a junior creditor's marshalling rights. This is the case with the purchase money securities. Similarly, a senior creditor can prevent a junior creditor from marshalling the senior security. This is the case with priority arrangements and certain covenants against marshalling (although the utility of the latter is highly questionable). **12.20**

BIBLIOGRAPHY

(1) AUSTRALIA

(a) Texts

C Cato, *Restitution in Australia and New Zealand* (1997 Cavendish)

M Cope, *Constructive Trusts* (1992 Law Book Company)

M Cope (ed), *Equity: Issues and Trends* (1995 Federation Press)

G E Dal Pont & D R C Chalmers, *Equity and Trusts in Australia and New Zealand* (1996 Law Book Company)

M Davies & A Dickey, *Shipping Law* (2nd ed 1995 Law Book Company)

S R Derham, *Subrogation in Insurance Law* (1985 Law Book Company)

W D Duncan & L Willmott, *Mortgages Law in Australia* (1996 Federation Press)

M Evans, *Outline of Equity and Trusts* (3rd ed 1996 Butterworths)

D Everett, *The Nature of Fixed and Floating Charges as Security Devices* (1988 Monash)

P D Finn (ed), *Essays in Equity* (1985 Law Book Company)

E A Francis & K J Thomas, *Mortgages and Securities* (3rd ed 1986 Butterworths)

M Gilooley (ed), *Securities over Personalty* (1994 Federation Press)

J Glover, *Commercial Equity: Fiduciary Relationships* (1995 Butterworths)

J Glover, *Subrogation* in P Parkinson (ed), *The Principles of Equity* (1996 Law Book Company)

W J Gough, *Company Charges* (2nd ed 1996 Butterworths)

J Greig & B Harrigan, *Enforcing Securities* (1994 Law Book Company)

W M C Gummow, *Unjust Enrichment, Restitution and Proprietary Remedies* in P Finn (ed), *Essays on Restitution* (1990 Law Book Company)

J D Heydon & P L Loughlan, *Cases and Materials on Equity and Trusts* (5th ed 1997 Butterworths)

F Jordan, *Chapters on Equity in New South Wales* (6th ed 1945 Sydney)

J Leslie, *Leslie's Equity and Commercial Practice* (1998 Prospect)

B McDonald, *Marshalling* in P Parkinson (ed), *The Principles of Equity* (1996 Law Book Company)

B McDonald, *Marshalling* in J A Riordan (ed), *The Laws of Australia* (1997 Release Law Book Company)

M McInnes (ed), *Restitution: Developments in Unjust Enrichment* (1996 Law Book Company)

K Mason & J W Carter, *Restitution Law in Australia* (1995 Butterworths)

R P Meagher, W M C Gummow & J R F Lehane, *Equity Doctrines and Remedies* (3rd ed 1992 Butterworths)

J O'Donovan & J C Phillips, *The Modern Contract of Guarantee* (3rd ed 1996 Law Book Company)

G E RICH, A NEWHAM & J M HARVEY, *The Practice in Equity* (1902 Law Book Company)

I C F SPRY, *The Principles of Equitable Remedies* (5th ed 1997 Law Book Company)

J G STARKE, *Assignments of Choses in Action in Australia* (1972 Butterworths)

R T J STEIN & M A STONE, *Torrens Title* (1991 Butterworths)

G P STUCKEY & C D IRWIN, *Parker's Practice in Equity* (2nd ed 1949 Law Book Company)

E I SYKES & S WALKER, *The Law of Securities* (5th ed 1993 Law Book Company)

E L G TYLER, P W YOUNG & C E CROFT, *Fisher & Lightwood's Law of Mortgage* (Aust ed 1995 Butterworths)

(b) Articles

D E ALLAN, *Security: Some Mysteries, Myths and Monstrosities* (1989) 15 Mon ULR 337

V ANNETTA, *Priority Rights in Insolvency – the Doctrinal Basis for Equity's Intervention* (1992) 20 ABLR 311

P BINGHAM, *The Surety's Right to Contribution* (1984) 12 ABLR 394

P BIRKS, *Equity in the Modern Law: An Exercise in Taxonomy* (1996) 26 UWALR 1

J BRYSON, *Restraining Sales by Mortgagees and a Curial Myth* (1993) 11 ABR 1

A BURROWS, *Understanding the Law of Restitution: A Map Through the Thicket* (1995) 18 UQLJ 149

P BUTT, *Is a Mortgagee Free to Choose how it will Apply the Sale Proceeds* (1994) 68 ALJ 814

S CHRISTIE, *Guarantor's Right of Subrogation* (1994) 10 BLB 21

G E DAL PONT, *Fair Shares: The Equitable Doctrine of Marshalling* (1996) 70 Law Inst J (5) 48

B F FITZGERALD, *Ownership as the Proximity or Privity Principle in Unjust Enrichment Law* (1995) 18 UQLJ 166

J GLOVER, *Equity, Restitution and the Proprietary Recovery of Value* (1991) UNSWLJ 247

R M GOODE, *Security: A Pragmatic Conceptualist's Approach* (1989) 15 Mon ULR 361

M GRONOW, *Secured Creditors of Insolvent Companies: Do They Get Too Good a Deal?* (1993) 1 ILJ 169

W M C GUMMOW, *Marshalling and Protected Assets* (1965) 5 Syd LR 120

L HOGG, *No Duty to Enforce Securities* (1990) 1 JBFLP 150

K KANJIAN, *Subrogation to the Security Rights of the Unpaid Vendor and Mortgagee* (1980) 9 Syd LR 176

W J KOECK & I M RAMSAY, *The Importance of Distinguishing between the Different Categories of Creditors for the Purposes of Company Law* (1994) 12 C&SLJ 105

J D LIPTON, *Equitable Rights of Contribution and Subrogation: Recent Australian Judicial Approaches* (1995) 13 ABR 21

J D LIPTON, *Sharing the Burden: Equitable Contribution and the Corporations Law* (1996) 70 Law Inst J (3) 49

L A McCRIMMION, *Protection of Equitable Interests under the Torrens System: Polishing the Mirror of Title* (1994) 20 Mon L R 300

D McGILL, *The Impact of Subrogation Rights upon Creditors' Management of Securities* (1997) 6 25 ABLR 118

M NEAVE & M WEINBERG, *The Nature and Function of Equities* (1979) 6 U Tas LR 24 and 115

J C NKALA, *Some Aspects of the Jurisprudence of the Floating Charge* (1993) 11 C&SLJ 301

A Nolan, *The Position of Unsecured Creditors of Corporate Groups: Towards a Group Responsibility Solution which gives Fairness and Equity a Role* (1993) 11 C&SLJ 461

Note, *Mortgagor's Rights* (1998) 72 ALJ 192

D Partlett, *The Right of Subrogation in Accommodation Bills of Exchange* (1979) 53 ALJ 694

D B Robertson, *The Lender-Borrower Relationship and the Subordination of Lenders' Claims* (1991) 2 JBFLP 69, 147 and 219

D B Robertson, *Subrogation and the Law of Restitution* (1998) 9 JBFLP 146

S Rodrick, *The Response of Torrens Mortgagors to Improper Mortgagee Sales* (1996) 22 Mon L R 289

D Wright, *The Continued Relevance of Divisions in Equitable Interests in Real Property* (1995) 3 APLJ 163

(2) CANADA

(a) Texts

G H L Fridman & J G McLeod, *Restitution* (1982 Carswell)

G B Klippert, *Unjust Enrichment* (1983 Toronto)

K P McGuinness, *The Law of Guarantee* (2nd ed 1996 Carswell)

R H McLaren, *Secured Transactions in Personal Property* (1981 Carswell)

P D Maddaugh & J D McCamus, *The Law of Restitution* (1990 Ontario)

A H Marsh, *History of the Court of Chancery and of the Rise and Development of the Doctrines of Equity* (1890 Carswell)

G E Palmer, *The Law of Restitution* (1978 Little, Brown & Co)

K R Palmer, *The Law of Set-Off in Canada* (1993 Canada Law Book)

W B Rayner & R H McLaren, *Falconbridge on Mortgages* (4th ed 1977 Canada Law Book)

D M Waters (ed), *Equity, Fiduciaries and Trusts 1993* (1993 Carswell)

(b) Articles

J Beatson, *Proprietary Claims in the Law of Restitution* (1995) 25 CBLJ 66

R C C Cuming, *Floating Charges and Fixed Charges of After-Acquired Property* (1988) 67 Can Bar Rev 506

R M Goode, *Is the Law too Favourable to Secured Creditors?* (1983–84) 8 CBLJ 53

L J Lysaght & G R Stewart, *Priority between Competing Secured Creditors: Exploring the Borderlands between Personal Property Securities Rules and the Common Law* (1995) 74 Can Bar Rev 50

B MacDougall, *Marshalling and the Personal Property Security Acts: Doing Unto Others . . .* (1994) 28 UBCLR 91

L D Smith, *The Province of the Law of Restitution* (1992) 71 Can Bar Rev 672

G G Triantis, *Debt Financing, Corporate Decision Making and Security Design* (1996) 26 CBLJ 93

R J Wood, *Enforcement Remedies of Creditors* (1996) 34 Alberta L Rev 782

(3) ENGLAND and WALES

(a) *Texts*

D E ALLAN, *Negative Pledge Lending – Dead or Alive* in R Cranston & R M Goode (eds), *Commercial and Consumer Law: National and International Dimensions* (1993 Oxford)

P V BAKER & P ST J LANGAN, *Snell's Equity* (29th ed 1990 Sweet & Maxwell)

H BALLOW, *A Treatise of Equity* (1793–1794 Strahan & Woodfall)

J BEATSON, *The Use and Abuse of Unjust Enrichment* (1991 Oxford)

W F BEDDOES, *A Concise Treatise on the Law of Mortgages* (2nd ed 1908 Stevens & Sons)

P BIRKS, *An Introduction to the Law of Restitution* (Revsd ed 1989 Oxford)

P BIRKS, *Restitution – the Future* (1992 Federation Press)

W BLACKSTONE, *Commentaries on the Laws of England* (New ed 1857 John Murray)

P I BLUMBERG, *The American Law of Corporate Groups* in J McCahery, S Picciotto & C Scott (eds), *Corporate Control and Accountability* (1993 Oxford)

E E BLYTH, *Analysis of Snell's Principles of Equity* (14th ed 1929 Sweet & Maxwell)

T BRETT, *Leading Cases in Modern Equity* (1887 W Clowes & Sons)

BRITISH COMPANY LAW AND PRACTICE (1998 Service CCH)

H BROOM, *Legal Maxims* (10th ed 1939 Sweet & Maxwell)

D BROWNE, *Ashburner's Principles of Equity* (2nd ed 1933 Butterworths)

W W BUCKLAND, *Equity in Roman Law* (1911 Cambridge)

E H BURN, *Cheshire & Burn's Modern Law of Real Property* (1994 Butterworths)

A BURROWS, *Essays on the Law of Restitution* (1991 Oxford)

A BURROWS, *The Law of Restitution* (1993 Butterworths)

A BURROWS, *Understanding the Law of Obligations* (1998 Hart Publishing)

C CAVANAGH, *The Law of Money Securities* (2nd ed 1885 W Clowes & Sons)

E CHITTY, *Index to All the Reported Cases Decided in the Several Courts of Equity and Bankruptcy in England and Ireland* (1886 Stevens & Sons)

E F COUSINS, *The Law of Mortgages* (1989 Sweet & Maxwell)

R CRANSTON (ed), *Making Commercial Law: Essays in Honour of Roy Goode* (1997 Oxford)

E R DANIELL, *The Practice of the High Court of Chancery* (5th ed 1871 Stevens & Sons)

P L DAVIES, *Gower's Principles of Modern Company Law* (6th ed 1997 Sweet & Maxwell)

S R DERHAM, *Set-Off* (2nd ed 1996 Oxford)

R A EASTWOOD, *Williams' Principles of the Law of Real Property* (24th ed 1926 Sweet & Maxwell)

R A EASTWOOD, *Strahan's Digest of Equity* (6th ed 1939 Butterworths)

I F FLETCHER, *The Law of Insolvency* (2nd ed 1995 Sweet & Maxwell)

I F FLETCHER, P DAVIES & D BENNETT, *Palmer's Corporate Insolvency* (1997 Service Sweet & Maxwell)

H C FOLKARD, *Law of Loans and Pledges* (2nd ed 1876 Butterworths)

J FONBLANQUE, *A Treatise of Equity* (1820 J & W T Clarke)

R FRANCIS, *Maxims of Equity* (4th ed 1746 Sweet & Maxwell)

LORD GOFF OF CHIEVELEY & G JONES, *The Law of Restitution* (4th ed 1993 Sweet & Maxwell)

G GOLDSMITH, *The Doctrine and Practice of Equity* (6th ed 1871 Butterworths)

R M GOODE, *Legal Problems of Credit and Security* (2nd ed 1988 Sweet & Maxwell)

R M GOODE, *Principles of Corporate Insolvency Law* (2nd ed 1997 Sweet & Maxwell)

A L GOODHART & H G HANBURY (eds), *Holdsworth's History of English Law* (7th ed Methuen & Co), Volume VI

A G GUEST, *Chalmers and Guest on Bills of Exchange, Cheques and Promissory Notes* (14th ed 1991 Sweet & Maxwell)

J HACKNEY, *Understanding Equity and Trusts* (1987 Fontana Press)

LORD HAILSHAM OF ST MARYLEBONE (ed), *Halsbury's Laws of England*, Volume 16 (4th ed reissue 1992 Butterworths), Volume 20 (4th ed reissue 1993 Butterworths) and Volume 32 (4th ed 1980 Butterworths)

H G HANBURY & C H M WALDOCK, *The Law of Mortgages* (1938 Stevens & Sons)

M B HAPGOOD, *Set-Off Under the Laws of England* in F W Neate (ed) *Set-Off as Security* (1990 IBA)

F O HAYNES, *Outlines of Equity* (5th ed 1880 Maxwell & Son)

E P HEWITT, *White & Tudor's Leading Cases in Equity* (9th ed 1928 Sweet & Maxwell)

A M HONORE, *Ownership* in A G Guest (ed), *Oxford Essays in Jurisprudence* (1961 Oxford)

J INDERMAUR & C THWAITES, *A Manual of the Principles of Equity* (1913 Barker)

P JENKIN, *Rivington's Epitome of Snell's Equity* (4th ed 1954 Sweet & Maxwell)

G W KEATON & L A SHERIDAN, *Equity* (2nd ed 1976 Professional Books)

D M KERLY, *An Historical Sketch of the Equitable Jurisdiction of the Court of Chancery* (1890 Cambridge)

LAW COMMISSION, *Transfer of Land – Land Mortgages* (Law Com No 204, Nov 1991)

R A LADBURY, *Rights of Set-Off as Security* in F W Neate (ed) *Set-Off as Security* (1990 IBA)

G MCCORMACK, *Reservation of Title* (2nd ed 1995 Sweet & Maxwell)

G MCCORMACK, *Proprietary Claims and Insolvency* (1996 Sweet & Maxwell)

G MCCORMACK, *Title Retention and the Company Charge Registration System* in N Palmer & E McKendrick (eds), *Interests in Goods* (2nd ed 1998 LLP)

S MCCRACKEN, *The Banker's Remedy of Set-Off* (1993 Butterworths)

E MCKENDRICK (ed), *Commercial Aspects of Trusts and Fiduciary Obligations* (1992 Oxford)

B MCLACHLIN, *Restitution in Canada* in W R Cornish, R Nolan, J O'Sullivan & G Virgo (eds), *Restitution: Past, Present and Future* (1998 Hart Publishing)

F W MAITLAND, *Equity* (1936 Cambridge)

D G M MARKS & G S MOSS, *Rowlatt on the Law of Principal and Surety* (4th ed 1982 Sweet & Maxwell)

O R MARSHALL, *The Assignment of Choses in Action* (1950 Stevens & Sons)

O R MARSHALL, *Nathan's Equity Through the Cases* (1961 Stevens & Sons)

J E MARTIN, *Hanbury and Martin's Modern Equity* (15th ed 1997 Stevens & Sons)

R E MEGARRY & H W R WADE, *The Law of Real Property* (5th ed 1984 Stevens & Sons)

C MITCHELL, *The Law of Subrogation* (1994 Oxford)

J A NATHAN, *Equity through the Cases and Judicial Exposition* (1939 Stevens & Sons)

F ODITAH, *Legal Aspects of Receivables Financing* (1990 Sweet & Maxwell)

PALMER'S COMPANY LAW (1997 Service Sweet & Maxwell)

N PALMER & A HUDSON, *Pledge* in N Palmer & E McKendrick (eds), *Interests in Goods* (2nd ed 1998 LLP)

R R PENNINGTON, *Company Law* (6th ed 1990 Butterworths)

R R PENNINGTON, *Pennington's Corporate Insolvency Law* (2nd ed 1997 Butterworths)

P H PETTIT, *Equity and the Law of Trusts* (7th ed 1993 Butterworths)

H POTTER, *An Introduction to the History of Equity and its Courts* (3rd ed 1931 Sweet & Maxwell)

J J POWELL, *A Treatise on the Law of Mortgages* (1822 S Brooke)

D D PRENTICE, *Some Comments on the Law Relating to Corporate Groups* in J McCahery, S Picciotto & C Scott (eds), *Corporate Control and Accountability* (1993 Oxford)

R L RAMSBOTHAM, *Coote's Treatise on the Law of Mortgages* (9th ed 1927 Stevens & Sons, Sweet & Maxwell)

G G G ROBB, *Nokes' Outline of the Law of Mortgages and Receiverships* (1951 Estates Gazette)

L G G ROBBINS, *A Treatise on the Law of Mortgages, Pledges and Hypothecations* (1897 Stevens & Sons, Sweet & Maxwell)

T A ROBERTS, *Principles of Equity* (1852 Butterworths)

F ROSE (ed), *Restitution and Banking Law* (1998 Mansfield Press)

F SCHULZ, *History of Roman Legal Science* (1946 Oxford)

L A SHERIDAN & G W KEATON, *Equity: The Nature of Equity* (3rd ed 1985 Chichester)

H A SMITH, *Analysis of the Principles of Equity* (1909 Stevens & Sons)

H A SMITH, *A Practical Exposition of the Principles of Equity* (5th ed 1914 Stevens & Sons)

J W SMITH, *Law of Real and Personal Property* (6th ed 1884 Stevens & Sons)

J W SMITH, *Manual of Equity Jurisprudence* (15th ed 1900 Stevens & Sons)

G SPENCE, *The Equitable Jurisdiction of the Court of Chancery* (1849 Stevens & Norton)

H J STEPHEN, *New Commentaries on the Laws of England* (1841–1845 Butterworths)

J A STRAHAN, *The Principles of the General Law of Mortgages* (3rd ed 1925 Sweet & Maxwell)

A TETTENBORN, *Law of Restitution in England and Ireland* (2nd ed 1996 Cavendish)

A THOMSON, *A Compendium of Modern Equity* (1899 W Clowes & Sons)

L B TILLARD, *Wilshere's Principles of Equity* (2nd ed 1929 Sweet & Maxwell)

A F TOPHAM, *Real Property* (10th ed 1947 Stevens & Sons)

E L G TYLER, *Fisher & Lightwood's Law of Mortgage* (10th ed 1988 Butterworths)

E L G TYLER & R OUGHTON, *Fisher & Lightwood's Law of Mortgage: Supplement to Tenth Edition* (1994 Butterworths)

A UNDERHILL, *Guide to Modern Equity* (1885 Butterworths)

G VIRGO, *What is the Law of Restitution About?* in W R Cornish, R Nolan, J O'Sullivan & G Virgo (eds), *Restitution: Past, Present and Future* (1998 Hart Publishing)

W W WATSON, *A Practical Compendium of Equity* (1873 H Sweet)

W F WEBSTER, *Ashburner's Concise Treatise on Mortgages, Pledges and Liens* (2nd ed 1911 Butterworths)

J J S WHARTON, *The Law Lexicon* (4th ed 1867 Stevens & Sons)

S E WILLIAMS, *Outlines of Equity* (1900 Sweet & Maxwell)

A M WILSHERE, *Analysis of Williams on Real and Personal Property* (3rd ed 1914 Sweet & Maxwell)

P H WINFIELD, *Jenks' English Civil Law* (8th ed 1947 Butterworths)

P R WOOD, *English and International Set-Off* (1989 Sweet & Maxwell)

P R WOOD, *The Law of Subordinated Debt* (1990 Sweet & Maxwell)

P R Wood, *Comparative Law of Security and Guarantees* (1995 Sweet & Maxwell)

P R Wood, *Title Finance, Derivatives, Securitisations, Set-Off and Netting* (1995 Sweet & Maxwell)

P R Wood, *Project Finance, Subordinated Debt and State Loans* (1995 Sweet & Maxwell)

S Worthington, *Proprietary Interests in Commercial Transactions* (1996 Oxford)

J S Ziegel, *What can the Economic Analysis of Law teach Commercial and Consumer Law Scholars?* in R Cranston & R M Goode (eds), *Commercial and Consumer Law: National and International Dimensions* (1993 Oxford)

R Zimmerman, *The Law of Obligations: Roman Foundations of the Civilian Tradition* (1996 Oxford)

(b) Articles

F O Adeoye, *The Anglo-American Law of Mortgages: A Quagmire for Creditors* [1993] JBL 544

J H Baker, *The Future of Equity* (1977) 93 LQR 529

N Bamforth, *Lord Macnaghten's Puzzle: The Mortgage of Real Property in English Law* [1996] CLP 207

J Beatson, *Benefit Reliance and the Structure of Unjust Enrichment* [1987] CLP 71

A Berg, *Duties of a Mortgagee and a Receiver* [1993] JBL 213

A Berg, *Charges Over Book Debts: A Reply* [1995] JBL 433

A Bidin, *Re Coslett: Equitable Interests and the Nature of Fixed and Specific Charges* (1997) 18 Co Lawyer 25

J Bird, *Restitution's Uncertain Progress* [1995] LMCLQ 308

P Birks, *Modernising the Law of Restitution* (1993) 109 LQR 164

M G Bridge, *Fixed Charges and Freedom of Contract* (1994) 110 LQR 340

M G Bridge, *Failed Contracts, Subrogation and Unjust Enrichment* [1998] JBL 323

A Burrows, *Restitution: where do we go from here?* [1997] CLP 95

R Calnan, *Proprietary Claims in Insolvency* (1995) 10 BJIB&FL 365

A Clarke, *Mortgagee's Powers of Sale: Contract or Statute* [1997] LMCLQ 329

H Collins, *Ascription of Legal Responsibility to Groups in Complex Patterns of Economic Integration* (1990) 53 MLR 731

V T H Delany, *Equitable Interests and 'Mere Equities'* (1957) 21 Conv (NS) 195

S R Derham, *Set-Off Against an Assignee: the Relevance of Marshalling, Contribution and Subrogation* (1991) 107 LQR 126

B Dickson, *Unjust Enrichment Claims: A Comparative Overview* (1995) 54 CLJ 100

A J Duggan, *Is Equity Efficient?* (1997) 113 LQR 601

A R Everton, *'Equitable Interests' and 'Equities' – in Search of a Pattern* (1976) 40 Conv (NS) 209

J H Farrar, *World Economic Stagnation Puts the Floating Charge on Trial* (1980) 1 Co Lawyer 83

E Ferran, *Floating Charges – the Nature of the Security* [1988] CLJ 213

E Ferran, *Lifting the veil* [1996] All ER Annual Review 47

L Gallagher & P Zeigler, *Lifting the Corporate Veil in Pursuit of Justice* [1990] JBL 292

G Goldberg, *Vivat ac vivat scintilla temporis* (1992) 108 LQR 380

R M GOODE, *Charges Over Book Debts: A Missed Opportunity* (1994) 110 LQR 592

R M GOODE, *Charge-Backs and Legal Fictions* (1998) 114 LQR 178

R GRANTHAM, *Refloating a Floating Charge* (1997) 1 CfiLR 53

R GREGORY & P WALTON, *Fixed Charges Over Changing Assets – The Possession and Control Heresy* (1998) 2 CfiLR 68

S HEDLEY, *Unjust Enrichment* (1995) 54 CLJ 578

M C HEMSWORTH, *Subrogation: The Problem of Competing Claims to Recovery Monies* [1998] JBL 111

L HO, *The Nature of Restitution – A Reply* (1996) 16 OJLS 517

J JEREMIE, *Gone in an Instant – The Death of 'Scintilla Temporis' and the Growth of a Purchase Money Security Interest in Real Property* [1994] JBL 363

N J MCBRIDE & P MCGRATH, *The Nature of Restitution* (1995) 15 OJLS 33

G MCCORMACK, *Proprietary Claims and Insolvency in the Wake of Westdeutsche* [1997] JBL 48

G MCCORMACK, *Charge Backs and Commercial Certainty in the House of Lords* (1998) 2 CfiLR 111

J E MARTIN, *Equitable and Inequitable Remedies* (1990–91) 1 KCLJ 1

A MASON, *The Place of Equity and Equitable Remedies in the Contemporary Common Law* (1994) 110 LQR 238

J K MAXTON, *Negative Pledges and Equitable Principles* [1993] JBL 458

R E MEGARRY, *Mere Equities, the Bona Fide Purchaser and the Deserted Wife* (1955) 71 LQR 480

P J MILLET, *Equity – the Road Ahead* (1995–96) 6 KCLJ 1

P J MILLET, *Equity's Place in the Law of Commerce* (1998) 114 LQR 214

C MITCHELL, *The Law of Subrogation* [1992] LMCLQ 483

C MITCHELL, *Subrogation, Tracing and the Quistclose Principle* [1995] LMCLQ 451

C MITCHELL, *Subrogation and Part Payments of Another's Debt* [1998] LMCLQ 14

C NAKAJIMA, *Lifting the Veil* (1996) 17 Co Lawyer 187

J NASER, *The Juridical Basis of the Floating Charge* (1994) 15 Co Lawyer 11

A J OAKLEY, *Proprietary Claims and their Priority in Insolvency* (1995) 54 CLJ 377

F ODITAH, *Assets and the Treatment of Claims in Insolvency* (1992) 108 LQR 459

F G RIXON, *Lifting the Veil between Holding and Subsidiary Companies* (1986) 102 LQR 415

T ROUGHTON, *Insolvency Set-Off* [1998] JIBL N–17

G SAMUEL, *Subrogation and Unjust Enrichment – New Feet in Old Shoes?* (1977) 93 LQR 344

G SAMUEL, *Subrogation and Unjust Enrichment – Old Feet back in Old Shoes* (1977) 93 LQR 494

R SCHULTE, *Corporate Groups and the Equitable Subordination of Claims on Insolvency* (1997) 18 Co Lawyer 2

D J SEIPP, *The Reception of Canon Law and Civil Law in the Common Law Courts before 1600* (1993) 13 OJLS 388

G P STAPLEDON, *A Parent Company's Liability for Debts of an Insolvent Subsidiary* (1995) 16 Co Lawyer 152

W STRAHAN, *The Marshalling of Mortgages* (1906) 22 LQR 307

C H TAN, *Automatic Crystallisation, De-crystallisation and Convertibility of Charges* (1998) 2 CfiLR 41

J ULPH, *Equitable Proprietary Rights in Insolvency: the Ebbing Tide?* [1996] JBL 482

P WATTS, *Restitution – A Property Principle and a Services Principle* [1995] RLR 49

P WATTS, *Subrogation – A Step too far* (1998) 114 LQR 341

A WILKINSON, *Piercing the Corporate Veil and the Insolvency Act 1985* (1987) 8 Co Lawyer 124

S WORTHINGTON, *Fixed Charges over Book Debts and other Receivables* (1997) 113 LQR 562

(4) IRELAND

(a) Texts

R KEANE, *Equity and the Law of Trusts in the Republic of Ireland* (1988 Butterworths)

A LYALL, *Land Law in Ireland* (1994 Oak Tree Press)

M O'DONNELL & F BRADY, *An Analytical Digest of all the Reported Cases, Statutes, and General Orders, in or relating to the Principles, Pleading, and Practice of Equity, in the several Courts of Equity in Ireland and the House of Lords* (1840 Hodges & Smith)

J C W WYLIE, *Irish Land Law* (1975 Professional Books)

(b) Articles

P DEVONSHIRE, *The Mortgagee's Power of Sale: A Case for the Equitable Standard of Good Faith* (1995) 46 NILQ 182

(5) NEW ZEALAND

(a) Texts

E C ADAMS, *Garrow's Law of Real Property* (1961 Butterworths)

G W HINDE, D W MCMORLAND, N R CAMPBELL & D P GRINLINTON, *Butterworths Land Law in New Zealand* (1997 Butterworths)

S KOS & P WATTS, *Unjust Enrichment – the New Cause of Action* (1990 NZ Law Society)

(b) Articles

T CLEAVER, *Marshalling* (1991) 21 VUWLR 275

P DEVONSHIRE, *The Mortgagee's Power of Sale: New Perspectives on an Old Theme* (1995) 16 NZULR 251

M LUEY, *Proprietary Remedies in Insurance Subrogation* (1995) 25 VUWLR 449

J MAXTON, *Some Effects of the Intermingling of Common Law and Equity* (1993) 5 Canterbury L R 299

T SCHUMACHER, *Marshalling* (1989) 5 BCB 89

S R SCOTT, *The Remedial Restitutionary Proprietary Remedy* (1995) 6 Canterbury L R 123

(6) SCOTLAND

(a) Texts

W M GORDON, *Roman Influence on Scots Law of Real Property* in R Evans-Jones (ed), *The Civil Law Tradition in Scotland* (1995 Edinburgh)

A M JOHNSTON & J A D HOPE (eds), *Gloag & Henderson's Introduction to the Law of Scotland* (7th ed 1969 W Green & Sons)

LORD KAMES, *Principles of Equity* (3rd ed 1825 Edinburgh)

T B SMITH, *A Short Commentary on the Law of Scotland* (1962 W Green & Sons)

D M WALKER, *Principles of Scottish Private Law* (4th ed 1989 Oxford), Volume III

(7) UNITED STATES OF AMERICA

(a) *Texts*

B E ADLER, *Secured Credit Contracts* in P Newman (ed), *New Palgrave Dictionary of Economics and the Law* (1998 Macmillan)

AMERICAN JURISPRUDENCE (1996 Lawyers Co-operative Publishing), Volume 53

C F BEACH JR., *Commentaries on Modern Equity Jurisprudence* (1892 Baker, Voorhis & Co)

M M BIGELOW, *Story's Commentaries on Equity Jurisprudence* (13th ed 1886 Little, Brown & Co)

Z CHAFEE, JR., *Cases on Equitable Remedies* (1939 Langdell Hall)

Z CHAFEE, JR., *Some Problems of Equity* (1950 Michigan)

Z CHAFEE, JR. & E D RE, *Cases and Materials on Equity* (4th ed 1958 Foundation Press)

CORPUS JURIS SECUNDUM, Volume 21 (1990 American Book Co) and Volume 55 (1948 American Book Co)

D R COWANS, *Cowans Bankruptcy Law and Practice* (6th ed 1994 West Publishing), Volume 3

J L ELDER, *The Law of Suretyship* (5th ed 1951 Greenwood Press)

W Q DE FUNIAK, *Handbook of Modern Equity* (2nd ed 1956 Little, Brown & Co)

J G HENDERSON, *Chancery Practice* (1904 T H Flood & Co)

R A HILLMAN, J B MCDONNELL & S H NICKLES, *Common Law and Equity under the Uniform Commercial Code* (1985 Warren, Gorham & Lamont)

W T HUGHES, *Equity – its Principles in Procedure, Codes and Practice Acts* (1911 Central Law Journal)

L A JONES, *A Treatise on the Law of Mortgages of Real Property* (1878 Houghton, Osgood & Co)

J KENT, *Commentaries on American Law* (7th ed 1851 W Kent)

C C LANGDELL, *A Brief Survey of Equity Jurisdiction* (1908 Harvard)

J D MCCOY, *Bispham's Principles of Equity* (11th ed 1931 Baker, Voorhis & Co)

T MOMMSEN, P KRÜGER & A WATSON, *The Digest of Justinian* (1985 Penn)

G E PALMER, *The Law of Restitution* (1978 Little, Brown & Co)

J N POMEROY JR., *Equity Jurisprudence* (3rd ed 1905 Bancroft-Whitney Co)

J N POMEROY JR., *A Treatise on Equitable Remedies* (1905 Bancroft-Whitney Co)

R POSNER, *The Economic Analysis of Law* (3rd ed 1986 Little, Brown & Co)

J RAM, *Law of Assets, Debts and Incumbrances* (2nd ed 1837 Baker, Voorhis & Co)

RESTATEMENT OF THE LAW OF RESTITUTION, QUASI CONTRACTS AND CONSTRUCTIVE TRUSTS (1937 American Law Institute)

RESTATEMENT OF THE LAW OF SECURITY (1941 American Law Institute)

(b) Articles

E S ADAMS, S H NICKLES & T H RESSLER, *Wedding Carlson and Schwartz: Understanding Secured Credit as a Fuzzy System* (1994) 80 Va L Rev 2233

B E ADLER, *An Equity-Agency Solution to the Bankruptcy-Priority Puzzle* (1993) 22 J Leg Stud 73

B E ADLER, *A Theory of Corporate Insolvency* (1997) 72 NYU L Rev 343

C H AVERCH & J P PROSTOK, *The Doctrine of Marshaling: an Anachronistic Concept Under the Bankruptcy Code* (1990) 22 UCCLJ 224

J D AYER, *Every Man a Scotchman: Some Comments on Kanda and Levmore* (1994) 80 Va L Rev 2169

D G BAIRD, *The Importance of Priority* (1997) 82 Cornell L Rev 1420

D G BAIRD & T H JACKSON, *Corporate Reorganisations and the Treatment of Diverse Ownership Interests: A Comment on Adequate Protection of Secured Creditors in Bankruptcy* (1984) 97 U Chi L Rev 97

D G BAIRD & T H JACKSON, *Bargaining After the Fall and the Contours of the Absolute Priority Rule* (1989) 55 U Chi L Rev 738

R L BARNES, *The Efficiency Justification for Secured Transactions: Foxes with Soxes and Other Fanciful Stuff* (1993) 42 Kan L Rev 13

L A BEBCHUK AND J M FRIED, *The Uneasy Case for the Priority of Secured Claims in Bankruptcy* (1996) 105 Yale LJ 857

L A BEBCHUK & J M FRIED, *The Uneasy Case for the Priority of Secured Claims in Bankruptcy: Further Thoughts and a Reply to Critics* (1997) 82 Cornell L Rev 1279

S BLOCK-LIEB, *The Unsecured Creditor's Bargain: A Reply* (1994) 80 Va L Rev 1989

J W BOWERS, *Whither What Hits the Fan?: Murphy's Law, Bankruptcy Theory, and the Elementary Economics of Loss Distribution* (1991) 26 Ga L Rev 27

J W BOWERS, *Kissing Off Economics and Misunderstanding Murphy's Law: Carlson's 'On the Efficiency of Secured Lending'* (1994) 80 Va L Rev 2215

W W BRATTON JR., *Corporate Debt Relationships: Legal Theory in a Time of Restructuring* [1989] Duke LJ 92

F H BUCKLEY, *The Bankruptcy Priority Puzzle* (1986) 72 Va L Rev 1393

C S BUSCHMANN, *Determination of Superior Equities in Cases of Marshaling and Subrogation* (1927) 2 Ind LJ 589

D G CARLSON, *Rationality, Accident and Priority Under Article 9 of the UCC* (1986) 71 Minn L Rev 207

D G CARLSON, *On the Efficiency of Secured Lending* (1994) 80 Va L Rev 2179

P CELLUPCIA, *The Insecure Place of Secured Debt in Corporate Finance Theory* (1988) 11 Harv J of Law & Public Pol 487

I DAVIES, *Absolute Title Financing in Commercial Transactions* (1985) Anglo-Am L Rev 71

R C DOWNS, *Piercing the Corporate Veil – Do Corporations Provide Limited Personal Liability?* (1985) 53 UMKCLR 174

J DRUKARCZYK, *Secured Debt Bankruptcy and the Creditor's Bargain Model* (1991) 11 Int Rev of Law & Eco 203

F H EASTERBROOK & D R FISCHEL, *Limited Liability and the Corporation* (1985) 52 U Chi L Rev 89

M EMAMZADEH, *Marshaling in Bankruptcy: Questioning the Recent Expansions to the Common Debtor Requirement* (1992) 30 Duquesne L Rev 309

D J GARDNER, *An Innovative Approach to Piercing the Corporate Veil* (1990) 25 Land & Water LR 563

R J GOEBEL, *Reconstructing the Roman Law of Real Security* (1961–62) 36 Tulane L Rev 29

B L GRAHAM, *Navigating the Mists of Metaphor: an Examination of the Doctrine of Piercing the Corporate Veil* (1991) 56 J of Air Law & Commerce 1135

S L HARRIS & C W MOONEY JR., *A Property-Based Theory of Security Interests: Taking Debtors' Choices Seriously* (1994) 80 Va L Rev 2021

S L HARRIS & C W MOONEY JR., *Measuring the Social Costs and Benefits and Identifying the Victims of Subordinating Security Interests in Bankruptcy* (1997) 82 Cornell L Rev 1349

J R HICKS, *The Foundations of Welfare Economics* (1939) 49 Econ J 696

T H JACKSON & A T KRONMAN, *Secured Financing and Priorities Among Creditors* (1979) 88 Yale LJ 1143

T H JACKSON & A SCHWARTZ, *Vacuum of Fact or Vacuous Theory: A Reply to Professor Kripke* (1985) 133 U Pa L Rev 987

P K JONES JR., *Roman Law Bases of Suretyship in Some Modern Civil Codes* (1977) 52 Tulane L Rev 129

N KALDOR, *Welfare Propositions of Economics and Interpersonal Comparisons of Utility* (1939) 49 Econ J 549

H KANDA & S LEVMORE, *Explaining Creditor Priorities* (1994) 80 Va L Rev 2103

H KARASIK & R KOLODNEY, *The Doctrine of Marshaling Under the Bankruptcy Code* (1984) Com LJ 102

S L KIMBALL & D A DAVIS, *The Extension of Insurance Subrogation* (1962) 60 Mich L Rev 841

S KNIPPENBERG, *The Unsecured Creditor's Bargain: An Essay in Reply, Reprisal or Support?* (1994) 80 Va L Rev 1967

H KRIPKE, *Law and Economics: Measuring the Economic Efficiency of Commercial Law in a Vacuum of Fact* (1985) 133 U Pa L Rev 929

F W KROGER & P ACCONCIA, *Marshaling: A Fourth Act Sequel to Commercial Tragedies?* (1989) 57 UMKCLR 205

A KULL, *Rationalising Restitution* (1995) 83 Calif Law Rev 1191

I D LABOVITZ, *Marshaling Under the UCC: the State of the Doctrine* (1982) 99 Banking LJ 440

M LACHMAN, *Marshaling Assets in Bankruptcy: Recent Innovations in the Doctrine* (1985) 6 Cardozo L Rev 671

J M LANDERS, *A Unified Approach to Parent, Subsidiary and Affiliate Questions in Bankruptcy* (1975) 42 U Chi L Rev 589

S LEVMORE, *Monitors and Freeriders in Commercial and Corporate Settings* (1982) 92 Yale LJ 49

L M LOPUCKI, *The Unsecured Creditor's Bargain* (1994) 80 Va L Rev 1887

J C MCCOID, *Set-off: Why Bankruptcy Priority?* (1989) 75 Va L Rev 15

R J MANN, *The First Shall be Last: A Contextual Argument for Abandoning Temporal Rules of Lien Priority* (1996) 75 Texas L Rev 11

R J MANN, *Explaining the Pattern of Secured Debt* (1997) 110 Harv L Rev 625

R J Mann, *Strategy and Force in the Liquidation of Secured Debt* (1997) 96 Mich L Rev 159

M L Marasinghe, *An Historical Introduction to the Doctrine of Subrogation: the Early History of the Doctrine* (1975) 10 Val UL Rev 45 and 275

M W Mosman, *The Proper Application of Marshaling on Behalf of Unsecured Creditors* [1983] Brigham Young ULR 639

Note, *Marshaling Assets and Securities* (1929) 15 Va L Rev 405

Note, *Subrogation – An Equitable Device for Achieving Preferences and Priorities* (1933) 31 Mich L Rev 826

D E Phillipson, *Development of the Roman Law of Debt Security* (1968) 20 Stan L Rev 1230

R C Picker, *Security Interests, Misbehaviour and Common Pools* (1992) 59 U Chi L Rev 645

L Ponoroff & F S Knippenberg, *The Immovable Object Verses the Irresistible Force: Rethinking the Relationship between Secured Debt and Bankruptcy Policy* (1997) 95 Mich L Rev 2234

A Posner, *The Rights of Creditors of Affiliated Corporations* (1976) 43 U Chi L Rev 499

S L Schwarcz, *The Easy Case for the Priority of Secured Claims in Bankruptcy* (1997) 47 Duke LJ 425

A Schwartz, *Security Interests and Bankruptcy Priorities: A Review of Current Theories* (1981) 10 J Legal Stud 1

A Schwartz, *The Continuing Puzzle of Secured Debt* (1984) 37 Vand L Rev 1051

A Schwartz, *A Theory of Loan Priorities* (1989) 18 J Legal Stud 209

A Schwartz, *Taking the Analysis of Security Seriously* (1994) 80 Va L Rev 2073

A Schwartz, *Priority Contracts and Priority in Bankruptcy* (1997) 82 Cornell L Rev 1396

B Schwartz, *Marshaling Assets for Benefit of Mortgagor* (1930) 5 Notre Dame L Rev 208

R E Scott, *A Relational Theory of Secured Financing* (1986) 86 Colum LR 901

R E Scott, *The Truth About Secured Financing* (1997) 82 Cornell L Rev 1436

J J Shalhoub, *Marshaling: Equitable Rights of Holders of Junior Interests* (1986) 38 Rutgers Law Rev 287

P M Shupack, *Solving the Puzzle of Secured Transactions* (1989) 41 Rutgers L Rev 1067

P M Shupack, *Defending Purchase Money Security Interests Under Article 9 of the UCC from Professor Buckley* (1989) 22 Ind L Rev 777

R M Stulz & H Johnson, *An Analysis of Secured Credit* (1985) 14 J Fin Econ 501

G G Triantis, *Secured Debt under Conditions of Imperfect Information* (1992) 21 J Leg Stud 225

G G Triantis, *A Theory of the Regulation of Debtor-in-Possession Financing* (1993) 46 Vand L Rev 901

G G Triantis, *A Free-Cash-Flow Theory of Secured Debt and Creditor Priorities* (1994) 80 Va L Rev 2155

B Weintraub & A N Resnick, *Marshaling of Assets in Bankruptcy Cases: the Spectre of Contance v Harvey Appears Again* (1984) 16 UCCLJ 384

B Weintraub & A N Resnick, *Compelling a Senior Lienor to Pursue Remedies Against a Guarantor – A Misapplication of the Marshaling Doctrine* (1985) 18 UCCLJ 178

B WEINTRAUB & A N RESNICK, *Subordination of the Guarantor's Subrogation Rights – the Marshaling Doctrine Revisited* (1986) 18 UCCLJ 364

E J WES JR., *Substantive Consolidations in Bankruptcy: A Flow of Assets Approach* (1977) 65 Cal L Rev 720

J J WHITE, *Public Policy Toward Bankruptcy: Me First and Other Priority Rules* (1980) 11 BJE 550

J J WHITE, *Efficiency Justifications for Personal Property Security* (1984) Vand L Rev 473

J J WHITE, *Work and Play in Revising Article 9* (1994) 80 Va L Rev 2089

INDEX

Apportionment, marshalling by
  Australia, in 11.28
  benefit of senior security, sharing 2.47, 11.20,
    11.21
  Canada, in 11.28
  contracting out of 11.27
  contribution, as instance of 5.48
  development of 2.18, 2.41–2.46
  entire burden of senior debt, prevention of falling
    on puisne creditor 11.35, 11.36
  exceptions to general rule 11.27
  general rule 11.22–11.24
  Ireland, in 11.28
  junior creditor's inchoate equity, effect of 11.14,
    11.17
  junior creditor's rights, derogation from 11.19
  law relating to 2.54, 11.18
  meaning 11.18
  New Zealand, in 11.28
  notice of junior security 11.25, 11.26
  order of priorities 11.24
  policy goals of security, and 11.37–11.40
  principle of 11.34
  priority-ranking, preservation of 11.36, 11.38
  redistribution, and 11.30–11.36
  residue of asset, entitlement to 11.23
  Scots law 11.22
  substitution of senior security 11.22
  third party, transfer of senior debt to
    11.31–11.33
  United States law 11.29
  unsecured creditors and 2.53, 10.01, 11.20
Assignment
  equity of redemption, of
    effect of 5.15–5.17
    mortgage, with 5.20, 5.21
    mortgage, without 5.18, 5.19
  interests in mortgaged assets, of 5.15
  proceeds of sale, of 9.17
  senior security, of, to junior creditor 3.28, 3.29
  substitution, alternative to 3.28, 3.29, 3.36, 4.02

Bills of exchange
  marshalling and subrogation compared 4.24–4.26
  subrogation, as category of 4.21, 4.24
Bottomry bonds
  marshalling and 2.40, 9.15

Chattel lease
  marshalling, and 9.37

Coercion theory
  Australia, in 2.58
  content of 3.01, 3.03
  development of 2.05, 2.06
  dominance of 2.21, 2.22
  election by senior creditor, preventing 2.27
  emergence of 2.14
  historical curiosity, as 3.02
  hybrid model *see* **Hybrid model**
  Ireland, in 2.21
  law regulating security enforcement, inconsistent
    with 3.06, 3.17
  legitimate expectation, protection of 6.04
  nineteenth century view, current theory differing
    from 2.61
  original doctrine 2.19
  post-realisation theory antagonistic to 2.23
  post-realisation theory distinguished 2.27
  revival of 2.57–2.61
    Australia, in 3.31
    cases concerning 3.30–3.34
  secured creditors, enforcement of securities by
    3.07–3.09
  senior creditor's freedom of action, encroachment
    on 2.19, 2.20, 3.04, 3.05, 3.06
  senior debt, impact on 6.42
  support for 2.22, 2.60
Common debtor rule
  assets owned by same debtor 2.33, 7.03, 7.06,
    7.07
  assets to be in existence 2.37, 7.02, 7.21–7.24
  Australia, in 7.05, 8.49
  Canada, in 7.05, 8.49
  common law countries, law in 2.53
  control of court, assets subject to 7.03, 7.04
  corporate veil, piercing *also* **Piercing the corporate
    veil**
  debts owed by same debtor 2.33, 7.03, 7.06,
    7.07
  development of 2.17, 2.18, 2.30–2.34, 2.37,
    2.38
  entitlement to marshall, effect on 7.01
  fraudulent avoidance of obligations 8.54
  Ireland, in 7.05, 8.49
  junior creditor, effect of marshalling by
    7.11–7.13
  multiple senior debts, senior security securing
    7.16
  New Zealand, in 7.05, 8.49
  proceeds of sale, proprietary securities over 9.24

Common debtor rule (cont.):
  redistributive nature of marshalling, consistency
    with 7.17–7.20
  requirements 7.02
  senior and junior securities, assets subject to 2.37,
    7.21–7.24
  senior creditor having equal rights of recourse
    authority for 7.26
    binding arrangement for 7.27
    efficacy of marshalling 7.28–7.31
    meaning 7.29
    nature of security 7.32, 7.33
    requirement of 2.38, 7.02, 7.25
  several senior securities, existence of 7.08
  single senior debt, existence of 7.08–7.16
  stipulations of 2.32, 7.02
  surety exception *see* **Surety exception**
  third party security holder, effect of presence of
    11.17
  third party transferee, effect of presence of 11.16,
    11.44, 11.47, 11.48
  United States law 8.49
  waiver 8.50
    English and US approaches 8.62–8.65
Conditional sale agreement
  marshalling, and 9.37
Consolidation of mortgages
  Australia, abolition in 5.02, 5.07, 5.08
  Canadian law 5.10
  countries in which abolished 5.02, 5.07–5.09
  creditor, power of 5.03
  equitable doctrine, marshalling as special instance
    of application of 5.02
  equity of redemption, assignments of
    effect of 5.15–5.21
    mortgage, with 5.20, 5.21
    mortgage, without 5.18, 5.19
  Ireland, curtailment in 5.06
  junior creditor, right of 2.07
  marshalling as basis for
    Ashburner's argument 2.08, 2.09, 5.02,
    5.12–5.14
    origin of 2.07
  marshalling as form of 1.03, 1.09, 5.01
  marshalling distinguished 2.08
  marshalling not being form of 5.22–5.27
  meaning 5.03
  New Zealand, abolition in 5.02, 5.09
  North America, in 5.10, 5.11
  origins of 5.03
  party holding united equities of redemption,
    against 5.26
  same mortgagor, creation of 5.25
  second creditor, restriction on 5.04
  statutory abolition of 5.02, 5.07–5.09
  statutory curtailment of 2.09, 5.02, 5.05,
    5.06
  sureties and 8.29–8.32
  United States law 5.11

Contribution
  adjustment of liability by 5.41
  agreement as to 5.31
  apportionment as instance of 5.48
  Australia, authorities in 5.44, 5.45
  burden of debt, distribution of 5.40
  co-debtor, recovery of over-payment by 5.30
  common liability bearing of 5.29
  confusion with marshalling 5.44–5.48
  equitable doctrine of 5.28
  exoneration, and 5.33–5.36
  interests protected by 5.39
  marshalling as form of 1.03, 1.09, 5.01, 5.28
  marshalling not being form of 5.37–5.43
  meaning 5.29
  origins of 5.43
  presumptive rule 5.31, 5.39
  principle of 5.28
  rights, status *qua* marshalling rights 5.42
  secured debts, share in security for 5.32
Co-surety
  access to securities 5.46
Covenants against marshalling
  effect of 12.01, 12.02
  equal rights of recourse, prevention of 12.06
  guarantees, in context of 8.33, 8.34
  superfluous, being 12.08
  types of 12.03, 12.04
  waiver of rights 12.05

Debtor
  enrichment of 4.48–4.50
  junior creditor's marshalling rights and 11.01
  personal representative, junior creditor and 11.02
  real representative, junior creditor and 11.02
Disponees *see* **Transferees**

Equitable charges
  fixed charge 9.07
  floating charge *see* **Floating charge**
  marshalling and 2.53, 9.25
Exoneration
  adjustment of liability by 5.41
  contribution, and 5.33–5.36
  origins of 5.43
  third party rights 5.33
  third party's right of, and surety exception
    8.18–8.20

Floating charge
  monitoring theory of security 6.23, 6.24
  transfer or disposition of security, consent to 11.63
  uncrystallised
    availability of marshalling 9.12
    junior creditor, and 9.14
    nature of 9.08

Guarantees
  covenants against marshalling 8.33, 8.34

Hire purchase agreement
marshalling, and 9.37
Hybrid model
Canada, in 3.35
coercion theory, and 3.33, 3.38, 3.39
general principle 3.35
junior creditor's security, protecting 3.39
post-realisation theory, not viable alternative to
3.37
United States, in 3.35, 3.36

Insurance
marshalling and subrogation compared
4.24–4.26
subrogation, as category of 4.21, 4.24
Inverse order rule
American doctrine, as 1.05
marshalling distinguished 1.06
principle of 1.05
right of transferee to apply 1.06

Judicial lien
marshalling, redundancy of 10.08–10.10
Junior creditor
assignment of senior security to 3.28, 3.29
competing secured creditors, and 11.02
consolidation, right of 2.07
exchange of security 3.22
first-ranking security, substitution of 7.19
inchoate equity 11.12–11.14
legitimate expectation, protection of 6.03, 6.04
loss, rectifying 2.15, 2.26, 4.06–4.12
meaning 1.13
priority-ranking
preservation of 2.25
regaining 3.24
proprietary interest, no 3.08, 3.23
right to marshall senior security, circumstances of
1.06
risk of damage, forestalling 2.18, 2.19
secured claim against debtor, protection of
2.04
security of senior creditor, access to 5.37
standing to marshall, having 2.30
substitution to security held by senior creditor
2.45
third party, position *qua* 11.03, 11.04
third party's security, destruction of 2.44
transfer *qua* senior creditor, as 3.08
unsecured creditors, and 11.02
Junior debt
meaning 1.13
Junior security
erosion of 3.23
meaning 1.13
scope of 7.24
secured status, protection of 1.01
senior creditor, erosion by 4.05
status of assets subject to 7.21–7.24

Lien
judicial 10.08–10.10
non-possessory
marshalling, and 9.12
proprietary security, as 9.10, 9.24
possessory lien, as non-proprietary security
9.10
vendor's
marshalling and subrogation compared
4.24–4.26
subrogation, as category of 4.21
Liquidators
third party, defeating junior creditor's right to
marshall, not being 11.02

Marshalling of securities
absolute entitlement, rejection of 2.30
apportionment, by *see* **Apportionment, marshalling by**
burden of debt, distribution of 5.40
classification, difficulty of 6.01
coercion theory *see* **Coercion theory**
common law countries, law in 2.51
confusion about 1.04
consolidation compared *see* **Consolidation of
mortgages**
contractual obligation, not relying on 5.52
contribution compared *see* **Contribution**
creditors eligible to invoke 2.16
death knell of 10.13–10.16
development of 1.07
employment of assets of debtor, reorganising
4.10
equitable doctrine of 1.01
expiration of date of redemption, not dependent
on 5.24
general principles, affirmation of 2.51–2.54
history of 1.03
hybrid model *see* **Hybrid model**
indiscriminatory expansion of rights 9.39
interests protected by 5.39
interests required for claim 9.01
juridical nature of 1.09
limits of 1.11, 2.17
major developments in, nineteenth-century cases
2.14–2.18
meaning 1.01
narrow remedy, transformation to 2.32
natural justice *see* **Natural justice**
non-security rights, extension to 9.26–9.29
origins of
eighteenth-century cases 2.05, 2.06
English law 2.13
marshalling of beneficiaries and legatees 2.02,
2.05
Roman law 2.10–2.12
seventeenth-century cases 2.02–2.04
other jurisdictions, in 1.12
policy goals of security, and 6.37–6.42

Marshalling of securities (*cont.*):
  post-realisation remedy, as *see* **Post-realisation theory**
  pre-requisites of *see* **Common debtor rule**
  priorities, acceptance of 1.02
  priority-preservation device, as 2.03
  puisne secured creditors, protection of priority-ranking 1.08
  quasi-securities *see* **Quasi-securities**
  rationale 6.02
  redistributive remedy, as 4.04–4.12 *see also* **Redistribution**
  restitutionary analysis, absence of 4.35–4.37
  rights described by 1.04
  securities to which applying 9.01–9.03, 9.34
  singular nature of 1.02
  specific performance compared *see* **Specific performance**
  subrogation, relationship with *see* **Subrogation**
  subrogation remedy, not 4.55
  theories of security *see* **Theories of security**
  treatment of 1.03
  United States, developments in 2.51
  unjust enrichment, and *see* **Unjust enrichment**
  unwarranted expansion of 9.30–9.33
  volunteers, by 5.55
Mortgages
  Canada, restriction of marshalling in 2.53, 9.25
  consolidation *see* **Consolidation of mortgages**
  equity of redemption
    assignee, interest of 5.17
    assignment with mortgage 5.20, 5.21
    assignments of 5.15–5.21
    same party, united in 5.18
    separation from other interests 5.23
  legal and equitable 9.06
  marshalling, and 9.12
  types of 9.06

Natural justice
  marshalling, basis of
    legitimate expectation, protection of 6.03, 6.04, 6.06
    rationale 6.02
    unsecured creditor, position of 6.05
Negative pledge
  marshalling, and 9.38
  monitoring theory of security 6.23, 6.24
Non-possessory lien
  marshalling, and 2.40, 9.12
  proprietary security, as 9.10, 9.24
Non-proprietary securities
  availability of marshalling 9.12, 9.13
  classification 9.05
  nature of 9.02, 9.03
  pledges 9.09
  possessory lien 9.10, 9.24
  proprietary securities, and 9.04, 9.05

  set-off, right of 9.24
  uncrystallised floating charges 9.08
Non-security interests
  extension of marshalling to 2.62, 9.26–9.29, 9.39, 9.40

Piercing the corporate veil
  capital contributions and 8.55–8.58
  common debtor rule, waiver of 8.50
  English law 8.53, 8.54
  facilitation of marshalling by 8.59
  fraudulent avoidance of obligations 8.54
  inequitable conduct towards junior creditor 8.51, 8.52
  policy goals of security, and 8.57, 8.68
  surety exception compared 8.59–8.61
  United States law 8.51, 8.52, 8.65
Pledge
  marshalling and 9.15
  non-proprietary security, as 9.09
Possessory lien
  marshalling and 2.40, 9.15
  non-proprietary security, as 9.10
Post-realisation theory
  acceptance of 2.52, 3.26, 3.27
  Australia, in 3.20, 3.26
  Canada, in 3.26
  coercion theory distinguished 2.15, 2.27
  coercive theory, dominance of 2.21, 2.22
  common law countries, law in 3.02
  content of 3.01, 3.18
  conventional theory of security supporting 6.43, 6.44
  freedom to realise assets, not interfering with 3.18
  giving effect to, alternative means of 3.28, 3.29
  hybrid model *see* **Hybrid model**
  legitimate expectation, protection of 6.04
  loss of junior creditor, rectifying 2.26, 3.25
  meaning 2.24
  nature of 3.21–3.25
  New Zealand, in 3.26
  preference for 3.19, 3.20, 3.27
  priority-position of junior creditors under 6.40
  priority-preservation without coercion of senior creditor 2.24–2.27, 3.25
  priority-ranking of junior creditors, preservation of 2.25, 3.22, 3.24–3.25
  reaction to 2.23
  result attained by 3.25
  securities, exchange of 3.22
  senior creditor's freedom of action, leaving untouched 2.25, 2.27
  subrogation, use of 2.28, 2.29
  substitution of junior creditor to security 2.15, 2.45
Prior securities
  marshalling and subrogation compared 4.24–4.26
  subrogation, as category of 4.21, 4.24

Priority arrangements
  effect of 12.11
  junior creditor, effect on 12.12, 12.20
  senior creditor and third parties, between
    12.09–12.12
Proprietary securities
  availability of marshalling 9.12, 9.13,
    9.15–9.24
  classification 9.05
  doctrine of marshalling only applicable to 7.32,
    7.33
  fixed equitable charge 9.07
  junior and senior creditor holding 9.22–9.24
  legal and equitable mortgages as 9.06
  marshalling
    availability of 2.39, 2.40
    holder entitled to protection of 9.04
  mortgage 9.06
  nature of 9.02, 9.03
  non-possessory lien 9.11
  non-proprietary securities, and 9.04, 9.05
Puisne secured creditor
  prior-ranking security, right to obtain access to
    1.04, 1.10
  protection of priority-ranking 1.08
Purchase money security arrangements
  debtor and third party, between 12.13–12.20
  junior creditor's marshalling rights, third party
    rights superior to 12.18, 12.20
  position of junior creditor 12.19
  priority-position 12.15–12.17

Quasi-securities
  examples of 9.35
  extension of marshalling to 9.39, 9.40
  meaning 9.35
  negative pledge 9.38
  set-off *see* **Set-off**
  title retention devices 9.37

Receivers
  marshalling and subrogation compared
    4.24–4.26
  subrogation, as category of 4.21, 4.24
  third party defeating junior creditor's right to
    marshall, not being 11.02
Redistribution
  common debtor requirement, consistency of
    7.17–7.20
  debtor's assets, of 4.07–4.12
  marshalling as remedy in 4.04–4.12, 4.17–4.19
  marshalling by apportionment, and 11.30–11.36
  marshalling, giving effect to 6.40
  non-security interests 9.39, 9.40
  quasi-securities 9.39, 9.40
  subrogation, nature of 4.17–4.19
  surety exception, and 8.21–8.25
  unsecured creditors, redundancy of marshalling by
    10.08–10.10

Restitution
  marshalling, analysis of 4.34–4.37, 4.40–4.54
  subrogation as remedy of 4.34, 4.38, 4.39
  subrogation, unifying principle for 4.03
Retention of title clauses
  marshalling, and 9.37
Romalpa clause
  marshalling, and 9.37
Roman law
  marshalling, origins of 2.10–2.12

Secured creditor
  duties owed by 3.09
  enforcement of securities by 3.07–3.09
  fair price, duty to obtain
    affirmation of principles 3.15
    law on 3.13
    persons to whom owed 3.16
    qualification 3.14
    reasonable care, taking 3.12
    time of 3.17
  good faith, duty to act in 3.10, 3.11
  junior creditor's marshalling rights prevailing
    against 11.02
Secured debt puzzle
  inquiry into 6.07
  theories of security 6.08–6.11
Securities
  priorities, problem of 1.02
Senior creditor
  enrichment of 4.44–4.47
  fair price, duty to obtain 3.12–3.17
  freedom of action
    encroachment on 3.04–3.06
    restriction of 2.06
  good faith, duty to act in 3.10, 3.11
  marshalling of securities doctrine, application of
    1.01
  meaning 1.13
  prejudicial enforcement by 2.04
  provision of credit, terms of 12.01
  right to enforce securities 2.03
  subsequent secured debt, lack of control over
    6.41
Senior debt
  meaning 1.13
Senior security
  assets subject to
    equal rights of recourse to 7.25–7.33
    status of 7.21–7.24
  meaning 1.13
  nature of 7.32, 7.33
  trustee for junior creditor, not 3.08
Set-off
  nature of 9.29
  extension of marshalling to 2.62
  marshalling, and 9.30–9.33, 9.36
  non-proprietary security, as 9.24
  proceeds of sale, of 9.17, 9.21

Set-off (*cont.*):
  right of, marshalling 9.23
  rights against assets of debtor 9.27–9.29
Specific performance
  contingencies 5.53, 5.54
  contractual obligation, relying on 5.51
  marshalling as form of 1.03, 1.09, 5.01, 5.49
  marshalling not being form of 5.50–5.54
  remedies of 5.51
  volunteers, position of 5.55
Subrogation
  categories of
    established 4.21–4.23
    independent, treated as 4.15
    marshalling, comparison of 4.24–4.33
    marshalling not being 4.32, 4.33
  developments in law of 2.29, 2.30
  effect of 4.02
  floating charges, and 9.14
  junior creditor, placing in position of senior credi-
    tor 4.02
  law of restitution, application of 4.34
  marshalling as an instance of
    comparison of 4.20–4.33
    lack of authority for 4.14, 4.35
    substitutive process 4.13
    texts considering 4.16
  marshalling not being remedy of 4.32, 4.33, 4.55
  origins of 2.12, 2.29
  post-realisation remedy, as 2.28
  redistribution of assets by 4.03
  redistributive nature of 4.17–4.19
  relationship with marshalling 1.03, 4.01
  restitutional remedy, as 4.34, 4.36
  restitutionary analysis not extended to marshalling
    4.52–4.54
  restitutionary model 4.03, 4.38–4.40
  restoration of benefit via 4.39
  surety, position of 8.48
  unifying principle 4.03
  unjust enrichment, redressing 4.34
Sureties
  access to securities 5.46, 5.47
  benefit of several securities, right to 8.32
  consolidation and 8.29–8.32
  debtor's assets, access to 8.27
  marshalling, application of term 8.28–8.31
  marshalling and subrogation compared
    4.24–4.26
  nature of rights, misconception as to 8.45–8.48
  rights of 8.26–8.32
  subrogation, as category of 4.21, 4.24
Surety exception
  ability of creditor to marshall senior security, con-
    cerned with 8.26
  Australia, in 8.13
  Canada, in 8.14, 8.18, 8.19
  common debtor rule, to 2.35
  common law jurisdictions, acceptance in 8.02

development of 2.35, 2.36
derivation of 2.36
efficacy of 2.55, 2.56
  questioning 8.02, 8.35–8.48
fallacious priority contest 8.45–8.48
Ireland, in 8.14
junior creditor holding security over debtor's asset
  8.11, 8.12
junior creditor's marshalling rights, limitation of
  8.09, 8.10
marshalling, permitting 8.05
meaning 8.01
narrow scope of 8.43, 8.44
New Zealand law 2.55, 2.56, 8.02, 8.16,
  8.35–8.48
operation of 8.06
part of senior debt, third party guaranteeing
  repayment of 8.10
piercing corporate veil compared 8.59–8.61
redistributive nature of marshalling, and
  8.21–8.25
third party, debtor obligated to 8.07, 8.08
third party's right of exoneration, and 8.18–8.20
United States, not accepted in 8.03, 8.17

Theories of security
  conventional
    policy goals 6.35, 6.36
    post-realisation theory, supporting 6.43, 6.44
    priority of secured creditors, reason for 6.36
    public policy, recognition of security as matter
      of 6.34
  debate on 6.07
  economic grounds, use of 6.11
  efficiency-based 6.08
  free-rider 6.25–6.27
  functional
    flaws 6.14, 6.15
    involuntary unsecured creditors, position of
      6.13
    little utility of 6.16
    meaning 6.12
    new priority rules, retrospective effect 6.14
    parity between secured and unsecured creditors,
      fallacy of 6.15
    preferential status of secured creditors, false
      assumptions 6.12
  informational
    creditworthiness and 6.33
    imperfect picture of security, providing 6.32
    main criticisms of 6.34
    pre-contractual cost-minimisation device, secu-
      rity as 6.31
    rationale for security, ascertainment of 6.30
  Kaldor-Hicks criteria 6.09, 6.10
  monitoring
    costs, reduction in 6.21
    creditors, monitoring by 6.21, 6.22
    floating charge, failure to explain 6.23, 6.24

lower rate of interest, charge of 6.22
main criticisms of 6.34
negative pledge, failure to explain 6.23, 6.24
post-contractual debtor misbehaviour under
  6.19, 6.20
rationale for existence of security, not providing
  6.29
supervisory purposes, security taken for
  6.18
private property-based 6.17
relational 6.28
secured debt puzzle 6.08–6.11
Third party
assets transferred to, effect on right to marshall
  11.03
junior creditor's right to marshall, enforcement
  against 11.01
marshalling to prejudice of 2.34
position of junior creditor *qua* 11.03, 11.04
rights, marshalling in presence of
  prejudice, effect of 11.06–11.09
  traditional treatment, propositions differing
    from 11.05
security holders
  marshalling by apportionment 11.18–11.40
  see also **Apportionment, marshalling by**
  privileged status 11.10, 11.11
  transferees/disponees, disparate treatment of
    11.15–11.17
security holders, privileged status of 11.10, 11.11
security in favour of 2.54
transferees *see* **Transferees**
undermining or excluding right to marshall
  absolute transfers or dispositions 2.48–2.50
  debtor, introduced by 2.41
  derivation of right 2.42
  effective rights 2.43
Trading trusts
marshalling and subrogation compared 4.24–4.26
subrogation, as category of 4.21, 4.24
Transferees
consent of senior creditor to transfer 11.62
development of 2.18, 2.41–2.43, 2.48–2.50
identity of 11.49
junior creditor's inchoate equity, effect of 11.14,
  11.16
marshalling rights, exclusion of 2.49, 2.54,
  11.14, 11.16, 11.41
Australia, in 11.55, 11.56
Canada, in 11.55, 11.56
general rule 11.42–11.44
Ireland, in 11.55, 11.56
New Zealand, in 11.55, 11.56
notice of junior security 2.50, 11.50–11.54
policy goals of security, and 11.57–11.63
third party, identity of 11.49
time of transfer or disposition 11.45–11.48

privileged status 11.10, 11.11
third party security holders, disparate treatment of
  11.15–11.17
Trustee in bankruptcy
judicial lien *see* **Judicial lien**
marshalling by junior creditor, and 10.14–10.16,
  11.02
United States law 10.03, 10.06, 10.07
unsecured creditor, marshalling on behalf of
  10.05, 10.08. 10.09

Ultra vires borrowings
marshalling and subrogation compared
  4.27–4.31
subrogation, as category of 4.21, 4.24
Undermining or excluding right to marshall
absolute transfers or dispositions to third party
  2.48–2.50
marshalling by apportionment, development of
  2.46, 2.47
subsequent conduct of debtor, by 2.41
third party claims
  derivation of right 2.42
  effective rights 2.43
transfers or dispositions by way of security
  2.44–2.47
Unjust enrichment
debtor, of 4.48–4.50
deprivation of benefit 4.41, 4.42
person enriched 4.43
redress 4.34
senior creditor, of 4.44–4.47
unsecured creditors, of 4.51
Unsecured creditor
enrichment of 4.51
involuntary, position of 6.13
legitimate expectation 6.06
marshalling, rights of
  extinguishment of 10.11–10.16
  redistribution, in context of 10.10
  trustee in bankruptcy, powers of 10.05, 10.08.
    10.09
  United States law 10.04
position after marshalling 6.05
right to marshall, lack of 2.05, 10.01
third party defeating junior creditor's right to
  marshall, not being 10.02, 11.02

Vendor's lien
marshalling and subrogation compared
  4.24–4.26
subrogation, as category of 4.21, 4.24
Voluntary arrangements
senior creditor and third party security holder,
  between 12.02
Volunteers
marshalling by 5.55